Preface

Some Generalities

There is a French expression that basically says the more things change, the more they stay the same. Though we think of the high-tech tackle of today and the modern improvements that seem to have been impossible earlier, that statement applies very well to fishing. An examination of the history of tackle, and of early rods, reels, lures, line and accessories, can lead to an appreciation of the tackle of today and to an understanding of its early evolution.

In addition, knowing about a broad variety of tackle and tackle history can make you a better angler. Seems impossible? Knowing about the specialty tackle of the past for certain species, types of fishing and fishing conditions can help you choose tackle of today that will best fill the bill for your purposes and needs. Knowing about the lures of the past and how they were manufactured and fished can lead to an appreciation of how to better fish modern lures, why they are made certain ways and how best to coax a fish to strike with our "just-invented" lures.

The New Is Often Really Old

It might also help you appreciate that nothing is new. Take, for example, the brand new rods in which the line goes through the blank and on which guides are not necessary. That idea goes back 125 years. How about the new hooks of the past five years with double barbs or barbs on the outside of the bend (obverse point)? Sorry, look to the original Van Vleck hook of 1907 for that idea. Fly fishing for striped bass? That was written about in 1845 and then later in 1865, in several books, even referring to the practice along the Potomac River just upriver of the nation's capitol. Fast-retrieve casting reels to "burn" lures through the water?

LEFT: *Old and new books, including fishing encyclopedias, are valued sources for information about the history of fishing tackle, equipment and techniques.*

Some early multipliers from approximately 180 years ago had gear ratios of 9:1. Modern star drags on casting reels for big bass, pike and muskie? That was developed at the turn of the century as a braking mechanism for handling big saltwater fish during a time when otherwise catching a 100-pounder was a rarity and a true angling feat. The list and the comparisons are endless.

Tackle Roots in England

Even when writing of North American tackle history, reference must be made to Europe and Great Britain. Although it is the melting pot of the world, the USA had, and continues to have, deep roots in customs and language from the English. Early tackle, books, ideas and comparisons of fish originated in England or Europe. Many of the early colonists were English, Welsh, Scotch, Irish, along with a mix of French, German, Spanish and other cultures.

The first fishing books of the early part of the country were by English authors and publishers. Only later did authors such as Thaddeus Norris, Frank Forester, Charles Hallock, Robert Barnwell Roosevelt, Genio Scott, Dr. James Henshall and others begin to formulate truly American thoughts, theories, fishing methods and tackle ideas.

Lost History

Some books, lamentably, were lost. Theodore Gordon, known for his truly American fly fishing ideas, along with other flies and theories (with fly fishing predating any mid-1800 baitcasting tackle and later introductions and developments of spinning and spincast tackle), broke away from English tradition to create the first original American dry fly. He tied trout and salmon flies and also experimented unsuccessfully with a bass bug. He had supposedly completed a book when, on May 1, 1915, he died of tuberculosis in his small cabin in New York. With the prevailing medical theory of preventing contamination, all his belongings, including his book manuscript, were burned.

Frank Forester, the preeminent writer of the early 1800s, committed suicide in his 50s, putting an end to the possibility of additional books and ideas from this popular fishing writer of only a handful of books at the time. (Frank Forester was the pseudonym of Henry William Herbert, an English gentleman from a wealthy family, who came to this country under mysterious circumstances and died in 1858.) His first book set the pace and the style for future fishing books and writing.

Izaak Walton's book, *The Compleat Angler,* has many American editions even though it is an English book that was first published in 1653 (most modern editions are from the fifth, 1676 edition, with Charles Cotton's work on fly fishing included). The earliest American edition (1847) was compiled by the Reverend George Washington Bethune. It contained

Our Fishing Heritage: Tackle & Equipment

Bethune's introduction and comments, which provided valuable insights into American fishing methods.

History Through Maybe's and Probably's

In addition to established facts here, you will also find some theories, some use of words such as "perhaps," "probably," "might have," "maybe," and similar conditional and probable statements such as "credited to" and "attributed to." That is unfortunate, because established facts are always good, though sometimes sporadic in history. Without this license, however, such a book would be less than it hopefully is and less than it could be. History is written with documents and accurately recorded deeds, and the preservation of "things" —tackle in this case, or the literature that refers accurately to tackle. It also includes some speculation, some trails, threads and leads with no end, some ideas and thoughts that may well be correct, but can't be definitively proven. That can apply to any and all history, not just fishing tackle history.

For example, noted in here is an exception to the commonly held "fact" that spinning reached this country only in the mid-1930s (followed by a decade-plus interruption caused by World War II) with the discovery that the first spinning reel was invented 100 years ago in Baltimore. The facts of this survive, but to date no reels have been discovered, leading to the tantalizing possibility that somewhere in the Baltimore area, near where I live coincidentally, there might be a never-before-seen spinning reel in the attic of some white-stepped row house, or in the basement of some decaying farm house, or in the musty ancient inventory of some hardware store or tackle shop.

Of course, that same spinning reel or other early rods, reels, lures or line spools might be in your attic, your basement, or found in summer open-air flea markets after resting unused in the dark for decades or even a century or two.

ABOVE: Spinners have not evolved much, as evidenced by these lures: early Hildebrant "spoon" (top); an early Skinner fluted spinner (center); a modern Mepps spinner (bottom left) and a modern Blue Fox spinner (bottom right).

The Evolution of Tackle

Tracing an exact history of reels— all tackle really —is a problem, because there were no steps or thresholds of tackle development and usage. Rather, there were gradual changes, such as the early use of reels, even multipliers being used on what we would consider fly rods for fly casting with flies. These reels, with their wide frame and narrow diameter, more closely resembled early casting reels and were sometimes even used on top of the rod and in a different position on the grip (above the hand as in casting tackle or below as in modern fly tackle). Thus, fly casting with reels of some sort perhaps first existed before the true upright-style fly reels of the day. In turn, casting reels might have led to the development of

ABOVE: Spoons have stayed the same over the years, and consist of two styles—fixed hooks (top and bottom right) and free-swinging hooks (center and bottom left). Spoons shown include a Heddon King Stanley (top); pearl finish and original red and white finish Eppinger Dardevle (center and bottom left); and Tony Accetta Pet spoon (bottom right).

the wide-frame fly reels of the early and mid-1800s. The distinct separations of types of tackle that we accept today was far more blurred in the past. In part, this was due to the lack of good reporting and dissemination of knowledge during the early infant years of tackle development.

Just as fly reels and casting reels and tackle might mix and evolve one to the other, the star drag of all modern freshwater casting reels had its birth in a saltwater drag system to handle big saltwater fish.

Work and Social History Mirrors Tackle and Fishing History

As our angling history progresses, we can have more precise information, more established facts, more details, more information. This is a result of gradually more leisure time as the Industrial Revolution slowly reduced working hours to provide more time, even if little more pay and disposable income. In time, workers did not have to slave for 10 hours a day, six days a week. With the advent of child labor laws, children went to school instead of toiling in factories and mills, and some at least had weekday afternoons, weekends and summers off for enjoying the sport of fishing. There were also more angling writers, more manufacturers, more catalogs of tackle made in America and more newspaper and magazine accounts where much of the history still lies. In fact, a treasure trove probably awaits some future writer with the time, ability and inclination to research and read thoroughly the over 350 sporting magazines and periodicals that existed early in this country. These sporadic accounts often predated the first fishing book of 1833 and no doubt contain gems of information on fishing and fishing tackle.

It is important to weigh tackle history and development against the social and technological developments of the time. When you read about early rod, reel and lure development in the 1860s, realize that it was not until 1861 that the two coasts were connected by the first telegraph. The Wright Brothers were trying to fly the first aeroplane (as they were called then) when the first wood plugs were developed at the turn of the century. Getting to fishing spots was difficult then also—the automobile was just being developed and in 1900 there were only 10 miles of paved road in the entire country. In 1917 steel workers would have had difficulty getting time to fish, although they were starting strikes to reduce the current working hours that were seven days a week, twelve hours a day (with some 14 hour days for the day shift). Times were tough and technology primitive by modern standards, but, even with that, some of the tackle and angling developments of the time were truly remarkable.

Ferreting Out Tackle History

Similarly, surprises and finds of tackle too are not uncommon, even with the constantly increasing competition of more collectors all the time. There

BELOW: Some lures, like these surface prop baits, have changed little over the 60 years covered by these examples. Shown are a 1905 Worden Combination Minnow (top); a 1947 South Bend Nip-I-Diddee (center); and ca. 1966 Smithwick Devil's Horse (bottom). Modern top water prop baits are very much like the Devil's Horse.

are over 5,000 members of the National Fishing Lure Collectors Club who are constantly searching out flea markets, auctions and yard sales, for buying and swapping lures and other tackle. Rods and reels have long been collected, but the first major push to collect reels began with the N.F.L.C.C. members in 1976.

Tackle history must also weave in other history, facts, interesting side roads and examinations of the habits and mores of the country. For example, the first American edition (1847) of the English book *The Compleat Angler,* by Izaak Walton, edited by Rev. Bethune, credited only "The American Editor," with no name credit. Bethune, a clergyman, wrote under a little-disguised pen name, perhaps a result of the earlier (18th century) philosophy that angling for sport was an idle pastime, to be shunned and avoided at best, and certainly not something for those doing God's work. But in his introductory notes he included facts and valuable information on the American fishing of the time.

Fishing Wasn't Always Proper, Particularly on Sunday

For the same reason as Bethune's anonymity, and in the same time period, anglers were in a Catch-22 situation. Work was often literally a dawn to dusk proposition, six days a week, with Sunday the only day off—and angling on the Lord's day was prohibited or discouraged by the mores of the time. Thus, much early angling, both by the necessity of survival and custom of the time, was "commercial," gaining fish for food. Of course, if a colonist had a little fun while fooling with fish, who was hurt and who was the wiser for it?

LEFT AND BELOW: *Exhibits in the National Fresh Water Fishing Hall of Fame and Museum recount both fishing history and also tackle history, as shown in these photos of early fishing rods (left) and antique outboard engines (below).*

Fish as Utilitarian Objects

Some early commercial fishing was with hook and line. So plentiful were the fish stocks that early settlers were restricted by laws and regulations as to the numbers of brook trout, shad or salmon that they could feed their slaves or indentured servants.

Fish also came in handy elsewhere. Some early farmers used the bony plates of giant sturgeon to protect and prolong the use of their wood plowshares. Indians earlier had used the scales of fish as graters and gar scales as arrow heads. In time, some tool manufacturers and makers of utilitarian objects delved into the increasingly popular sport of fishing. The American Fork and Hoe Company

LEFT: Rod guides have changed radically over the years as evidenced by these examples. **Left to right:** an early roller guide, wire wrap guide, two-ring guide, agate guide, early Fuji ceramic guides, chrome plated guide, snake guide and modern one-foot ceramic Fuji guide.

BELOW: Handles, reel seats and grips on rods have also changed over the years. **Top to bottom:** wood handle on oak homemade muskie rod; sliding ring reel seat on tubular steel Kingfisher rod; offset reel seat on True Temper solid steel rod; modern cork grip on Berkley spinning rod; EVA foam grip on modern Shimano Catana casting rod; and modern skeletal reel seat and foam grip on Berkley Series One spinning rod.

became True Temper, which made steel rods, and Kentucky watchmakers and gun makers such as Snyder and the Meek brothers became the earliest manufacturers of true, castable baitcasting reels.

Commercial Efforts, Imports and Stockings

Initially, commercial fishing was the only true fishing done, although early on those with means undoubtedly tried some of the English recreational angling methods in the streams and rivers. Even 100 to 150 years ago, some writers worried about the excessive killing of fish both by commercial and by recreational anglers. Many recreational anglers considered angling a sport, albeit a sport that would—or should—provide food for the table.

The conflict between commercial and recreational fishing continues to exist, perhaps even more, at least in the saltwater arena, where long-used fishing grounds such as the Georges Banks have collapsed and regulations do not seem to go far enough in protecting adequate stocks of major species. Other practices have also affected sport fishing. Considered an esteemed food fish, carp were brought from Europe to ponds on the banks of the Hudson River prior to 1850, whereupon a break in the dam released the fish into the Hudson. So valued was this fish that a law was passed to protect the escaped Hudson River carp from harm. Other carp, stocked in water supply reservoirs around Baltimore, MD, were passed out to interested parties, often at the request of Congressmen. Brown trout from Europe first stocked in 1883 retained a longer and more hospitable reception. Proceedings of the Fourth International Fisheries Congress in the Bulletin of the Bureau of Fisheries note efforts to stock trout in other countries (New Zealand, Argentina and Italy) and to raise both freshwater and saltwater fish. The stocking of trout to Argentina paved the way for the fabulous fishing there reported by Joe Brooks on The American Sportsman TV show in the 1960s and for the continued good fishing there today, as well as the phenomenal trout fishing in New Zealand.

Our Fishing Heritage: Tackle & Equipment

Stocking native smallmouth and largemouth bass around the country in watersheds originally unknown to them, moving rainbow trout from the Rockies to the East Coast and elsewhere, and moving Eastern brook trout to the West Coast may have improved fishing opportunities, but also added fish populations to areas new to them and further changed and diluted fishing opportunities while introducing fish that competed with native fish populations. This changed the native biology, ecology and angling opportunities. Some changes were for the better, some for the worst.

Fishing Suffers in Sport Acceptance

Prejudices against fishing have existed in the past and unfortunately continue to exist today. Fishing does not get the respect it should on the sports pages of American newspapers, which primarily consider only those sports that involve throwing or hitting a ball, watched by people packed into stadiums and shown on TV. Fishing is often a solitary sport, certainly not practiced before a packed throng of 50,000 spectators. Individually or in small groups, however, fishing is practiced by upwards of 50 million people nationwide.

Over the years, even fishermen had their prejudices against other fishermen. Dry fly anglers—initially copying the English—eschewed nymph fishermen; bass anglers looked down on those after catfish; the growing sport of saltwater big-game angling made a competition of it all that the bluegill fisherman cared little about and perhaps could not fathom. Efforts to counter this through an umbrella group of all fishermen have been tried, the most recent, at this writing, United Fishing Association.

The Varieties of Fishing

Through it all, angling, especially freshwater angling, has grown from a simple hook and line to a hook, line and rod, to the addition of reels, to various methods of trolling, still-fishing, pitching (swinging the line onto the water without a reel, much like the current popular bass methods of flipping and pitching), fly fishing, baitcasting, spinning, spincasting, using various live baits, prepared baits, lures and lure-and-bait combinations. All this has been aided by accessories as simple as a net or stringer or pliers and as complex as modern depth finders and GPS systems, along with special fish grips, thermometers, downriggers, outriggers, planer board systems, color gauges, pH meters, *ad infinitum*.

Here then, is a look at our collective angling history, with some theories confirmed, some perhaps skewed along the way, and some interesting side trips into the world of tackle and fishing history.

ABOVE: *In addition to rods, reels, lines and lures, anglers need a variety of other equipment and accessories such as these waders, gaff, net, tackle box, stringer, scale, scaler/knife and fly box.*

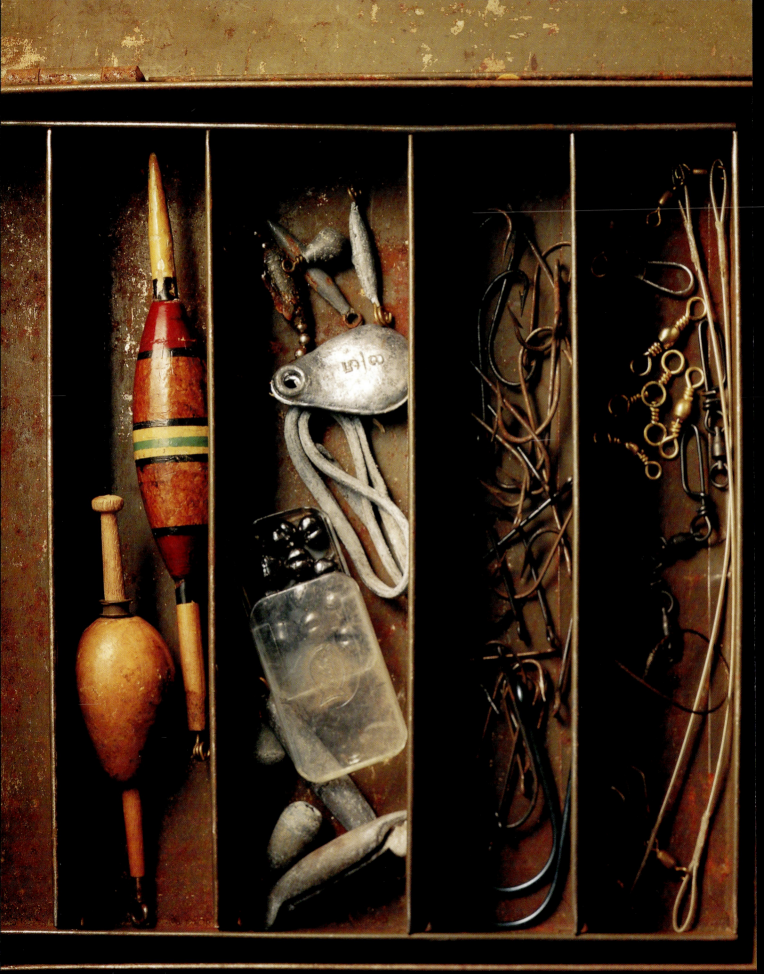

 # Hooks & Terminal Tackle

Hooks as Basics and Basic Hooks

Unless considering methods of hand-tickling trout without any tackle at all, or "noodling" under banks to grab giant catfish, fishing—recreational fishing—still requires a hook and a line as the bare basics.

Hooks did not start as hooks. The first method to catch fish by means of a line, no doubt for utilitarian, commercial or survival/subsistence purposes, was a gorge, in which a primitive line was tied to the middle of a stick pointed on both ends. Bait on the stick—turned parallel to the line—enticed the fish to swallow it, then a pull on the line turned the stick so as to jam the point into the stomach or throat of the fish for landing. In time, these gorges might have become bent from the pressure of the fish resisting capture. Regardless, in time the gorge evolved into a crude precursor of the double hook of today, where the center of the gorge was bent down to form a loop or eye and the shanks of the hooks, and the ends were bent up to form early hook points.

Single Point Hooks, But No Single Material

In time, hooks with a single point developed. Hooks of different ages and cultures have been made of bird talons, eagle beaks, sea shell, lashed-together twigs and branches, cactus spines, honey locust twigs with spines, bear fangs, reindeer horn, tortoise shell, human bone, stone, whale tooth, copper, brass, bronze, gold, iron, steel and clear plastic. A hook from the Bronze Age looks remarkably similar to those manufactured today. It has a slightly long shank, similar to a Limerick bend, a turned-out straight point (although this might have occurred from fighting a fish), a typical barb and what would be called a loop eye, in which the shank forms the eye and then is

LEFT: *Even the ancients used lures, as evidenced by this abalone shell and bird talon hook. The lure is less than three inches long, and from the Palau Island area of the Pacific. The talon is secured to the abalone shell lure with palmetto fibers, and pearl beads on the rear serve as an additional attractor.*

BELOW: *Photo of the Improved Van Vleck hook of 1907 shows both the outside barb and also the double barb. More recently, outside barbs and double barbs have been promoted as "new."*

turned back parallel to the hook shank. Hooks with a simple "ball" eye were also formed by primitive man. Studies of all native Indian tribes revealed many ways of taking fish, including the use of hooks, lines and sinkers.

Hook drawings and paintings have been found throughout the world, including inside Egyptian pyramids. As metallurgy developed, so did metal hooks. Bronze hooks (the Bronze Age was about 4000 B.C.) have been found in Bavaria and Switzerland; copper hooks in Wisconsin. In what is now Columbia, South America, a gold fishhook was found when excavating a tunnel for a mine; other gold hooks have been found around the Amazon. Steel hooks were used prior to the Christian era, 2,000 years ago.

Hooks as Important Imports

In the colonies, there is little doubt that the first hooks came from England. Early on in the Americas virtually everything had to come from abroad, until crafts and manufacturing developed. Also, hook making was firmly established in England and Europe by the 12th century. Steel forging was learned from the Knights Templar in Spain and was quickly adapted for hook manufacturing. Tempered steel hooks were available by the mid- to late 1600s.

In 1651, hook maker Charles Kirby, of the same name as the hook design, went into business and for a time dominated the English hook industry. He was even listed in Izaak Walton's 1653 book, *The Compleat Angler.*

Manufacturing Trends in Hooks

In the late 1700s hook manufacturing shifted to Limerick, Ireland, and the O'Shaughnessy family, then back to Redditch and Kendall, England. Most of today's names for hook styles and bends come from the names of the original designers or from the names of the towns where hooks were manufactured.

Because early America was primarily an English colony, much of the imports must have come from Great Britain. Certainly, along with tea—some of which went into the Boston harbor—hooks for fishing were among those early imports. Hooks from France go back 200 years with the VMC brand. O. Mustad started manufacturing in Norway in 1832 and soon after started exporting to the United States and to other parts of the world.

Want to Make a Hook? Good Luck!

Basic early hook making started with wire clipped to length, barbed with a blade, then sharpened by hand. The sharpened wires were bent on hook benders that formed the shape and the eyes. Tempering was accomplished by heating batches of hooks in a furnace for 15 to 25 minutes, then hardening and strengthening them by quenching them in a bath of fish oil or water. This made the hooks very brittle, so they were reheated slightly to reduce the temper, then scoured in tumbling tubs of sand to remove scale. The hooks were then finally finished by japanning (using two baths of a tarry liquid for the hook coating) or bluing (as gun barrels are blued by acid baths). More recent coatings have included everything from gold to color dyes, to special finishes for saltwater such as tin and cadmium. Cadmium has recently been proven to be environmentally damaging and thus discontinued.

American pioneers made their hooks by hand, working with carved-wood hook forms to bend the wire into shape. The entire process is described in Ken Reinard's book, *The Colonial Angler's Manual of Flyfishing & Flytying* (1995). In it, Reinard notes that much of the tackle of the 1770 angler—hooks, lines, flies and rods—had to be made in the home workshop and required some time both to make and to fish, as well as disposable income to allow this recreation.

The method of making hooks by hand obviously led to a lot of variations in size, bend, gap and shank length, but a general rule that might have been followed was to make the shank length anywhere from two to four times the gap measurement. Today, this range of proportions would cover most regular-length hooks and long-shank hooks for streamers.

The Eyes Don't Always Have It

Early fishermen might have found it difficult to make eyes in hooks, particularly in small hooks. This might be why many flies through the turn of the century were tied on eyeless hooks, first wrapping the gut snell (leader) to the hook with tying thread, then tying the fly on the hook and covering the snell or "arming" of the hook with the fly dressing. Often these steps were combined, first tying thread to the hook, then wrapping the overlapping hook shank and end of the gut, then working the thread to the bend of the hook and beginning tying the fly, gradually working forward before tying off at the end of the eyeless shank.

Hooks for flies and lures were made prior to 1850, with some mayfly patterns shown on eyed hooks in an English book. Hooks from most companies were made by hand, some even into the 1940s.

Early U.S. Hook Makers

The identity of the earliest hook maker in the U.S. has been lost to antiquity, but it was probably established by the mid-1800s. Prior to that hooks were sold, perhaps manufactured, as per the catalog cover of Dame, Stoddard & Kendall, which was considered the oldest tackle shop in the U.S. It started operations in 1800 in Boston as Bradford & Anthony. The cover of the third edition of their catalog (presumably sometime in the early 1800s) lists them as "Importers, Manufacturers and Dealers in Fish Hooks, Fishing Tackle and Angling Implements."

SQUID/FISH HOOKS

Not really designed for recreational fishing, squid hooks were made by many companies for snagging squid, which often come to the surface at night. These hooks were first developed over 100 years ago, with the first patent filed in Newfoundland, March 2, 1886, by Canadian James Scotland and French citizen Francois Cordon. "Our invention will be found very useful in fishing for caplin, squid, herring, and various other small fish," so states part of the claims for their invention.

Their cylindrical device consisted of a transparent tube into which phosphorus or other light-producing materials could be placed as an attractant. The bottom of the device held twelve curved hooks. Similar styles, some with straight hooks or spines and some with curved, are still made today. They are made with a metal or lead frame for weight in jigging and sinking, and have "hooks" that surround the main body of the lure.

Some makers, or "manufacturers," of other tackle also made hooks, such Samuel Phillippe of Philadelphia, who is better known and credited as the first to make a complete split-bamboo rod.

Small hook manufacturing facilities such as Phillippe's probably produced hooks that were regionally sold and used. This is most likely considering early transportation of the 1800s (boat, canal barge, railroad and difficult coach rides over impossible roads) and considering the early manual methods of manufacture used to make hooks.

Hook and needle manufacturing were closely related. Hooks were nothing more than a needle bent into a hook shape and fixed with an eye on one end (although sometimes not even that) and a point and barb on the other. Methods for

16   *Our Fishing Heritage: Tackle & Equipment*

making hooks by hand utilized "hook benders" often farmed out to families as a cottage industry, the finishing and tempering later done at a central factory location.

Hook Benders—The Tools, Not the People

Hook benders resembled nothing more than a short dowel, almost like the end of a broom handle, the flat end of which was carved and fitted with a metal form designed to catch the point end of the hook. The straight wire was then bent around the form to make a hook. The same thing could be done today by fixing nails into a board in a hook shape, with one nail at one end designed to catch the point and prevent its moving as the wire is bent around the nailed form. In fact, it is presumed that some early hooks were made this way, which might explain why some hook styles have sharp bends in them. The fewer the nails used in the bend area, the sharper the bends in the resulting hook. A prime example of this is the Scottish-developed Sneck, bent almost like the open end of a box, or a squared-off "J."

Hooks Go Heavy Industry

Hook making changed. By 1880, Norway's Mustad plant had three hook-making machines, in which wire went in one end and hooks came out the other. The machines then (and now) were highly guarded, with lifetime secrecy agreements signed by workers involved with these machines, and the machines located in special locked and guarded parts of the Mustad factory. In time, Mustad hooks were exported from Norway to America and gained a solid foothold in the fishing industry here.

Gradually, more foreign hook companies followed. VMC, a 200-year-old French hook company, along with a host

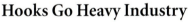

TOP: *The Colonial angler used carved wood forms to bend fish hooks from wire and needles. This form shows how the wire is held in place and bent around the form to make the bend of the hook.*

ABOVE: *The completed hook would have a long shank and although eyeless, would otherwise look like modern hooks. Hooks bent around forms like this after being barbed and sharpened on the end.*

TOP: *Tools required by the Colonial angler for making hooks include a small anvil, hammers, lengths of wire, pliers, hook forms, tweezers and sharpening stones, along with some infinite patience!*

ABOVE: *Wire for making hooks was first barbed with a small, sharp chisel as with this example. The point was sharpened by repeated strokes on a sharpening stone.*

Hooks & Terminal Tackle

SPRING TRIGGERING HOOKS

ABOVE: A short-lived spring hook from the 1980s was very similar to the spring- and lever-operated sockdolagers of the past that would cause a second hook to impale a fish taking a baited hook.

Many of the early patents for fishing tackle were for various styles of spring-operated hooks. In fact, the earliest patent known in this country for a fishing tackle device was for a spring-loaded double hook. These worked by the fish biting on one hook and pulling free a second hook that, through spring or leverage pressure, would impale the fish through the outside of the mouth while the original hook remained in the mouth.

Some of these have been incorporated into lures, with the idea that tension on the lure or pressure from the fish biting the lure triggers the hooks to fly out from a hiding place and hook the fish. Many were separate from any lure, and made with the idea of creating a truly weedless hook, since no hooks would be exposed to catch weeds or snags, whether fishing bait or lures.

One idea from the 1980s revisited an idea of 75 years prior. The idea was for a hook that worked like ice tongs of the 1940s in which gripping the handles of the ice tongs would cause increasing and continuous pressure on the ice. In fishing, the ice-tong hooks were rigged normally to a soft-plastic worm, with the line tied to a short extension arm on a second hook that was held in place with a clip. When the fish took the worm and pulled on the first hook, the leverage of the line pressure would cause the second hook to come down and impale the fish between the two hooks with a pincer movement. The idea, perhaps considered too complex or too unsportsmanlike, soon died. The earlier spring hook designs also died in time, perhaps then as a result of the higher cost of making the hooks and their increased complexity, along with the perceived unsportsmanlike purpose of impaling the fish on two hooks.

Another spring hook incorporated eight large hooks and eight smaller hooks, spring-loaded more like a trap than a hook. It sold under the name Eagle Claw. This was not, however, the Eagle Claw of the Wright & McGill Company, but an 1877 version from the B. F. Smith Co. Something about the concept can be told from the ads, which also suggested catching not only fish, but when rigged differently could also be used to capture mink, muskrats, raccoons, bears, wolves, panthers, etc. Naturally, these came in different sizes!

RIGHT: 1940 style of sockdolager double hook in which the fish is hooked on the top hook and the bottom hook swings up to impale the fish (as pictured in ad also shown).

Our Fishing Heritage: Tackle & Equipment

of Asian companies such as Daiichi, Tiemco, Maruto, Owner America, Gamakatsu and others, have gained footholds in the U.S. hook market. The English, of course, were never really out of the picture, with Partridge selling hooks made in Redditch. Recently, Partridge was bought by Mustad, although the Partridge name continues as a separate subsidiary, with the hooks still made in England. Most of these other hook companies have specialty niche markets, often in saltwater or the fly tying fields.

American Hook Makers

The largest and best-known American manufacturer of hooks was, and is, the Wright & McGill Company of Denver, CO, makers of the Eagle Claw hooks with their curved points. The company was started in 1925 by Andrew McGill with Stan Wright as financial manager. Initially, it was a fly tying company, based on patterns and fly tying earlier done by Drew McGill. The Eagle Claw hook design with the curved-in point was developed in 1926.

This basic curved-in point design was also made by the Kingfisher Tackle Company under the name Falcon Grip hooks. Other companies making curved point hooks between 1926 and 1952 included O. Mustad, Weber Company, Driscoll & Bruch and Pflueger. By 1930, Wright & McGill decided to make its own fish hooks for fly production and in the early 1930s hired an engineer who made them a hook-bending machine, albeit a hand-operated one. Even so, it allowed them to turn out barbed fish hooks in one operation, replacing 37 separate hand operations previously necessary.

Other American hook manufacturers included the Enterprise Manufacturing Company, Pflueger (with their start in 1864, and which in ads up through the 1930s emphasized with a subheading that it was pronounced "flew-ger"), P & K Company, The Jamison Company (which in 1924 made both bent-shank barbless and squared Sneck hooks for spinnerbaits), and William DeWitt of the Shoe Form Company, whose assets were later sold to O. Mustad and Sons in the 1950s.

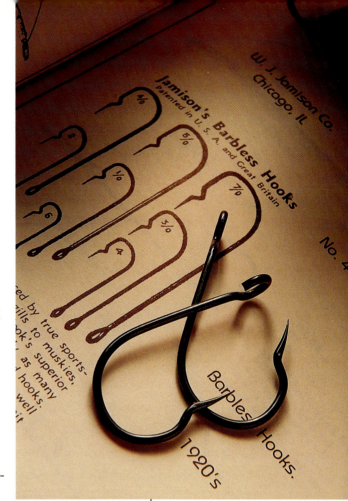

ABOVE: *One of the many styles of a modern kinked-point barbless hook that is very similar to the Jamison hooks pictured in the ads.*

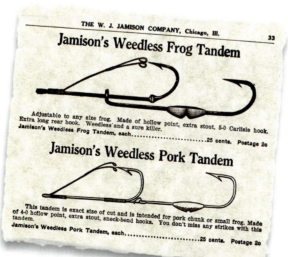

Hooks & Terminal Tackle 19

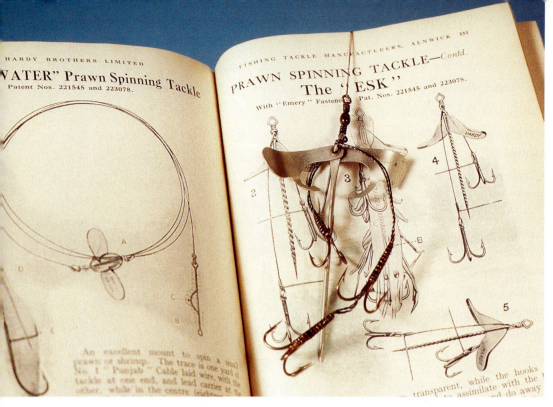

LEFT: This small size Archer-style spinner was often used for fishing minnows and impaled the minnow on the center shaft and side blades that would rapidly spin the minnow. They were often advertised and also illustrated in books, as shown here.

Specialty Hooks

Along the way, hooks have been designed for certain purposes. Hooks with extra-strong shanks have been designed for large fish such as catfish and a lot of saltwater species. Fine-wire hooks are used for dry flies, both to float the fly and also to lessen its visibility. Trebles are made with shorter shanks than in the past, simply because most used in lure manufacturing today are attached to the lure using small split rings that are secured to molded-in hook hangers in the lure. The split ring increases the distance from the hook point to the body of the lure. Today, short-shanked single hooks with a turned-up eye for easy snelling are today standard for steelhead and salmon fishing with eggs or egg sacks.

Long-shank hooks are used for minnows, with long-shank double hooks inserted through the body of a dead minnow trolled or drifted along the bottom. Double hooks with an attached safety-pin device are designed to hold a minnow or insect in place. They are available today from Mustad, just as they were 100 years ago in the Crane hook (the inventor's name), and in the Nostealum hook from Eppinger in the 1940s. Similar hooks were available from Herter's, a popular mail-order company, in the 1960s and 1970s.

World War II Also Affects Hooks

With World War II and the Nazi invasion of Norway (the home of Mustad), Mustad hook supplies to the U.S. were cut off. Military contracts for many tackle companies became the order of the day. The Wright & McGill Co. got a military contract to supply fish hooks for survival packs of pilots flying the North Atlantic. The fish hooks, called Iceland hooks, were to aid the downed pilots in life rafts to catch their own food until rescue. In the war years, the hooks were snelled in a Boulder, CO, plant by the wives of servicemen, a practice followed by other companies including the Horrocks-Ibbotson Company.

But this did not mean the end to developments and inventions. In 1942, a double-barbed hook (one on the inside of the point; one on the outside, so that the point was more like a spear) was developed by the Driscoll-Bruch Company of Portland, OR. It also had a curved-in point similar to the Wright & McGill Eagle Claw design or the earlier Falcon Grip design of Kingfisher.

Jig Hooks and Other Hooks

Jig hooks, with an upward-bent shank, are necessary to hold the lead bodies of jigs in place when molded onto the hook shank. Since these are made only to be molded into a lead head to make the modern jig, there is still a chicken-and-egg question as to the origin of this style of hook. After all, you don't make a hook like this if you don't have a market for it from a jig manufacturer, and you don't become a jig manufacturer without a source of hooks on which to mold the head. Anyway, it seems that the first of these hooks were made by Bill DeWitt's Auburn Fish Hook Company, in Auburn, NY. The manufacture of these hooks was continued by Mustad when that company bought Auburn in the 1950s. Later Mustad transferred manufacturing of the jig hooks to Norway. About five years later, Eagle Claw started making jig hooks.

Circle hooks, in which the point curves back toward the shank (much like a bent-in and exaggerated Eagle Claw hook), were developed for the long-line commercial market, but were sold to recreational anglers in the 1950s. They are being popularized again for sport fishing. This is a trend in some saltwater bait fishing and chumming to catch fish in the corner of the mouth rather than have the fish swallow a hook and bait which, would make catch-and-release impossible.

More Specialty Hooks With Modern Lures

Specialty hooks have also developed as tackle has changed. When Nick Creme poured the first of the modern worms in molds on his kitchen table in 1949, the next question was how to hook it. Early worms usually had molded-in hooks, with the two or three hooks connected by leader material, with spinner blades and beads on the leader forward of the worm. A loop allowed tying this rig to the end of the line.

ABOVE: Many different types of hook rigs became popular over the years. Included here are bare hooks designed to hold minnows and frogs, special pork rind rigs, June Bug spinners for fishing worms and minnows, muskie bucktails, and spinner/fly combinations.

EARLY CIRCLE HOOK DESIGN

Some of the earliest hooks developed by man resemble the hooks that are increasing in popularity today. The circle hooks of today were originally developed for long-line commercial fishing and have a point sharply bent back toward the eye or hook shank (thus the appearance of a circle). Hooks like these were used in the 1930s by commercial Japanese fishermen. They were also sold for sport fishing as early as 1952. They are not unlike hooks of hundreds or thousands of years ago from the Sandwich Islands (today called Hawaii). These were made of shell and resembled a circle, through they lacked the barb found on most of the modern circle hooks.

ABOVE: *Zane Grey wrote about fishing before he wrote his popular western novels. He was later absorbed by big game angling. Here Grey is shown sorting out tackle during one of his trips to Australia.*

LEFT: *Zane Grey was recruited by companies to endorse their tackle, which he did with Ashaway line and, separately, special swordfish hooks.*

Later use evolved into sales of unrigged worms and soft plastics, using hooks to rig the worm Texas-style. This simple and now almost universal method of worm rigging from the 1950s, was to run the hook through the head of the worm, out the side, with the point buried in the body of the worm. This led to the development of the offset hook in which the shank makes two sharp-angled bends near the eye, the better to bury the hook eye into the head of the worm and hide it, the bends preventing the worm from sliding down on the hook shank and ruining the rigging. Companies such as Wright & McGill, Mustad, Owner, Gamakatsu, Tru-Turn, Mister Twister and others all cater to this market with a wide variety of special worm-hook designs, including this basic off-set pattern.

Old Hooks, New Hooks

Not all hook designs are as new as we think. A "recent" invention is the double-barb hook, presumably better to hold fish. An even more recent concept is the so-called obverse barb, that is, the barb on the outside of the wire bend, not on the inside. But both of these ideas go back to a Van Vleck hook of 1907, made in Ohio. The larger hook was designed for tarpon fishing in the tropics; the smaller hook for bass. There are also hooks of old that resemble modern hooks. Thus, an Evans saltwater hook from the 1930s resembled in shape

THE CHANGING PURPOSE OF HOOK DESIGNS

Some hook designs are developed for one purpose, but then are later used for another purpose. The Sneck hook was originally developed in Scotland by, and for, fly fishermen. The unusual design is almost like the three sides of a square, with sharp bends at each corner rather than a rounded bend. In fact, writer Thaddeus Norris wrote that he had never heard or read of any plausible reason for this shape of hook. This becomes particularly evident today with increased testing that shows that the sharp bends in this hook make it weaker than otherwise identical hooks with round bends. However, in 1918, almost 60 years after its original development, this "fly fishing design" hook was incorporated into the Shannon Twin Spinner, an early spinnerbait made by the Jamison Company.

the keel hook that was later developed in the 1960s for fly fishing. Some of the very early efforts by primitive man and others used in the 1930s by commercial Japanese fishermen are echoed today with the increasing popularity of circle hooks for lures, chumming and even flies.

Modern Hooks

Modern hooks have gotten better and better, with slight refinements of bend, wire, temper, shape and specific purpose, but no real basic changes from the simple eyed hook of Macedonian times several thousand years ago. One of the first fishing tackle patents in this country was for a spring or leverage "ice tong" hook, called in the early 1800s a sockdolager. This came back in the 1980s as a style of worm hook—but it did not stay around long. Neither did transparent hooks of tough Lexan plastic that came and went (they had to have a thick diameter for strength that would be equivalent to steel hooks of the same size). Colored hooks are also recent—and old at the same time. In the 1990s, companies started making hooks in colors to match soft-plastic worms and lures or the salmon eggs and lures used for steelhead fishing. Early lure companies did color coding on a primitive scale by using nickel-plated

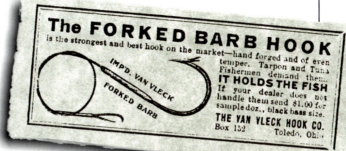

hooks on bright or light lures and dark japanned hooks on dark lures. One recent change is the "chemical sharpening," about which the manufacturers are very secretive, but which basically involves in part a controlled chemical (acid) drip on the point to make it needle sharp.

Better Hooking Designs

Problems with hooks prematurely sliding out of the mouth of a fish led John W. Campbell in 1959 to invent the Tru-Turn hook and in 1960 to create the Tru-Turn Company. The hook design, first played with by John as a kid, was patented after he retired from the military and needed something to do for additional income to help support his family. The hook is unusual in that the

TRANSPARENT HOOKS

One theory of hook making is that if the fish can't see the hook, it is more likely to take the bait or lure. The extreme of this was the development in the 1980s of a transparent hook of Lexan plastic. Lexan is a very strong plastic, although the hooks made were still far larger in shank diameter than any steel hook. The concept never took hold, and the idea, and the hooks, faded from the fishing scene after a brief stint of publicity.

BARBLESS HOOKS: A RECENT INVENTION?

With catch-and-release fishing becoming even more popular for all species and types of fishing, barbless hooks are also increasing in popularity. However, this is not the new idea that it seems. In the 1890s, the Edgar barbless hook was advertised, showing a hook in which the shank was turned over to make the eye, then bent down to make a spring bar in back of the hook point to prevent a fish from being lost. But it had no barb on the point.

Some hooks today have a bend in the wire in place of the barb, but the Williams Barbless hooks, made by Lacey Y. Williams of Oak Harbor, OH, in 1910 had the same basic design and theory. Later, on July 29, 1924, the W. J. Jamison Company patented their barbless hooks in both single hooks and snelled worm styles in sizes 8 through 7/0. The hook featured the same kink in the wire just in back of the point as did earlier hooks. These hooks were also used by some of the lure companies, such as the Outing Manufacturing Co. of Elkhart, IN, which used the hook in their Porky Getum, a metal bait with two single up-pointed hooks. The Outing Manufacturing Company was bought by Heddon in 1927 and the lures were discontinued.

To make hooks barbless today, just use pliers to pinch down the barb or file off the barb—but be careful to not weaken the point.

---

shank is curved sideways, this better to torque the hook to rotate in the fish's mouth when setting the hook, causing the hook to engage the fish rather than just slide out. Initially, John bought straight hooks and bent them in a small manual machine, then later had companies such as Mustad, Wright & McGill and VMC make them.

Finishes and Designs

The cadmium finishes for saltwater were once popular but then discontinued because they were found to be environmentally unsound. They were replaced by stainless steel, tinned or various special proprietary finishes. A quality saltwater hook was not made until the mid-1960s, when the Z-Nickel hooks began to get popular (although they had soft and weak points). They were later eclipsed by stainless steel hooks such as the Eagle Claw 254SS and 66SS.

Fly hooks also evolved from the straight-shank hooks of the recent past with hooks of the 1980s and 1990s made with special down-bent shanks for nymphs, up-bent shanks for swimming nymphs, extended doubled-shanks for extended-body dry flies and curved-shank hooks for scuds and freshwater shrimp.

Hook prices have obviously risen over the years from the days when a box of 100 fly tying hooks might have cost a buck or two, to prices of $25 per 100 or higher for some specialty hooks and far more for big-game saltwater hooks. Still, considering that the sport needs at least a hook and a line, hooks are still one of the necessities and, considering the quality today, a bargain at that.

ABOVE: Sinker styles have not changed much over the past 50 years as shown by these examples of bank, bead chain, clinch-on and in-line sinkers from this old tackle box.

Terminal Tackle

Introduction

Terminal tackle has long, perhaps always, been a part of fishing tackle. If drifting a bait with a primitive bone hook was the tactic, then a method of getting the bait down to the big fish was necessary; thus, the sinker. Even if only stone was used, it was still a primitive fishing sinker. The same was true for the weight required for slinging a bait out with a hand line, then later for trolling a lure or bait deep while rowing slowly across a lake, and still later for casting with baitcasting or spinning tackle. Floats have similarly been around a long time, at least for the past 500 years.

Swivels That Sometimes Didn't

Swivels to prevent line twist (sometimes successfully, sometimes not) came into being at least by the 1770s. Edward Pole listed "box and plain swivels" in his ads that began in 1774. Swivels are mentioned in Smith's *Natural History of the Fishes of Massachusetts* (1833) as being necessary to keep a bait spinning in the water to attract trout.

John J. Brown in his 1849 book, *The American Angler's Guide,* notes that swivels are in common use and he even suggests that they were developed in America and not used in England or Europe. "Swivels are used for 'spinning' bait, and for preventing entanglement of the line," he writes. "They are placed in various parts of the tackle, but usually on the gut-length, or leader, and should be a necessary appendage to the equipment."

Plates in *The American Angler's Book* by Thaddeus Norris (1864) show box swivels both with and without a "hook" or snap that, other than being open (and thus described as a "box" swivel), are identical to simple barrel swivels

Hooks & Terminal Tackle

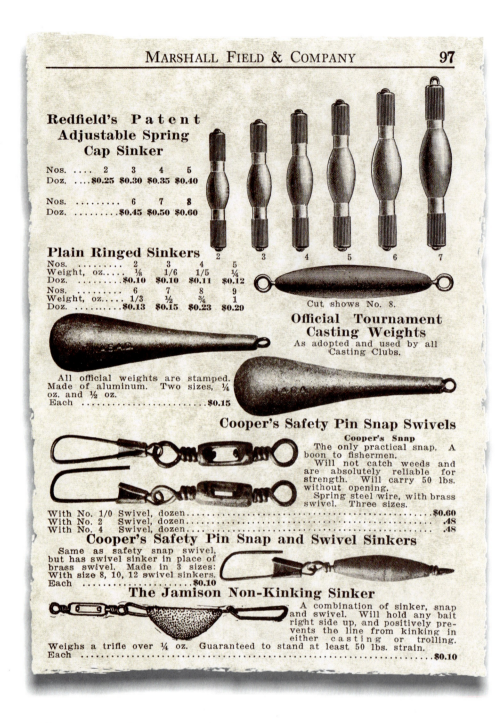

should be used for freshwater, and brass swivels for salt-water fishing."

Swivels, both as an in-line necessity and combined with a snap for adding lures or hooks, were subsequently developed in many styles, as evidenced by Harlon Major's 1939 book, *Salt Water Fishing Tackle*. He lists a wide variety of swivels and snap swivels including the popular barrel swivel used today, along with variations including the open box swivel, the heavy-duty toggle swivel, the big-game Siwash swivel and the tiny Apex swivel.

But swivels, at least according to Major in his book, didn't always work. He outlines this in a section describing some tests on a new teaser that twisted the line. He added a swivel, then a second swivel, then a third and finally all the swivels in his tackle box—three feet of swivel hardware—and still found the teaser twisting.

Ball-Bearing Swivels

Ball-bearing swivels were introduced in the early 1950s by Sampo, after the development of this design by a young inventor, Oney Johnson. Prior to this, swivels were the standard box, barrel or Crane style. One swivel that might have been a stepping stone for

used today. "Swivels are necessary when the bait is required to spin or revolve," writes Norris. "The box-swivel is used by looping the leader or bottom through one ring and the line through the other. When it is necessary to disengage the bait and snood from the leader, as in trolling for Pike, the hook-swivel is convenient, and in many cases indispensable. All bottom fishers and trollers should be well supplied with these useful little articles; steel swivels the ball-bearing swivels was the Luxon Tunalin swivel for offshore use in which a metal ring formed the swiveling surface between the two brass swivel parts. Initially designed and used for saltwater, ball-bearing swivels gradually became accepted for any angling situation where twist was a problem. Later, Sampo met competition from similar ball-bearing swivels by Berkley and some foreign companies. For absolute assurance in minimizing line twisting, ball-bearing swivels are the only answer. Sampo makes the only ball-bearing swivel manufactured in the U.S.

Sinkers

Sinkers have been around as long as fishing. Dame Juliana Berners in her work on fishing (*Treatise on Fishing With an Angle*, 1496) speaks of sinkers as common at that time and also gives some good practical fishing tips on using sinkers, tips that are just as valid today.

"Your lines must be weighted with lead," she writes. "And you must learn that the lead sinker next to the hook must be a good foot away or more. And the amount of the lead must be according to the size of the line. There are three kinds of sinkers for a running ground-line. For the ground-line ten sinkers joined together must lie on the bottom, before the float. Nine or ten small sinkers must be used for the running ground-line. The float lead shall be so heavy that the least nibble of any fish must drag it into the water. And you must make your sinkers round and smooth so that they do not get stuck under stones or get tangled in the weeds." A woodcut accompanies the text showing the various ways in which sinkers are used for different fishing situations.

These "nine or ten" sinkers listed and shown might be what we today would call split shot that is clamped onto the line as needed and which spreads the weight along the line. At least, the woodcuts indicate that they were used the same way.

Early-season trout fishing, as described by Jerome V. C. Smith, M.D. in *Natural History of the Fishes of Massachusetts,* 1833, refers to using a stout salmon rod, single-action reel (although multiplying reels are referred to and were in use at the time), large hooks and a weight or sinker, "… about the size of a musket ball." In the same text, he describes using a "… single shot of the size called B …" as being absolutely necessary for fishing a bait for trout.

The fact that little has changed in the general assortment of angling sinkers available today can be exemplified by a description of sinkers from Thaddeus Norris in 1864 (his *American Angler's Book*). "In bottom or bait fishing, sinkers of various sizes and shapes are used; the weight proportional to the tide or current. Those in general use are split shot. The sliding sinker is oblong with a hole running longitudinally through the centre. The advantage of this is, that the bait may drift off with the tide while the sinker is comparatively at rest. The swivel sinker is a combination of sinker and swivel, which allows the bait and snood to revolve; it is seldom used." Thus, he affirms that split shot is, and has been, popular, while otherwise describing what we today call egg sinkers and dipsy or bass casting sinkers. Similar bell sinkers have a lead eye—not the half-swivel.

During the same period, anglers were using short lengths of lead pipe, bent into a shallow curve, and fastened at each end to the line to make the precursor of the various types of in-line trolling sinkers (keel, crescent and bead chain) used today.

Modern Sinker Styles

Today, sinkers consist of dozens of different styles. Surf-fishing sinkers alone include a dozen styles for sandy beaches; even more when rocks and reef conditions are included. River anglers have specialty sinkers designed to drift or drag when presenting baits and lures in deep holes. Trolling anglers have various keel-like sinkers designed to prevent line twist; bobber and bottom fishermen have their own choices of styles for a variety of fishing situations.

The Rubber Cor sinker was developed in 1949 by the Water Gremlin Co. It had a rubber center that allowed twisting it onto the line anywhere and was a major development in sinkers. Other sinkers were developed for specific needs, such as the pointed bullet-like center-holed sinkers for worm fishing that developed as a result of the need to get the new early 1950s plastic worms down to the fish. Sinkers can also be lures, such as the hooks added to the long, fish-shaped codfish jigs to make a deep-fished lure.

Sinkers can range from tiny split shot weighing a small fraction of an ounce to those of several pounds to get a bait down a few hundred feet for North Atlantic cod fishing. Though it's hard to equal the fun of seeing a fish take a surface lure or fly, getting down is often the best way to get fish, get lots of fish and get big fish. Sinkers, in their many varieties, have always allowed us to do that and in their infinite variety allow us to do that even better today.

Floats and Bobbers

Just as Dame Juliana Berners described sinkers, she also described floats and how to make them. Then, in 1496 and now, 500 years later, cork was an important ingredient, as the good lady shows in writing about making floats:

"Take a good, clean cork without too many holes, and bore it through with a small, hot iron, and stick a quill through it that fits exactly and lies straight. The greater the float, the greater the hole and the greater the quill.

"Make it wide in the middle and small at both ends and particularly pointed at the nether end, as may be seen in the following figures. And smooth your floats on a grindstone or a tile-stone.

"See to it that the float for a one-hair line is no

ABOVE: This dealers display of floats was locally used by Tochterman's, a Baltimore tackle shop still in business since starting in 1916. The floats were colored by wraps of thread, much as guides are wrapped on rods.

larger than a pea. For a two-hair line, the float should be as large as a bean, and for a twelve-hair line, as large as a walnut. And for every line, the float should be in proportion to the number of hairs used.

"Every kind of line that is not used for fishing on the bottom must have a float. The running ground-line must have a float. Only the line that lies stationary on the bottom can be without a float."

Cork, Quills and Red Cedar

That same concept of float, although perhaps not as small as described for the one-hair lines (about two-pound test), can be found today. More materials were used in time, and John J. Brown in his *American Angler's Guide* of 1849 writes: "Floats are made of quills, cork, and red cedar, of various sizes, adapted to the current or water, or the peculiar description of angling, and are of two shapes, egg and oblong.

"The float used for trout is generally made of quills or cork and cannot be too light for fishing in clear streams; where the current is strong or the water muddy, a larger float may be used without inconvenience.

"For bass, pickerel or salmon, there are two kinds of floats employed, the cork, and that made of hollowed red cedar, which are made of different sizes, varying from three to eight inches in length, and of neat proportions. Those of red cedar are very light, and much preferred in angling for bass and weakfish, in the vicinity of New-York."

Thaddeus Norris, in *The American Angler's Book*, 1864, briefly notes the use of floats as follows: "Floats are

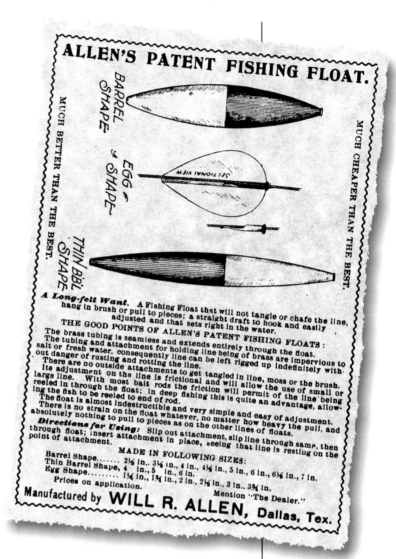

made of cork, hollow wood or quills, of a great variety of shapes and sizes. The quill is preferred for the Roach, Chub, and other fish that bite delicately. The size of the float should always be regulated by the weight of the sinker; the shape is a matter of fancy. I have whittled shapely floats out of the bark of a pine tree."

Floats even inspired companies and tackle shops, such as Tochterman's in Baltimore, a tackle shop now run by third generation Tony Tochterman. The business was begun by Tony's grandfather in 1916 who converted his candy store into one selling bait and hooks and then added large perch and pike floats, which they made in their home above the first-floor shop. Float fishing in the nearby brackish rivers and creeks for yellow perch, white perch, bass and pickerel became a way of life for some fishermen. Most personal piers had a float rig in the water, or one ready to use. Eventually Tochterman's stocked and sold everything for fishing, and at one time even had a wholesale business supplying regional stores with tackle.

Some Different Floats

Along the way, there have been some strange floats, such as some 1905 patents and floats. One of these was a Cullum & Boren (Dallas, Texas) slip float (line runs through the float and is held in place with a supplied stop). It was made of pyralin in solid colors and available in several sizes in both barrel and egg shapes, perhaps following the earlier writings of Brown. Dallas must have been a hotbed of float manufacturing, because during the same time period a similar slip float by a Will R. Allen is written about. The material used is not stated, but the float was available in barrel, thin barrel and egg shapes and in up to eight sizes for the barrel float.

Though the above had the line slip through the center axis of the float, the same time period also produced the J. M. Mast Mfg. Co. float in egg shape with fixed peg ends that had a "buckle tip," which allowed fixing to or removal from the line at any time.

In 1925, Boyer Manufacturing, makers of Winona reels (a simple side-mounted "casting" reel), also offered a Winona celluloid float that resembled a porcupine quill and looked as if it was used the same way, that is, with an eye at one end and a band in the middle to hold the line. Ideal Tackle Co. of Alexandria, VA, was also an important float manufacturer.

A different type of float was produced in 1947 with the Nibble Nabber, which was a tapered float but with a spring arm that would release when a fish nibbled on the bait. The spring arm supposedly drove the hook home. Whether it worked or just bounced around the float is questionable, because it was never again seen.

The Red-and-White Plastic Floats and Bobber Stops

Floats of wood and cork stayed pretty basic until the 1940s when plastic started to be used for much angling tackle, including the still popular and ubiquitous red-and-white round float with spring hooks for fixed or slide fishing. The original Dayton float with the snaps on both ends was advertised in magazines as early as 1947. Bobber stops—small devices designed to fit inconspicuously to the line and, together with a sliding bead, allow casting floats that would slide down the line and allow fishing deep— gained acceptance. Several styles were available, with one of the most popular being the Fred Arbogast model which included a small spring wire that when twisted onto the line and, when stretched, gripped the line. It could then be cast with spinning or casting gear and stopped by a bead captured on the line, the bobber sliding along the line as the sinker pulled

LEFT: *Old floats of cork, wood and plastic were made in a vast array of styles, colors and designs, as shown in this assortment.*

down the bait. Anglers also discovered that they could do the same thing with a rubber band girth- or clove-hitched to the line, then trimmed.

The same effect was achieved by the Helin Rollaflote, introduced by the Helin Tackle Co. in 1950. It allowed an angler to select the depth to be fished, reel the float all the way to the tip of the rod and cast. The float would slide along the line to allow the bait to reach a predetermined depth.

In the South, anglers fishing live bait such as crickets, hoppers and catalpa worms for bream (sunfish) and bass used very lightweight porcupine quills for floats. This may have laid some of the groundwork for the 1980s, imported floats from Europe. These began to gain popularity as fishing for crappie, panfish, perch and similar species gained more fans. These floats were sold individually in a wide variety of styles and in sets. In this, they copied the English and European match-fishing methods where anglers would have a set of a dozen or more floats, the correct float chosen for the fishing conditions, water, current, depth, bait and species sought. The idea of a one-float-fits-all was changing and still continues in this country with tackle shops and catalogs carrying slip and fixed floats.

Live & Natural Bait

Some Thoughts on Fish Foolers

Fishing with bait was, and is, a basic method of catching fish. Using natural foods of the quarry, even chumming them to the area with ground-up bait as an attractor, remains a popular method. That doesn't mean that using live bait is without concern, at least for some baits and some fishing.

"Many years ago," writes William C. Vogt in his 1928 book, *Bait-Casting*, "when I hooked a frog through his lips, he reached up with his little baby-like hands, and took hold of the shank of the hook and tried as hard as he could to pull it out of his mouth, while drops of blood dripped from his chin. The sight was so touching that then and there I resolved never to use another live frog for bait." That concern might be why today there are far fewer frog harnesses made and sold than were popular 50 to 150 years ago, and why fishing topwater artificial lures—some of which closely resemble frogs—has become so popular. (Hooking live frogs is likely not as "touching" as the method used in the Bengal area of India for baiting crocodiles, the bait being a live puppy!)

More Reasons To Not Use Frogs Today

Today, there might be other, if less emotional, reasons for not using frogs. Recent studies indicate that frog populations worldwide are markedly down, while leg and body deformities are increasingly being found on frogs in many areas. With global warming, pollution and acid rain being named as possibilities of this ecological problem, the fact remains that frogs are less popular than they once were when frog-hooking harnesses were a staple in most tackle shops.

Early Baits—And the Ubiquitous Worm

Just what was used initially for bait is anyone's guess, because bait fishing has been written about less than fly fishing. Both were little described until the mid-1800s, even though settlers were here in the 1600s. The one exception to descriptions of bait fishing was the baits and bait preparation sometimes described in detail in early publications.

Early baits, as might be expected, were anything easily obtainable, with the earthworm and its many variations being the main ingredient of many angling expeditions. The methods of using worms and even gathering worms has not changed much in 150 years, according to an account in the *American Angler's Guide* (Brown, 1849).

"The most common Bait used in this country for ensnaring almost all varieties of the finny tribe that inhabit fresh water," Brown writes, "is the common earth-worm, or, as it is called, dew-worm, dug-worm, and the angle-worm; which latter, from its universal use in angling, would be the most proper name. It can generally be obtained by digging a foot or two in the ground, except in sandy soils, which produce clear streams, and where the fly will be found the better bait. Another method, recommended by Blaine, is to walk cautiously over close cut lawns, or clean fed meadows, with a candle or lantern, during the night. If the weather be moist, and the search be conducted with a very light tread, almost any quantity may be procured; for as they are blind, it is not the light but the motion which disturbs them. When they are not wanted for immediate use, a good plan is, to wet some straw, or hay, and lay it on the ground for a few days, by which means they will be brought to the top, and can be easily gathered. Another, and more expeditious plan, practiced by Walton, and others, is to take the green leaves of the walnut-tree, and squeeze the juice into fresh or saltwater, and pour it on the ground, which will make them rise in a very short time."

Products exist today that are also designed, when diluted in water, to cause worms to rise to the surface where they may be more easily gathered. Some anglers have used soapy water for the same purpose. Tools—some electric—have been produced to achieve the same purpose. For those buying worms, the general opinion is that the best worms come from Canada, where they are supposedly harvested from golf-course greens.

Ground and Paste Baits

Early baits also included a host of other natural and made-up baits and pastes. Some early books list white grub worms, grasshoppers, minnows, trout or salmon roe (or spawn as it was called then), wasps, beetles, flies, caterpillars, locusts, other insects, frogs, (in whole or in parts, sometimes with the legs skinned to make them white and presumably more attractive to fish), shiners, mullet, goldfish, shrimp, (for saltwater, although in modern times they are often used for catfish and other species in freshwater), shedder crabs, soft-shell clams, Marsh worms, brandlings (alternately streaked with red and yellow ringlets), little gilt-tail or tag worms, red-worms, peacock-red worms (or black-head worms), maggots (or gentles, a name originated in England), caddis larva, dock grubs, oak grubs and a bunch of other date-named worms, grubs and baits.

Some of these were named as the best baits for specific fish, such as the grasshopper as an excellent

bait for trout and the minnow (of many types, though unnamed) ideal for trout, pickerel and salmon. In his writings, Frank Forester mentions ground-up fish as bait (perhaps chum) as attracting saltwater gamefish.

Some paste baits from the 1700s and 1800s involved strange mixtures of items such as putrefied meat (often from game such as rabbit), honey, stale bread and flour all mixed together.

Roe: Tops for Trout and Salmon Then and Now

The top bait for trout was trout or salmon roe, just as it is today. As then, it is used today either singly on a special short shank hook or tied up in roe bait bags, or tied as a fly and used with split shot to get deep for the "chuck-and-duck" fly fisherman.

"The trout or salmon Spawn, however, takes the lead as the best trout bait in the world; so much so that many Anglers in Europe deem it unworthy a sportsman to use it," writes Brown of its use 150 years ago.

A similar bait was shad roe, found only during the shad runs in April and May. In fact, Thaddeus Norris, in 1864, writes derisively and disparagingly of the "shad-roe fisherman" as one of lesser character, going to fish on Sundays with a kettle of shad roe for bait (when fishing on Sunday was not considered proper or gentlemanly), often with a flask of rye liquor, catching pansize rock and white perch and after a day of fishing smeared and smelling of shad roe. Norris noted that this "species" of angler is found in Philadelphia, and rarely elsewhere. Sorry, Philly!

Other Worms and Baits

Worms were always a standard for bait for all species of fish, especially trout and panfish. Francis, in 1867, wrote in his *A Book On Angling* that many worms are used, referring to the various baits as red heads, brandlings, or gilttails, lob or dew worms, dock or flag worms, green stink worms and blood worms. Though published in England and written for that audience, it is likely that some of the books came to America and that similar worms (as mentioned by Brown) were used here for our native fish, just as the worms

ABOVE: *Containers to hold bait were always popular with anglers.* **Front to back:** *some typical containers (front two containers) to hold worms, crickets, and minnows; Lewis metal floating bait bucket and relatively modern plastic minnow buckets.*

Live & Natural Bait 35

>
> ### BASIC SPREADERS GO BACK A-WAYS
>
> Spreaders are wire devices, bent in a slight curve, with a line tie on the convex center of the curve and a snap for a sinker on the concave center of the curve. Fasteners on each end hold snelled hooks for bottom fishing. Some have extendable wires, which slide together for storage, apart for fishing. They are widely used in bottom fishing for species such as flounder and sea bass in saltwater; or fished mid-depths for crappie and perch in freshwater.
>
> They are currently available everywhere, but they are not new. "A friend has lately shown me a Chinese contrivance, which was brought over many years since by an old East India merchant; it may have caused the introduction of the 'bow-dipsy' in Philadelphia," writes Thaddeus Norris in his book, *The American Angler's Book* of 1864. "This is a piece of whalebone bent at right angles, each side or arm being fifteen to eighteen inches in length, with a snood attached to the ends. It is lowered to the bottom by means of a hand line, and a conical leaden sinker fastened ten or twelve inches beneath the angle. It is well adapted for taking small fish in any rapid tideway (especially White Perch), where they collect in schools and bite rapidly. It is braced by lateral pieces of cord, which cause the whalebone to give and resume its position as the fish takes the bait—making it almost sure to hook him. I have heard of forty dozen White Perch being taken in the Delaware by three fishermen, in the last two hours of an ebb tide, with this strange-looking contrivance."
>
> Most spreaders today are of brass to prevent rusting and are curved rather than bent, but otherwise not unlike the above in appearance or use.

were used in Europe for tench, carp, roach, gudgeon and dace.

Some terms are questionable. The blood worm reference describes not the saltwater mud flat bloodworm harvested from the Northeast flats that we are used to, but, based on his description, a tiny worm of "extremely small size and slender proportions (making it) next to impossible to get it onto a hook at all." These worms might have been the ½-inch-long larvae of *Chironomous* midges, referred to in aquarium books as "blood worms." Another possibility could be tubifex worms, found in slow and stagnant areas of streams and sold in this country to feed aquarium fish, and now implicated in the "whirling disease" that is adversely affecting trout populations throughout the country, particularly in the West. Of course, those names could be inclusive of several species, particularly in those days of rapid scientific findings and taxonomic name changes. Conflicting names were even given to gamefish. From 1850 to 1974, the rockfish (striped bass) of the Atlantic Coast had its scientific name changed five times.

Strange Baits

Other baits listed included meal worms (really grubs) and maggots (also called gentles at the time) preferably bred in a bullock's liver, which was obviously easier to obtain 100-plus years ago than it would be today from your local supermarket.

Caddis larvae taken from the stone and twig cases and threaded onto a hook, grubs of moths, leeches, cockroaches, grasshoppers, crickets, stonefly larva, beetles, slugs, snails, small frogs, large frogs, rats, mice and small birds were all tried as baits.

These are not unexpected and, even today, hard and soft lures that resemble frogs, mice, rats and even small birds have been tried. Live rats, mice, frogs and especially birds are little, if at all, used today. The difference is perhaps a societal change, in our current concern over humane use of animals, when compared to the 18th and early 19th century when dogfights, cockfighting, bear-baiting, bull-baiting, buffalo-baiting and similar activities were popular entertainment both in England and in the colonies.

Early Terrestrials—Bait, Not Flies—And Some Chumming

The early use of grasshoppers, crickets and beetles predicted the later popularity of these in fly patterns as written about by Vince Marinaro and Charles Fox in the late 1950s and early 1960s, with the baits used for chumming of feeding trout in south-central Pennsylvania before the artificial fly was thrown into the feeding lane. In this, then and now, the standard method is to locate a trout visually or through the rises, then toss a few baits (jassids, beetles, hoppers or crickets) into the feeding lane to condition the trout, followed by a cast or tossed fly imitating the bait into the same lane.

One of the strangest and earliest methods of chumming, long predating Marinaro and Fox, involved a dead groundhog. The method was to shoot a groundhog, slice it open, then drape it on a sturdy branch that would overhang the water. After about seven to ten days, the groundhog would be ripe with maggots, which would drop into the water. Trout would gather beneath this bountiful feast like kids in front of a candy store. The fishing method was to tie on a light colored fly or maggot imitation, drift it straight downstream into the feeding lane, and hang on!

Scoured Any Worms Lately?

There were also early (mid-1800s) methods of "scouring" worms so that they would be clean, active, tough and look good in the water. This was a system to remove the dirt in the alimentary canal of the worm and to make them clean and red. The methods used today are not unlike those early methods in which worms were placed in washed, moist moss, which would clean them of the earth in their digestive tracts after a few days. The suggestion was that worms could be kept this way for a long time by changing and washing the moss every three or four days. It was noted that dead or sickly worms were to be removed immediately, lest they affect the other, healthy worms. Today, commercial worm bedding is available for the same purpose as the moss used then.

Some anglers use coffee grounds, arguing that after a few days, this makes worms clean and bright. Also, today you can do the same thing by keeping worms in a specially prepared commercial worm bedding, such as that by Buss Bedding. This also "scours" the worms for immediate use. In the 1700s and 1800s though, commercial worm bedding was not available. They had the next best thing, because in those agricultural times, most farms had a pile of wood chips from cutting and splitting wood for the stoves, fireplaces and furnaces. Even on the hottest days, the center of the chip pile would remain moist and cool and usually full of clean red wigglers, along with a red-headed white grub or two.

Live & Natural Bait

Baiting and Hooking Worms

Baiting with worms was also similar then to methods of today. One method was to run the hook point into the worm a little below the head, then thread the hook through the worm to within a quarter-inch of the tail, with the hook shank well-covered by the worm.

For two worms, the method was similar, hooking below the head, but then exiting the worm in its middle, then hooking into the middle of the second worm, threading the hook up to within a quarter-inch of the head. With the two worms meeting on the hook shank, the hook would be completely covered with the worms. A trick also mentioned was to thread the first worm up onto and over the "arming" of the hook.

The "arming" of the hook is the point where the hook is tied, snelled or whipped onto the line, thus the worm would hide this part and slide up onto the line as well. The same method of running the worm over the arming is suggested for large worms, entering the point in the head of the worm and threading down to the tail. Similar techniques are done with all types of worms.

Getting Grubs on the Hook

The possibility of grubs slipping down on the hook shank or off of the hook is also addressed, with many anglers taking their tips from as early as the 1676 edition (fifth edition) of *The Compleat Angler*, by Izaak Walton, but specifically from Charles Cotton's description of baiting. For this, grubs were to be baited after first tying the hook to the line or leader and leaving a very short length of stiff hair or gut protruding from the knot or junction (arming) of the line and hook. The grub was then hooked below the head, the hook run through the body, until the head of the grub rested on the protruding gut or hair, placed there to keep the grub in place. This same method works today for the large Euro-larvae available from bait stores.

In short, this early method of stabilizing a live grub is not unlike the method of toothpick-pegging the head of a plastic worm in modern day bass fishing or using a length of leader or wire to hold the head of a ballyhoo in place for saltwater big-game trolling. Caddis larva (then spelled cadis) were threaded two or three to a hook, or sometimes singly, but together with a worm or artificial fly.

Pastes and Making and Preserving Roe

Pastes were also common, although as an imported idea from England, presumably less used here than in Great Britain. The exception might be the catfish and carp pastes sold today, along with canned or frozen chum that is used primarily for saltwater fishing. Trout or salmon roe was considered a paste, although in reality, directions for its preparation are not unlike those of today when the roe is preserved by being immersed into hot water, separated from the membranes that hold it, then rinsed in cold water, after which it is dried for 24 hours. Following this, two ounces of rock or bay salt and a quarter ounce of salt peter (spelled salt petre in early directions) was placed with a pound of roe, then hung up to dry again for 24 hours, after which it was further dried before a low fire or in the sun. To bait a hook with the roe, a piece the size of a hazelnut was recommended, or a piece that would fill up the bend of the hook from point to shank and thus hide the hook.

Shrimp paste was prepared similarly (presumably by cutting up the shrimp tails into bait-size pieces). Cheese paste from old or new cheese and mixed with stale bread, sweet paste of mixed bread and honey and bread paste of moistened bread worked into a dough-like consistency were also popular. Dyes were also used to color the baits, particularly the pastes, to give them the appearance of fish spawn.

Baits You Could Cast

With the influx of casting tackle by which lines were spooled on revolving-spool reels and lures cast and retrieved for fish, baits changed to those that could be cast. That's how baitcasting came to be named, since the early casting reels were developed in the 1810 to 1825 period, prior to the great development and expansion of lures and crankbaits later around

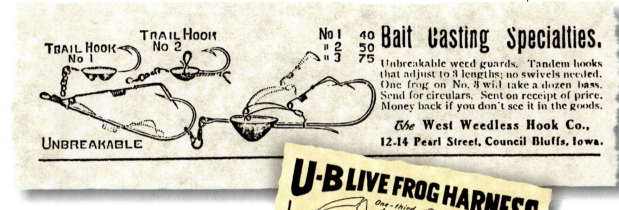

the turn of the century. Baitcasting early on was quite simply casting with bait.

For baitcasting, frogs (along with the mice, rats and most other small creatures) became popular, with frogs and minnows of various types the most likely target of bait hunters then. Small mice were often used, sometimes at night, when fishing for big brown trout. Anglers learned quickly that the big trout, particularly brown trout, quickly became meat eaters. A 1939 *Pennsylvania Angler* magazine article notes that a 19½-inch brown trout that had been caught had a small ground squirrel in its stomach.

Frog Harnesses, or the Spanish Inquisition?

Frog harnesses were not lures, but were usually wire configurations with accompanying hooks, some hanging off the apparatus; others were designed to be hooked into the frog. One, the Prevost Patent Combination Frog Hook from the 1890s, was really a harness that hooked the frog by the lips, with two additional hooks, one through the skin of the knee of each leg. Twitching the line caused a sleeve to slide on the device to pull the legs forward to simulate a kicking motion and make the frog more lifelike, if less life-preserving and more painful to the frog. Three sizes were available. Ketchum's Frog Casting Frame Gang from 1904 was just that. Size 3/0 single rear hooks were hooked through the frogs legs, while a treble on each side of the body caught anything missed by the single hooks.

The 1900 Crosby New Frog Tandem harness, in weed-guard and plain styles, used only two single hooks. The front hook went through the frog's lips, the rear hook hung free and a rubberband secured the body of the frog to the long-shank rear hook. Other frog harnesses and hooks followed, most built around the lines of securing the frog by means of bands or clamps or hooking him

Live & Natural Bait

in various ways. In 1937, the Pflueger catalog listed a Hanson Frog Harness that did not harm the frog, but was a weedless rig and that allowed the frog to swim freely. The harness was still listed through 1952. Herter's sold frog harnesses in the 1960s. All of these harnesses for frogs and other baits were to entice the increasingly popular gamefish—the largemouth bass, chain pickerel, northern pike and muskellunge.

Minnows Held on a Hook

Minnows and baitfish also often ended up in harm's way with the many hook riggings designed to hold them as bait for everything from trout to bass to pike. One of the early ones was the 1910 model of the Eckhardt Minnow, sold as a "Life Preserving and Weedless Hook," that also incorporated a wire weed guard. Judging by the illustration in an ad, the body of the minnow appeared to be caught between the inside bend of the hook and the spring of the weed guard. "This is a combination hook that will keep your minnow alive, continually swimming in its natural position, and attracts fish where other hooks fail," notes the ad copy. It continues, "This is the only hook that preserves the life of the minnow." If your dealer did not carry it, the manufacturer would sell it to you direct, for 10 cents, but it asked that you also send two cents for postage.

Archer spinners, made in England but no doubt sold here in the 1890s and up to World War II, had spinner blades that were hinged to the shaft and swivel, with in-pointing pins or spikes designed to pinion the head of a dead minnow used for trolling, the fins spinning the bait slowly in the water. It was lures and bait rigs like this that coined the phrase "spinning" (spinning of the bait in the water) long before the term spinning applied to the advent of fixed-spool tackle. Five sizes were made; the small trout and salmon sizes had free swinging trebles attached. Hardy's or Hardy's Alnwick rigs were similar with points, like an Iron Maiden, pinioning the dead minnow. L. L. Bean offered two sizes at 70 cents each in their 1939 catalog.

Other bait rigs were also designed for dead minnows, such as the W. J. Jamison Company Sure Catch Minnow Hook and the similar Sure Catch Grasshopper Hook. Basically, these were double hooks on a long shank that formed a pointed baiting needle that was designed to run through the minnow (usually through the vent and out the mouth). The eye of the needle/shank was secured with an eyed clip hook to which the line was tied. The grasshopper hook worked on the same principle, but was smaller. Grasshopper hooks ranged from size 8 and 1 inch long to size 1 and 2½ inches long; the minnow hooks were from size 1/0 and 2¾ inches long to size 6/0 and 5⅜ inches long. Today, the same style and design of hook is available from the Mustad Company, some 80 years after the early ads for this design.

Lip Hooking and Corsetting Minnows

Lots of hooking rigs were little more than a small short-shank hook rigged or soldered to the forward end of a large, long shank hook. Minnow rigging with these involved hooking the minnow through the lips with the small forward hook and running the large hook through the tail or skin of the body. Some, like the U. B. Minnow Harness from Jamison, had an additional wire frame for holding the body of the minnow, which was hooked only through the lips to keep it alive longer.

The Minnow Corset was made with two single

LEFT: *Three types of early (and fragile!) glass minnow traps. Front center, one with funnel holes in the sides; front right, a trap with a funnel hole in the rear; and rear, a trap with two open ends, each holding a wire mesh funnel. Note the wire handles on two of the traps by which to carry them. All are from the very early 1900s.*

hooks, side-by-side and spring-loaded, and with a bracket attached to the shank of each hook. The spring would clamp onto the minnow, with the brackets gripping the sides to prevent its loss. It was promoted as a "live bait lure" (although really a rigging and not a lure at all) for "minnows, shrimp, crawfish," but they also included liver and pork rind in the mix.

The Pachner and Koeher Minnow-Saver hook of the 1930s worked similarly, except that the brackets were replaced with a pin that went through the back of the minnow to pin it between the two hooks.

During the same period (1930s), South Bend had a similar double hook that would hold the minnow parallel to the two hook shanks, a spring holding the body with the lips pinned with a small forward hook on the rig. Water Gremlin had a single-hook spring-loaded clamp that would hold a lip-hooked trolling minnow behind a spinner blade on the rig.

Anglers combined some of these rigs with a June Bug spinner (most likely from Hildebrandt) to make a spinner/bait rig, using either minnows or a tangle of worms.

Chaining Up Minnows

Some rigs went to extremes. The Log Chain Live Bait Hook was designed to lip- or tail-hook a bait, the eye of the hook attached to a tiny chain that was half-hitched around the body to drag the minnow through the water.

Easily Seen If Not Easily Eaten

Other methods were designed to hold minnows without harming them, although their ultimate fate was probably the same regardless. The Detroit Glass Minnow Tube Company of Detroit Michigan made glass tube rigs with hooks attached by metal bands.

Live & Natural Bait

LEFT: *Clear plastic or glass tubes, rigged with wire frames to hold hooks and a line tie, were used early on to hold live minnows. The idea? To protect the minnows while keeping them visible to the fish. The wire frog harnesses (bottom) were designed to hold frogs that were a popular bait in the early days of bait casting.*

The minnow was slipped into the tube, which was then capped. The minnow, "… will remain alive all day," according to ads run in the 1910s of this bait holder that was equipped with four treble hooks. Hopefully the minnows so encased did not get claustrophobia.

The same company at the same time also advertised a "Live Minnow Cage." This was a tapered, torpedo-like spring-wire cage with free flow of water, a treble hook at each end and a line tie on top and about one-fifth of the way back. Finally, it sold a "Live Minnow Holder," which appeared to be a double hook with a spring clip on the upper part of the shank, the minnow pinned by the dorsal fin under the clip and pinioned into the belly by the two hooks.

Other companies had clear minnow tubes similar to that of the Detroit model. Pfeiffer's (no relation to the author) Live Bait Holder Co. had two models of clear glass minnow tubes, one with four treble hooks and one with three. The smaller "trout size" version of the minnow tube with three trebles had the tail treble dressed with bucktail and attached by means of a split ring to a glass ring molded into the tail of the glass tube. You have to wonder how that held up when a big fish hit! The Charles C. Kellman company had a glass tube rigged with two single hooks. These also came in small fly-rod sizes, which are very rarely found today.

Clear celluloid was used for some tubes, such as those by the Joseph M. Ness Co. of Minneapolis, MN, which made the Nifty Minne clear celluloid tube with five trebles and a propeller spinner blade on the front and the A. J. Baldwin company, which manufactured the Baldwin Live Minnow Bait. That had a wire frame sporting three trebles around a clear celluloid tube. Most of these devices were made in the 1900 to 1915 period, but that was not always the case. One from 1947 was a Bass Oreno-shaped lure of clear plastic called the live lure. This allowed insertion of the minnow by removing the head of the "lure." The plastic would also magnify the bait.

Plastics Enter the Bait Game

Plastics other than celluloid entered the minnow and bait rigging methods in the 1940s with the Hotternell Bait Holder from the Martin Fish Lure Company. This plastic head, or cup, was designed to hold the head of a minnow, the minnow clipped in place at the head and then with a hook through the tail. These are not unlike the various cut bait or plug bait fishing heads and rigs sold today for salmon trolling, or the similar plastic heads such as the aptly-named Hoo Nose (for holding a ballyhoo by slipping the rig over the nose of the bait) for rigging saltwater ballyhoo for big game offshore.

All Types of Bait Hooks

Other bait hooks evolved over a period of time. Early on, hooks were made with one or more slices into the shank that were designed to hold the bait in place, just like Eagle Claw hooks from the Wright & McGill Company and similar hooks available today from other companies. This idea is thought to have originated with the Sealy Hook Company of England in the 1930s, later picked up by Eagle Claw in the 1940s and by Mustad in 1953.

Most of the spring and snag hooks (one of which had 12 large hooks and 12 small hooks—not exactly sporting!) came from around the turn of the century. Gradually, the concept of sport and using bait changed a little, then a lot, so that today, most hook rigs for bait are plain, hooking minnows with single hooks through the lip for trolling, through the back for still-fishing and through the tail for live-lining bait.

For paste and prepared baits, the treble hook remained popular, particularly those made with a loose spring around the center shank to which baits like prepared catfish baits, carp dough balls and similar concoctions would better adhere.

Pork Rind—The Bait for Lures

Pork rind is a bait, but one that is most often, but not exclusively, used with lures. Some early weedless hook rigs used pork rind strips, chunks and eels alone, but most pork rind was and is designed as a trailer to spoons, spinnerbaits, jigs, etc.

The first pork rind is credited to Lutz in 1892. That company's eel, which continued through the 1960s, was a popular bass bait in the then-fledgling bass fishing tournament scene. The most popular and successful pork rind manufacturer today is the Uncle Josh Bait Company, which was begun in 1920 by Alan P. Jones and his fishing buddy Urban Schreiner. Both fished for bass in the lakes around Fort Atkinson, WI. They would fish plugs early in the morning, then switch to live frogs after the sun was up.

One day, so Jones related in recounting the history of the company in 1976, they could not find frogs around Lake Jordan, where they were fishing, so they decided to "make" a frog from something else, such as pork. They went to a butcher shop, obtained a slab of pork fat back with the rind, carved and whittled and came up with a rough facsimile of a frog. They caught bass on their new baits, and from that day on left the real frogs alone and the plugs in their tackle boxes. With Jones in the dairy, sausage and meat-packing business, the idea of the lure and the company was a natural.

The company formally started in 1922 with white baits, later dyed green to make them look more frog-like. They had some problems with early dyes, and also with preservation (and the smell of some early ship-

ments of ill-preserved baits), but soon solved these spoilage problems. Shortly after the pork frog, they developed four other baits: the Pollywoggler (a tail chunk with red yarn whiskers); the Bass Strip; the Fly Strip; and the oval Pork Chunk. Better dyes came along after World War II, as did more shapes—eels, lizards and leeches—and various sizes of strips. Pork, with or without a lure, was here to stay.

Artificial Lures

Introduction

Lures started with flies. In the broad sense all flies are lures, but not all lures are flies. Flies, and later lures, gave the angler lots of advantages. For those with sensibilities about harming another form of life by impaling bait on a hook (we'll forget for a moment the goal of impaling a fish with the bait or lure), lures eliminated the squirming of a worm, the distress and efforts to dislodge the hook by frogs and the throes of a hooked minnow. Ken Reinard, author of *The Colonial Angler's Manual of Flyfishing & Flytying,* quotes John Gay on the subject. John Gay, an English writer describing the sport in his 1720 book, *Rural Sports,* writes:

> *"Around the steal no tortured worm shall tweine*
> *No blood of living insect stain my line*
> *Let me, less cruel, cast the feathered hook*
> *With pliant rod across the pebbled brook"*

There is even evidence of primitive lures made by native Indians. In the mud of a small Florida island—Key Marco—was found what probably was a primitive Indian fishing lure. A double hook made of deer antler was wrapped to a sea shell (pen shell) measuring one by three inches and with a pearly luster, closely resembling spoons that we use even today. In the past 50 years, manufacturers have included natural shells in some spoons and spinner blades for this same pearl luster.

Lures also made fishing more convenient and economical, since minnow buckets, worm boxes, cricket cages, bait cans and the like became unnecessary. Also no longer a factor were the time and difficulties of catching, caring for, feeding and transporting the little critters to the fishing spot, then keeping them alive and under control while fishing. Lures have allowed carrying a few or a lot of bait imitations that would cause fish to strike and get caught on the attached hooks. "Clean, convenient, effective and humane," Heddon was to say later in its 1929 catalog when introducing its Luny and Little Luny frogs and other lures with frog finishes as a substitute for the real thing.

Is Walton's Described Minnow the First Lure?

There is ample evidence of lures made during Walton's time, and in fact written about by him, as follows in an exchange between "Piscator" and the others in this tale of anglers as follows from his book, *The Compleat Angler:* "And here let me tell you, what many old anglers know right well, that at some times, and in some waters, a minnow is not to be got; and therefore let me tell you, I have (which I will show you) an artificial minnow, that will catch a trout as well as an artificial fly, and it was made by a handsome woman that had a fine hand, and a live minnow lying by her: The mould of body of the minnow was cloth, and wrought upon or over it thus with a needle: the back of it with very sad French green silk, the paler green silk towards the belly, shadowed as perfectly as you can imagine, just as you see a minnow; the belly was wrought also with a needle, and it was a part of it white silk, and another part of it silver thread; the tail and fins were of a quill which was shaven thin; the eyes were of two little black beads, and the head was so shadowed, and all of it so curiously wrought, and so exactly dissembled that it would beguile any sharp-sighted trout in a swift stream."

Never mind for the moment the run-on sentences and the resultant need for excessive punctuation, since this seems to describe an artificial minnow, not a fly, that was made to closely resemble a live minnow in shape and subtle color shadings. It is described so matter-of-factly that it appears that these were not new or unknown at the time when written about in 1653. With the distinction made between flies and this well-described minnow, it also makes the point that this was not a fly, or tied like any fly of the period. It was a lure. It also might have been a precursor of the cloth-bodied English Phantoms later used in the 1700s and up through the 1800s in England that were also imported here, and also resulted in some American copies.

Whether or not early fishermen realized the several reasons why fish strike is not known. Today, we assume, and indeed have some evidence, that fish: strike to eat, as when taking a lure that resembles suitable food; strike to remove a danger from a nest area, as will bass in removing a plastic worm from a bed; strike from anger, as fish can sometimes be tricked into doing from repeated casts to a given fish or spot; or strike competitively to keep another fish from getting the bait as dogs do with a bone or food bowl. As an example of this, it is not unknown to catch two fish on one two-treble hook lure on one cast, or to have one or more fish trying to take the lure or fly from the hooked fish's mouth right up to the boat. Probably the Helin Flatfish with its wide-spread belly-hook hanger with three or four trebles has been responsible for more double catches than any other lure.

It is likely that the first notable lure developed for fishing was made after realizing that fish would strike an artificial object, thinking that it is food. This again was referenced by Walton after his description of the effectiveness of the artificial cloth minnow, noting that trout have been caught with up to 160 minnows in their belly. (That's what Walton said—not the author!)

From the Beginning to the 1800s

Flies Are King

Although some additions of feathers and carvings to early hooks by primitive man might be considered lures, the only early lures were flies, mentioned almost 2,000 years ago. This earliest proven description of a fly is from the writings of Claudius Aelian (170 to 230 A.D.), who included a little about fishing in his book, *On The Characteristics of Animals or Natural History.* He does not state the species of fish other than to note that they have speckled skins (quite likely brown trout or perhaps a char, like an Eastern brook trout, which are still found in the area today), and that they rise to the surface to take flies. He also noted that live flies are not used, because they change color and wither and are thus unfit for fishing. (There are earlier references to fly fishing, but scholars are not sure if they refer to artificial flies or natural flies placed on a hook. As with any history, there are differences of opinion.)

Of making the fly, a popular translation (it was written in Greek) is: "They fasten red [crimson red] wool round a hook, and fix on to the wool two feathers which grow under a cock's wattles, and which in color are like wax. Their rod is six feet long and their line is the same length. Then they throw their snare, and the fish, attracted and maddened by the color, comes straight at it, thinking from the pretty sight to get a dainty mouthful; when, however, it opens its jaws, it is caught by the hook and enjoys a bitter repast, a captive."

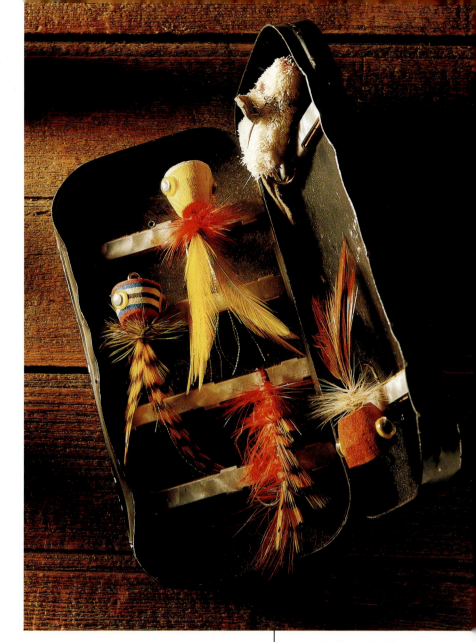

Even-Earlier Fly Fishing?

One researcher suggests an earlier mention of fly fishing by the Roman poet Martial (40 to 104 A.D.), although this was for a saltwater fish, the sea-parrot, and, if true, would be the first mention of what is thought of today as the "new" sport of saltwater fly fishing.

Regardless, fishing with flies, making rods (no reels yet) and tying flies continued without demonstrable change into the 1400s with the 1496 description of 12 flies for the 12 months of the year by Dame Juliana Berners with *A Treatise On Fishing With An Angle* (hook). This carried over

ABOVE: Modern colorful foam bass bugs often echo the styles, colors and patterns of the past, when deer hair bugs were made in these designs and colors.

Artificial Lures

into the 1676 fifth edition of Izaak Walton's *The Compleat Angler,* in which Charles Cotton contributed a section on fly fishing.

Colonial Fishing

Colonial fishermen into the late 1700s fished the same way as they had in England for 300 years, perhaps even longer. Long, cumbersome rods of typical English style were used, although these ultimately proved to be less effective for American-style fishing. Ken Reinard in researching his book on colonial angling, (*The Colonial Angler's Manual of Flyfishing & Flytying,* 1995, Fox Chapel Publishing, Lancaster, PA), notes that many early anglers had to be tackle makers and tackle tinkerers, making or tying not only their own flies, but also making the hooks on which the flies were tied, making lines and making rods. No reels were used early on, sparing the early angler the most difficult task of tackle construction.

Fly fishermen of this period usually fished several flies at once, the fly on the end of the leader (often called cast during that period) the stretcher; the flies farther up the leader called droppers. This also allowed fishing so that flies just barely touched or skimmed the surface. It wasn't dry fly fishing, but it was fishing with flies on the surface or in the surface film.

Bobs and Bass Bugs

American Indians in the late 1700s used a method of fishing that encompassed modern techniques of flipping and pitching, a precursor of a deer hair fly and a skittering method. The naturalist William Bartram noted this in journal writings from his view of angling methods used by Southeast Indians in the late 1760s. That he used the term "reed" for "rod" in a second reference, and that he referred to "green trout" when in fact the fish were bass are the only necessary explanations for this early method of lure/fly fishing. Trout as a term for bass is still sometimes used in the Southeast.

"They are taken with hook and line," writes Bartram, "but without any bait. Two people are in a little canoe, one sitting in the stern to steer, and the other near the bow, having a rod ten or twelve feet in length, to one end of which is tied a strong line, about twenty inches in length, to which is fixed three large hooks, back to back. These are fixed very securely, and covered with the white hair of a deer's tail, shreds of a red garter, and some particoloured feathers, all which form a tuft, or tassel, nearly as large as one's fist, and entirely cover and conceal the hooks; this is called a bob. The steersman

LEFT: *A selection of colonial flies, in a large fly book of the period, tied with the short leaders of horse hair and ready to fish. Note that the early anglers used interconnecting loops for their line/fly attachments, just as do many modern anglers.*

SKITTERING, BOBBING AND SPATTING

The Indian method of skittering a "bob" of deer hair wrapped up with a hook when fishing for bass was described by William Bartram in the late 1700s. The method, somewhat revised, is still popular today using pork rind and a cane pole. It is also not unlike methods of flipping, whereby a long (usually 7½ feet) stiff rod is used with a short line and flipping reel (or one with a free spooling/drag lever switch) to drop a lure such as a jig or worm into tight snag-filled places to wrest bass out of the cover. Pitching is similar also, but practiced at slightly greater distances from the angler.

The skittering technique was also suggested as a good method in 1951 by *Sports Afield* angling editor Jason Lucas who noted that a long pole, short line and big bass bug was an effective way to fish for bass, dropping and working the bug around snags, weeds, pads and the like. He called it spatting, and suggested one angler work the rod while a buddy maneuvers the boat along the shore.

Eric C. Fare advertised a method of guaranteed bass fishing for nine years in *Outdoor Life* magazine. His method—a skittering technique—would be revealed to the reader for $15.

ABOVE: *The spinner fly on the right is a Buehl that is very similar to a latter E-Z spinner fly pictured in the 1939 Horrocks-Ibbotson catalog. The main difference is that the E-Z lure has a Sneck (squared bend) hook; the Buehl does not.*

paddles softly, and proceeds slowly along shore, keeping parallel to it, as a distance just sufficient to admit the fisherman to reach the edge of the floating weeds along the shore; he now ingeniously swings the bob backwards and forwards, just above the surface, and sometimes tips the water with it; when the unfortunate cheated trout instantly springs from under the weeds, and seizes the prey. Thus he is caught without possibility of escape, unless he breaks the hooks, line or rod, which he, however, sometimes does by dint of strength; but, to prevent this, the fisherman used to the sport is careful not to raise the reed suddenly up, but jerks it instantly backwards, then steadily drags the sturdy reluctant fish to the side of the canoe, and with a sudden jerk brings him into it."

Substitute modern equipment and you have a perfect current description of flipping with casting tackle or casting with a fly to the edge of a weedline while a trolling motor controls the distance from the shore (perhaps one of the side-scanning controlled motors that will maintain distance automatically?), teasing the bass into striking, while working the shoreline thoroughly. Bass hooked this way, whether for fun

Artificial Lures

or tournament fishing, are fairly rapidly and unceremoniously jerked into the boat as was done almost 250 years ago.

Apparently the first recorded mention of recreational fishing in the New World was with a fly (wrapped or "true" fly, in contrast to the "bob" above) in the colonial New York area (not a state then), by Sir William Johnson, who dapped flies in the mid-1730s on New York's Kenyetto Creek to catch brook trout. Most of the flies through this period were made on hand-bent or home-made hooks.

Other lures might also have been used during this period. Reinard's book on Colonial fishing notes a May 27, 1784, receipt from Edward Pole, to a General Cadwalader who along with rods, lines and trolling hooks bought "2 Artificial Chubbs & 2 Minnows." This might record the first sale of lures or flies in this country. Could these "artificial chubbs and 2 minnows" be cloth or other minnow imitations or lures, such as were described by Walton? And could the English cloth-covered Phantom lures of the 1700s and 1800s be direct descendants of the cloth minnow described by Walton?

Even prior to this, native Americans used plug-like lures to catch fish, according to Scott and Art Kimball's book, *Early Fishing Plugs of the U.S.A.*, which described these primitive lures used for gathering food, along with trolling lures used in the Hawaiian Islands for capturing bonito. Great Lakes Indians made wood minnows or fish-shaped lures that would be attached to a pole by means of thongs to move around and attract fish, most often pike and muskie, for spearing. Along the upper Mississippi River, the

TOP LEFT: *A very early style of J. T. Buel trolling spinner made in Whitehall, NY (note location in photo). It featured a box swivel and originally had a red feather on the treble hook.*

BELOW LEFT: *A second generation of Buel spinner, smaller than the above model, but with a full feathered treble hook and barrel swivel. Made in Canton, NY.*

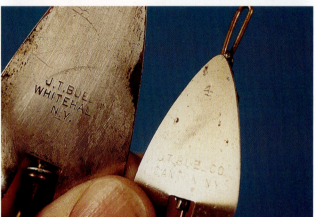

natives used shell lures, possibly with a hook, to capture fish. Eskimos used ivory plug-type lures or "squids" for fishing in their Northern waters.

From the 1800s to the 1850s

Metal Enters the Market

Imports from England between 1800 and 1810 included the Phantom Minnows and Devon lures that were perhaps the first lures used other than sewn minnows, flies or the primitive hook/lures of Indians and Eskimos. These Devons resembled a cigar on a wire shaft, a line tie at one end and a treble attached to the tail end. Blades that resembled pectoral fins amidships spun the lure and gave rise to the term "spinning," which was practiced with hand lines or by trolling, not with the modern spinning tackle, which had not been invented then.

The first patent for a United States-developed lure was for a metal spoon (really a spinner) invented a half century after the first English lures entered the country. It was credited to Julio Buel, who got the idea during a mishap while fishing as a boy.

When Julio T. Buel was 15 in 1821 and living with his family in Castleton, VT, he often fished the local streams for trout and trolled with bait for lake trout in Lake Bomoseen, about six miles north of his home and accessible by horseback. Once he was fishing the lake from his small rowboat and after a productive morning, boated the oars to let the rising breeze drift the boat back toward shore. He ate his lunch during this time, finishing his bread and meat. He was having a dessert of fruit from a jar, which had been prepared for him by his sister. The boat hit a rock, Julio lurched, and the German silver tablespoon he was using tumbled into the clear waters. Julio watched as the spoon twisted and turned in the water. When it was just about to disappear, it was grabbed by a large lake trout.

That night he "borrowed" another spoon, sawed off much of the handle, soldered a hook to the concave side of the blade and drilled a hole in the handle stump to which to tie the line. On his next visit to the lake, after talking his brother into doing his morning chores, Buel trolled by rowing back and forth over the spot where the trout had hit the previously lost spoon. This time he got a hit, hooked the trout, almost lost his rod but eventually landed the fish. He caught a second and as most of us might do, took his time going home down main street with the two trout tied to the pommel of the saddle and prominently displayed for all to see. He told fascinated anglers and townsmen where he had caught the trout, but not how or on what. These were the first catches of trout on a lure made in this country.

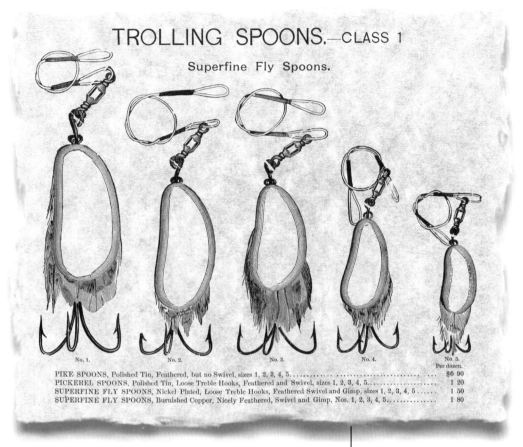

The Dawn of Lures in America

Young Buel eventually confessed to the fate of the two spoons and started making spoons for anglers eager to buy his new product for catching fish. Eventually he made his Buel spoons of nickel silver metal (an alloy of nickel, copper and zinc), stamped with dies to form the spoon curvature, painting the convex side red. For hooks he used trebles. Some of his spoons sported feathers; others remained bare. Despite the popularity of his spoons, he continued learning his main trade as a furrier.

He left home in 1827 and started business in Whitehall, NY. He then sent some spoons to Frank Forester, the pen name for Henry William Herbert, who had emigrated from England and began writing articles, later books, on the out-

WHAT'S IN A NAME?

Names are important in lures, and how they develop is another aspect of fishing tackle history. For example, the Crystal Minnow, the first lure made by the Enterprise Manufacturing Company (Pflueger) when it started advertising in 1883 (no earlier ads have been found), was first advertised and spelled as the Chrystal Minnow. The hollow glass lure was available in either luminous or nonluminous body.

The Dardevle was so named by Lou Eppinger of the Eppinger Lure Company only after first naming the famous spoon the Osprey. The Osprey spoon got its name from the birds that soared above the Ontario lakes where the young Eppinger tried his first homemade model and fished it for a month in 1906. After the end of World War I, the Osprey was renamed the Dare Devil in honor of the name the U.S. Marines were given by the allies, according to the book, *The Spooners,* by Harvey W. Thompson (1979). Later it was again renamed the Dardevle, although pronounced the same. This, it was felt, would go over better in the Bible Belt and Northcentral states, where seeing the word Devil in print was about as welcome as the later Scopes (monkey) Trial.

The same philosophy (and fear) led Jack Smithwick to first name his Devil's Horse lures as Devels Horse. He felt that people would not want to buy a lure that had the name "Devil" in it, even though this slim, two-prop top water lure was and is a top lure for largemouth bass.

There were some scandalous names (for the time) such as the Little Egypt from Al Foss developed in 1916 and named for the popular belly dancer of the 1893 Chicago World's Fair. The bare-breasted Virgin Mermaid lure caught more fishermen than fish. The Heddon Zaragossa, a wide-swinging, sashaying, walk-the-dog surface lure, was named by a Heddon Florida salesman when the lure was in the prototype stage. Salesmen were shown the lure—and its action—early in a week-long sales meeting and told to come up with suggested names by the end of the meeting. The Zaragossa name won. He later revealed to Charlie Heddon that it was named for Miami's Zaragossa Street, where young "working girls" plied their trade from pink-lit windows along the street where they could advertise their wares. "When I saw the action of that lure, this was the only thing I could think of," he explained.

ABOVE: *A very rare lure made in limited quantities in 1935 by a New Jersey jeweler and sold more as a novelty than as a serious fishing lure.*

Some lures were named for their folksy sound and for stage performers. The Uncle Josh brand was named for a stage comedian of the 1920s (when Uncle Josh began); the company founders rented boats on a fishing lake from a farmer who talked like the comedian.

doors. Forester wrote about them in the *Spirit of the Times,* an early sportsmen's publication, bringing acclaim and demand for the spoons and forcing Buel to make a decision. Further publicity came at the same time when he sent spoons to John Brown, author of the 1849 *American Angler's Guide* and a New York City tackle dealer. The result was the J. T. Buel Company, established in 1848 to make fishing spoons. From the start they were behind in orders as anglers stopped by to pick up spoons or sent in orders by mail. Buel began his company in 1848, but he did not patent his lure until 1852.

Fly Fishing Remains Strong

Flies continued to be the favored artificial bait, even with the increasing popularity of spoons. Most of the flies were tied on homemade hooks until about 1850 when American companies started to import and manufacture hooks and tackle. Anglers of the time were either fishing flies in the small streams for trout, trolling bait or spoons for lake trout or fishing frogs as bait for bass and pike. Fly fishing gear became the stream and trout fishing tackle, and bait and trolling methods were used for other angling.

Fly fishing at the time was often practiced using a "cast" of flies, this being a selection of three or more (three was common) flies, with one fly tied to the end of the leader (the point), the others tied to droppers. This also often led to the method of using a long rod and allowing the curve of the line between the rod tip and the point fly in the water to drop or "dap" the dropper flies along the surface.

Flies remained popular for trout and salmon mostly, but also occasionally for other species such as bass, panfish, pike or anything else that could be caught near the surface. Tackle such as the sinking and sinking-tip lines for fishing deep with the fly had not yet been invented. Saltwater fly fishing presumably had begun, as noted by Paul Schullery in his 1987 book, *American Fly-Fishing.* He noted an English reference from 1843 where the writer claimed to have fly fished in fresh and saltwater for more than 40 years. This would place the first reference for saltwater fly fishing about 1800, assuming we forgive the very early reference by Martial (40 to 104 A.D.) of fishing with a fly for sea fish.

There are some very early references to saltwater fly fishing in England. Richard Brookes, in the fifth printing (1781) of his book, *The Art of Angling,* refers to bass as being caught in "sea and rivers." Thus, he includes saltwater, although the species of bass is not noted. He further notes that these bass can be taken several ways, including using the same methods used for mullet. Under "Mullet," he notes that bass are "bold feeders" and can be taken on most flies that attract trout.

In the U.S., there are a lot of references to fishing with flies for striped bass and shad, both popular coastal fish that make anadromous runs into freshwater and brackish water areas. Jerome V. C. Smith wrote in his book, *Natural History of the Fishes of Massachusetts* (1833), about fly fishing for sea-trout (sea-run brook trout, not the true saltwater seatrout), along with an occasional detested (Smith's feelings) sculpin, presumably also on the fly. Later, Robert Barnwell Roosevelt writes in his book, *Superior Fishing* (1865), that striped bass can be taken on a red-and-white fly, casting into the Potomac River at Great Falls, just northwest of Washington, DC.

After 1850 to 1875

Spoons and Metal Lures Go Big Time

At the time of Buel's death in 1886, a *Whitehall Times* newspaper article told of Buel's continuing struggle to fill orders for his lures, which were widely known for their fine quality, as well as for being first rate fish-catchers. As a result of demand for Buel spoons and lures exceeding available supply, competitors came into being, perhaps one of the first being Floyd Ferris Lobb, according to Harvey W. Thompson's book, *The Spooners.* He developed a brass, then later a copper and nickel, spoon, about the same time that Buel established his company, but after he had been selling lures for some years. Most of these early spoons were, as might be expected, shaped like the bowl of a teaspoon or tablespoon.

But other shapes and other metal lures were developed and did evolve. Kidney-shaped spoon blades were also used, and some were shaped more like a spinner than a spoon, with the line tie and hooks on opposite ends of one shaft, the blade revolving around the shaft by means of a clevis. Fluted- and ribbed-blade spoons, perhaps first devel-

ABOVE: *Size number 3 Skinner fluted spinner made in Clayton, N. Y. Note the old box swivel attached.*

oped by G. M. Skinner, also became popular. Skinner patented his spoon design in 1874, and it soon gained fame as a muskie lure. Similar fluted and revolving spoons (really spinners) from Buel and Pflueger soon followed. Skinner also patented a red/white enameled spoon (spinner, really) that won a first prize in lures at the 1893 Chicago World's Fair.

Though most of these early spoons were really spinners as we would think of them today, other designs were also developed in this period. In 1859 the Haskell Minnow and the Haskell Musky Minnow, along with a third size, debuted. They were made of copper with a double hook at the tail and looked like a small metal minnow with stamped gills and eyes and realistic tail, dorsal fin and ventral fins. Currently, the Haskell Minnow commands the highest lure price in the collectibles market. In part, this is because it has a three-dimensional shape that, in essence, makes it a "plug," if not a wood plug, which would follow later. It is, however, considered the first plug manufactured in the U.S.

More Metal Lures

Although the Haskell Minnow realistically resembled a minnow, other metal lures were designed to resemble other creatures. In 1870, the S. Allcock Company of Reddich, England, introduced the Maybug Bait, a small 1⅝-inch-long metal bait with wings and body followed by a red yarn-wrapped treble hook that resembled an insect. Twenty-two years later, in 1892, Pflueger introduced a similar-looking and same-name lure, designed to be used on the end of a short line and skittered around pads and weeds for bass and panfish.

About the same time as the Skinner patent, H. C. Brush patented (in 1876) his lure variously called a trolling spoon or floating spinner and also sometimes described as being like a floating spinnerbait. It really wasn't, however, because the wood that made the lure float was in line with the shaft of the lure, the blade revolving around the shaft, just as does a Mepps spinner today.

Some lures looked and acted like nothing alive. The metal 1855 Bate's Patent Serpentine Spinner looked like a

Artificial Lures

skinny football with a fin that spiraled around the full length of this lure and came with a removable treble hook. The treble was particularly unusual in that it was the eye of the hook, not a loop in the lure, that opened for removal from the lure.

Some lures developed concepts that were later used by more modern lures and lure companies. One was the J. B. Christian 1868 patent for a lure on an in-line shaft and propeller-like blade followed by a red woolen yarn or rubber (both mentioned in the patent) body around the shank of a long treble hook. Other examples would be the Bass Bait and the Twin Bass Bait from W. D. Chapman of Theresa,

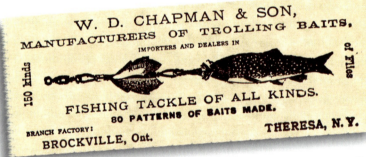

NY, developed in the 1880s. These had broad spinner blades with opposing fins that would look right at home 120 years later on a modern buzzbait. They were on a straight-line spinner shaft, not unlike the straight-line buzzbaits sometimes still available in modern bass lures.

More Metal In the Salt

Saltwater was also being increasingly fished during this late 1800 period: in brackish-water situations, coastal saltwater for stripers, blues and seatrout; and in the late 1800s, the beginnings of offshore angling for the finny giants. Codfish jigs, along with some early fixed-hook trolling spoons, were commonly used in saltwater deep jigging and trolling, respectively. One jig used in the Northeast around 1890, the New England Cod Fish Jig, consisted of an 18-ounce, metal, fish-shaped lure with two single 7/0 hooks running out the mouth.

Rubber Lures, Wood Decoys

Lures of natural rubber were made as early as 1865 by Pflueger. The Pflueger model consisted of two trebles with a small revolving spinner blade on a shaft in line with and in front of the rubber body.

It was during the 1850s that wood fish attractors— the decoys used for ice fishing by spearing in the upper Midwest, were also developed, perhaps following or copying some native American ideas for capturing fish in winter. Fly fishing and flies continued to gain popularity, although many of the flies were not yet American in design, style or origin. Thaddeus Norris in his *American Anglers Book* (1864) showed all British flies in plates of wet fly and streamer patterns. Some flies might also have been the precursors of the soft plastics of today. Nymph and stone fly imitations that were most likely gutta percha (a rubber-like material made from the sap of some Asian trees) are illustrated in Genio Scott's *Fishing in American Waters* of 1888.

Fly Fishing, and in Saltwater Too!

During this period, the gradual shift from English- to American-style flies continued slowly. Most books illustrated flies of English design and patterns. And fishing with the "bob," the deer hair skittering lure described in 1764 by Bartram continued, although it was not always considered fly fishing.

This period also saw perhaps the first fledgling but serious efforts in saltwater fly fishing, with books describing fly fishing for striped bass in New England and the mid-Atlantic states. Books published in 1849

ABOVE: *Early styles of spinners. **Left to right:** two Buel spinners, American Hendryx spinner from 1886, large Muskill spinner (ca 1937) with feather treble and box swivel, Pflueger American spinner (top), Skinner fluted spinner (bottom), and Pflueger McMurray spinner that was made as early as 1894.*

and 1864 described the fishing with red and white flies, sometimes cast and sometimes drifted in the current. Robert Barnwell Roosevelt has been criticized in some circles for using this technique. Feeding line into the current may not be exactly considered fly fishing, but since the IGFA allows making a cast and feeding out line to where the fly is 120 feet from the angler, it makes it a little more difficult for any of us to snobbishly sniff at these techniques of the past.

Lures from 1875 to 1900

More Metal and the Birth of Wood

More variations of metal spoons and spinners evolved during this period, along with the importation from England of metal lures with built-in propeller blades, variously called Devons, Phantoms and Caledonians, all designed to spin the lure in the water, presumably to resemble a twisting minnow. Variations of these included the 1885 Allcock Cleopatra, with seven segments in the jointed copper body and the typical short opposing fins for spinning, and the 1890 Allcock Paragon Minnow, with minnow-shaped body, glass eyes and spinning fins followed by a treble hook with a red yarn wrapping. Except for the addition of the spinning fins, it resembled the earlier Haskell Minnow.

A similar lure was made in the U.S. by W. D. Chapman with his 1897 Safe Deposit Bait that resembled a minnow (the Paragon Minnow, for example) with opposing spinner tail and side fins.

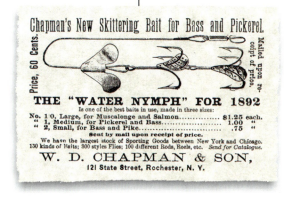

Artificial Lures

LEFT: *Many types of early hook hangers were used, including cup, screw eye, toilet seat, South Bend plate style and staple.* **Left to right, top to bottom:** *South Bend Bass-Oreno, Heddon Dowagiac Minnow, South Bend Better Bass-Oreno, Helin Flatfish, and Shakespeare #6527.*

Pflueger Tackle Begins

Ernest Pflueger and his Enterprise Manufacturing Company began in Akron, OH, in 1864, but the first advertisement found for the company was from 1883, which listed only the Dexter Spoon and the Chrystal Minnow (later spelled Crystal Minnow). The Dexter Minnow had a hammered finish, not unlike the hammered spoons from Hopkins or the metal jigging lures from Bay Du Noc of today. The Dexter Spoon has a swivel on the front and a feathered treble at the rear. The Crystal Minnow was a smaller version with a propeller-like blade on the front and a free-swinging feathered treble on the back. It was available only in a luminous model, the glow-in-the-dark lures a favorite theme of the Pflueger Company.

A Pflueger Flying Helgramite from the same 1883 period had twin metal spinning blades with three treble hooks and was first made by Harry Comstock for a few months before Pflueger bought him out.

Rubber lures (as opposed to rubber flies, which began earlier) continued during this period. Pflueger introduced rubber (and later, wood) fish decoys in 1895 along with a metal-finned, through-wire construction rubber fish lure designed for muskie and fitted with three single hooks. The eyes, scale patterns, color shading and gills would make it accepted by any modern angler as not unlike some PVC plastic fish imitations sold today by Felmlee and Renosky. By now, most of these pre-1900 rubber lures have dried up, and one is rarely found.

There was also a lifelike hand-painted Hastings Rubber Frog, hollow and with two upright single weedless hooks. This was later bought by the Jamison Company and put into its line shortly after the turn of the century.

Hildebrandt Begins 100 Years of Metal; Others Start and Fail

The Hildebrandt Lure Company started in 1899, and it is still family owned, run by fourth-generation Mark Hildebrandt. Though metal spinners, spinner-fly combinations and spoons have been its main-

58   Our Fishing Heritage: Tackle & Equipment

HOOKS AND MORE HOOKS

Most lures today have a reasonable number of hooks on them, often a single or one treble on spoons, single hooks on spinnerbaits, buzzbaits, jigs and soft-plastic lures, single treble on spinners and one to three (two is a popular average) trebles on top water lures and crankbaits.

Lures of the past were designed with the theory of maximum hooks for maximum catching ability. Many crankbaits by Heddon, Creek Chub, Moonlight, Pflueger, Shakespeare and South Bend had five treble hooks per crankbait. A Heddon Musky Minnow #300, with props fore-and-aft from about 1925, had four trebles on the sides with extra large trebles on the tail and belly for a total of six trebles in all. An anonymous Indiana lure maker, listed in Fishing Lure Collectibles, by Dudley Murphy and Rick Edmisten, shows a Weedless Collared Bait from 1915 that sports weedless treble hooks, each point protected by a wire guard with a ball end. The lure shows three trebles around the body in back of the popping face, three farther back along the belly and one tail hook, for a total of seven trebles in all on a 5¼-inch lure.

stay, the company has also manufactured some bass bug fly rod lures and some bass casting lures.

Many other lure companies started and after a short or long haul, failed, are no longer around or were incorporated into other companies through take-overs and mergers. The noted Abbey & Imbrie Company of 1885 made lures, but was later absorbed into the Horrocks-Ibbotson Company. The Andrew B. Hendryx Company of New Haven, CT, was also a maker of popular metal lures, but it is also long gone. James Hastings of Chicago created and sold hand-painted rubber frogs that had two single hooks, weed guards and a molded-in belly weight. Later this product was sold by the Jamison Company.

Wood Carves an Important Niche in American Lure Making

It was during this period also that wood lures began to appear. The most notable example and story of this is that of the idea behind the James Heddon and Sons Lure Company. The story goes that close to the turn of the century (it could have been as early as 1890, according to one report attributed to his son Charles) James Heddon was whittling on a stick of wood while waiting for a friend to go fishing or hunting (you pick; both stories have been told) at a millpond or Dowagiac River (pick again). The friend showed up, Jim

ABOVE: Very early Heddon 200 with capped tail, metal collar (to splash water) and screw-and-cup rig hook hangers.

Artificial Lures

HOOK ATTACHMENTS

Hook attachments in lures today often consist of a split ring to attach a single or treble hook to the hole stamped into a metal spoon or a split ring to attach a treble hook to a wire molded in hook hanger in a plastic lure. In some cases, the wire in the lure goes completely through the lure to connect the line tie and all hooks, though, in other cases, the hook hanger is simply a small wire device that is locked into the lure when the two parts of the lure are assembled after being injection molded, often using ABS or Butyrate plastics.

In older lures of wood, the through-wire construction was sometimes done with a wire running the length of the lure from the line tie to all the hooks, the wire on the outside belly of the lure. The idea was that even if the lure were shattered by a big fish (as can happen in saltwater fishing for cubera snapper, big bluefish and the like), the wire would keep the fish hooked and prevent its loss. Heddon used both wire and line (string) for this external rigging in some of their saltwater lures.

In more typical cases, it was done by through-drilling the lure front to back, then drilling side holes that would attach the hooks using spacers or swivels. The Manitou Minnow, made by Bailey and Elliott in the Rochester, NY, area around 1905 and which came with a tiny wrench for assembling and disassembling the lure, is one example. Another of this design is the Pflueger Monarch Minnow in which the line tie shaft would unscrew from the tail hook, the entire hook assembly coming off of the lure.

Other lures had a variety of hook hanger designs, most evolving from simple screw eyes inserted into the tail or belly of the wood lure. Through its history, Heddon used 22 different hook hanger arrangements.

In saltwater, through-wire construction was important to hold the fish should the lure get bitten in half. One example was a catch of a Cubera snapper on a Creek Chub Giant Pikie, in which the wood body was completely destroyed, and only the wire and hooks remained when the fish was landed.

Some unusual hook attachments were the two trebles tied eye-to-eye with line strung through a hole drilled in the body of the lure in the Pflueger Trory Minnow of 1899. This positioned the hooks a little ways from the lure body. A similar arrangement was found in the Kent Double Spinner Artificial Minnow from 1898 with the two side trebles connected through the body with string and closely resembling in shape and design the Pflueger Trory. These designs perhaps were precursors of the wire attachments between the hooks and the screw eye in the Helin Flatfish and Fishcake lures. The little fly rod F-2 and F-3 models seemed to have a staple for a hook hanger. On some spoons and large crankbaits, the hook was held loosely by a split ring (spoons) or screw eye (wood lures) but held the hook close to the body by means of a clip or snap that secured the shank of the hook until the fish hit.

Early worms had built-in hood riggings, with the Burke Company using a small light chain running through the center of the molded worms as a hook hanger. The chain also provided some weight.

ABOVE: Early Heddon plugs were often topwater lures, such as these three. **Top to bottom:** *Heddon Dowagiac Minnow "Double 00", Heddon Glass Eye Vamp and Heddon Weedless Widow with single hook and twin weed guards (shown upside down).*

Heddon threw the stick into the water, whereupon a bass struck at it or struck at it repeatedly, knocking it into the air several times (you pick the version).

Heddon who had previously been involved in politics, newspaper publishing and beekeeping (he was a published, acknowledged expert in the field) began making lures with his son William in 1898, making a wood frog that had two legs and double hooks fore and aft. The frog lure was made for friends and personal use, and never available commercially. A few years later, in 1902, he, however, did start his company with his two sons, William and Charles.

Fly Fishing Includes Bass, Along with Trout

Of course fly fishing and sales of flies continued during this period, with flies often being advertised as being available with gut loops (drawn silk gut), metal-eyed hooks or with a single strand of gut spliced into the fly. Flies were still being imported from England, although Theodore Gordon, considered the dean of early American dry fly fishermen and tyers, was popularizing the American dry fly, as contrasted with the earlier English Halford-style dry flies and method of tying and fishing.

Lures Between 1900 and 1920

The Expansion of Lure Development and Lots of Wood

This period might be thought of as the wood lure period, although wood lures preceded the 1900s and also continued well past this era into the 1950s. After the development of the early frog, really before the company had been formally formed, James Heddon and Sons brought out their first lures under the company name and over the years became a major force in American lures and tackle making. In Carl F. Luckey's book, *Identification and Value*

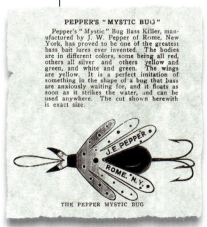

Artificial Lures

LEFT: *Various types, lengths and styles of metal and plastic lips on diving crankbaits.* **Clockwise from upper right:** *Bomber, Rapala Count Down, Paw Paw Fire Plug, Heddon River Runt, Rebel Deep Runner, Heddon Deep Six and Heddon Widget (center).*

Guide, Old Fishing Lures and Tackle (4th edition, 1996), his list and description of Heddon lures covers 71 pages—and that does not, of course, include the rods, reels and other tackle that Heddon made or was involved with over the years. Clyde Harbin of Memphis, TN, who goes by the name of The Bassman, has made a study of Heddon, publishing collections of Heddon catalogs, videos on Heddon lures, and other works revolving around his vast collection of tackle. Others have been heavily involved in collecting and the historical aspects of tackle, some even making part or all of a living from it.

Heddon Goes Wooden

Heddon's first offerings under his company (1903) as James Heddon and Son (William) were for a slim, tapered surface bait, known as the Dowagiac, but better known to collectors as "slopenose." This is due to the shape of the nose, almost like that of a pencil point, albeit an off-center pencil point aimed up and with a metal collar around the neck of the lure, slanted so as to cause the lure to ride up and splash water.

The Model 100 series with props fore and aft and the various Model 200 Dowagiac "Expert" Minnows followed from 1904 on. The earliest models had an external belly weight to sink the lure, not unlike something that an angler today might do to add a bell-shaped sinker to the belly of a lure to help it get down.

All of these early lures resembled the slim, tapered torpedo shape of the Devons that were first fished and imported from England in the early 1800s, but with one big difference. The Devons were designed to spin (thus the very early references to "spinning" as a method of fishing and also "spinning" tackle, which was not at all related to our modern fixed-spool spinning methods). Two opposing fins on the body of the lure spun the entire lure around, making swivels necessary and also most likely twisting line then as it would today, swivels or not.

The difference is that the Heddon lures and other lures of this type, while designed to be fished underwater, had revolving props that would spin, fore, aft or amidships, while the body of the lure would not—or should not—spin.

Colors in Heddon and other lures quickly became important, with the 1906 catalog referring to the Dowagiac "Expert" Minnow as having a red collar and blue snout, the rest of the lure white. During 1907, the so-called fancy-back finishes started, later called crackle back and other names by several companies, and reintroduced several times over the years. It resulted, so the story goes, from a rush order for some lures and the efforts to dry the paint rapidly in Mrs. Heddon's oven. The heat must have been too high, with the result that the paint crackled and separated from the undercoat to reveal the crazed finish effect.

62   *Our Fishing Heritage: Tackle & Equipment*

Jamison Offers Wood and Metal

Other lure companies also started and flourished during this period. The Jamison Company began in 1904 with its popular Coaxer, patented January 3, 1905. The fly rod model came in three sizes. This resembled more of what we would call a fly rod bass bug today. A larger casting model had a surface-skittering body, horizontal transverse hole to take red felt or leather "wings," red feather tail and a single hook. The weedless model had the point up; a convertible model had a removable double belly hook.

This was the lure that won a June, 1910 *Field & Stream*-advertised challenge fishing match thrown down by William J. Jamison that only Anson B. Decker of Decker Baits picked up. The three-day judged-and-refereed fishing contest was won by the Coaxer. The score of the Lake Hopatcong, NJ, contest was 28 bass for the Coaxer; 16 for the Decker.

Jamison Also Develops the Spinnerbait

The Jamison Lure Co. also invented and developed the spinnerbait concept as we know it today. The Shannon Twin Spin had a 1917 patent-pending mark, and though developed by Jamison, was the invention of Jesse P. Shannon. The original lures included box swivels, and various models came in different sizes with bucktail (polar bear early on) or feather trailers. There was also a model called the Porker for the addition of pork rind. Bass, fly rod and muskie models were available, and all used the squared Sneck hook style.

Decker and Others

Decker was another lure company that began during this period (ads date the lures back to 1907), producing a blunt, cigar-shaped topwater wood plug with either three trebles or three single hooks (angler's choice) and a large rotating propeller blade amidships between the head and body of the lure.

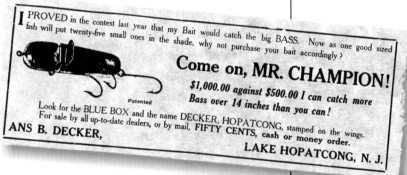

(Although this bait was not produced earlier, a talk given by Anson Decker in 1933 [as related in Carl F. Luckey's book] notes that Decker claimed that he developed the lure in 1880 when a pike ruined the cloth body of an English Phantom, so he replaced the cloth with a wood body. He perfected the final form by 1882,

Artificial Lures

and he and his father continued to fish it for 10 years, keeping it a secret during that time. Sometimes it is difficult to figure out who was first with what, and when that was!)

The similar Pflueger Globe was introduced about 1912.

There were other lures of about the same design at the same time, or perhaps preceding the commercial introduction of the Decker Bait. These included the Yellow Kid (named for a popular turn-of-the-century comic strip character) in the Wm. Mills catalog, and a Jersey Queen lure by a Jacob Mick who lived near Decker in New Jersey and geographically, at least, had some connection.

Creek Chub Lures

Other companies continued with their lure designs at this time. Creek Chub began as a company in 1906 with its first lure, the #100 Creek Chub Wiggler. This offered a slightly different version of lures of other companies in that it was a floating/diving lure with a metal plate or lip, just like the molded plastic crankbaits of today. In 1917 the #300 Crawdad lure was added. This was a "backward" running lure, later followed by similar designs and running style in the Bomber and Hellbender. It had a natural crayfish coloration and rubber legs on the bottom to make it more life-like. Pikie Minnows followed about 1920 with a Z-shaped (or stair-step) lip design, spawning a whole series of similar lures of different sizes and styles that continued into the following decades.

Creek Chub also contributed in other ways to lure development, such as the method patented in 1919 of spray painting through mesh netting or tulle to produce an accurate simulation of fish scales on a lure. This technique is still used today, even by do-it-yourselfers.

Pflueger and Fish Hooks

Pflueger, which started in 1864 as the American Fish

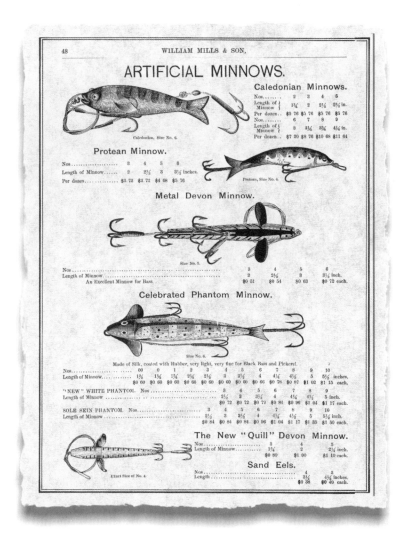

Hook Company and went through various names including Akron Fishing Tackle Works, the Enterprise Manufacturing Company and finally Pflueger Fishing Tackle, had its greatest development of lures beginning about 1906. The company, of course, also made reels and rods and continued to produce a lot of metal and other lures and terminal tackle.

It was early in this period (1900) that Pflueger debuted its Pflueger Competitor Wooden Minnow (shaped like a cigar or similar lures of other manufacturers of this period) and the Pflueger Trory Wooden Minnow, shaped like a fish with a fishtail. Both had propellers fore and aft. The Trory Minnow had side trebles, connected to the lure with string tied through a hole in the side of the plug. The Competitor sported three trebles; the Trory five trebles.

Other lures of the same general shape followed through this period. One variation of this in a wood lure were the various Kent Floaters from the 1910 to 1920 period. They were short lures looking like a fat Southern bullfrog, with fore- and aft-props. The similar but slim Tiny Torpedo from Heddon would follow later.

Shakespeare Plays with Lures

The William Shakespeare Co. Of Kalamazoo, MI, established in 1897, produced some early reels, but did not produce its first lure until 1901. This Revolution, as it was called, was similar to the prop-in-the-center-of-the-plug idea of Decker, but with the two props, separated by a bead so that they could spin unencumbered, and placed farther back in the lure. In essence, there was more wood body in front and less behind the props, in contrast to the Decker design. The February 5, 1901, patent granted Shakespeare however, shows the reverse, with a small acorn head and longer body, but also with the two propellers. Some of the Revolutions of this period were also made of aluminum and painted, although most of them were wood.

Shakespeare also produced some rubber lures. The 1902 Sure Lure was a hollow rubber tube that resembles the tube lures of today (without the tentacles or tail skirt), but it had a shaft through the tube, a treble on the tail and a rotating propeller ahead of the tube.

Rush and the Banana Shaped Plugs

J. K. Rush and the Rush Tango lures that were patented and introduced in 1914 ushered in two things: a lawsuit from Fillmore M. Smith and Henry S. Welles from an earlier-issued patent; and a new development in lure

ABOVE: *Banana shaped lures were popular early and continue in popularity today.* **Left to right, top row:** *Heddon Tadpolly with glass eye and L-hook rig from 1920s, Heddon jointed Game Fisher from the 1920s, and South Bend Tease-Oreno with tack eye from the 1940s.* **Bottom row, left to right:** *Helin wood Flatfish from the late 1930s, wood Lazy Ike from the mid-1940s, Heddon Tadpolly Spook from the late 1950s, and plastic Swim Whiz by Homer LeBlanc.*

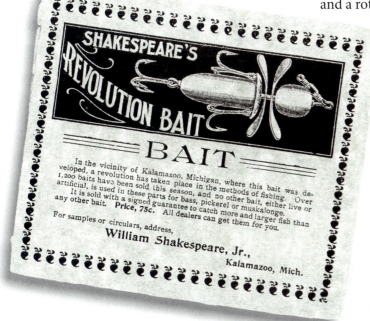

Artificial Lures

ABOVE: *Banana lures include the typical curved shape from companies such as Lazy Ike, Heddon and others. This design allowed companies to manufacture wobbling floating/diving lures without making and fastening a separate metal lip.*

design in which the lure was designed to dive under the water, caused by a downward sloping of the front of the wood body.

These curved bowling pin or banana-shaped lures with the sloping head were not unlike later lures such as the Heddon Tadpolly, and the more curved, banana shapes of the Lazy Ike, South Bend Tease Oreno and the Helin Flatfish that were yet to come. The early models did have an unusual line tie that in place of a wood screw eye used a machine screw that went right through the thin lip and was secured in place with a nut. Later models had the standard screw eye.

Most of these lures had two trebles, although the small sizes had only one screw eye, and the larger muskie sizes had either two double hooks or one single hook. Some fly rod 2¼-inch-long Troutangos and 1½-inch Troutiger Tangos, each with one double hook or a treble hook, were made around 1920 (Troutangos) and 1923 (Troutiger Tangos).

South Bend and Other Companies

South Bend was another lure company with major influence and which produced lots of lures during this fertile period after the turn of the century. It had actually started as the Worden Bucktail Bait Company of B. F. Worden in 1894, but eventually became the South Bend Bait Company around 1910. Shakespeare sold some of the early lures in its catalog; South Bend lures were like the early Shakespeare Revolution lure. Early wood lures resembled the tapered surface and swimming sinking plugs with propellers fore and aft and five trebles on many of the models. Late in this period, and extending into the decades following, were the various "Oreno" models (Bass-Oreno, Babe-Oreno, Troll-Oreno, etc.) that resembled a blunt cigar in shape but with a sloping curved front end to cause the lure to dive. This achieved the same diving result as the earlier Rush Tango, but was a different shaped lure and still lacked a metal diving lip, although an early-model Rush Tango did have a metal reinforcing plate.

The first jointed lures also appeared during this time period with the Animated Minnow made by the K & K Manufacturing Company of Toledo, OH. It was doubly unusual in that the hinge of the two parts of the lure was two sets of interlocking screw eyes, not the single set or the pinned metal plate that became popular later.

More Metal

Metal lures continued in popularity, with Buel and others expanding their line and more competitors entering the market. One of these was Lou Eppinger, who in 1906 at the age of 29 found himself fishing Ontario lakes for a month-long vacation and doing quite well on a spoon that he invented. The spoon was the Dardevle, first called the Osprey, and was made by forming both convex and concave sides to the lure, and also varying the thickness of the blade to give it more action. It then, and now, has proved to be a formidable weapon for not only pike and muskie, but for a host of fresh- and saltwater

LEFT: Modern spinners from a number of companies all incorporate the basics of a body on a shaft and a blade that revolves around the shaft on retrieve. Mepps alone is said to have more than 5,000 different color, size and model variations.

Artificial Lures

LEFT: Some spinners used a figure "4" shaped blade as with these examples. **Top row, left to right:** Pflueger Snapie Spinner and Al Foss Little Egypt pork rind lure. **Bottom row, left to right:** Weezel Bait Co. Wessner Feather Weezel and Al Foss Shimmy Wiggler pork rind lure.

BELOW LEFT: Two styles of the original spinnerbait—the Shannon Twin spinner by Jamison. Upper left, straight body model; lower right, jointed body style in which the hook/skirt and body were jointed.

The Saltwater Influence

During this period, saltwater fishing began to blossom, with catches of increasingly larger fish on improved rods and reels. The drag systems in reels were constantly being improved. The result was also the development of larger spoons for trolling for the larger saltwater fish, along with the development of jigs. In the style in which we know them today—with the lead head on the bent shank hook, eye above the body of the lure and a tail of bucktail or fur—they are basically a 20th century lure, and initially used only in saltwater. Most estimates and evidence show that the jig continued as a popular lure for inshore saltwater fishing until about the 1940s, probably after World War II, when smaller sizes began to be used for freshwater fishing with the then-new spinning tackle.

fish. It comes in everything from fly rod sizes to huge lures, such as the 3½-ounce Husky Devle.

Over a period of time it has evolved into a broad line of metal spoons, including single-hook weedless casting spoons, jointed spoons, clicker models, thin trolling blades, thick-blade deep-fishing styles and a range of sizes for everything from fly rod to surf fishing, trolling and vertical jigging.

A lot of other spoons and spinners were developed during this period. Metal lures that we would call double spinners, single spinners, June Bug spinners and some spinning minnows were produced, along with the continuation of the lure that started it all—the Buel spinner with the kidney-shaped blade still used in both single- and double-blade models.

One exception to this late development was the 1906 Jamison Underwater Coaxer that had metal body and trailing red feather tail with weedguard. These, along with the

68 Our Fishing Heritage: Tackle & Equipment

early Jap feathers and molded "jigs" on straight-shank hooks, were the precursors to the jigs of today that are molded on the right angle bent shank hooks.

Realize that during this period anglers still had little time to fish. In 1917, striking steel workers were trying to demand an end to the 12-hour day, seven-day work-week that was prevalent in the industry. Hours like that left precious little time for fishing—or anything else.

The Pork and Plastic Period

It was also during this period that Al Foss introduced the first of his line of metal lures—metal bodies, preceded by a spinner blade, with a single hook (often weedless) on the back of the body to hold a chunk or strip of pork rind. These included his

Little Egypt, Skidder, Jazz Wiggler, Dixie Wiggler, Frog, Mouse, Shimmy Wiggler #5 and perhaps the first of the plastic lures, the Oriental Wiggler #3 with a celluloid body in place of metal. Later, ads referred to this as pyralin, another early plastic.

Metal or early plastics were not the only materials used for these types of lures. Some spinner blades were made of mother-of-pearl and some, such as those by the S. Doering & Company of Brooklyn, NY, and the Haynes Bait Company of Akron, OH, had mother-of-pearl body and blades.

SPECIAL PROPS OR INTERNAL PROPS ON LURES

Most props and turning blades on lures were on the front or back, often like miniature propellers. But there were others, often unusual lures that had other means of making the same type of fuss. The Chippewa Bait of Immell Bait Co., 1913, had a plug-like frame and internal horizontal spiral "screw." Blades

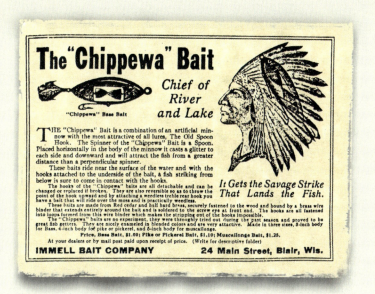

could be changed or replaced if broken. The Old Fighter from the Beaver Bait Co. was a River Runt-like lure with deep cuts in the side. On each side a wire ran from front to back of the cut-out area, with two propeller blade spinners separated by beads on each side. The cut-outs allowed room for the blades to turn. Pecos River Tackle Minnow made a plastic crankbait around 1945 that had a round hole, straight through the center sides, with a vertical pin that held a rotating spinner blade. Bill Norman used to have a slab-sided surface bait with a center hole holding a blade that turned like a paddle wheel when retrieved. In 1937 Shur Bite had an almost identical lure.

Flies: Gaudy But Catching

Flies retained their popularity during this period. Trout flies continued to be invented, while bass flies with the large gaudy wings of guinea, ibis and other feathers remained popular. Jamison had made the first fly rod bugs with its fly rod Coaxers. Bass flies of the period looked like nothing used today. They had large wings in bright colors and would most closely resemble a bright oversized modern steelhead fly. Hair-bodied

bugs of the Henshall style had previously been developed in the late 1800s, but now solid bugs of cork and balsa came along. After the turn of the century, bass fly fishermen had their choice of bugs such as the Jamison cork Coaxer, Heddon's Wilder-Dilg series of bullet-head bugs, Peckinpaugh's similar Floating Feather Minnow, South Bend's Feath-Oreno Minnows and Callmac bugs and Shakespeare's Kazoo Reed bugs. Bugs from Creek Chub and Pflueger would come later.

The 1920s Through 1940

Lures of Plastic and Other Materials

The 1920s through the 1940s saw a lot of new companies entering the market, with some of the original old-time companies dropping out or being absorbed by other companies. Some existing lure companies such as Heddon expanded into other areas of tackle such as rods, reels, lines and accessories. More metal-making companies joined the marketplace, with

LURES WITH A NATURAL CONNECTION

Lures have also been made more attractive, at least in the eyes of their manufacturers and makers, by covering them with natural materials. Examples have been coverings of frog skin, snake skin, feathers and fur. The Charles C. Kellman Company of Detroit, MI, a one-man home business in the 1930s, was a major manufacturer of such lures. The Duckling, Feathered Frog, and Feathered Wiggler all looked like their name (small duckling, swimming frog and minnow) and were covered with the appropriate color and type of feathers. Kellman also used feathers and fur in combination with wood to make a number of lifelike lures for fly rod fishing (which would have served several decades later for spinning). The small lures resembled grubs, ladybugs, hellgrammites, grasshoppers, dragonflies, crickets, mayflies, beetles, frogs, tadpoles, minnows, snakes and cicadas.

Paw Paw made its 1938 Croaker surface bait with a real frog skin covering. The casting size cost $1, and the fly rod size cost 60 cents. Its ad stated, "BIG FISH are Always After MY SKIN."

Examples of other natural coverings on lures were the Musky Monk by Marathon, which looked like an old-time shaving brush with a body and tail of tied-in hair (bucktail?) and the Mouse Bait from an unknown maker, which featured leather tail and legs tacked to a wood body to make it look like a mouse. The Weezel Sparrow lure used duck feathers, not sparrow, as the name would indicate. Lures currently available at this writing include the Wrats—fur covered surface and shallow running lures that resemble mice, rats and small muskrats.

Johnson producing the Johnson Silver Minnow, the Johnson Caper and the Johnson Sprite. Of those, the Johnson Silver Minnow, a weedless single fixed hook lure remains the most popular. The Johnson Silver Minnow celebrated its 75th anniversary in 1995.

Heddon introduced its Spook lures made of Heddylin in 1930. Heddylin was like pyralin, an early plastic (so Heddon said; it might have been the same thing). The original lures made with it were called Spooks, since you could see through the translucent lure as if it were a real translucent minnow. "They are extremely life-like and resemble real fish-flesh," said the catalog copy. "Made of Heddylin (like Pyralin). These ghostly go-getters' will outlast a dozen ordinary wooden lures, even when grabbed by fish with sharp teeth. A new bait free if yours does not live up to the guarantee." Along with the transparent Super Dowagiac Spook with whirling spinner blades front and rear, Heddon also made some saltwater lures called the Shrimpy-Spook and the Sea-Spook.

Arbogast Joins the Fray

In the late 1920s, Fred Arbogast started making metal lures, and in 1930 purchased a house in Akron, OH, for offices, manufacturing and marketing facilities. Though the company is often thought to have started in 1930, Carl Luckey notes in his book that there was a June 1926 ad in *Hunting & Fishing* magazine advertising Fred Arbogast's Spin-Tail Kicker. The original lures had a typical oval spinner blade tail in back of a hackle collar, and later models had a forked fish-tail blade in place of the oval blade. A similar lead-molded Arbogast Cock-Tail Kicker lacked any tail

ABOVE: *Over the years, eyes on lures have varied widely. Top to bottom, some examples of typical lure eyes include: old wood minnow with glass eye, Storm Thin Fin with large molded-in plastic eye with eye pupil detail (left center), minnow lure with luminous glowing painted eyes (right center), red head/white body wood lure with tack eyes.*

blade, but had flared hackles as an attractant. These were plain metal precursors of the Tin Liz lures that were to follow in about 1930. The Tin Liz (named after the slang term for the early Ford motor cars) lures were a series of finely painted lures that were molded of metal (lead) on a long shank, single hook, with a flapping tail spinner blade, usually the forked fish tail model. These were beautiful little lures, resembling fish (the species of fish varied with the type of the lure). Their first lures were the various Tin Liz series with the Tin Liz Spintail, the Tin Liz Minnow and Big Tin Liz featuring dorsal and ventral fins and painted very realistically. Some other Tin Liz lures even surpassed these as being more lifelike, typically with a more realistic representation of fins and the same fine detail in the painted finishes. The Sunfish Tin Liz, Tin Liz Three Fin, Tin Liz Walleye, New Tin Liz Snake and Musky Tin Liz resembled, respectively, sunfish (either sunfish or crappie), a dace or darter, yellow perch (the frequent prey of walleye, this perhaps explaining the name), pike (often called snakes then) and muskie. There was also a Twin Liz that featured two separate hooks joined by a V-shaped wire to presumably resemble a small school of fish and a fly rod size Tin Liz and Hawaiian Wiggler.

Around 1936, Arbogast started making the Hawaiian Wiggler series of lures that were similar to some earlier Al Foss lures, particularly the Shimmy

LURES FOR DISPLAY

Sometimes lure manufacturers made large lures for display purposes, either for their dealers or more often to advertise their wares at a booth at a sportsman's or trade show. Creek Chub did this with a large Pikie minnow for store display. The lure is 17¼ inches long with an 11¼-inch circumference. A photo exists of a small boy holding the lure, the lure over half the height of the boy. The M-F Manufacturing Co., a molder of soft-plastic lures, did the same with a giant plastic worm weighing about 20 pounds and measuring about five feet long.

ABOVE: An "angler's prayer" on a plaque, often with a large fly, was used in shops and also sold for display in an angler's den. These are from Herter's (left) and Glen L. Evans (right).

A Heddon display sign for tackle shop counters (that may or may not have been distributed) showed a young lady in a very small bikini bottom, arms folded across her breasts, with references to the advertised lure working best with a "short stiff rod," along with a quote from the girl, "When it comes to bait action, I'll G-string along with Heddon."

ABOVE: Large lures, specially made by manufacturers for dealer's use and to attract customer attention, were often found in the past. This store display soft-plastic crayfish from Gene Larew weighs 28 pounds and is 42 inches long. Note the rod and reel and the Mann's 11¾-inch lure next to it!

72   Our Fishing Heritage: Tackle & Equipment

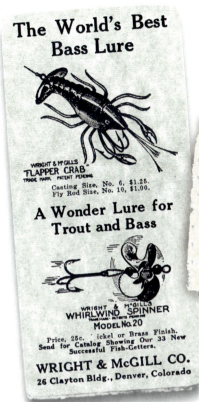
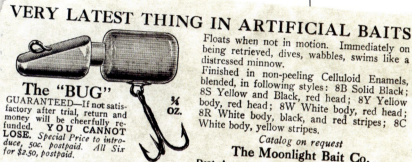

Wiggler. These had the eyed fish-head design that was similar to the Tin Liz series, but with a shaft and spinner blade joined to the front. What really made this lure was a later Fred Arbogast invention, patented March 15, 1938—the rubber Hula skirt. This rubber skirt made the Hawaiian Wiggler and the similar Sputterfuss (which came later, in 1936) into classic in-line spinner-baits and also paved the way for other similar skirts, once the patent ran out. Today, skirts—not of rubber, but of modern synthetic materials including vinyl, Spandex, Living Rubber, etc.—are used on safety-pin style spinner-baits, in-line spinnerbaits, buzzbaits, jigs, offshore trolling lures and trolling and casting spoons and are incorporated into lures such as plastic worms and tube lures. The fact that Fred Arbogast worked for the Goodyear Rubber Company in Akron until starting his company might have had something to do with the development of the rubber skirt style that today graces so many lures.

Arbogast followed with wood lures—both topwater and crankbaits—the first of these being the Jitterbug, named after the popular dance of the era. As with so many experiments in trial-and-error lure design, this one started with a cigar-shaped chunk of wood carved from a broomstick (sound like James Heddon's frog lure development?) with a spoon blade attached crosswise to the front to make it a diving lure. It didn't work, and was thrown into a drawer to languish for about 10 years until 1934 when he found it during a friend's visit. They continued to modify it until coming up with this classic surface lure in 1938. The idea was not ignored by other manufacturers. A similar Paddle Plug from Millsite Fishing Tackle, Waddle Bug from Makinen Tackle Co., Gurglehead from Trenton Mfg. Co. and the Skipper from Hom-Art Bait Co. (with a hole in the front plate) all had similar angled plates that made these lures look and work similarly to the original Jitterbug.

Artificial Lures

ABOVE: Left, an original Worden Minnow with fore- and aft-propeller blades, crackle back finish and early glass eye. Right, a South Bend Min-Buck Minnow which, other than the dressed tail, is almost identical to the Worden lure. South Bend bought out Worden and improved on their original idea.

RIGHT: An evolution of diving lips can be seen in these three lures. **Top to bottom:** Creek Chub scale finish #200 Wiggler from 1918 with early style 1919 unmarked tin lip, Creek Chub #100 Wiggler with extended tin lip for deeper diving, and modern molded-in clear plastic lip on modern diving crankbait.

Hollow Metal Floaters and More Wood

Not all surface lures were wood, or even the new plastic that as a hollow lure would work on the surface and which would later be the basis for the floater/diver crankbaits. The Outing Company made both surface and floating-diving lures of hollow metal; two parts (top and bottom or right and left sides) were stamped, then fastened along the seams. The diving lures had metal lips attached to go deep. The company was bought by Heddon in 1927, and the existing lures were sold off as close-out specials.

Other lure companies continued production and introduced more lures with more innovation in design. In 1924, Creek Chub brought out the Darter with the sloping face and horizontal cut in the head to make it swim shallow. It was probably the first walk-the-dog lure. Later there was a spinner and midget version. More Pikie Minnows were also introduced in different sizes and styles.

The Plunker, basically a cupped-face chugger style of surface bait for bass, was introduced in 1927, following the Pop It fly rod lure in 1926. This also seems to be the first large lure with a true cup, or concave, face, in contrast to the scooped or straight slope faces of other similar lures.

One of the most famous lures of all times, from the standard of record fish caught, was also intro-

duced during this period. In 1925, Creek Chub debuted the Wiggle Fish, the lure that George Perry used on June 2, 1932, to catch a 22-pound 4-ounce largemouth bass, perhaps the top catch in terms of publicity for the Creek Chub Bait Company and a record that still stands today. A replica of this jointed, lipped diving lure with the metal tail flap was produced in 1992.

The Wee Dee and an early surface Ding Bat were also introduced during this period. These were short stubby lures. The Ding Bat also came in a diving model.

Heddon during this time introduced jointed Game Fisher lures (1923) and the one-piece Tadpolly lures (1924), first in wood and later in plastic. These were similar to the much earlier Rush Tango. Among other offerings was the Darting Zara, similar to the Creek Chub Darter, the single-hook Walton Feather Tail and the Heddon-Stanley Ace, a spinner-spoon metal-body lure with a wobbling action.

The Heddon Luny Frogs, introduced in 1927, were made of pyralin, an early plastic. The Frogs resembled a swimming frog with cocked legs that on some models—not all—were reinforced by a molded webbing between the legs.

Lures for Special Markets

Though the bass market was big and getting bigger, all these lures would catch other fish. Some lures were produced for other specific markets and species, such as the Musky Vamp, the King Wig-Wag (for Pacific Northwest salmon), and the Salt-Water Special and Sea-Spook for saltwater fishing. The Sea-Spook (1930) was also unusual in that it was plastic and transparent to resemble the partial transparency of many saltwater baitfish. The screws holding the hook hanger in place were clearly visible. Other companies had similar offerings for the expanding saltwater markets, as well as lures for muskie, pike, walleye, lake trout and Pacific salmon.

Pflueger went more into the diving baits at this time, using an unusual metal diving lip in the shape of an open taco shell or V that fit into a cut-open mouth in lures like the O'Boy Minnow (1924) and the Pal-O-Mine lure (1924 and later). The slim celluloid molded Live-Wire lures with front and rear props were different in that they had raised dorsal fins, which, as a result, resembled a sculpin.

Shakespeare continued to produce a wide variety of plugs, including the Bass-A-Lure that had the cut mouth and lip arrangement of the Pflueger lures, but also had not only a scale finish, but also painted-on gills and pectoral fins that then, (1934) predicted the similar features of fins, lateral lines, gills and such that would be pad printed on lures 50 years later. Some Shakespeare lures of this time also featured a small belly fin, often just in front of the belly hook and

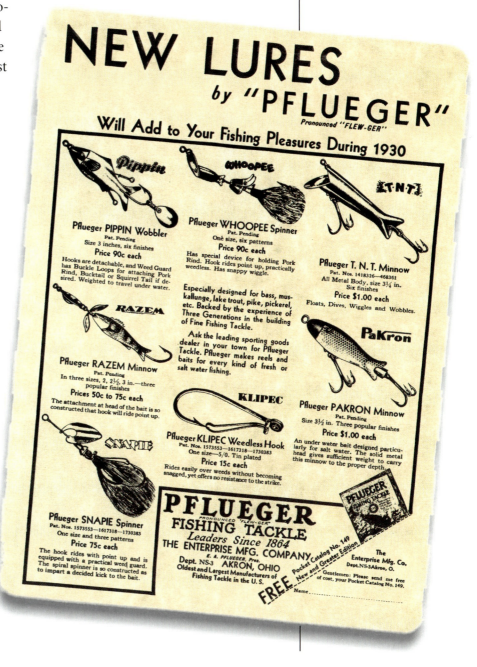

Artificial Lures

looking like a tiny keel. The Striped Bass Wobbler, Kazoo Wobbler, Waukazoo Surface Spinner, Tantilizer and Strike-It were just some of the surface and diving lures that had this feature.

Whether by design or accident, it is obvious that many lures of many companies at any one period often resembled lures of other companies. In some cases, the companies with similar lures were from the same area. One further example to some of those already mentioned is the Plug-Oreno from South Bend, produced in 1929 and very similar (two single hooks, pork rind attachment, weed guards and frog finish) to the 1927 Creek Chub Weed Bug.

South Bend did continue to make more lures with the basic "Oreno" design and name, including a big, eight-inch long, saltwater Tarp-Oreno from 1922 that sported two large single hooks for the tough Southern tarpon.

Other companies in the sporting field also got into the fishing tackle business during this time. One was the Winchester Company, the manufacturer of firearms. Some of their lures (they also produced rods and accessories) were with slope faces and cut mouths to run shallow like the Creek Chub Darters. There was also a wide variety of surface, subsurface and diving lures.

Sonic lures in which the body vibrates rapidly on retrieve really started with the Pico Perch in the late 1920s but didn't really hit their stride until the 1950s with increased publicity gained through competition with Fish Hawk, Whopper Stopper with their Bayou Boogie and, in 1957, the Sonic from Heddon. The early lures from Pico were made of wood, but by 1950 most companies had switched to plastic. In 1971, Homer Circle, the Angling Editor of *Sports Afield* magazine, named the Pico Perch as one of the top 10 lures of the time.

ABOVE: *The history of eyes in lures can be seen in these examples, all of which are South Bend Bass-Orenos, with the exception of the third from the left which is a Shure Strike (made by Creek Chub).* **Left to right:** *no eye, glass eye with black shadow, plain glass eye, tackle eye, molded eye and pressed eye.*

A general trend during this entire 20-year period was for more variety in lure design to make lures do more things and to dive deeper than before. There were also trends in finishes and in jointed lures, some of which had several different sections rather than the typical two sections. Hook hangers also varied as manufacturers tried to make better and more secure attachments. (Heddon used as many as 22 different hook attachments over the years.) Eyes varied from painted, to painted tacks, to glass, to plastic to molded (in plastic lures).

Jigs, Spoons and Trolling Lures

The saltwater field was rapidly expanding with lures as both inshore and offshore trolling from boats continued to grow in popularity. It was also a time when the well-to-do could engage in this often-expensive hobby, and when the fishing grounds were rich for exploration and rich with angling rewards. Jigs were developed, most likely from the early commercial codfish lead jigs used in the late 1800s. Up to the 1940s, many jigs were primarily lead slugs with a hole through the center and fur or feathers wrapped to the back (the so-called Jap feathers) or jigs on a straight hook designed more for trolling than for casting or jigging.

Trolling spoons also became increasingly popular during this period, including the popular Pflueger Chum spoon, Tony Acetta Pet, Huntington Drone, MetaLure, Clark Spoon, L-Y Yates, Crippled Alewife, Hopkins, Wob-L-Rite, Seneca, Doctor, K-B and many others. Most came in a series of sizes, but they were often large, and well suited for striper trolling on the East Coast. The size 23 Tony Acetta Pet spoon measured over 12 inches from line tie to bend of the fixed hook and that did not include the five to six inches of

BIG COMPANIES GET BIGGER

As various classic lure companies have fallen on hard times, or the descendants of the originators have no interest in the company, companies are sold to larger parent companies that, through combined marketing and manufacturing efforts, allow them to continue. Examples include the Pradco Company of Fort Smith, AR, parent company of old-time classic lure makers such as Rebel, Cotton Cordell, Arbogast, Heddon, Bomber, Smithwick, Creek Chub and Lazy Ike, and new companies such as Riverside, Excalibur and Real Craw. Most of these older companies are basically crankbait manufacturers; the new companies include soft plastics and scents.

Luhr Jensen of Hood River, OR, has 11 divisions of companies that used to be separate, including Luhr Jensen, Les Davis, Genuine Crankbait Brand, Tony Accetta, Kwikfish, Crippled Herring, John L. Walleye, Classic Woods, and others.

Yakima Bait Company now includes classics such as Yakima, Worden's, Helin, Poe's, Hawg Boss and Charley's Worms. Knight Manufacturing bought the assets of Creme and Burke Flexo-Products.

ABOVE: *Pflueger All-In-One #3500 lure with facetted rhinestone eyes. This lure came with four interchangeable lips that made it four lures in one, each with different actions.*

yellow feathers on the end. A size 21 Pet measured just under nine inches not counting the feathers, about the same size as a #34½ Huntington Drone. These were all single, fixed-hook lures. All companies, however, made smaller sizes of these. Some, such as the weedless Pet, became popular for bass fishing. Development of spoons continued, including fixed single hook and swinging treble hook styles from Eppinger (Dardevle), Hofschneider, Red Eye, Paul Bunyan, Williams, Wilson, South Bend, Johnson and others.

How I Spent My Summer

In 1937, 15-year-old Berkley Bedell started tying and selling flies from his home in Spirit Lake, IA. Unknowingly, young Berk Bedell had started a business that 64 years later (by the turn of the century) was to become one of the dominant forces in fishing tackle—Pure Fishing, owner of Berkley, Fenwick, Abu Garcia, Red Wolf, and Coleman Family Fishing companies. Today, this worldwide business is run by Berk's son, Tom Bedell.

In time, Berkley Bedell went from tying flies to making lines, developing nylon-coated steel lines, Berkley Trilene fishing lines, rods such as the Lightning Rod, scent and taste filled Power Baits and low-stretch lines such as FireLine. Today, Pure Fishing has companies in 12 countries, distributors in 38 other countries, with 1400 workers that speak over 20 different languages. What did you do to earn money in your spare time when you were 15, other than mow the neighbor's lawn or deliver newspapers?

Lures in the War Years and After—1940 to 1950

War Wounds the Tackle Industry

This period saw the United States increasingly involved in and then completely committed to waging a war from 1940 through 1945. As a result, most lure and tackle development slowed, for several reasons. This was the period of gas rationing. Most anglers, if they had a car, did not have the ration tickets to go far for fishing. There were also increasing numbers of young men being drafted for the war effort who, once in the military, had neither the time nor money to fish.

Furthermore, as the U.S. increasingly geared up for the war, first by helping the allies through lend-lease programs of arms and materiel and second with our subsequent involvement in the war, the raw materials were just not there. An example is the Arbogast Jitterbug with its shiny metal lip that made it wobble side-to-side. During the war, those produced had a red or black plastic lip, which was thicker and did not perform as well as the metal lip.

Some other companies switched from treble hooks to single or double hooks on their lures, trying to make do with what was available. This was particularly a problem for the Helin Company with their Flatfish and the wire outrigger arrangement to hold two belly treble hooks. They had to switch to singles or doubles. Hooks were no longer available from Mustad, and even after the

Artificial Lures 79

war years, hooks were back ordered for as much as two years. Glass eyes from Germany for wood lures were being used less and less and disappeared with the advent of war. The 1947 Creek Chub catalog stated that they were 18 months behind in filling orders as a result of the war.

Many companies could not produce lures or catalogs. South Bend stopped lure production during the war. To retain public interest in their lures and fishing, they instead ran fishing contests with photos of the winners printed in annual brochures.

There were ads that showed new lures that were influenced by the war effort, such as the Bomber (Bomber Bait Co.), named because it looked like a bomb, certainly on everyone's minds in those days of 1942 when the prototypes were made. The lure had a slim football shape with bomb-like fins at the head end to make it dive and featured a stylized resemblance to a backward-scuttling crayfish.

Creek Chub made the Dive Bomber in 1942 that was an all wood (no metal diving lip) floater/diver with a angled lip in the face. It was later called the Kreeker, and changed from the war-time popular "victory" finish, which consisted of three dots and a dash and a large sideways V in the gill plate position. The three dots and a dash spell V in Morse code, the wartime symbol for victory that all hoped would— and eventually did—come a few years later. (In 1916, Rush made a World War I "Victory Finish" on its Tango lures. The finish was different, however, in that it was green back over yellow with red scales over silver, and a light colored belly.)

Development of fly rod lures continued through the war years and into the '50s, although there were fewer produced after the war than prior to the war. Creek Chub made nine fly rod lures after 1940, but only two after 1950. Several other companies started then, such as The Gaines Co., a Pennsylvania firm that popularized cork fly rod poppers and sliders and is still in business today. Companies, such as Peckinpaugh (bought by Tony Accardo), Orvis, South Bend, Shakespeare and others, also made fly rod bass bugs and lures.

This was also a period with less emphasis on lures and increasingly more on rods and reels, including that new-fangled method, spinning.

Heavy Metal

Many metal baits, spinnerbaits and spoons did not survive the war years. Other lures did better. One spinnerbait that did become popular was the 1941

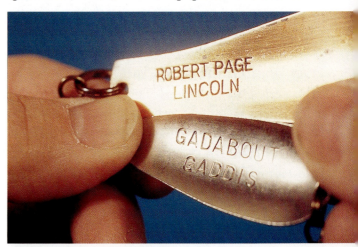

TOP: *Some companies made special lures marked with the names of fishing writers and personalities. Top, a 1940 Robert Page Lincoln spoon, named for the popular writer of the 1930s-40s and made by Superior Door Catch, makers of the popular K B spoons. Bottom, a Gaddabout Gaddis spoon labeled with the nick name of Roscoe Vernon Gaddis, a popular TV fishing show personality of the 1950s and 60s.*

ABOVE: *Early Johnson Silver Minnows, which have been around since 1923, came in paper boxes like these and noted on the box that they were plated with pure silver (left) or 24 carat gold (right).*

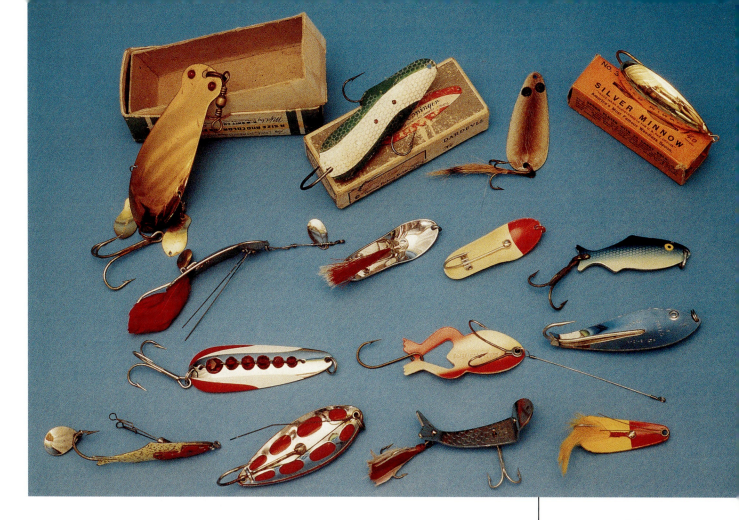

spinner from Pflueger that was its answer to the previous Jamison Shannon Twin Spin. The lure had a spoon base (rather than a weighted head, as with other spinnerbaits then and now) with a spring arm with two wire weedguards that ended with two spinner blades. Bomber also debuted a spinnerbait called the Bush Wacker with a single arm and blade (in contrast to the Jamison and the Pflueger with two arms).

Jigs and lead head lures and a whole spate of metal spinners began to increase in popularity after the war. Some of this transition might have occurred with tran-sitional fish, such as the shad that are basically saltwater species that make anadromous spawning runs into East Coast rivers each spring. A popular lure from 1941 was the Quilby Minnow, sometimes called the Quilby Streamer, and its fancy version, the Quilby Wab-Tail, which had a spinner-blade flapping tail. It was great for spinning, and fly rod sizes were introduced in 1948.

The lure was made by the Pequea Works of Strasburg, PA, and consisted of a weighted

ABOVE: **Top row (left to right):** *Early K-B spoon with fish-shaped bangles on each side of the spoon, on original box; Winged Dardevle with fold-out hooks, sitting on top of original Osprey box; Mousie Devle by Eppinger; gold Johnson Silver Minnow on box.* **Second row:** *Heddon King Stanley spoon; Pflueger Chum spoon with bucktail; Pflueger Chum spoon, no bucktail but painted; Pflueger Last Word spoon.* **Third row:** *Red and White Witch by Alcock, Leight, and Westwood of Canada; Heddon Spoony Frog; L-Y Yates spoon.* **Bottom row:** *Pflueger Pipin spoon; Sunspot spoon by South Bend; Wicked Wiggler by Creek Chub; Weezel spoon by the Weezel Company.*

Artificial Lures 81

turkey quill body, painted with a red head and eyes and calf fur tail. The body was molded in the quill of a low-melt lead-like material called Wood's metal, and it was thought that the sheen of the metal through the translucency of the quill was necessary to attract the shad during their coastal runs. That later proved to be untrue as competitors, or those not willing to go through all the steps necessary to make this lure, began to mold similar look-alike lures of lead that resembled the original, but had painted bodies. The Jamison Underwater Coaxer existed between 1906 and 1923.

ABOVE: *Three early Mepps spinners, noting size differences and also patents. Left to right; size #5, size #4 and size #3. Left and right lures have both British and French patents only; the center lure has these plus a note of U. S. Patent Pending.*

But even in the 1940s and the early '50s, there are few references to jigs, and most were in regard to saltwater. A 1942 fishing and vacation guide published jointly by *Field & Stream–Outdoor Life* shows two-page photos of lures "…used in trolling and jigging…" Lead lures are shown, but they more closely resemble the so-called squids that were used along the coast for stripers, rather than the feathered or bucktail jig we know today. None shown were made with the bent shank jig hook commonly used by modern manufacturers.

Light Metal

Spinning, though invented as a tackle method 50 years prior, was formally introduced to the public before World War II, in the 1930s. This method of casting lighter lines as a "bridge" between the fly and the heavier lures of baitcasting required lighter lures.

Lighter lures were also considered an advantage for everything from trout to panfish to smallmouth, because the larger, heavier lures of casting tackle were often too big for these species.

The first lures for this new system of fishing were spinners and light spoons made of metal. Many of the companies making the rods and reels also made or imported the lures. By 1950 a wide range of lures had been designed specifically for this "new" tackle. The

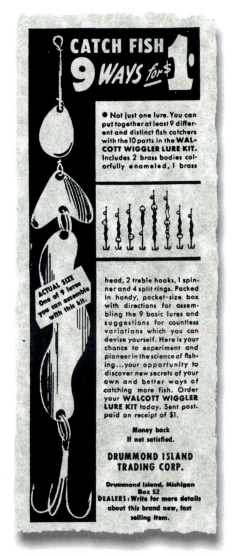

82   *Our Fishing Heritage: Tackle & Equipment*

Mepps, C. P. Swing, Thommen T-Flirt, Monti-Spinner, Riss Findory, French Olympique, Garcia Voblex, Erne St. Claire Tail-Lite, Panther Martin, Swiss Filvit Flirt, Devons, Abu Reflex, and Airex lures became popular spinners. Some few of these, such as the Mepps, still remain.

Popular spoons included the Dardevle, Wob-L-Rite, Thommen Dolly Midget, Falcon, Swiss EGB Bunker, Les Davis Hot Rod, Thomas Hi-Fi Minnow, Thomas Buoyant Minnow, Thomas Fighting Fish, Thomas Cyclone Spoon, Al's Goldfish spoons, Seneca spoons, Phoebe, Abu Charmer and others. Obviously, metal was big in the first decade of spinning in the U.S. The Orvis Company sold a wide range of spinning gear, and in A. J. McClane's 1952 book, *Spinning for Fresh and Salt Water Fish of North America,* there is a photo of 18 popular spinning lures from Orvis—all metal—all spinners, spoons or Devons. All were imported, reflective of the European influence and popularity of spinning at the time. Most of the spinning lures at the time where small—usually weighing about ⅛ to ¼ ounce.

More Wood and Plastic Baits

Some companies were able to introduce some new lures. The free-swinging paddle blade Crazy Crawler was introduced in 1940, and other companies debuted new lures or made modifications to old ones or adjusted their production to cope with the shortage of raw materials as a result of the war. As with most

ABOVE: **Top row (left to right):** *Porky Getum coated with Celluloid; Oriental Wiggle, made of Pyralin, by Al Foss; Heddon Pyralin Vamp; early 1935 Heddon Jointed Vamp made of Tenite; South Bend Bass Obite made of Tenite; Red and White trolling spoon (Troller) made of Pyrashell by Bill DeWitt.* **Second row:** *Modern plastics were better, but early lures still required better lips since the plastics were sometimes opaque; the lure to the right is a modern clear plastic that results in a clear lip.* **Bottom:** *A very tough lure for toothy fish (Jawbreaker), made of hard foam plastic.*

Artificial Lures

LURES WITH LOGOS AND SPECIAL DESIGNS

Lures have been made that resemble spark plugs, beer cans, soft-drink cans and the like, often by name manufacturers who do them as a special novelty issue in conjunction with the company whose brand appears on the lure. Other lures that are different and not originally sold on the open market include standard lures that have labels or logos of other companies or organizations. Jamison had a Miller High Life bottle lure that looked just like the beer. There was also a Schlitz beer bottle spoon. Fred Arbogast made a novelty bait in the shape of a corncob, with two trebles, in honor the DeKalb Corn Co. Some more current examples would be a series of Vortex Lures (crankbaits) in the late 1980s and early 1990s. These were their standard crankbaits (although not so standard in that they had battery-operated lights) with logos of Coors, Coors Light, Keystone Beer and Keystone Light and a rattling slim minnow labeled Coors Light, The Silver Bullet.

Among others, Mann's did an RC-labeled crankbait, Dardevle a "Sport Show" stamped spoon, Luhr Jensen produced a green BP logoed spoon and JWA Associates, which owned Johnson lures and also produced SpiderWire, made a few Johnson Silver Minnows with the SpiderWire spider over a red/black swirl painted convex side.

Poe's lures, after it was bought by Browning, produced a few black crankbaits and some hookless key chains with the deer's head Browning logo. TNN gave out some minnow crankbaits with TNN or TNN Outdoors printed on the sides. Around the time of the Gulf War, Storm produced both desert camo finish and red, white and blue stars and stripes Thunderstick Juniors and Deep Thunderstick Juniors.

At shows, particularly trade shows, new lures are sometimes signed by the designer for special presentation to dealers, distributors and the press. Luhr Jensen did this for several years with designer Tom Seward's name and the lure introduction date before he went to work for Worden's Lures. Luhr Jensen did the same thing with Sam Griffin-designed wood lures, supplying them in wood boxes with a clear plastic lid, and wood shavings surrounding the lure in the box.

Pradco, through their Cotton Cordell company, did this with signed or stamped lures by Cotton Cordell with several lures including a 25th anniversary model in 1992 of the 1967 Fred Young Big O. It was done in conjunction with B.A.S.S., which was also formed in 1967, as part of a B.A.S.S. collector series.

Some lures have been specially stamped for certain organizations, such as for members of the Outdoor Writers Association of America and usually distributed at their annual conference. Examples can be found with Burke lures (1984 in Traverse City, MI), Storm Lures (Marco Island, FL, 1988), Rebel (1978, Virginia Beach, VA) and Arbogast (Niagara Falls, NY, 1991 and Bismarck, ND 1992).

---

lures, there were later imitators, in the case of the Crazy Crawler, a similar 1949 Le Boeuf Creeper in two sizes for bass and muskie from Hew Plastic Sales.

Toward the end of this decade, smaller plugs and other lures also gained ground as spinning became increasingly popular. The smaller plugs and topwater lures were usually just reduced-size versions of existing lures designed to capture the spinning market. Some of these smaller versions of the big lures did not work as well in the water and weren't as effective. Smaller spinnerbaits and heavily weighted flies were also introduced then and promoted for spinning. These flies seldom weighed more than ¼ ounce but were far heavier than would be used for fly

fishing and were specifically geared for the spinning market.

More and more plastics and fewer and fewer wood lures were being produced as the 1940–1950 decade continued, with Pflueger one of the last lure companies to switch to plastic for lure bodies. The Helin Company switched from wood to plastic in 1948, making larger models easier to make through the injection molding process. Six new models of Flatfish were added, two of which were fly rod size. Mackinen Tackle Co. began conversion to tenite plastic in 1946, completing the switch in all lures the same year. Its Makilure baits, which were very similar to the South Bend Bass-Oreno, were very popular in the Northern states.

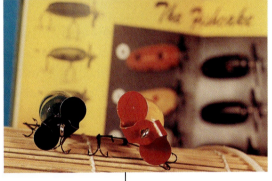

TOP: Fishcake top water lures from Helin were made with both right turning black plastic props and left turning red plastic props. These two sizes both had the double treble hooks on the wire rig as with the Flatfish, also made by Helin.

ABOVE: Fishcake lures with the right-turning black prop (left) and the left turning red prop (right). The catalog in the back relates the red-turning props to the reds or communists that were a great fear in the 1950s when this lure was popular.

Artificial Lures

Lures from 1950 to 1975

The Push to Plastic (Soft and Hard)

By 1950, the glory days of lure manufacturing were, if not over, certainly diminished. Most of the basic styles and types of lures that we use today were developed by then, plastics had come into being and special tackle boxes for holding lures had been developed. Lures, some of them great, were developed in the next 50 years, but the groundwork of lure design had already been prepared.

Nick Creme, Soft Plastics and Competition

A year before this period began, Nick Creme started a business. It was in 1949 that Nick Creme virtually created an industry in his kitchen and basement, melting plastics and trying them in molds to make a soft-plastic imitation of a live worm. Ultimately he succeeded, and the soft-plastic lure is more popular today than ever. To be sure, soft lures had been attempted, developed and used before—rubber insects and minnows, gutta percha baitfish and the like—but none had neither the softness required of such a lure nor the long life and durability required for continued sales. The difference is that the earlier rubber lures were rubber; the "rubber" worm, now called the plastic worm, is really a PVC (polyvinyl chloride) plastic, which, according to reports, will endure for 1500 years!

ABOVE: Early soft rubber lures predated the soft plastics that were to come later. As evidenced by the condition of these early rubber lures, they did not have the flexibility, durability or long-life of the plastics of today.

ABOVE: *This is just a small sampling of the modern soft plastics that include not only the worms, grubs and tube lures shown here, but also lizards, crayfish, frogs, leeches, rats, shrimp button-tail minnows and other similar lures found in modern tackle boxes.*

Nick Creme and his wife Cosma developed the technology in their kitchen and basement and by 1951 had a Wiggle Worm ready for the market. A jobber sold nearly 10,000 packs of the worms at the 1951 Cleveland Sports Show. Creme also started the expansion of lures beyond just simple earth worms, a move that continues today with soft lure manufacturers. Creme added maggots, fat grubs, corn borer and weed worms. In the late 1950s Creme moved to Tyler, TX, built a plant and continued to make a wide variety of soft plastics. The company was sold to Knight Manufacturing in 1992, when owner Wayne Kent combined it with his business and shortly thereafter also purchased assets of the Burke Flexo-Products Co.

DeLong lures started in the 1950s, offering 35 different colors of soft-plastic worms, along with saltwater soft-plastic baits, freshwater tadpoles, minnows, eels, and fly rod lures including hellgrammites, insects and crayfish. They also advertised a permanent special taste and odor, which predated scent offerings by more modern companies. Burke carried a similar line of soft-plastic worms and insects for panfish and fly-rodding, as well as foam lures.

More companies followed in the 1960s, with Tom Mann, later of bass tournament fame, starting Mann's Lures, which made and makes both soft-plastic and hard-plastic lures. Mann's started in 1956 when Tom start-

Artificial Lures

THE KITCHEN CONNECTION

Many of the early lure companies began as an offshoot of a hobby of making home-made lures, and began in the kitchen or had a kitchen connection. The idea for the first and second spoons came from a silver teaspoon dropped into the water and engulfed by a lake trout. Julio Buel was fishing from a boat for lake trout in Lake Bomoseen outside of his home in Castleton, VT. The boat hit a submerged rock and jarred Julio into dropping a silver spoon into the water as he was finishing a bowl of cut fruit at the end of his picnic lunch. He watched it as it twisted down in the clear depths, only to see a large trout lunge for it. "It was a fine, silver tablespoon, from Germany," Buel later related.

James Heddon, with his sons William and Charles, started his lure company in 1902 in their kitchen. William J. Jamison also used the family kitchen as his first manufacturing facility in 1905 when making the Coaxer, his first lure and a cork surface bait. A farmhouse kitchen in Akron, OH, was where the first Pflueger lures of the new Enterprise Manufacturing Co. were made when the company started in 1864. Nick Creme, inventor of the soft-plastic bait (true rubber baits had been around since the late 1800s), first melted the plastic for his lures in the family kitchen, running the pots of molten plastic to the basement where the plastic was poured into the molds to form the first plastic worms still used today.

Then, too, there was the Kitchen Sink lure, a novelty item that looked just like a small sink with a hook attached. For another kitchen connection, there is also the Fork Lure, made like the business end of a fork (perhaps a play on the business end of the spoon used by Buel?).

TOP: *This assortment of fly rod poppers from The Gaines Company is drying after being painted using aerosol spray paints, netting and templates to achieve scale finishes, designs and eyes.*

RIGHT: *Here a worker in The Gaines Company sprays the finish on a rack of fly rod poppers.*

Our Fishing Heritage: Tackle & Equipment

ed tying jigs in his Shawmut, AL, home. He became a game warden and, during that time, carved a little piece of lead into the lure that would become the tailspinner Little George, named after Alabama governor and friend George Wallace. One million of the little lead lures sold in 1973 alone. (Other companies followed this concept, with Abu Garcia making a similar Dazzle Tail.)

In 1968, Tom had decided to devote full time to the lure business, moved to the banks of Lake Eufaula, started the soft plastics with the Jelly Worm and was soon employing 100 people. A side trip involved his relationship with the Humminbird depth finder made by Techsonic Industries, after which he sold the bait company to Techsonic. The company was sold again in 1985. Today, the company makes a wide range of soft-plastic lures, continues to make metal lures like the Little George and also makes a wide range of hard-plastic baits.

FlipTail was another soft lure company of the 1960s. All companies at the time had a problem in that the plasticizers used would soften and melt the tackle boxes and destroy the finishes of hard baits. Ultimately the tackle box companies switched from styrene to polyethylene and other better plastics that were not only worm proof, but also tougher and better plastics for the purpose. Today, there are dozens of companies that make not only worms, but also lizards, crayfish, grubs, snakes, crayfish, rats and frogs.

Hollow Vinyl Lures

As with a lot of anglers who had ideas for lures, Harry Ehlers wanted a lure that held a concealed hook or weedless hook that would allow him to fish in the weedy spots favored by bass and other species. His concept was for a soft, hollow-vinyl plastic body against which would fit upturned double hooks. The idea was for the hollow lure to collapse to expose the hooks and hook the fish on a strike. This snag-proof lure, with a proprietary method of injection mold manufacturing, developed into the Snag Proof Manufacturing Co. The first lures were made and sold by mail order in 1957; the company was formed in 1961. In time it expanded its line from the original frog to poppers, mice, worms, crayfish, leeches and other lures to form a family of hollow plastic collapsible lures.

Naturally, because success breeds competition, several other lure companies manufactured lures with the same idea, including Mann's with its cigar-like Ghost and Gobblin lures, various Frogs, Rats and Poppers; and

LEFT: *Enduring lures will continue to last and continue to catch fish. Here, top to bottom, are both old and new Mepps spinners, Rapalas and Johnson Silver Minnows.*

The Big O

One of the most popular lures that came out of the 1960s was the Big O, a fat minnow or baitfish wood crankbait first carved in 1967 by angler Fred Young. It was during that summer that Young was recovering from back surgery, and carving lures, whittling out a balsa lure that became the Big O. He named it after his brother Odis, who tested the lure. It was also the first year of Ray Scott's Bass Anglers Sportsman Society and bass tournament fishing. Although the two did not form a marriage, they did make a propitious acquaintance. Early bass pro anglers on the tournament trail such as Blake Honeycutt and Bill Nichols used the Big O to win tournaments; the fame of the fat lure was established. There were even stories of the lures being rented on a daily basis at fish camps, after the renters put down a healthy deposit in case

Southern Lure Co. with its Scum Frogs and Tiny Toads. In the category of nothing-is-really-new, the same concept of hollow, soft-skin lures was first thought of and patented in 1901, using latex liquid rubber instead of the modern plastics. Prior to that, in 1895, the James T. Hastings Company produced a hollow rubber frog, with upturned hooks that extended in back of the body!

of loss. The 3,700 or so that Fred Young carved, each signed and numbered, sold for about $10 to $15 each in the '60s, a handsome price to pay for a lure when a Whopper Stopper Hellbender was selling for $1.25, a Heddon Zara Spook for about $1.75 and a Mepps spinner for under a buck.

The 3½-inch-long Big O design was bought by Cotton Cordell lures, which was later bought by

90   *Our Fishing Heritage: Tackle & Equipment*

ABOVE: Many lure companies are understandably proud of a successful lure, and often will issue commemorative lures, plaques or other memorabilia to mark the occasion. Here, several Rapala lures are shown on top of a Rapala catalog along with a plaque marking the 20th anniversary of the original Rapala and a boxed example of the same lure.

Pradco. Pradco is a parent corporation owning a number of modern lure companies. Other companies tried to cash in on the craze, making lures of a similar shape, and often with a similar name, such as the Bill Norman Big N.

The Start of Storm

Storm started with a surface lure, the Glop, a bobbing, action-filled banana-shaped lure that worked great, but was difficult to manufacture. The date was 1964. The lure did not last long, but the company did. In 1965, the Thinfin, a slim, shad-like diving lure that could resemble a number of slab-sided baitfish, (and which is very close to a shad), debuted. It was available in a number of finishes.

This was followed by the Hot'N Tot, a metal-lipped lure originally designed as a bass bait, but shortly proving better on walleye and, in the right bright colors, on salmon and steelhead. The Wiggle Wart followed in 1975, leading to a series ranging from Wee Warts to Magnum Warts.

Normark and *Life* Magazine and Fishing

The slim shallow-running Rapala was just some "Finlander plug," as a friend described his lure to Ron Weber in 1959 when Weber first saw it while being outfished on an outing for pike. Weber bought a few that were just then becoming available, then ordered 500 from Lauri Rapala, patriarch of the then-fledgling company. Weber then contacted Ray Ostrum about selling a few out of his store in Minneapolis, and the lure started to take off. They then proposed to the Rapala Company an exclusive deal for selling in the U.S., a deal to which Rapala immediately agreed. Outdoor writers began to publicize the new type of lure that closely resembled in action and shape a slim minnow. The lure worked, and worked well, and sales were good, even though it was selling for $1.95. Most other lures were selling for about $1.

The big push came in 1962 when the Rapala was featured in the same issue

Artificial Lures 91

LEFT: Various early metal jigs and lures did not include the popular jig shape on the bent shank hook that we know today. **Top to bottom:** 7/0 size 18-ounce New England cod fishing jig ca 1890; 1906 lead Jamison Underwater Coaxer that was perhaps the earliest lead jig type of lure designed exclusively for freshwater fishing; and tin body jig designed for surf fishing that allowed shining the lure in the surf sand and also bending the lure slightly for more action on the retrieve.

of Life magazine that covered the suicide and life of Marilyn Monroe. By 1965, the lure had eight winners in the annual *Field & Stream* Fishing Contest and 11 winners in the *Sports Afield* Big Fish Contest. The original lure was followed by more sizes, deeper divers and more finishes. In 1970 the company started seriously courting the saltwater market with tougher lures for the tougher fish, and in 1975 debuted the first of its jointed models. It was in that same year that the 25th million Rapala was sold.

Mepps and Other Spinners

A spinner with a blade revolving around a shaft was the first patented lure with the Buel "spoon" in 1852. Other lures came along, but the basic spinner idea remained, and some of the early lures introduced here after World War II for the then-new spinning tackle market were small spinners. That's how the Mepps came into being from a 1938 French invention. The lure was given to Todd Sheldon by a returning WWII soldier. Sheldon first tried it on the Wolf River in Wisconsin in 1951, where it caught four trout weighing 12 pounds. The first spinners that were sold in Sheldon's tackle shop in Antigo, WI, were obtained by Frank Velek, the G.I. who gave Sheldon the spinner. Velek got the early inventory for Sheldon by corresponding with a French girl and exchanging nylon stockings for spinners. The lures sold too fast (or the stockings wore out too slowly), so that soon stock was coming directly from the French factory. By 1960, sales had topped 500,000. By the mid-1990s, over 350 million Mepps had been made, and there are 5,000 different variations of Mepps spinners.

Other companies got into the business. Some, such as Hildebrandt, which was already making spinners, increased their output and geared lures to the new spinning market. Lures by Abu Garcia, C. P. Swing, Blue Fox, Normark, Harrison Hoge, Caliber, Worden's and others were common place in the 1950s to 1960s and continue today.

92   Our Fishing Heritage: Tackle & Equipment

Jigs Start to Get Popular

With the advent of the bass tournaments and the later similar popularity of crappie and walleye tournaments, jigs became more widely used. Manufacturers made more variations, in different styles for a variety of fishing, from slow trolling to hopping jigs along the bottom. Originally, jigs were made with fur or hackle tails. Then rubber skirts were tried, the same as those originally developed years earlier by Fred Arbogast. Then molded skirts were developed to slip over a molded ridged collar on the lure to hold it in place, along with loose skirt material held in place with tiny O rings. Skirts changed from rubber to eventually include plastic, silicone, Spandex (Lumaflex) and molded soft plastic (PVC). In the 1960s, fishing a jig with a Hoochy skirt in California was called

LURES WITH HOLES IN THEIR HEADS

In an effort to create even more splash and noise in surface lures, some were made with holes in their heads. Some diving lures were also made this way. Collectors often call these water sonic lures, because the water runs through the lure.

One of the first of these was the 1909 (patent date) E. J. Lockhart (Wagtail Minnow Mfg. Co.) Water Witch or Pollywog that was cigar shaped with a hole in the bottom front that exited through a smaller tapered hole in the top back. The 1914 Eureka Wiggler was a similar cigar stick-like topwater lure with a hole on the underside that was expelled through two holes about half way back on the top.

The Master Biff Plug from 1926 was a simple-looking little wood chugger style, but with a hole in the flat head and holes on the side to expel water. The Bag-O-Mad lure from Bill Harrington Bait Co. had two holes in the front notched-wood lip, each hole exiting through the side of the lure. Even Creek Chub had a water sonic lure with their 1933 Jigger that had a hole that ran top to bottom through the topwater plug, with a metal lip or scoop in back of the bottom hole to help direct water through the hole.

More recent diving lures were those made by Aquasonic Lures of Cibolo, TX, that had five different plugs with holes through them. Its plastic Undertaker lipped diving lure had a hole in the head (above the lip); the water shot out through slots in the belly and back.

One lure that had a hole that was not important to the action was the 1970s Fincheroo that had a large straight-through-the-side hole in back of the line tie but forward of the hooks. The idea was to slip your finger into the hole to land the fish.

The most recent version of a lure with through-hole design is the 1999 Merlin Lures Pathfinder that combines a hole with scent. The plastic crankbait has a hole that allows water to enter the gill area and run through pores in the back. A central compartment holds a sponge designed to hold scent, so that the exiting water creates a scent trail.

Artificial Lures

tule fishing, for the tules, or shoreline reeds, where it was done.

Special lures for special circumstances were developed, such as the Bass Buster crappie jigs that had a simple ball head, with a hackle tail and hackle-wrapped chenille body in bright colors. Because most of the larger jigs were fished on the bottom for bass and walleye, weed guards were developed including wire guards, the molded-in brush guards and the molded- or glued-in Y guards. And long after rattles became popular in crankbaits and topwater lures, rattles began to be added to jigs, usually molded into plastic sleeves on the shank of the hook or attached with a short length of flexible rubber tubing.

Sonic Lures Continue—The Rat-L-Trap

By the early 1970s, the sonic lure crown was switching from the Pico Perch, Heddon Sonic (new in 1960), Hawk Fish and Whopper Stopper to a new lure company, the Bill Lewis Company Rat-L-Trap. All of these lures were small, flat tapered-body shapes that would set up a rapid vibration on a fast retrieve. The big difference with the Rat-L-Trap was that it was the first lure specifically designed with built-in rattles (shot in a large sound chamber). Often in shallow water and fishing from an aluminum jon boat, you could feel resonance vibrations begin in the hull of the boat.

The Beginning of Blade Baits

In 1959, Heddon introduced a new type of lure that was a flat blade, with several holes for line ties on the dorsal part of the lure, a weighted head/belly and a belly and tail treble hook. It was called the Sonar, and came in three sizes. The three line tie holes on the top were for fixing a snap, with the holes adjusting the running depth of the unusual vibrating lure.

The lure worked but languished for a while. It was not until the early 1990s that other lure companies got into the blade bait business. Popular current lures of this design are the Heddon Gay Blade, Heddon Sonar Flash, Luhr Jensen Ripple Tail, Cicada and the Silver Buddy, all designed for both casting and vertical jigging.

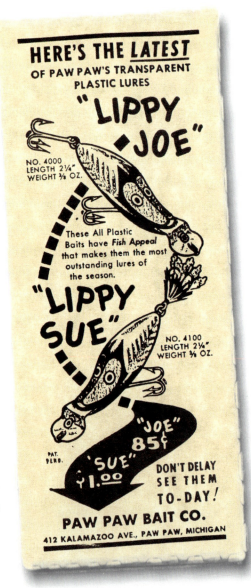

Lures from 1975 to the Present

More Lures and More Variety of Lures

Many lures and varieties of lures have been developed over the past 25 years, but most of these fall into categories of previously established designs. Topwater lures, crankbaits (they used to be called plugs), spinner-baits, buzzbaits, spinners, weedless spoons, structure or jigging spoons, trolling spoons, jigs, soft plastics of all types, hard-plastic saltwater trolling lures and soft-plastic trolling skirts continued to be invented, expanded and explored as lures for both fresh- and saltwater.

Some lures stayed pretty much the same. Topwater lures continued to have chugger-cupped faces, fore- and aft-props, skipping lips, skipping heads, some with holes in the head to throw water and some just simple cigar shapes to wake or walk-the-dog. All were designed

to work on the surface as something swimming along or injured and fluttering on the surface, and all were designed to attract gamefish.

Spinnerbaits, too, stayed pretty much the same. Twin spin (on two shafts as with the original Shannon Twin Spin), two blades (on one shaft—a common rigging today) and single spin all retained popularity and had specific purposes for specific fishing situations. In-line spinnerbaits such as the Erie Dearie and other brands for dredging the bottom for walleye also became popular and continue to have their following.

Most of the lures that remain today as they were in the past are metal lures—Hopkins jigging spoons, the Johnson Silver Minnow, the many styles of the Eppinger Dardevle, Accetta Pet trolling and casting spoons, spinners and spoons from Hildebrandt, Prescott and K.B. Explosions of lure brands occurred in some specific categories, namely the slim minnow-like baits, following the popularity of the Rapala and the wide range of possibilities, following Nick Creme's soft-plastic worm development.

More Slim Lures Follow Rapala

Following the popularity and increasing sales of the Rapala, competition soared. It seemed as if every hard-lure company followed with its version of the lure that made it into magazine. Some were made of balsa as was the carved Rapala; others were molded of plastic. Heddon, Rebel, Cotton Cordell,

ABOVE: *Many species spawned their own particular tackle and became some of the early niche fishing tackle for manufacturers. One example was muskie fishing that in the 1940s and 50s was responsible for books, special stiff rods, larger wide spool reels and larger lures in topwater, medium running, spinner and spinnerbait styles, as shown here.*

Artificial Lures

LEFT: Some lure manufacturers would have their lure designers at sport and trade shows to autograph lures and tackle. This example is a balsa wood Bagley lure signed by designer Jim Bagley.

This was not unlike a previous idea—the 1939 Garland Cork-Head Minnow that had a cork head that fit over the slim "dowel" of hardwood that was an extension of the rear wood body. The idea was to make the head of the lure float higher in the water because of an "unbalanced specific gravity" through the use of two materials.

Storm, Bagley, Mann's, Norman, Whopper Stopper, Smithwick, Rat-L-Trap and others came up with their versions.

One problem with any of the balsa lures is that balsa is a light but fragile wood, and subject to damage and also hook-pull-out. One way to solve this was achieved by Bagley with its balsa lures when the company began to make them with a harder wood center, almost like a dowel. The hook hangers and line tie fastened into the harder wood. A sleeve of balsa was placed over the core and glued in place so that the final lure had both the look, weight, feel and action of an all-balsa lure and the durability of a hardwood lure.

Care had to be taken, however, with the new hollow plastic slim baits. A weed-removal trick was to slap the lure across the surface of the water to slough off any water weeds as a quicker, easier and less messy way to take weeds off of lure hooks than pulling them off by hand. The problem was that when done with the Whopper Stopper Hellcat lures that the author liked and used, the result was often two halves of a lure, the slap against the water breaking the lure apart.

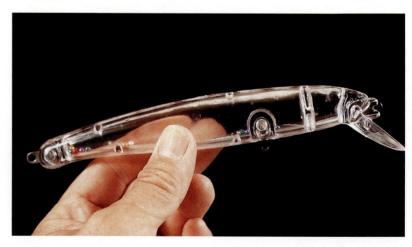

RIGHT: Some lures were made clear, but most clear lures were made that way so that the finished painted lure would have a clear transparent lip that would not show to the fish. This example shows a shallow running minnow-type lure, molded from two halves and with the line tie and hook hangers sandwiched between the two halves before sealing them together.

Lure Colors and Color C-Lectors

In the early 1980s, Dr. Loren Hill developed a system of determining maximum visibility of certain colors in lures by using a light probe that could be dropped to any given depth. The preferred lure color could subsequently be read on a hand-held instrument dial. Many lure companies bought in on the idea and advertised their lures as finished in Color C-Lector colors. At the time, Fenwick made a tackle box with compartments keyed to the colors to make lure selection easy.

Some Odd Lures

Some odd lures have always cropped up during lure development, even in recent years. Some ideas have been good, others not so good. One good idea was found in the Whopper Stopper spinnerbait. Rather than using a painted lead body that would chip and could be damaged, they encased the lead body in a thick, tough plastic shell that could not be damaged.

Whopper Stopper also had some crazy ideas, such as the late 1970s top water lure that internally had a small spring fixed to the inside of the lure at the rear of the plug and a lead weight at the other end of the spring. The idea was that chugging, working and popping the lure would cause the spring to move, making the weight vibrate the lure during a pause in lure action. It worked—but not that well—and did not last long.

Lazy Ike (not the original company, which had been sold by this time), in the early 1990s, introduced a lure with three interchangeable lips. The concept was to create one lure that would run shallow, medium and deep. The lips could be changed with a small supplied screwdriver. The lure seemed to disappear after a few years.

The idea of making a single lure that could be adjusted to run to several depths has always intrigued lure makers, and one design in the 1980s utilized clear diving

Artificial Lures 97

DIFFERENT, SOMETIMES OFF-COLOR BUT NOT OFF MARKET

Some lures are decidedly gimmicks and designed more for the joke value than for their fishing ability. In many cases, the "joke," if you wish to call it that, may be slightly suggestive, off-color or definitely offensive and racist. Some examples of the slightly suggestive lures are those that have been sold from about the 1950s on that resemble a mermaid (the Virgin Mermaid), with exposed breasts and usually with hands folded above and in back of the head, treble hooks attached to the tail and belly areas. Off-color lures have been sold recently that resemble the male anatomy. Sometimes lure manufacturers just have a little fun for their reps, the press, some dealers and the like, as was one nonproduction model of a soft-plastic lizard from a small lure manufacturer. The lizard came in a bag labeled Big Buford and looked like a regular unrigged dark purple lizard lure until turned over to reveal a well endowed "male" lizard with the appropriate parts molded of red plastic.

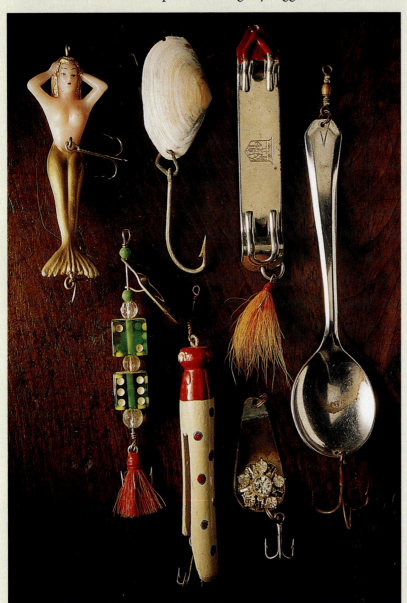

ABOVE: Novelty lures are numerous, yet seemed more popular in the 1940s and 1950s than today. Examples from both anglers and tackle manufacturers include, top to bottom: Virgin Mermaid lure from Stream-Eze, Lucky 7 dice lure, clothespin lure, shell lure, Sparkler Fish (patented July 10, 1911, manufacturer unknown), can opener lure and silver spoon lure.

98 Our Fishing Heritage: Tackle & Equipment

fins on the side of the lure, almost like pectoral fins on a fish, rather than a clear diving bill. An internal ratchet mechanism allowed adjusting the angle of the fins for different depths. These concepts again were not new. The same idea of a lure with external side-mounted adjustable planes to make the lure dive at different angles—or work on the surface—was developed, advertised and sold as Pepper's Yankee Aero Bass Bait by Joe E. Pepper of Rome, NY, in 1918! In 1949, Millsite had a double-ended slope-face lure with a line tie at each end to run shallow or deep, depending upon which end was fixed to the line.

It was also possible to run a lure to the side as with a buzzbait from the late 1980s that allowed adjusting the arm to run the lure at an angle to the right or left. The idea was to have a lure that would more easily run parallel to structure, riprap or the length of a pier even with the angler at an angle to the preferred lure path.

Soft Plastics Ring Up Hard Sales

With the realization that soft-plastic worms worked so well, many manufacturers soon thought up new baits. In time, there were not only worms and the grubs, maggots and caterpillars that followed immediately, but also a lot of other soft plastics. Crayfish, lizards, rats, frogs, snakes and more insects were developed. Bing McClellan of Burke focused on panfish, trout and bass with soft-plastic baits that resembled crickets, caterpillars, grasshoppers, beetles and other "bugs." He also had a line of soft-plastic worms, along with

ABOVE: *One face of a two-part aluminum mold used to manufacture large quantities of soft plastic baits. Injection molding of the PVC material into one opening in the mold then shoots the molten plastic through gates and sprue holes to reach each lure cavity.*

Artificial Lures

his Flex Plug lures that were, in essence, closed-cell soft-plastic crankbaits and topwater plugs. The hook-to-line tie connection was via a chain through the plug, molded into the plug as it was made. The crankbaits also had molded-in metal lips.

As the soft-plastic industry developed, new manufacturing methods allowed the use of different color tails, "blood lines" through the center of the worm and lamination. Ironically, the industry started with open face (one sided) molds that produced a molded worm with only one side, then progressed to two-side molds to make round worms. In the late 1990s, companies went to "hand poured" worms that were made in open-face molds. The hand-poured worms had gained popularity with some of the bass pros at the time and were thought to be superior to the mass-produced molded worms.

One different technique of making soft plastics was tried by Rebel with its Redneck lizard, which featured a groove molded around the neck into which fitted a contrasting-color gill-like collar. Some similar techniques were also used by companies making soft-plastic tails with outrigger "arms" of soft plastic.

Tube lures of soft plastic also entered the market during this period. One of the first of these was the Knight Tube Worm that was developed in 1977. The four- and six-inch worms had molded skirt tails and a hollow body, and were really a precursor of the shorter, thicker tube lures available today from most of the worm and soft-plastics manufacturers and that came out of California in the 1980s.

One new idea in the fall of 1889 was Herb Reed's concept of a new type of soft-plastic lure that could be worked underwater like the Zara Spook topwater walk-the-dog action. The result, after 2½ years of research, was the patented Lunker City Slug-Go, since copied by almost everybody (with most eliminated through defense of the patent). The slug-type of lure could be rigged Texas style, and short twitches would cause it to dart off in any direction, and proved immediately to be an effective bass lure. Variations of this lure such as the slimmer-tailed Lunker City Fin-S and a host of imitations make this lure type and this method of fishing currently popular with no sign of waning.

Harder Soft Plastic for Saltwater

The family of PVC plastics (polyvinyl chloride) is used to make everything from fly line coatings to soft-plastic lures to drain pipe and plumbing fixtures. In making soft-plastic lures, a difference in the plasticizer in the plastic will make a difference in the hardness and durability of the lure. Add a lot of plasticizer, and you have lures that can be just slightly harder and more durable than a bowl of Jello. Remove plasticizer, and you have the tougher worms, fish tails, shrimp and grubs popular for saltwater fishing. Remove even more plasticizer, and you have even

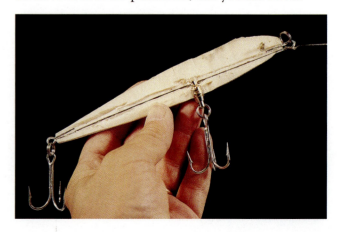

RIGHT: *This hard plastic foam lure that has been sawn in half lengthwise shows the through-wire construction that connects the line tie, belly hook and tail hook so that a fish cannot be lost, even if the lure body is destroyed.*

tougher "drier" plastic that is still flexible. This is used to make the skirts and soft-plastic trolling lures for saltwater. In essence, you have vinyl, which is flexible in sheet form but is far tougher than any freshwater plastic worm. These include the various trolling skirts from Sevenstrand and Weber, along with similar skirts and molded squid from Moldcraft. Most of these lures are designed to be skipped on the surface in a boat wake. They are large, often as long as 18 inches.

Combo Hard and Soft Plastic Lures

The L'il Tubby was one of the first of the combination lures, after the lure companies figured out how to reduce or stop the chemical reactions between soft plastics and hard plastics. The L'il Tubby from the mid-1970s had a lipped egg-shaped body with a keyed slot in the tail to take a mated soft plastic curved tail.

The company was bought from Tubby Tackle by Storm, and then discontinued in the 1980s. Today, in the late 1990s, the concept is coming back with some of the large bass plugs such as the A. C. Plug and the Castaic Baits. Berkley also introduced combination hard- and soft-plastic lures, with their Power Bait series of lures that incorporated a hard plastic forward head with line tie and hook hanger, and a slot system to hold the mated soft-plastic tail.

RIGHT: *Large lures like these were made for both saltwater and also freshwater pike and muskie fishing.* **Left to right:** *Jointed Rapala deep diver, Creek Chub Plastic Pikie in chrome finish, and Creek Chub Giant Jointed Pikie that weighs four ounces and is 14 inches long from line tie to tail hook. This far right lure had all the hooks and line tie connected, to prevent fish loss.*

Artificial Lures

LEFT: *Jerry Gibbs, Fishing Editor of* Outdoor Life *magazine, photographs one of the several test tanks and facilities for testing lures at Berkley. Water flows through this tank to show the action and fishing depth of lures. Dr. Keith Jones of Berkley (in the background) checks the performance of two lures in the tank.*

BELOW: *Dr. Keith Jones of Berkley checks the action of two lures in a flow-through test tank at the Berkley plant in Spirit Lake, IA. Facilities like this allow manufacturers to thoroughly test lures before bringing them onto the market.*

The Race to Go Deep

In the early 1980s there was a sudden desire among crankbait companies to get deeper for the increased interest in year-round bass fishing. Year round, more bass in the winter and summer are deep off of breaklines and thus not reachable with the standard River Runt/Bass Orenos of the past and certainly not with the shallow-running original Rapalas. The race to the depths had some early interest in the 1950s and 1960s with the Bomber Water Dog and the Whopper Stopper Hellbender.

Serious interest began with the companies racing for an honest reachable 20-foot depth with a lure on a cast—not while trolling a long light line where it would be possible with many lures. This started with four companies in 1986 advertising a 20-foot-plus crankbait. The companies and lures were the Mann's 20 Plus Deep Hog, Angler's Pride (Crankbait Corporation) TD 20, Bomber Mag A and the Bagley Rattling DB3 Magnum. This spurred other companies into the same race, with lures now reaching 30 feet or more when cast, as with the Mann's 30 + and the Luhr Jensen Deep Secret.

Let There Be Light

The ability to light up the darkness with a lure has always been a dream of lure makers. Some of the earliest lures were made with luminous paint, either on the outside of a wood lure or on the inside of a glass or, later, clear plastic, lure. Pflueger had some early designs and patents on this idea, and many lure companies followed in the early days of lure manufacturing.

The idea was that a few minutes of sunlight would "charge" the lure and allow it to be more visible to fish when retrieving deep. The second step, which requires more of a leap of faith, is that by being more visible, the lure is also more likely to be struck. Today, lures are still made with luminous finishes, although today the tip is to carry a small inexpensive electronic camera flash to charge the lure as required.

Batteries and regular lights have also been used to illuminate lures. Vortex, first in the late 1980s and then again in the mid-1990s, pushed such lures. They produced several designs, all of which came with watch-size batteries that were inserted into a special battery compartment in the lure that was sealed with a screw lid and O ring. The tiny LED in the lure would flash intermittently, varying with retrieve speed. Similar fresh- and saltwater lures by Sadu Strobe Lures were available in the late '90s.

The idea of a battery operated bulb in a lure is also not new, because in 1937 both the Research and Model Co. of East Hartford, CT, and the Lloyd & Co. of Chicago, IL, both had such lures. Both operated with pen light batteries and a tiny bulb, with one ad noting that the light will run for three hours and that batteries are replaceable for 5 cents. Of course, this was 1937. They were molded of translucent or transparent plastic or pyralin and the Research and

Artificial Lures 103

Model Co. models had heads that screwed into the body. Both wobbling and spinner heads were available, in red, black and white, with bodies available in white, green and yellow. An addendum to the ad from Lloyd and Co. is as true today as it was then, stating, "Note—to be used with light only where game laws permit."

The idea wasn't even new in 1937. Though not completely described, a similar battery-operated and lighted lure, probably of glass, was sold as the Glow Worm by the Electric Submarine Bait Co. in 1916.

Chemical light sticks were also used in lures, with the tiny 1½-inch- and 2-inch-long light sticks just like the larger counterparts designed for emergency use. Some were designed to fit into specific lures, others were made to fit onto any lure by means of a short length of rubber tubing fixed to a hook or spinner wire. LumaLure made a wide range of these lures, including spoons, spinners and jigging lures, each with compartments or clips to take the light sticks. To add to the choices, the light sticks were available in yellowish-green, blue and red. Abbey & Imbrie had a Glow Body Minnow in 1920 that had a glass tube body, the inside of which was coated with a luminous radioactive material.

Companies making soft plastics got into the phosphorescence business with worms and other lures in which the tail or the entire lure would glow underwater. One company with an entire line of lures based on this was Advanced Lure Inc., with its Lazer system of lures (LazerTail worms, LazerGrub, LazerShad and LazerLizard).

Salts, Scents or Nonsense

The idea of creating a lure with a scent that would attract fish has been around for a long time with various "secret formulas," but it became most popular with the surge in tournament bass fishing. What developed was the marketing of various scents, tastes and concoctions in liquid, spray, gel or solid form that could be sprayed on lures or into which lures could be dipped or soaked. The first popular brand was Fish Formula, but soon others followed, including Berkley, Wisconsin Pharmacal, Bait Mate, Dr. Juice, Nature's Scent and others. At one point there were approximately 50 different manufacturers of various scents and taste formulations. Some of the tastes were natural, such as fish, earthworm, and crayfish. Others were far from natural fish food, such as anise, garlic, peach and boysenberry.

Initially, a lot of lure manufacturers got interested in the scent idea. Arbogast made a Hula Popper with a hole through the center, the hole holding a wickable material that could be soaked with scent. Some lures were designed with lidded, lattice-work compartments to hold bait, solid scents or gel scents. Worm weights and jigs were made with a flocked surface to hold scent. Many worms were originally scented with anise oil (like licorice) and other scents. Snag Proof sold a scent wax to smear on their lures, Dr. Juice had scents in many flavors, and Fish Formula ultimately produced scent with glitter in it to simulate lost scales of a baitfish. Masking scents to eliminate the smell of human pheramones and baitfish pheromone scents to appeal to fish were also sold.

One of the most successful of the companies entering this field was Berkley, which got into it after hiring Dr. Keith Jones in 1985. In 1985 they came out with their Strike, then in 1987 introduced Solid Strike, in 1988 their Power Baits in dough and tub formulas and in 1989 plastics impregnated with Power Bait formulations.

The whole scent and taste idea spawned other lures and accessories. Culprit brought out a hollow worm that could be filled with their Burst scent, Mann's produced soft-plastic tube lures with open-cell inserts to hold scent, and some spinners even had a compartment for holding gel scent or a rattle. Salt as an addition in soft plastics came even earlier than scents. In 1981 Gene LaRue patented the idea of salt impregnation in lures, with companies using the idea paying a royalty for the privilege.

Rattling Up Fish

Rattles have long been used in lures, but they hit the big time in the early 1970s when Bill Lewis introduced his Rat-L-Trap. The 1940 Millsite Rattle Bug was the first lure to deliberately use rattles as noise in a lure. Prior to that, sonic lures such as the Bayou Boogie (Hawk Lures and later Whopper Stopper in the early 1950s) and the Heddon Sonic (1957) were made, but without any rattle. All of these lures did have a weight in a forward compartment and fishermen ultimately found out that some of these weights were slightly loose and thus made a clunking noise on retrieve—and also seemed to catch more fish. Bill Lewis made his lip-

Artificial Lures

LEFT: *Making slim lures and placing the line tie on top of the lure or the back makes a lure that vibrates rapidly in the water. Add rattles and you have the modern sonic and lipless crankbaits. Top, an old Chatter Chub; left, a modern Bill Lewis Rat-L-Trap; and right, a Frenzy by Berkley.*

together. As with the Rat-L-Trap, they used a casting and diving weight in the front and loose rattles held in the larger rear compartments so that they would rattle around and make noise with the action and vibration of the lure during retrieve. Anywhere from two to about 30 rattles were used in dozens of different lures as everyone got on the bandwagon.

Since then rattles have been built into topwater lures, jigs, spoons, spinnerbaits, sonic lures, and other lures. Separate rattle compartments and

less Rat-L-Trap with a forward weight for casting and diving deep and a rear compartment to hold loose shot. That, along with the buoyancy created by this rear chamber and the light tail hook, allowed the lure to vibrate rapidly on retrieve, causing the shot to rattle.

In the mid-1980s, companies such as Venom, Hart, Woodies and others began making the rattles that today are available in aluminum, plastic and glass. Initially they were designed as worm rattles—push one of these small pill-shaped pieces into the soft-plastic head of a worm and have it make noise as it crawls along the bottom. That worked, and they sold, but then other manufacturers of crankbaits started molding rattle chambers into their lures, which were molded in two parts and then glued or welded

chambers that can be easily fastened to the line or to any hooks or lure are available for use in any fishing. Do-it-yourselfers were encouraged to glue and fasten rattles to every lure imaginable. Rattle lures were also designed that did not use the steel or copper balls, but depended upon the rattling of lure parts or blades to make noise. An example would be some of the jointed spoons or the jointed blade in the Mann's Undulator spinnerbait or the various "clacker" style of buzzbaits in which the turning blade hit another blade to create noise. Today, a new rattle emphasis is with worms and Carolina rigs in which clicking and clacking balls and beads of steel and glass are threaded onto the line in front of the worm to rattle and make noise as the worm is retrieved.

Our Fishing Heritage: Tackle & Equipment

Biology and Fisheries Studies Affect Lure Design

All lure manufacturers have design and testing facilities. In fact, Rapala has made an advertising point of tank testing every lure before it leaves the factory. Perhaps the most advanced facilities today for designing (not just testing action) of lures is located at the Berkley factory in Spirit Lake, IA. Under Dr. Keith Jackson, the company has developed a variety of tank systems for testing lures. One of the most innovative is an oval tank (like a race track) with dividers that separate the center into "walled cages" to hold and separate fish. A battery-operated motor on a track runs around the oval pool holding an arm from which is suspended the current lure being tested and a video camera to record the results of fish seeing the lure. Gates can be opened to release bass and watch them as they ignore, show interest in or attack the lure. There are no hooks in the lure to injure the fish.

In this research, Dr. Jackson has tried soft-plastic exact-imitation replicas of crayfish, then made similar lures that lack various parts of a crayfish, such as the claws, legs, head, tail, antennae, etc. The results are surprising, since they show that bass don't like the big claws so often seen on soft-plastic lures, but really favor a "crayfish" that is nothing more than the tail. Might this be why the simple soft-plastic grub on an unpainted lead head is so effective for both smallmouth and largemouth?

Other research involves testing the action of lures, shape of lures and colors of lures to check for effectiveness. At this writing tests have only been done on bass and in clear water (dirty water would be difficult to view with the video camera), but this seems to be the first really scientific approach to lure design and testing under controlled conditions.

One trend among the hard-bait manufacturers is for more realistic and lifelike finishes on lures. These are not photo reproductions, but more artistic, natural-looking renditions of baitfish that are now found on topwater lures, crankbaits, lipless sonic lures, spinnerbait blades, some jigs and even on some of the soft plastics.

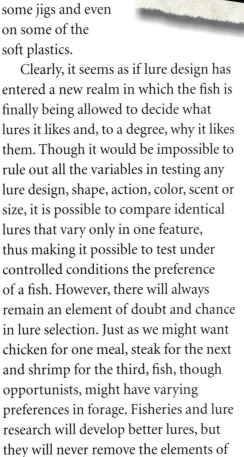

Clearly, it seems as if lure design has entered a new realm in which the fish is finally being allowed to decide what lures it likes and, to a degree, why it likes them. Though it would be impossible to rule out all the variables in testing any lure design, shape, action, color, scent or size, it is possible to compare identical lures that vary only in one feature, thus making it possible to test under controlled conditions the preference of a fish. However, there will always remain an element of doubt and chance in lure selection. Just as we might want chicken for one meal, steak for the next and shrimp for the third, fish, though opportunists, might have varying preferences in forage. Fisheries and lure research will develop better lures, but they will never remove the elements of chance or random choice.

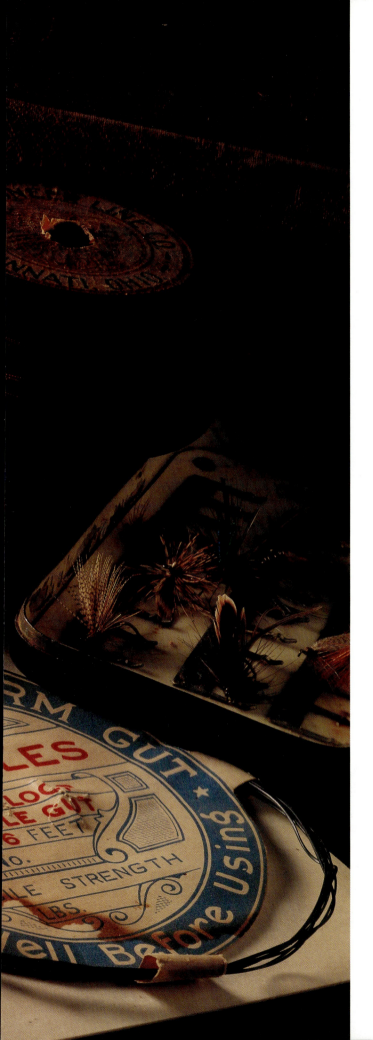

Knots & Connectors

Introduction

Tracing the evolution of knots and connections for fishing is even more difficult than following the development of tackle. Tackle, through patents, magazine ads, catalogs, circulars and references in books, leaves a trail that, though not always easy to follow, is at least manageable. Knots are not so much inventions as they are developments, happy accidents, trial and error efforts and experiments. Just as knots today continue to be developed and refined, so were knots of the past.

In the past, it is likely that knots were developed with only rudimentary knowledge of the principles of making knots and of the characteristics important to knots. There were no easy, accurate and inexpensive ways to determine knot strength as there are today through simple and easily obtainable line-testing machines and industrial tension gauges. Also, different materials were used, and tackle had different requirements.

Knots Before Eyed Hooks

For example, early flies (the first common "lures," because hardware lures had yet to be developed and all other fishing was with bait) were often tied on hooks which lacked eyes, so were, instead, permanently fastened by lengths of silk gut. The gut was wrapped or lashed to the fly hook before the fly was tied, and the snell, or length of gut, ending was attached to the line with a tied loop. Thus, tied loops became important, (as they are today, although for different reasons) along with the connections for tying the end of the line or leader to the loop on the end of the fly snell.

LEFT: *A worker at Berkley tests knots on their lines, using modern sophisticated equipment such as this industrial test gauge. Computer technology shows how knots stretch and fail.*

tying together varying lengths of different diameters.

Knotting the Knots in Place

Knots for tying directly to the eye of a hook or to a sinker or float were also important. Most of these knots are similar to those used today, although improvements and refinements have been made over the years. In some cases, knots must have been known as weak, ineffective or subject to becoming loose. Provisions and recommendations were made with some knots for additional hitches or connections to prevent knot slippage, or to wrap the tag

Line-to-Line Connections

Knots were also important for connecting different pieces of line, both for tying together hair lines that were no more than about three to six feet long per section and for tying lengths of gut to make up a leader, much as tapered leaders are made today by

SOME DRAWINGS OF GOOD KNOTS ARE NOT GOOD DRAWINGS OF KNOTS

Both historically and currently, knot illustrations often leave a little, or a lot, to be desired. The angler's single knot, illustrated in Norris (1864), rather than shown joining two lines with an overhand knot (as it is described) is shown as a short length of line tied into an overhand knot with a long running line. Currently, directions for an in-line dropper loop are often wrong, because the directions for looping the line and folding over the double strands through which the loop is inserted are counter to the illustration that shows the knot made with repeated overhand knot turns. The single water knot (Norris, 1864) and double water knot (Norris and Henshall, 1881) were illustrated so that the bends of the overhand knot would jam against each other and make for a less strong and bulkier knot than they would if alternated around the main lines to mate with each other, as with current knots, such as the mating ends of the Homer Rhode loop.

Our Fishing Heritage: Tackle & Equipment

ends of a knot to the main line with fine thread, whipped to finish the thread wrapping and then sealed to prevent damage to this final protection against unraveling or untying.

Knots Vary with the Line

Presumably knots may have varied with the materials used, just as some knots do today. Historically, horsehair, braided or twisted lines of cotton, spun silk, linen and flax, later braided lines of silk, nylon, Dacron and recently gelspun polyethylene and monofilament lines of nylon have been used. Leaders of horsehair, silkworm gut, nylon monofilament and most recently fluorocarbon have been used between the line and the hook or lure.

Current Knots and New Lines

With current lines, the knots that might be ideal for monofilament will not always work with braided Dacron or gelspun polyethylene. Special connections for braided lines are required, either as modified knots with more turns, or some splices and more complex knots that are a must to gain back some of the strength that would otherwise be lost if using typical knots for monofilament. One of the main problems with braided lines such as Dacron and the newer gelspun polyethylenes is that the standard knots that work on monofilament tend to cut braided lines.

Wire Is Wiry and Tough to Tie

Wire also has special requirements. For single-strand wire, special twists, such as the haywire twist, are most common. For braided wire, some special and often simple knots (such as the figure-eight knot), along with the use of leader sleeves crimped in place with special pliers, are most common. Some new braided wire lines include fine wire stranding combined with the polyethylene braid strands of the "super" lines to make tough, bite-resistant wire lines into which standard knots can be tied.

Knots and Knot Tying of the Past

What is known about early knots is that often the simple knots used historically are not as strong, efficient or slip-proof as are modern knots. Quite frankly, some of the knots used 100 or more years ago

THE WEAK LINK

Do you think that knots are not important? Think again, because the knot is usually the weakest link in any fishing rig. Most of the smallest swivels and snaps test in the 20- to 30-pound range. The smallest ball-bearing swivel by Sampo tests at about 10-pound strength. Most line (except for IGFA lines used for tournament and record fishing) will test above the stated test on the spool. Most hooks chosen are appropriate for the tackle and line and may bend slightly, but rarely break while being fished. A weak knot of, say, only 50-percent, however, will reduce the strength of a 12-pound line test to only six pounds; a knot of 75-percent strength will break at about nine pounds of tension on 12-pound test line.

Knots can also wear in time and with use, particularly with some heavy jigging lures. Knots also wear when fished around rocks, structure or over sandy bottoms or when you're fishing for toothy fish. That's why serious and successful anglers will use the best possible proven knots for their chosen line and will frequently test and retie knots during the day to maintain maximum line and knot strength.

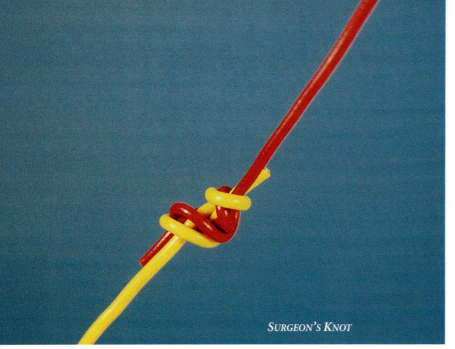

SURGEON'S KNOT

Ironically, the angler's single knot, which is nothing more than an overhand knot in two overlapping lines, would place a kink or bend in the lines at this connection, rather than the lines lying straight as with the angler's double knot (surgeon's knot of today). Today, the surgeon's knot is often used; it is ideal for connecting monofilament leaders to line or joining monofilament leader sections. Henshall also wrote of this knot and noted that it is a knot used for ligating arteries, and that in the 1880s it was known as the surgeon's knot, by which it is still known.

Norris also includes a water-knot in his book, this being what we today call a fisherman's knot, which is little, if ever, used for fishing. It was also used for joining lines or leader sections and is nothing more than overhand knots tied in the end of each of the joining lines after the lines have been overlapped; the overhand knot was tied around each of the standing lines. Later, in 1881, Henshall describes this knot as a single water-knot and also describes a double water-knot, which involves two turns or loops around the standing line before running the tag end through the loops

look very risky in terms of slippage or loss of a leader or hook. Furthermore, proper preparation was necessary to prevent breakage.

"Gut should be soaked in hot water for at least ten minutes to insure a compact, secure knot in tying leaders," writes Thaddeus Norris in his book, *The American Angler's Book,* published in 1864. "If on the stream, the ends may be held in the mouth a few minutes to soften them. Any attempt to tie a knot in dry gut will cause it to break, or fracture so as to endanger its strength," he continues.

We also know that a lot of early knots were not named, requiring drawings or lengthy instructions in print each time they were mentioned in literature to show others how to tie them. Some knots were named, but not always with the names that we give them today.

Early Line-to-Line Knots

The angler's single knot from Norris (1864) was nothing more than an overhand knot tied with the ends of two lines overlapping. The angler's double knot was similar but required an extra turn in the overhand knot to make what we today call a surgeon's knot and described by Norris as a good knot for tying together two lines.

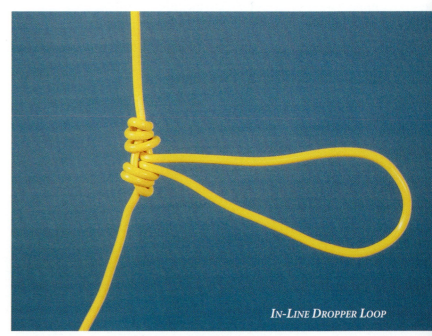

IN-LINE DROPPER LOOP

112   Our Fishing Heritage: Tackle & Equipment

and pulling tight. This is done on both sides of the knot, then tag ends pulled tight and finally the knot pulled tight.

The single water knot can be found today in some books where it is named the fisherman's knot, but is not widely recommended, since it has poor strength.

Adding a Dropper, With Risk

A big advantage to either of these knots, according to both authors, was the ability to open the knot by sliding the two separate parts or hitches apart, then inserting a dropper loop with an overhand knot tied in the end, finally pulling the water-knots tight to secure the dropper. The idea was that the dropper would sit at right angles to the main knotted line or leader, keeping it from tangling in the line and would not slip out as a result of the overhand knot. This also sounds very risky as to the possibility of the overhand knot of the dropper or snell pulling out between the two parts of the main line knot.

Square Knots Are Weak Knots

Another knot used was the square knot, also known as the reef knot, although this was noted by authors of the time as subject to loosening. The suggested method of tying this "very safe and strong knot" (it wasn't and isn't) was to wrap and whip the ends with fine silk thread, whipping the end and then sealing it with shellac or varnish. The same wrapping and whipping procedure was also suggested for the single water-knot. This wrapping, whipping and sealing process would, of course, prevent tying knots on the water, as modern anglers do, because it would take 24 hours for the varnish or shellac to cure; otherwise

TESTING KNOTS

Although books and articles on current knots and knot strengths are good, not every book contains every knot that you might want to test. There is an easy way to test knots, however, without any expensive line-testing machine or other equipment. To test two different line-to-line knots, cut several feet of line into three portions. Tie the ends of two strands with one known knot and the other end of one of these strands to the remaining line with the other new knot you wish to test. The result will be a single strand with two knots in it. Make sure that you know the identity of each knot. Wrap one end five or six times around a wood bucket handle and secure the tag end with a knot or tape. Wrap the other end five or six times around a one-inch dowel or broom handle held horizontally in a vise or other clamp. Make sure that the bucket is off the floor, then gradually fill it with sand until one of the knots breaks. This is the weaker of the two knots. Use the same method in about 10 tests to make sure of your results and knot strength.

You can make the same test for line-to-hook/lure knots by tying a short length of line to two identical large hooks, using a different knot in each end. Hang the bucket on one hook and hang the other on a firm support. Pour sand into the bucket until one knot breaks. Another method is to clamp one hook in a bench vise and pull on the other hook with Vise Grip pliers until one knot breaks. Naturally, wear safety goggles and any other necessary safety equipment in all such tests. With all methods, test several times to check results.

To make sure that each knot is as strong as possible, and pulled up tightly, moisten it with saliva as a lubricant before tying.

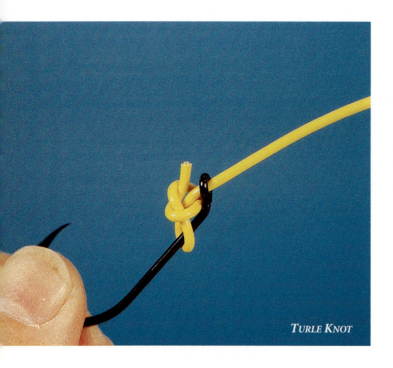
TURLE KNOT

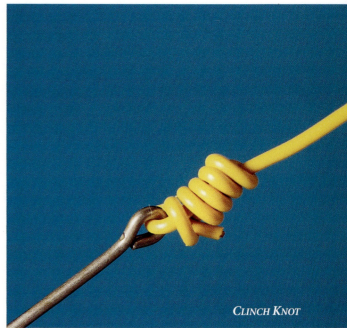
CLINCH KNOT

it would turn white upon contact with water and also would not properly protect the whipping from water damage. Today, nail or needle knots would be used to attach a monofilament leader to a fly line, although the knot would still be protected with a sealer, usually something flexible such as Pliobond.

Early Line-to-Hook Knots

Knots to tie a line or leader to a hook were apparently little used prior to the turn of the century, although eyed hooks and some fishing lures (plugs and spoons) were available. One of the earliest knots used was apparently the Turle knot (named after a Major Turle), one still used by some trout fly fishermen, although more in disfavor today than some other knots such as the improved clinch and the Palomar. The Turle knot was used primarily with flies, because these were the only artificials prior to the mid-1800s development of the spoon and the very late 1800s development of wood surface lures and underwater plugs.

The Clinch Knot By Any Other Name

In Lee Wulff's 1939 book, *Lee Wulff's Handbook of Freshwater Fishing,* there is a description of a timber hitch that is identical to the clinch knot of today. He does suggest some variations, such as tucking the tag end of the line through the eye of the hook when using a turned-up or turned-down eye hook to give the leader a straight pull on the hook. A variation of this with an additional tuck of the tag end back through the loop formed is to forestall the possibility of it becoming untied with heavier lines.

Whipping a Hook to a Gut Leader

Methods were in place for tying onto hooks lacking eyes. The basic method described in most early books involves hooks without eyes and only a straight shank or perhaps a flat or grooved shank for more purchase when whipping and wrapping a gut or linen snell to a hook shank. The basic method was to overlap the gut or line and the hook shank, then with fine silk thread, overlap the tag end and carefully wrap the entire shank, making sure that touching, even coils of, silk secured the leader to the hook. To secure the silk thread, instructions were to hold the tag end parallel to the hook shank and overwrap this with several turns of the thread, in effect making a modern fly-tying whip finish. One hundred or more years ago, this was called the invisible knot. Alternatives to this were two or more half hitches, also described and illustrated in some books.

THE CHANGING NAMES OF KNOTS

Knots have changed names over the years, and sometimes even gone back and forth on the same name. Some examples of current knots and their other names or past names (along with approximate dates) are:

PRESENT KNOT NAME	PREVIOUS OR OTHER KNOT NAME
Surgeon's knot	Anglers double knot (1860s) Surgeon's knot (1880s) Two-fold water knot (1940s) Double surgeon's (1950s, 1990s) Simple knot (1960s)
Surgeon's loop knot	Two-fold open-hand eye knot, Gut loop (1940s) Double thumb knot (1960s)
Overhand loop	Common loop knot (1880s) Single open hand eye knot (1940s)
Overhand knot	Angler's single knot (1860s)
Figure-eight loop knot	Flemish open hand eye knot, End loop knot (1940s)
Fisherman's knot	Water-knot (1860s) Single water-knot (1880s; in the 1860s a double water-knot has two turns around line before tucking in tag end) Single buffer knot (1920s) Waterman's knot, Halibut knot, True-Lover's bend, English, Englishman's, Angler's knot (1940s)
Turle knot	Major Turle's eyed-fly knot (1930s) Major Turle's knot (1940s) Turtle knot, Turl knot (1940s, in jest or ignorance)
Tucked sheet bend	Figure-eight knot (1900s) Lorn knot (1940s)
Slip sheet bend	Tiller hitch, helm hitch (1880s)
Knotted sheet bend	Becket hitch (1880s)
Bimini or Bimini twist	Twenty-turns around knot, Twenty-times around knot, Double line knot, Rollover knot (1940s)
Trilene knot	Blood knot (1990s, Australian) Double clinch knot (1950s; without final tuck) Double-loop improved clinch knot (1960s)
Clinch knot	Timber hitch (1930s) Half blood knot (1990s, Australian)
Improved clinch knot	Pendre knot (1950s) Locked half blood knot (1990s, Australian)
Uni-knot	Grinner knot (1940s) Duncan loop (1950s) Vic Dunaway's Uni-knot (1960s)
Offshore swivel knot	Catspaw Hitch, Hook Hitch
Homer Rhode loop knot	Fisherman's eye, Fisherman's, Waterman's, Englishman's, True-Lover's knot (1940s)
Perfection loop knot	Angler's loop (1940s)
In-line dropper loop	Dropper loop (1940s)
Whip finish (used in fly tying)	Invisible knot (1880s)

Knots & Connectors

PERFECTION LOOP

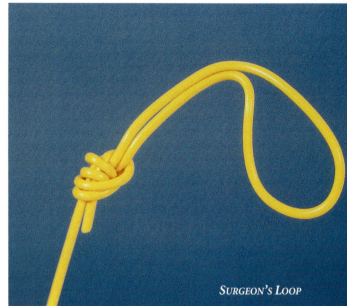

SURGEON'S LOOP

Loops, Then and Now

In addition to tying the line or leader to the hook shank with fine silk thread, anglers formed gut into small or large loops, with both ends of the loop wrapped and whipped onto the hook shank to make a large "eye" by which the hook or fly could be attached to the rest of the leader or line. For this attachment, loops were tied in the end of the leader or line, then secured to the gut-eyed fly using interconnecting loops. The method of tying loops and connecting them is still used today, mostly in fly fishing where it allows easy and immediate adjustments and changes in leaders, tippets, shock tippets and the like.

Making Loops

Loops for these interconnecting attachments in lines and leaders were made using several tying methods. One was the perfection loop knot, still used today. Another was the same as the figure-eight loop knot used today, in which the line is doubled, then tied into a figure eight. This knot was unnamed in some literature and writings, but called the end loop knot in others.

Still another unnamed knot was really poor, since it was nothing more than an overhand knot in a doubled over end of line. This knot places the loop

WHY KNOTS CHANGE

Knots improve over the years as new methods of connection are tried, tested and used. Knots must be easy to tie to make them acceptable to anglers. Lefty Kreh, co-author with Mark Sosin of *Practical Fishing Knots, II*, suggests that the change in materials dictated a change in knots. For example, while silkworm gut was widely used from the early 1800s until the early 1940s and the development of nylon, it was a very weak and often unreliable material. As a result, the knots used did not have to be that strong, since they were strong on a percentage basis when compared to line strength.

The change to nylon monofilament, which is much stronger per diameter, made past knots very weak and thus required the development of new knots. Most of the new knots in use today are variations and combinations of snells, clinch knots and twists.

116   *Our Fishing Heritage: Tackle & Equipment*

at an angle to the main line, something that should be avoided in loops and knots and is avoided in the figure-eight knot, the perfection loop knot and also the surgeon's loop. The surgeon's loop is nothing more than an overhand loop with an additional turn of the loop through the knot that results in the loop staying straight with the line.

Interconnecting loops were not used in all cases for connecting lines and leaders. For example, with any loop knot formed, one connection used a sheetbend, which every Boy Scout learns, although then they were often tied with an overhand knot in the end of the connecting line to prevent slippage and were called a becket hitch. A similar knot did not have an overhand knot in the end of the connecting line but instead had the tag end of the line folded back on itself, for instant loosening. This was known as the tiller-hitch or helm-knot (1940s), although today it is called the slip sheet bend.

Another knot used in a prepared loop was nothing more than the completion of a square knot, with an overhand knot in the end to prevent slippage; a variation of this involved the same square knot with the tag end tied in an overhand knot around the main line.

Knots, Changing and Improving

Knots today have not changed that much from the basic good and strong knots of the past. More technology has gone into understanding knots, however, with the line companies having a vested interest in this and promoting knot understanding and technology. As knots became more complex and required more wraps (the improved clinch has more wraps than the Turle used for the same line/hook connection) it was also realized that friction was a problem, both in pulling a knot tight and also in the build-up of heat that could weaken the line. This was particularly a concern with nylon monofilament. The solution was a simple one—saliva—to lubricate the knot, allow it to be pulled tight and reduce the heat on the line from the friction created.

Glue Is Not New

Glues were also used, although this again is not a new idea. Some 100 years ago, anglers used shellac or varnish on knots as protection against their coming apart. This occurred after the more time-consuming method of wrapping the tag ends of knots to the main line with silk thread. Today, the instant super glues are used, such as Fishin' Glue or Zap-A-Gap, in the very liquid formulas (not the thicker gel types) that allow the glue to wick into the knot and help prevent slippage

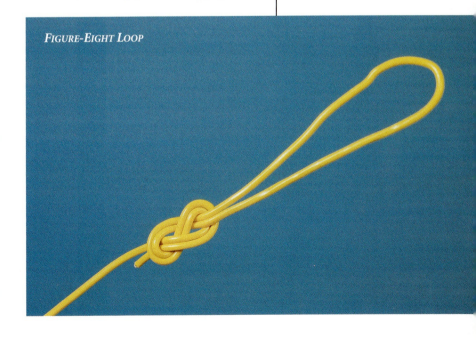

FIGURE-EIGHT LOOP

and the resulting knot failure. In effect, it increases knot strength.

These additions of glue, and the earlier use of wrappings, did not mean now or then that weak or poor knots could be used. In fact, much of knot research and development today is for knots with high knot strength that are also easy to tie. Having a very strong, efficient knot that is difficult to tie might result in it being tied incorrectly and, thus, actually be weaker than a simpler knot that can always be tied correctly.

Knot Strength

Most modern good knots are in the 90-percent-of-the-line-strength-or-better category, though 95 percent and above should be the goal. The exception to this are those knots that are tied with heavy monofilament for bite protection, and where knot strength is less critical. For example, a good loop knot to retain lure movement (tight knots restrict lure action) in a heavy bite or shock mono is the Homer Rhode knot. However, this knot tests only about 50 percent of the line strength. This is not a problem if you're tying this in 50-pound-test mono where the knot strength is only 25-pound-test, if you are using this as a final leader tippet in conjunction with 12- to 15-pound-test line.

No-Knot Connections

No-knot connections for standard lines (mostly monofilament) have also been invented of late, most typically wire connections that attach to a hook eye, the line then wrapped around the wire connection and secured without knots. Some of these connections are made using a doubled line for added strength and security. An example is the Berkley no-knot system, which consists of a link that fastens onto a hook eye or lure; the doubled line is twisted around it to secure it.

Fly Fishing and No-Knot Systems

A system for fly fishing from the 1940s used a small barbed eyelet that could be inserted into the end of a braided fly line (or the braided core of a modern PVC coated fly line) to which the leader could be tied. Even with a recommended wrapping of thread

ABOVE: *This Berkley Not-A-Knot system does not require tying a knot, since the line is doubled, looped over the end hook, wrapped around the shank and then run through the loop to hold a lure or hook.*

on the end of the line, it still did not work well and tended to cut the line internally. For the end of the leader, a small hook-shaped device was developed in the 1950s, available in three sizes, for easy hooking (no knots) to a fly. The ads claimed that it was light enough to be floated by a dry fly. Both these devices are still available today.

Other Connectors

Small, plastic football-shaped connectors, which worked similar to the metal connectors of a bead chain lamp pull, were also designed for fly fishermen, although sometimes used by other anglers for line-to-line or line-to-leader connections. Similar plastic connections were made to allow adding a looped leader snell into a line at any point. These also are available today.

Braided Line Connections and Knots

Braided line also required different connections. Braided nylon and, before

ABOVE: *Special metal attachments for fly fishing have included barbed metal eyelets for insertion into the end of a fly line. This makes attaching a leader much easier. Small clips for attaching fly to tippet are more common.*

RIGHT: *Special braided plastic sleeves and loops can be slipped over the end of a fly line and held in place with wrappings or shrink tubing. These loops allow for interconnecting loop connections of fly line and backing, fly line and leaders, and leader sections.*

Knots & Connectors

BIMINI TWIST

Palomar for its higher strength, even though it is harder to tie and pull tight correctly. Pull slowly and carefully using saliva for lubrication with a two-turn or three-turn Palomar.

Wire Knots and Connections

Wire requires different connections than those used for monofilament. There are several possibilities. Wire was not introduced as a fishing line until perhaps the early 1900s, when braided, twisted and single-strand wire was all first developed. Connections for wire were not knots, per se, since most wire could not be tied into the tight-binding bends required of a true knot.

Each type of wire required different connections. Lead-core wire could be tied using standard knots, because the line is really a braided outside sleeve (nylon today) with a single-strand lead core, almost like fuse wire or the wire used in fly tying to weight flies. The pound test of these lines is, and always has been, in the braided sleeve, not the lead core, and ranges from about 12- to 60-pound-test.

Single-strand wire was, and is, very stiff, and requires a twist that does not create sharp bends in the wire which might weaken it. The best solution is the haywire twist, in which the wire is run through the hook eye or swivel, then back parallel on itself, the two strands are spiral-twisted together (not one twisted around the other), finally ending with a tight coil wrap, where the end is bent to be broken off clean and close to the line. This did go by another name initially, and was known as the piano twist in the 1930s.

Braided Wire Knots

Braided wire (really twisted) can be tied into one knot—the figure eight—for connecting to a lure or

that, silk, were once used for casting lines. They have been largely supplanted today by nylon monofilament. Braided Dacron line became popular in the 1940s but did not have the proper knot strength when tied with knots that were proving ideal for monofilament. The line tends to cut itself in a tight knot. Thus, wraps such as the Bimini twist, spider hitch and others are best for making the initial knot. This leaves a loop or doubled line that then has twice the line strength when compared to tying with a more standard knot; this doubled line is used to tie an improved clinch, Palomar or other knot.

Splicing and Splicing Needles

The other solution with some Dacron and Dacron-blend braids is to splice them, and some spools are sold with small splicing needles that allow running the needle (really a miniature latch hook tool) into the center of the hollow line, through it for a distance, then out the side to capture the main part of the line and pull it into the hollow center to form a loop or to connect two lines without knots.

The newer gelspun polyethylene lines are very strong for their diameter and again require different knots, often the same ones used for Dacron. One exception to this is the Palomar knot, which has high knot strength, although some knot experts prefer the two-turn-through or three-turn-through

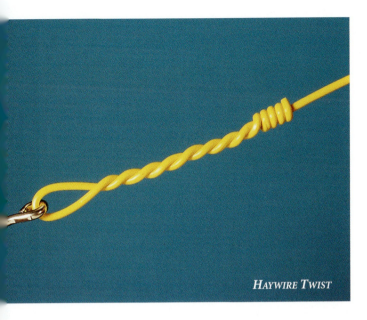

HAYWIRE TWIST

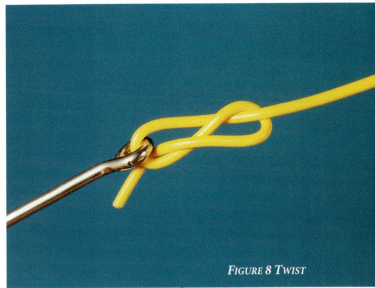

FIGURE 8 TWIST

hook. This simple knot looks ineffective (and it is if used on anything other than braided wire), but it is very simple and holds securely on multistrand wire.

Leader Sleeves for Mono and Wire

Braided wire and mono can also be connected using leader sleeves, which are brass, aluminum or other metal through which two strands of the wire are inserted; the sleeve is then crimped with special pliers to make a firm connection. There are many sizes and types of sleeves, with two basic types (round and oval) requiring two different types of crimping tools. Depending upon the type, they can be used on monofilament, braided wire and nylon-coated braided wire.

The New Knotty Wire

A new type of wire, initially available from Fenwick and American Wire in the late 1990s, combined wire and gel spun polyethylene fibers. It does allow tying standard fishing knots while retaining the advantages of wire to protect against toothy fish. Knots can include standards such as the improved clinch knot, the Palomar, blood knot, loop knot and those initially developed for monofilament, the earlier braided lines of silk and linen and gut leaders.

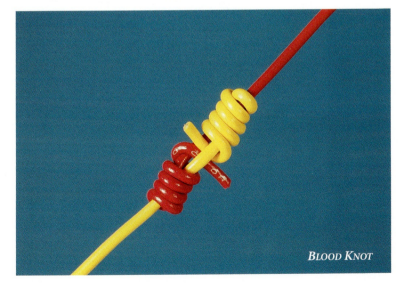

BLOOD KNOT

Knots & Connectors

# Lines

Introduction
When recreational fishing began late in the 15th century, and continuing into the late 19th century, hair lines were in vogue. Hair lines were fishing lines made from the hair of a horse tail, several strands gathered together for added strength. The maximum length was about three to six feet (depending upon the horse), with strands knotted together to get lines long enough for fishing. Tapering, to make a thinner line at the fly or hook end to less likely scare the fish, was possible by merely reducing the number of strands with each knotted length. Alternative methods were to overlap the several strands of hair at varying lengths, so as to twist or braid them into a continuous length without knots.

Indian Lines
Indians used lines for fishing with hooks made from bent wood and twigs, spines and bones. In the Pacific Northwest, Indians made line of bull kelp, a seaweed that has a long stem of up to 25 meters. The kelp was soaked in freshwater, stretched and twisted. Similar lines for fishing were made of whale sinew (tendons and ligaments), and the inner bark of cedar (primarily for heavier lines for halibut fishing). When a long line was desired, lengths were knotted, using what appears to be the fisherman's knot. Certainly these lines were not used for sport fishing as we know it, but they were early lines that were used for bottom fishing and trolling.

Early Colonial Lines
Typically, lines originally used in the Colonies, when some brief leisure time allowed for fishing, were made of hair, vegetable fibers, linen, flax, silk or cot-

LEFT: *Re-enactor Ken Reinard, portraying a Colonial fisherman of the late 1700s, in Colonial garb and with Colonial tackle, fishing flies on a small stream in Pennsylvania.*

ton. Horsehair was still popular well into the 1800s. There might be some confusion in some of these lists (which vary with different writers), because some references list both linen and flax. Flax, made from slim erect plants, is the raw material used to make linen (and also used to make linseed oil); the word flax also means to weave or interweave, a method of braiding. Lines were twisted or braided; twisting by means of a linewalk and braiding by means of braiding machines or by plaiting, a method also described.

The lines were based upon the raw materials available at the time. Thus, though horsehair was initially used, along with vegetable fibers from the strong strands of kelp (sometimes called sea-grass although sea-grass was also a term for raw silk used to make lines), linen, cotton and silk. Furthermore, though horsehair was the line of 500 years ago, it was also mentioned favorably in books in the 1920s. The 1923

CASTS DIDN'T HAVE ANYTHING TO DO WITH CASTING

"Casts," as described through the turn of the century, referred not to what you did with the line to get the fly or lure to the fish, but, instead, what we today would call leaders. Often companies would advertise salmon, grilse and trout "casts," these being tapered horsehair or gut (monofilament not yet having been invented) tied with water knots or fishermen's knots to join sections of silk gut drawn from mature silk worms. A cast was a leader; a "whip" was that leader with the flies attached, as described by Thaddeus Norris in 1864.

Similarly, a lot of terms no longer in use were used for the gut or leader of early fishing outfits and for the snell tied to a fly or hook. Common terms for these were snell, snood, snooding, snead, sid and tippet. The middle four of these terms are mostly English. Also, the "arming" of a hook and line is the connection, knot, whipping or splice used to connect the leader or line to the hook, lure or fly. It is English in origin, but used by the early fishing colonists into the 1800s.

ABOVE: *Casts of horsehair and gut were used to attach eyeless hooks to the leader, wrapping the gut or leader onto the hook with thread. These are on hooks, ready for bait fishing, and clearly show the "arming" (the point at which the leader is fastened to the hook).*

124 *Our Fishing Heritage: Tackle & Equipment*

Sportsmen's Encyclopedia, compiled by William A. Bruette (Forest and Stream Publishing Co., New York), noted in over five pages of text and illustration how to make and use horsehair lines and their many attributes.

Linen, Cotton and Silk Lines

Linen was made from flax bought by the early line companies, often from four different sources. Thus, in some cases, skeins of flax, spun to order in Germany, Ireland, France and Belgium, were combined to make lines. This was done for the same reason that today different nylons are combined to make monofilament line, the different nylons each having slightly different properties that would help make a line with the proper balance of tensile strength, abrasion resistance, limpness, knot strength, diameter, etc. The various materials, 100 or more years ago, were combined to give the lines a balance of strength, durability, knot strength, etc.

The cotton was also spun from "selected stock in this country," as one catalog noted, and run off onto drums that allowed running off the thread without tangling. The silk, also spun here from imported silk fibers, was made by gathering and spooling silk from silkworm cocoons. This silk is very fine, with 3,200 yards of it weighing only one ounce. A thread of 2,000 yards, in some instances, was possible from one cocoon without a break. Silk lines were also called sea grass, Japanese grass and catty grass. This is the same silk as that used to make silk or gut leaders used in fly fishing until the late 1930s, but it was made from a different process.

Silk Lines Are Not Silk Leaders

The process of making silk lines is completely different from that of making leaders, even though the same silkworm is involved. In making silk lines, the Japanese silkworm is allowed to make its cocoon, which it does at a certain stage in its life, alternatively eating mulberry leaves and resting, then spinning the cocoon around its body. Line manufacturers carefully unwind the silk from the cocoon after soaking it in water to remove an adhesive gum. The fine silk is run off onto skeins (called "books" in the trade at the time), then sold. The strands are doubled and twisted several times to make different size threads, which are then spooled for the braiding machines.

LINE-MAKING AS PRACTICED BY THE COLONIAL ANGLER

TOP LEFT: Materials for making hair lines and leader include the horsehair, scissors, thread and combed-out horsehair. Note: the horse tail shown is for illustrative purposes only.

TOP RIGHT: Horsehair leaders were made by attaching the strands to the hook, then braiding or plaiting the strands to form a single line as shown being done here.

MIDDLE: Here a completed heavy horsehair line has been tied to the end of the cane pole.

ABOVE: Arming a hook with the horsehair leader or line used by tying it to the eyeless hook using a thread wrapping around the hook shank.

Lines

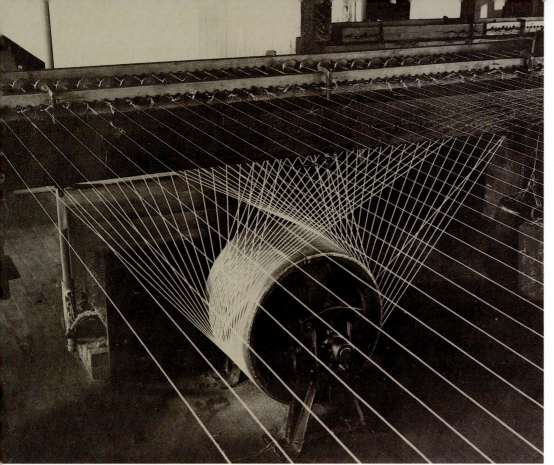

LEFT: *Cradles like this were used to twist strands into lines, here shown in the Ashaway plant in the 1930s. The strands of line (linen at first) were twisted and rotated around each other using this cradle and trolley system. These twisted lines were very popular back then.*

Walking to Make Lines

Line walks used to make twisted lines were long narrow sheds. They started at a few hundred feet, but by 1933 they grew to 725 feet in length. These walks had a machine at one end to twist the lines, the bobbins holding the individual threads or strands moving on a car along the walk after the ends were tied to the twisting machine. This both released strands as they were twisted and allowed the 24 bobbins or drums on the car to be twisted into eight strands (each three strands twisted together), after which an additional

Silk for the gut or "cat gut" of fly leaders and the early snells and loops on eyeless hooks was also made from the silkworm. In this process, when the silk in the silkworm sacs was considered ready, the silkworm was killed by being dropped into a bath of vinegar, then cut and pulled apart. The silk in the silk sacs of the worm pulled out like thin taffy and solidified on contact with the air. The two parts of the worm were pegged at each end and allowed to dry. The size of the gut was determined by how far the silk was pulled and by the thickness of the gut. Different diameters of gut were then tied together to make tapered leaders, just as knotted leaders of monofilament are created today.

LINE MAKING WAS ONCE A TOUGH PROFESSION

Using fishing lines is fun, but it wasn't always fun making them. The original twisted-linen lines were made by stretching (walking) strands of the yarn or threads a long distance, tying the strands at one end and twisting them by means of a wheel at the other end to create the twist in line such as linen Cuttyhunk. Originally, lines were made by fishermen during their off season, with no sheds, just laying the strands out on a path.

Later commercial development led to line walks—long sheds, some of which were over 700 feet long. That kept the rain and snow out, but these were unheated, and air conditioning was still many decades away. Since most line manufacturing was in New England, this had workers toiling under extreme cold in the frigid winter and extreme heat in the closed sheds in the humid summer months, for little pay and no unions to fight for better conditions.

126   *Our Fishing Heritage: Tackle & Equipment*

twist was given the line, and the line doubled to twist upon itself to prevent later unwinding.

The Start of Ashaway Lines

One of the first commercial line walks, and a precursor of the Ashaway Line & Twine Company, was made by Captain Lester Crandall, a Rhode Island fisherman. He commercially fished out of the village of Ashaway, named for the nearby Ashaway River, and he first made lines for his commercial fishing. He made his lines during the off season, twisting the lines with a large wood wheel after laying the separate strands out along a path paralleling the river. Soon his lines were noted as better than others, and in 1824 he left fishing for line manufacturing. In 1838 he built a dam across the river to provide water power for his machinery.

His orders increasingly came from sport fishermen, including those of the Schuylkill Club, a Philadelphia

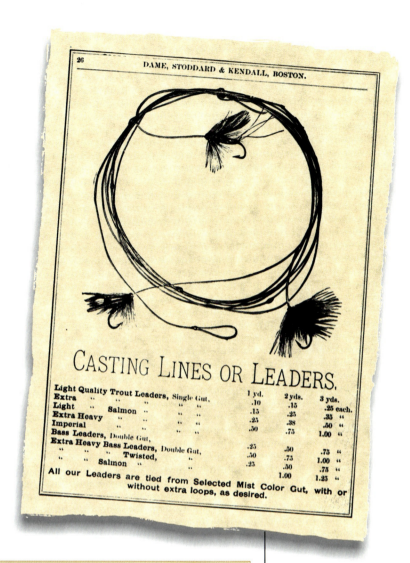

ARE FIBER OPTICS PART OF OUR FISHING FUTURE?

According to Berkely, a major tackle manufacturing company, research is underway that would place computer chips into future lures, the chips providing information about depth, retrieve speed and other data to the angler. Computer chips are now inexpensive enough to make this possible, particularly with the escalating price of some crankbait lures. Transmission of this information to the angler would be through lines of fiber optics, previously thought of as primarily for phone, computer and cable TV. The problem with this development is that present fiber optics do not combine the required small diameter and high strength of monofilament, thus making immediate application unlikely. Will this change and will fiber optic lines and computer chip lures become a part of the future tackle box? Stay tuned.

LINE LOGOS

At one time, the Ashaway Line & Twine Company used the swastika as part of the logo for its lines. In 1919 its Western Union cable address was Swastika-Westerly and its envelopes, letterheads and even line spools

boasted "manufacturers of Swastika Brand." There was even a swastika on the company water tower. The swastika was square, not diamond shaped, and in a circle formed by a rope that was tied at the bottom with a square knot, with Swastika Brand encircling the logo inside of the rope. Later logos shows the lettering removed, and the name Ashaway curved around the outside of the circular symbol. During Ashaway's use it was not thought of as a symbol of anti-Semitism or Nazi oppression. The symbol was last used by Ashaway in their 1933 catalog, in the very early days of Hitler coming to power as Chancellor in 1933. The swastika logo and symbol was completely discontinued by 1934.

The swastika, both in Nazi and reversed fashion, has been used for hundreds, perhaps thousands of years, by the Hopi Indians, Buddhists and in Japan. It was frequently used as a good luck symbol. Some anthropologists and archeologist think that it was a simple early symbol for a running man. Thus, Ashaway was only using a prevalent, popular and stylistic art form, popular at the time and not a representation of anything evil or politically incorrect.

sport-fishing club begun in 1732. As early as 1830, Captain Lester was selling line for sport fishing through tackle dealers.

The L. Crandall & Company, formed with Crandall's son H. L., was established in 1854, making twisted lines in a 480-foot-long covered line walk.

Cuttyhunk for Quality

"Cuttyhunk," a term for quality linen line, was originated by the company in the late 1870s. It was named for a small, early White settlement in Massachusetts, situated on an island called Poo-cut-o-hun-kun-oh by the Indians, shortened to Cuttyhunk by the early settlers. In 1865, the Cuttyhunk Club was formed nearby to cast for, and catch, striped bass, casting from the shore or from specially built piers as an early form of surf fishing. The club suggested the name for the quality Crandall lines, and a marketing term was born.

Beginning Braiding

In the early 1900s, the line walk was lengthened to 725 feet, and braiding machines were first installed for making braided silk lines. Braiding is different in that each strand is woven in and out of other strands. To accomplish this, power-operated braiding machines were used. These had the separate bobbins mounted on pins that traveled in elliptical, figure-eight tracks that crossed each other's path, braiding the line together. From eight to 16 strands (and bobbins) were used to make braided lines this way, which was a slow and obviously more expensive process. It, however, made the best lines for casting and was also used for making tapered fly lines prior to changes in line manufacturing in the 1950s.

Ashaway first used braiding machines to make silk fly lines beginning in 1906, then shortly thereafter began making braided silk casting lines. Lines were sometimes given strange names by today's standards. For example, Ashaway named one of its lines the Joseph Jefferson for a then-beloved (and since forgotten) stage star, and later renamed their Cuttyhunk lines in honor of big game angler Zane Grey.

"Thread" Lines

Back then, the linen lines were not listed by pound test, but by the number of threads, or strands, in each line, with each thread testing about two to three pounds. A standard of lines used until the 1950s was to measure lines by thread, thus catalogs would list line in 6, 9, 12, 15, 18, 21, 24, 27, 30, 36 and 39 threads. These would respectively test about 18, 27, 36, 45, 54, 63, 72, 81, 90, 108 and 117 pound test. These lines were not inexpensive, even by modern standards. In the Ashaway catalog of 1906, a 300-yard spool of the best Ashaway "Original Genuine Cuttyhunk" line, 9 thread (about 27-pound-test) sold retail for $19; a 300-yard spool of 36 thread (about 108 pound test) sold for $38.80.

World War I stopped production of sportfishing lines, with companies making silk cords for powder bags, ammunition and other war material. In 1919 Ashaway returned to domestic production of fishing lines, and in 1939 discontinued

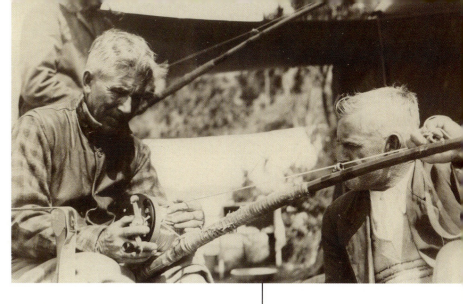

ABOVE: *Linen and silk lines, after a day of fishing, had to be removed from the reel, washed if used in saltwater, and dried before respooling onto the reel. Here, Zane Grey respools linen line on his big game reels with the help of a New Zealand guide.*

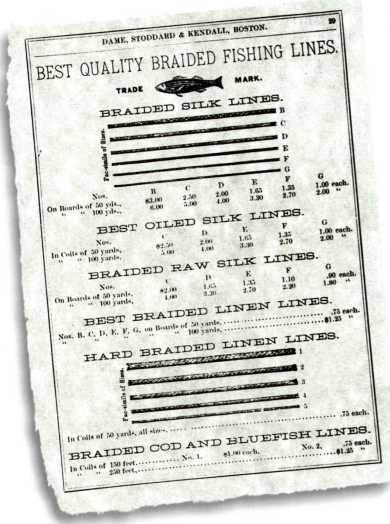

Lines 129

LEFT: *Even though lacking the gelspun, modern wire and monofilament lines of today, the angler of the past had many lines to choose from. These included Kingfisher Silchrome wire leader, Block Island line by Ashaway (under the 1933 discontinued Swastika label), Irish linen trolling line, Airex braided spinning line, Cortland nylon line and US Line Co. imported linen.*

sales of commercial fishing lines. In 1926 tapered fly lines were introduced, and in 1934 trolling line marked with a different color each 10 yards made its debut.

Other Line Companies

Other companies were producing line during the same period. The B. F. Gladding Co., started in 1817, was a major manufacturer of silk casting lines, silk fly lines and later nylon casting and fly lines. Gladding continued in business until the late 1980s, although the company got out of fishing line production in the 1960s after buying out the South Bend Bait Co.

Some companies were in line and cordage manufacturing long before they got into fishing lines. That was the case for the Gudebrod Company, formerly Gudebrod Bros. Silk Co., which started in 1870, ultimately involving six Gudebrod brothers in various parts of the company business. They got into fishing lines about 1945, according to David LeGrande, in a letter to the author. Early catalogs (1947-1950) show their heavy influence on lines through the many types

they made then, including silk tapered and level fly lines, nylon tapered and level fly lines, nylon and silk braided casting lines, nylon and silk braided lines for the new spinning tackle (initially, monofilament was not universally well received), specialty nylon ice fishing lines, specialty nylon and silk saltwater braided lines, while still carrying linen lines. They were also beginning to carry flosses for fly tying and thread for both fly tying and rod wrapping.

Nylon Monofilament Arrives!

Nylon monofilament line began with the development of nylon in 1938 by the DuPont Company. Early application for fishing was realized when some researchers took the early stranded material, wound it onto fishing reels and tried it for fishing in Brandywine Creek, which ran past the research labs in Delaware. Although the line then was crude by today's standards, it proved good enough to spawn an industry.

In fact, Ashaway, after getting some samples of the new nylon line from DuPont, began to market the first commercial product made of nylon yarn with their January 20, 1939, debut of Ashaway Nylon Bait Casting Line. DuPont later developed its Stren from the raw material that the company was manufacturing. Until the sale of the fishing line division by DuPont to Remington Arms Co. in the early 1990s, it

130   *Our Fishing Heritage: Tackle & Equipment*

was the only part of the company manufacturing a finished product. All other sales were through different divisions that made raw materials available to the final OEM (original equipment manufacturer) company.

Today, nylon monofilament line is made and sold throughout the world. Major U.S. companies, such as Stren, Shakespeare, Berkley and Cortland, make line in the U.S. but also export it. Some monofilament lines sold here such as Maxima, Ande, Five Star, P-Line, SeaGuard, Hi-Seas, Triple Fish, VMC and others are made elsewhere, from Europe to Asia, but sold through U.S. distributors.

The concept of making monofilament is a simple one, even though it requires major investment and extensive knowledge of the nylons and processes involved. Most of the processes today are closely guarded secrets; the final manufacture is controlled by computers. The basic process involves chips of nylon fed through a silo or conveyer belt system to ovens where it is melted. The molten nylon runs through holes in the bottom of the oven (like a sieve or colander) into a temperature-controlled water bath where it starts to cool immediately.

The strands are picked up from this point, brought out of the water bath and run over and around several large drums, the line stretched between each drum. Usually there are several drums close together, then a long run before

TEST LINE AND CLASS LINE

The label on lines showing their breaking strength is done in two different ways. One is "test" line, the line that most of us buy. The other is "class" line, used by those anglers interested in records and in some tournament fishing.

Test lines are, in essence, guaranteed by the company to test at least the strength listed on the label. Thus, a new, properly cared for line of eight-pound-test will test at least eight pounds, often with a margin of a few pounds more, sometimes up to 10 or even 12 pounds. Thus, the line will not break unless you or the fish pull more than eight pounds (not counting knot strength).

Class lines are a result of record-keeping organizations such as the International Game Fish Association (IGFA) and the National Fresh Water Fishing Hall of Fame and Museum keeping records by line test. In this, to avoid someone entering a catch and using line labeled eight pound but obviously much stronger, class line categories were developed. These state that the line must break below the line test category. Thus, to enter a fish for record in the eight-pound line class, the line must break at or below eight pounds.

Actually, this is a little fudged also, since the eight-pound class used in the above example is really a four-kilogram class, and four-kilograms weighs 8.81 pounds. Thus, a catch on a line testing up to 8.81 pounds would be accepted into this category. Check with IGFA and NFWFHFM for details on this.

SEWING THREAD FOR LINE?

With the vast array of lines available today, anglers would scoff at the idea of using sewing thread for fishing line. This was not always the case, however, and both sewing thread and common packing twine were sometimes suggested as emergency fishing lines for baitcasting tackle.

Wallace W. Gallaher, suggested sewing thread in his book *Black Bass Lore*, published in 1937, two years before the DuPont invention of nylon and the subsequent development of monofilament line. He notes that No. 8, or even finer, sewing thread would work in a pinch, cast well and will land bass of fair size. He also suggests linen sewing thread into which a little oil has been rubbed.

Sewing thread could also be used as a stunt. Ted Kesting, writing the introduction to Jason Lucas' book, *Lucas on Bass Fishing* (1947), stated that Lucas had once played and landed a 36- pound salmon on sewing thread, a feat that took 14 hours! The type of tackle wasn't mentioned, but it probably had to be fly fishing gear. Lucas, it was stated, did it just to prove that it could be done.

---

reaching a second or even third series of stretching drums. The stretching controls the strength and diameter and other important properties. Finally the line is wound onto large spools, after which these spools are used to fill the small spools bought by consumers or the larger service spools used by dealers to fill customers reels.

Along the way, nylon was tried in many different forms. In 1962, Stren introduced an oval mono for baitcasting to reduce backlashes. Oval or flat mono was also made by Cortland as their Cobra, designed as a flat running line for fly fishing (used between a shooting head and the braided backing line). Today it is improved with Teflon impregnation for faster and farther shooting. Other brands, such as Amnesia and 14/40 or 7/20 from Stren, have also been used for this. Stren's 14/40 or 7/20 were designed as flat line for casting tackle and could not be used with spinning gear. The name gave the picture that Stren wanted to promote: the thickness of the line through the flat surface was the same as 14- (or 7-) pound-test line, though the actual pound test was 40 (or 20).

Special Lines, Including Dacron

Special lines with special characteristics, or for special purposes or species, have also been introduced, most in the last 15 years. Some lines, primarily of different materials, got a head start on the specialty market. Dacron, a braided line made of Dacron polyester fibers or strands developed by DuPont, came onto the market in the mid-1950s. It had the advantages of low stretch for the time and easy splicing using splicing needles to make loops and connect lengths, but poor knot strength with the standard monofilament line knots of the time. Special knots such as Bimini's had to be used. Lead-core lines were developed about the same time, using braiding machines to braid a cover around a core of lead wire that was fed through the center of the braiding machine as it made the line.

Other lines followed. Thus, ice fishing lines from Cortland (both braids and monos) and cold-weather lines from Fenwick (monos) are designed for extra limpness in cold weather, often with extra abrasion resistance for protection against ice. Usually you can't have both abrasion resistance and thin diameter in a line, so Berkley years ago introduced their Trilene XL (extra limp) and Trilene XT (extra tough).

No-Nylon Leader Materials

In the mid-1990s, companies such as Fin-Nor, Cortland and others introduced fluorocarbon line (really leaders). This is made of a different material than nylon monofilament, although made in approximately the same way through the melting, extrusion through dies, cooling and stretching procedure. The advantage of the fluorocarbon over nylon monofilament is that it has a refractive index closer to that of water and, thus, is theoretically less likely to be seen by fish in clear-water fishing situations. Because of the high cost of these lines and their specialized purpose of less visibility, they are usually sold in leader coil spools for use as leaders on the end of trolling, casting and spinning lines or as leaders or tippets when fly fishing. In 1999 reel-fill spools of fluorocarbon have become available.

Color In Lines

Colors have also been added to lines, with the pink and green colors of Ande monofilament long recognized by offshore fishermen. Other brands have responded with similar colors. Just about everything from clear to dark green or black is available today. Camouflage lines also became popular, first used with the braided casting lines of the 1940s and today found in casting lines such as the Cortland Cam-O-ES Mono, Saltwater Cam-O Mono and Cam-O-Flage lines. These lines change every few feet between two to four colors to help disguise a lure to the fish.

Lines with higher visibility were introduced to help anglers become "line watchers." This was, and is, particularly important in surf fishing and offshore trolling, where knowing line position is important both to pinpoint the location of a lure or bait and to

LINES FOR EMERGENCY KITS

Just as Wright & McGill provided hooks for the emergency kits supplied to all fliers and ship personnel, and in all life rafts during World War II, so Ashaway provided the line for these survival fishing kits. The reason was to allow downed servicemen and merchant marines to catch and eat raw fish, since it had just been determined (by Gifford Pinchot, head of the Forestry Service under Teddy Roosevelt and twice governor of Pennsylvania) that nearly all saltwater fish could be safely eaten raw and that the juices from the fish would supply life-sustaining liquid. These emergency survival skills were counted on to produce fish that would save men's lives, and, unknowingly, echo the later demand for sushi and ceviche.

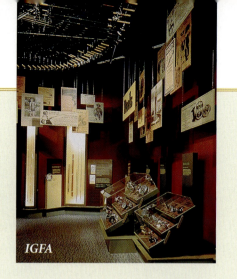

IGFA

FISHING FOR THE RECORD BOOK

There are two organizations that keep records on catches of big fish. They are the International Game Fish Association (IGFA), 300 Gulf Stream Way, Dania Beach, FL 33004, telephone (954) 927-2628, fax (954) 924-4299, E-Mail: IGFAHQ@aol.com, Web site http://www.igfa.org; and the National Fresh Water Fishing Hall of Fame and Museum, Hall of Fame Drive, POB 33, Hayward, WI 54843, telephone and fax (715) 634-4440. The International Game Fish Association keeps records for fresh- and saltwater, regular tackle and fly fishing as follows: 2, 4, 6, 8, 12, 16, 20, 30, 50, 80 and 130-pound-test classes, and 2, 4, 6, 8, 12, 16 and 20-pound-test tippet classes for fly. All entries must be on lines testing below the listed class.

The National Fresh Water Fishing Hall of Fame and Museum keeps records in fresh water only in 2, 4, 6, 8, 10, 12, 14, 15, 16, 17, 20, 25, 30, 36, 40, 45, 50, 60, 70, 80, 130-pound-test and unlimited line classes for all but fly fishing in which records are kept in 2, 4, 6, 8, 10, 12, 14 and 16-pound-test tippet categories. Tests are made based on given parameters for each line class.

For detailed information on entering a catch, current records, ordering information for their record books and membership, contact the two organizations.

know the position of a hooked fish. It became somewhat important in freshwater fishing when trolling for those same reasons and when line watching while bait fishing, plastic-worm fishing and flipping for bass.

The first of these lines, which was introduced by Stren in 1964, was a clear-blue high-visibility line that basically included whitening agents, not unlike those used in laundry detergents to brighten clothing. Berkley was scared off of this process by a Stren patent, and in 1972 Stren debuted its high-visibility Golden Stren, which was used a lot in saltwater. A Florida regional fluorescent-orange line had a short life of a few years. Stren continues with fluorescent-yellow lines today.

About the time the patent expired, 17 years, Berkley brought out its Hi-Viz lines in clear/bluish color and, more recently, its bright chartreuse Solar line. Shakespeare has its Sigma high-visibility clear-blue fluorescent line, Ande has a yellow and a high-visibility green line (appropriately called Envy) and mail-order catalogs such as Cabela's and Bass Pro Shops have introduced their own house brands of high-visibility lines.

Other Braided Lines: Gel Spun Captures Imagination, and Fish

Braided lines were once all Dacron. Today, however, lines of gel-spun polyethylene have been introduced, starting with about 20 companies in the early 1990s. That list has been whittled down some to companies such as Gudebrod, Berkley, Cortland, SpiderWire, Mason, VMC, Versitex and Western Filament. Stren has Kevlar line made of a different material, but with the same intent as with the Spectra gelspun lines. The purpose of any of these lines is for more sensitivity, less stretch (really the same thing as more sensitivity), smaller diameter (for pound test when compared to mono), stronger (when compared to same diameter as mono) and good abrasion resistance. These have not replaced mono in the eyes of expert anglers but are being extensively used in trolling, deep jigging, pitching, flipping and, in some cases, as backing on fly reels where they offer more line capacity.

Wire and Other Lines

Although the above braided and monofilament lines satisfied early and most current fishing situations, there are fishing methods that require different lines. One writer noted that in 1908 he saw the first of the then-increasingly popular method of fishing deep for lake trout in New York, at first using a three-way drop-sinker rig with 16 ounces of lead, the lure or bait at the end of 20 feet of line off of the second ring of the three-way swivel. Initially, silk or linen lines where used with these sinkers of up to 32 ounces of lead, although this allowed little fight by even the large lake trout. Among the first lines without lead to get deep were copper wire lines, first used, according to one description, in western New York state about 1912. In fact, trolling with wire line was sometimes called "pulling copper." The wire was attached to a wobbling trolling spoon (perhaps such as one like Buel's early trolling spoon) and trolled right on the bottom. The one problem with this was that the lack of stretch in the wire often resulted in lake trout hitting and the hook pulling out. Springs (curtain springs) were tied in the line just ahead of the spoon, but were deemed not worth the tangle.

ABOVE: *Wire line (used while trolling deep for lake trout) was wound onto a simple reel with a large-diameter spool. The reel shown here sports copper line. Other trolling lines shown include Kingfisher stainless steel wire line and American Fishing Monel stainless steel leader wire.*

MISTAKES DO HAPPEN

Fishing tackle companies have long been concerned about the protection of the environment, as noted by acts (Dingell-Johnson and Wallop-Breaux) that created a self-tax on manufactured and imported goods. The funds from these taxes are distributed by the federal government back to the states for waterways protection, biological fisheries studies, boat-ramp construction for fishermen and similar related works. However, accidents do happen. The demise of the B. F. Gladding Co. of South Otselic, NY, in the late 1980s came in part as a result of legal and financial damages incurred when chemicals from their plant accidentally leaked into a nearby river, causing pollution and fish kills.

At one time, the B. F. Gladding Company, was a major producer of all types of line, including lead-core lines, twisted linen lines, braided lines, monofilament lines and fly lines. It began in 1817, according to a 1935 catalog statement that referred to its then 118 years of manufacturing experience.

Lines

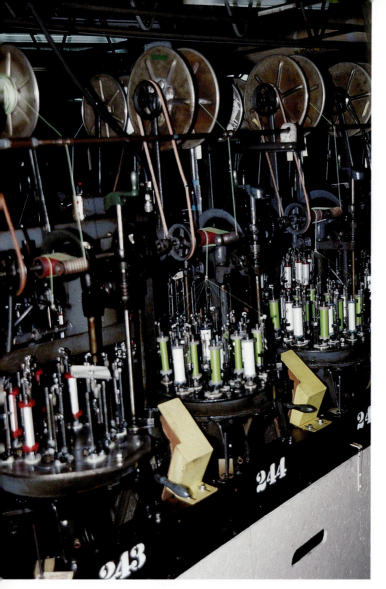

ABOVE: *Braiding machines like these were used to make braided casting lines, trolling lines and fly lines. Fly lines required intricate changes of the spool and bobbins to make the tapers required of double and weight forward tapered lines.*

Another solution was lead-core trolling lines, which were made by using basic braiding machines. In this, the lead core (like fuse wire or lead wrap used in fly tying) was fed through the center of the braiding machine, the covering of threads braided around it. The strength was in the covering, not in the core, and usually only one or two lead-core diameters were used, despite the 12- to 60-pound-test range of lines available. These also were made in multiple colors, not for camouflage in this case, but for measuring the amount of trolled line that had been let out. In most cases, the line color changed every ten yards for depth and distance coding.

Fly Lines

American Fly Fishing

Exactly when fly lines were first used in this country is subject to conjecture and interpretation. Some early fishing with flies was done with lines attached to the tip of the rod. Anglers did not play out the line during the cast and off of the reel as with modern fly fishing and fly casting. Yet, reels were used early, and there is evidence that some lines were tapered as are modern lines. Jerome V. C. Smith, writing in his 1833 book, *Natural History of the Fishes of Massachusetts,* notes that double-tapered lines were used even then. "The fly-fisher, if he has learnt the art of throwing the fly, may proceed with less caution; his greatest delight is to overcome distance by the length of the line, rather than by the length of the rod," writes Smith. He follows with, "Lines are generally made of an equal size from one end to the other, but a better way is to make them like a whip-lash, that is, larger in the middle than at the extremities, for this gives an impetus in casting the fly." This seems to establish two things: the casting by allowing line to flow through the rod rings or guides; and the manufacture and use of double-taper lines that become thinner at both ends.

Fly lines come in several basic tapers, all designed for this tackle in which the line is cast and the fly is just carried along by the line. As a result, fly lines are and were thick, so designed with weight to be cast, albeit by a method of repeatedly false casting rather than casting a lure with one stroke of the rod as with baitcasting and spinning tackle.

Lines, as they developed for fly tackle, were initially made using all hair, silk and hair, then all silk, then all nylon, then a PVC coating over a braided or mono core. Some early writings note that silk and hair lines were not good, particularly with the floppy loose rings then used as guides (like some modern hook keepers), and that the "fuzzies" of the line caused by the horsehair ends sticking out of the braid impeded the flow of line through the guides.

DYING AND USING EARLY HAIR LINES

Back when horsehair was the only reliable material for fishing lines, specific instructions were given for its selection, dying and use. In Dame Juliana Berners' book, *Treatyse of Fishing with an Angle* (1496), she notes that line must be taken from the tail of a white horse, using the longest and finest hair possible. Other writers suggested the use of stallion hair, arguing that the urine staining from a mare would both color and weaken the tail hairs. Berners also suggested that the hair be dyed into colors, each to suit different water and fishing conditions. Suggested colors, with instructions for dying and seasons for each use, included yellow, green, brown, tan, red-brown and "dark." The undyed white hair was also used, primarily for flies when fishing for trout, greylng (today spelled grayling), roach and dace.

Instructions were also included for separating the hairs into three equal bundles, the bundles then attached to a line-twisting machine that would result in the finished line. Lines of different amounts of hair were used for different fish, as follows:

One hair—minnows;
Two hairs—small roach, bleak, gudgeon and perch;
Three hairs—dace and large roach;
Four hairs—flounder, small bream and large perch;
Six hairs—large bream, tench and eel;
Nine hairs—small trout, greyling, barbel and large chub;
12 hairs—large trout;
15 hairs—salmon; chalk-line dyed brown, together with a wire leader—pike.

Fly Line History

Early on, fly lines were made of horsehair, as were regular lines, although this was considered a poor material with the many knots or overlapping strands required to join the sections or make braids. Sections were generally no longer than about three to six feet, the length of the hair in a horse's tail. Stallion hair was favored, the argument being that the urine-stained hair of a mare would make the line weaker. The bristly hair, coupled with the freely attached rings (like a present day hook keeper) in fly rods, must have made this a terrible casting combination, even with the fly casting method of feeding line as the line is worked back and forth in false casts.

Frank Forester referred to a line coated of naphtha and India rubber that might have been the first coated fly line. Later on, beginning about 1906, fly lines were braided of silk threads on braiding machines. Earlier lines of braided or twisted

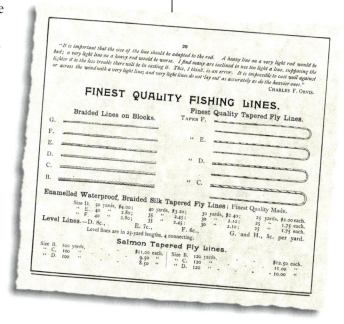

Lines 137

hair, or hair and silk, were largely replaced by the "...really elegant tapered and enameled waterproof braided silk-line," according to James Henshall writing in 1881 in *The Book of the Black Bass*. "The latter is the line par excellence for all kinds of fly-fishing, being smooth, round, polished and perfectly waterproof, and is just stiff and heavy enough to favor a perfectly straight cast, without looping or kinking, qualities that are peculiarly essential to this mode of angling." He further notes that they are made in several sizes for trout, salmon and bass and, as today, average about 25 to 30 yards in length. Most modern fly lines are about 80- to 105-feet in length (27 to 35 yards).

Lines then were tapered, as are lines now, but with different tapers and made differently. Initially, it appears that a typical taper was in one end only, the thicker belly of the line tapering to a forward fly end that was about one-half of the diameter of the belly. Lines by Hall & Sons in the 1800s were tapered at both ends, just as are double-tapered lines of today.

Silk Fly Lines: Level and Tapered

Silk lines, after the development of braiding machines, were braided, rather than twisted or otherwise manufactured. Some of the early lines were made by the Ashaway Line & Twine Manufacturing Company in 1906, actually predating by several years

LINE SIZES, THEN AND NOW

Early silk, and later nylon, lines were rated by diameter, and given a letter designation by which anglers bought their lines. Silk lines from the 1880s were also sold by a number system, although different from the number system used today with fly lines. Both level and double-taper fly lines were available in the late 1800s. These diameter, number and letter designations are as follows:

OLD NUMBER SIZE	OLD LETTER SIZE	DIAMETER	MODERN NUMBER* FLOAT	SINK
—	AAAA	0.075"	11	13
—	AAA	0.070"	10	12
—	AA	0.065"	9	11
—	A	0.060"	8	10
—	B	0.055"	7	9
1	C	0.050"	6	8
2	D	0.045"	5	7
3	E	0.040"	4	6
4	F	0.035"	3	5
5	G	0.030"	2	4
—	H	0.025"	—	—
—	I	0.020"	—	—

*The above modern numbers are approximate to the older letters, because through the early 1960s when the change was made to numbers, silk and nylon varied by one line size, and level, double-taper and weight-forward taper lines all differed slightly. That's also why the above treats sinking and floating lines differently, because the diameters for the weight and sink rate were different before the change in the 1960s.

silk casting lines for baitcasting tackle. Back then, though, lines along with other forms of tackle such as rods and reels, were sometimes interchangeable between different forms of fishing, unlike the distinct differences that we appreciate today.

Lines were made level, in which the entire line was the same diameter. Tapered silk lines were introduced by Ashaway in 1926, although they were apparently in use sometimes after the 1830s, as indicated above. Double-taper lines were commonly sold in the 1870s to the 1890s, in various sizes with 42 yards a common length. The development of silk fly was for two basic types of tapered lines. The double taper is a line tapered from a long, thick belly to a thin, short length at each end.

Weight-Forward and Specialty Lines

Weight-forward tapers presumably began about 1933 with the Cortland Line Co. and were designed for distance casting for the increasingly popular bass bug fishing. They had a heavy casting belly toward the front, tapering on both ends to a very short front section and a longer thinner level end at the rear. These were designed for casting big flies and bass bugs long distances with the fly rod. Following this, shooting tapers were developed, just in time to cash in on the increasing popularity of saltwater fly fishing. These were nothing more than short lengths (about 30 feet) of a thick shooting "head" to which a braided or mono running line was attached to make long casts. They were developed on the West Coast under the influence of Myron Gregory and others, many in a San Jose fly casting club. Initially they were sinking lines, sometimes cut from sections of lead-core trolling line, and later made in floating versions also.

Fly Line Weights and Sizes, Then and Now

Since a thin leader was and is used between the fly line and the fly, pound test of any fly line was not important. Size (really weight) was and still is the important factor, because almost all lines have a core that will be stronger than the tippet of the leader used with the line. Since all silk lines were standard as to weight for a given diameter,

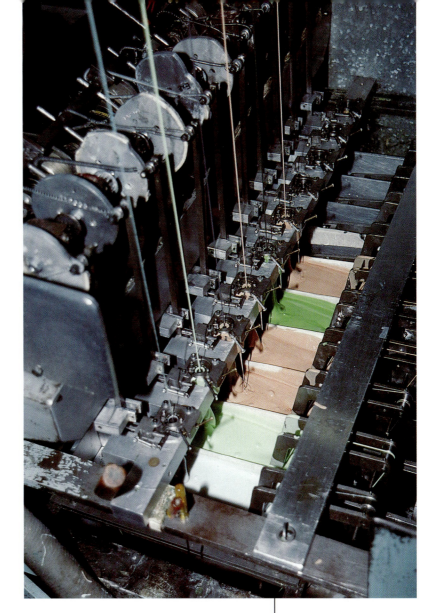

ABOVE: *Modern fly lines are made with a braided or monofilament core that is run through a bath of liquid PVC coating, then run vertically through a heated "silo" to cure the finish on the line. Here, the braided cores are coming out of the colored baths of PVC to make different fly lines.*

Lines 139

the industry adopted a letter designation for diameter of all lines. An HDH indicated the front, belly and rear tapers of a popular double taper; GAF indicated the sizes of the front, belly and rear running line of a weight-forward taper. A single letter, such as a B, C or D, indicated the size of level lines. In the late 1800s number sizes were used in addition to the commonly accepted letter sizes, with a size 3 or 4 the equivalent of a size E or F, respectively. These were not the same numbers later used in more modern and current fly line weight designations.

Braided Fly Line Construction

The method of construction then was different, in that the taper was formed by the braiding machines, just as were some, though not all, other lines of the late 1800s. The braiding bobbins travel on racks on a metal table, feeding individual threads in and out of the other threads to make a braid. "The tapering is done," so quotes Henshall from a June 6, 1880, article in *The New York Times* of the Henry Hall & Sons plant at Highland Mills, New York, "by simply dropping out a strand at regular intervals; but the machine has to be readjusted each time to secure a regular braid."

According to Leon Chandler, who worked for the Cortland Line Company since the age of 19, in 1941, tapers were made by periodically stopping the 16 bobbin machines and changing some of the bobbins to those with a larger thread size, doing this regularly as the braid continued to form the taper. As many as 96 thread changes were made for each line. An operator would be in charge of eight braiding machines, which would make one line each in an eight-hour shift.

The lines were then joined end to end, and run repeatedly through oil baths and heated to impregnate the lines with oil. Leon Chandler seems to remember the enameled lines as a later invention, although Henshall notes them (if he is correct in his description) in his 1881 book. They were supposedly less expensive and had a surface coating that could—and would—crack, allowing water penetration to sink the line.

Later, after the DuPont invention of nylon, nylon fibers were used in place of silk to braid tapered fly lines. This also worked well with the World War II effort, since silk was increasingly difficult or impossible to get from the Asian countries where the silk was produced from silkworms. The braiding method of changing line sizes to make the tapers was still used.

Initially, oil and enameling methods were used to coat and protect the nylon braided lines, just as with the previous silk lines. The oil coating on the nylon, however, proved no better or worse than when used with silk. The big advantage was that the nylon would not rot and required less care than did silk lines.

Nylon to the Rescue?

The new vinyl plastics were also used to coat the lines, moving away from the enameled or oiled finishes. Though initially accepted, these nylon coatings, which were more like a thin, clear vinyl sleeve, were subject to cracking and peeling. Cortland, Ashaway, Newton, Marathon, Horrocks-Ibbotson, U.S. Line, Sunset and Gladding were popular line manufacturers of both nylon and silk lines in the early 1940s into the 1950s.

At the same time, it became evident that nylon was lighter in weight than the silk, thus a thicker line (heavier line and different letter) had to be used for the same rod and casting performance previously achieved with silk lines. This was because rod manufacturers were listing the line size on the rod and were basing this on the earlier standard silk lines first in use. Thus, those used to an HDH double-taper lines or GBF weight-forward tapers, switched to HCH and GAF respectively when fishing nylon. This, and the later introduction of neutral density and sinking lines of different weights for a given diameter, led to problems by consumers in picking lines for a particular rod. Different nominal sizes might be needed when picking silk or nylon lines or picking floating or sinking varieties.

CASTING FLIES WITH SPINNING TACKLE?

Several years ago, Angler's Engineering introduced its Statech Spinfly lines that were thick, short lengths of a fly line-type design for attachment between the spinning line and a leader to enable casting a fly with spinning tackle. The concept is that the short line can be false cast once or twice, then released and cast with an open bail reel.

The idea is not new. In the early 1950s, several companies tried the same concept to bridge the differences between spinning and fly fishing. Thommen had both sinking (¼ ounce) and floating (⅙ ounce) Fli-Tossr lines in short lengths, Gladding produced an AeroSpin line that was a ¼-ounce, 15-foot-long torpedo taper line and Airex sold a ¼-ounce 16-foot floating torpedo spinning taper. All were designed for casting flies with spinning tackle.

Another system, not using any special lines, involved a clear casting bubble that could be used for weight when casting a fly with spinning gear. The bubble had a cap to allow filling with water or mineral oil (recommended) for added weight. Usually the bubble was tied to the line with a short length of line between the bubble and the fly, but writers of the period also described other ways to use it by placing the bubble at the end of the line and adding a fly or two as a dropper. These casting bubbles were made clear since an actual bubble would not scare fish.

A New Line-Size Standard

This led the industry association, the American Fishing Tackle Manufacturers Association (AFTMA) in 1963 to develop number designations based on weight, not the diameter of lines of the letter system. The then-new number system allowed the line and rod manufacturers to designate lines for their rods and lines to be made based on weight rather than diameter, and knowing that they would all be castable with a rod matched for a given line size. Weight, or line size, was determined by the first 30 feet of each line (less any level tip section).

In 1999, the fly industry association, American Fly Fishing Trade Association (AFFTA), changed this slightly to better conform to the heavier rods, heavier lines and longer casts made by warmwater and saltwater fly anglers, by measuring the first 40 feet of lines 7 weight and heavier and by making other minor changes. At the same time, it established a standard numerical sink rate system for the increasingly popular sinking and sinking tip lines.

Plastic Coatings, and Line Design Changes

The first plastic coating for fly lines was made by the Cortland Company with their 333 fly line. The surface was a thin coating of PVC that unfortunately was subject to cracking and thus also sinking—not good for a so-called floating line.

The entire manufacturing method of making fly lines was changed in 1945 when Leon P. Martuch and two partners got into the fishing tackle business as Scientific Anglers. They started with the idea of making fishing rod tubes of magnesium, but the end of the war and the surplus of cheap aluminum tubing spelled the end of that venture. They then introduced three new products for fishermen, a fly floatant, a line floatant and a leader sinker and developed the name Scientific Anglers.

They contracted to sell these products to the B. F. Gladding Co., a major manufacturer of fishing line. In 1951 they signed another contract with Gladding for consulting services. This led to the development of a casting line lubricant, as well as a fly line coating applied over a braided core. Contractual disputes with Gladding led Scientific Anglers to develop a second method of coating braided cores to make fly lines, which it then sold to Gladding in return for the original patent. The method invented was a way of continually running the braided core line through a bath of liquid PVC, the line then going through changeable diaphragm blades to control the amount of PVC coating retained on the core line.

The change in the diameter of the hole in the diaphragm (today controlled by computer) allowed for any tapering desired. Heat curing ovens rapidly dry the PVC coating. At about this time, that is, 1962, Leon L. Martuch, the son of Leon P., joined the company as treasurer and eventually became president in 1964. Under the son further line innovations were introduced. For instance, the original Scientific Anglers AirCel floating lines used steam to form small air bubbles in the PVC coating. The later development of the AirCel Supreme used tiny hollow glass bubbles, called microballoons, in the PVC coating to aid in flotation. This allowed for exact control of the degree of flotation so that the hollow core of the braid was no longer a necessary ingredient in the flotation process. In time, more lines were added, including bass bug and saltwater (weight-forward style) tapers, and later more WetCel lines—the Wet Cel I (intermediate) and the Wet Cel Hi-D (fast sinking). Shooting heads were also introduced.

PVC and High-Floating or Fast-Sinking Fly Lines

This PVC coating also allowed for other wide-ranging changes in lines that previously floated only through the application of oil or waterproofing compounds to keep the line in the surface tension. Beginning in 1968, they started using 3M microballoons (microscopic hollow glass balls) to aid in flotation of the lines. Tungsten replaced lead in 1983 to make better (and more environmentally friendly) sinking lines. By running the line through different baths and dies, it was possible to make

ABOVE: *Monofilament is created from heated nylon drawn through dies. The end product is stored on large spools like these. These spools are then used to fill the service spools used by dealers, and the smaller spools used by anglers.*

sinking tip lines in which the end (five to 35 feet) sunk and the rest of the line floated.

PVC is not the only coating used, and some manufacturers (notably Air Flo of England) use Kevlar (no stretch) braided cores for some of their lines and a coating of polyurethane. Clear lines were developed by the line companies in 1986.

Today, fly lines from Gudebrod, Cortland, Scientific Anglers, Royal Wulff, Teeny, Rio, Air Flo, Orvis, Bass Pro Shops, Cabela's, McKenzie, Sage, Bean and others (many of these made by the larger companies such as Cortland and Scientific Anglers) vary tremendously. There are 850-grain sinking lines from Teeny, triangle tapers from Royal Wulff (in which the belly tapers progressively thinner as you approach the fly end of the line), sinking tip lines, sinking lines, interchangeable tip lines from McKenzie, and saltwater, big game, tropical, spey casting and other specialty lines from Cortland. Scientific Anglers has even more, with specialty tapers and formulations for bonefish, pike, stripers, tropical fishing, nymphing, bass bugs, salmon, tarpon, billfish and various wind and sink-rate conditions.

Lots of Lines for Any Type of Fishing

Once, lines were made of a few materials in a few ways for a few types of fishing. Today, anglers can choose from hundreds of lines for spinning and casting, hundreds of tapers and sink or float rates for fly fishing and dozens of types of lines for trolling and big-game angling. You can get lines with specific characteristics for cold-weather fishing, ice fishing, tropical climates, high-abrasion resistance, thin diameter, controlled stretch, almost no stretch, lines in every color of the rainbow, even lines with vanilla scent.

Line making that was once an inexact art at best is now a precise science, with manufacturers and research chemists dialing into a computer the characteristics of the line that will come out of the line machine and onto the reel. Together with the hook, line is the one basic to all fishing, and one that we often take too much for granted. Anybody want to go back to horsehair, silk or linen?

Lines 143

Rods

Introduction

Early rods did not use reels. Even without a reel, a rod offered advantages over a hand line because it provided increased leverage and "casting" (or flipping) ability to get a fly, bait or lure to the fish. Often, early rods had lines tied to the tip top, or sometimes the line half-hitched around the rod every few inches all the way to the butt. This was for added strength and also insurance against losing a catch, should the rod break from the weight of a fish.

Early rods were also long, since the prevailing theory of the time, from at least the 1400s through the end of the 1700s, was to use a long rod and short line and to keep a hooked fish literally under the rod tip as you played it. Often England's topography required fishing from high banks or along brushy streams, thus requiring long rods. To fish with a short rod was the mark of an unethical, unprofessional or unknowing angler or sportsman.

Such long rods were not unlike those made by earlier fishermen following the direction of Dame Juliana Berners who wrote about making lines, rods and tying flies. Her writing appeared in her contribution, *A Treatise on Fishing With an Angle,* published in 1496 as part of a sporting book on hunting to the hounds and falconry in the *Book of St. Albans.* That, of course, was not the first mention or display of rods or recreational fishing as we know it, since the Roman Claudius Aelian wrote in the 2nd century A.D. about a Macedonian method of fishing using a rod and line of six-foot length each and casting (Flipping? No reel was involved.) an artificial fly to catch trout. Some Chinese drawings from the 12th century show anglers with short rods, to which is fixed a reel. History also tells us that the Egyptians used rods about 2000 B.C.

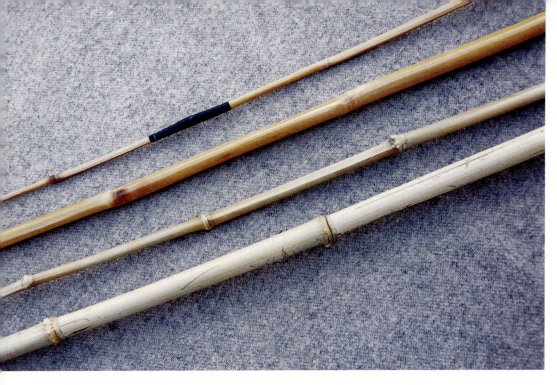

LEFT: Locally available cane was used for rods by the colonial angler as shown here in a modern recreation of an early cane rod. Note the upper section which has been damaged and repaired with a thread wrap.

BELOW LEFT: Reproduction of early cane rod with metal ferrules, as might have been used by the colonial angler. Ferrules like these were made from metal sleeves and tubing.

BELOW RIGHT: Tools needed to make early colonial-style rods included a knife to cut off the branches of the cane and a file to trim and dress the nodes on the cane.

Early Colonial Rods

Early rods were mostly imported from England along with other goods of the colonists in the 1700s. The rods were the long instruments that afforded maximum pliancy to prevent a fish from breaking off while providing length to allow the line that was tied to the end to swing a bait far away from the bank to the lie of a trout or other species. Most often it was a trout, especially a brook trout, which was the only trout native (although really a char) to the East.

Rods originating in this country were most likely nothing more than long switches of willow or similar straight branches to which line was tied for fishing. As with other tackle such as flies, hooks and lines, most colonial anglers with the interest, time and some money for sport fishing made their own tackle. Rods were simple, not unlike those of the mid-1600s of Izaak Walton, and often made in three, four or more sections that were wrapped and spliced together for fishing. The line was most often tied to the end of the rod.

"Commercial" rods were most likely English or European, 14- to 18-feet long, made in three or four sections. By the early 1800s, American rod makers, whether making rods for their own and friends' use or for commercial sale, were established. Brown, in the *American Angler's Guide,* published in 1849, notes that American rod makers had made substantial improvements over the past 10 years. Allowing time for writing and printing, this puts the manufacture of "good rods" (as defined at the time) as beginning around 1835, with some rod manufacturing prior to that.

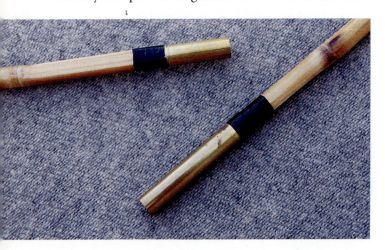

Early Rod Construction

Rods then were made with spliced joints in which the overlapping pieces were tied together with heavy wraps (much like a guide wrap on a rod today), the rod only taken apart at the end of the season for storage. Other rods were made with ferrules or joints, with these in the mid- to late 1800s referred to as "trunk rods," "pack rods," "tourist rods" and "walking cane rods." These are all designed for easier handling of the rod in travel, much of which was by horse, carriage, boat or train at the time, the advent of the automobile was still decades away.

In all these early rods, the butt was often hollowed out, using a red-hot iron, with this hollow both to lighten the rod (rods were measured in pounds, not ounces!) and sometimes to serve as a storage area for the upper sections. Often these were made to disguise the rod as a walking stick or cane, something noted in a number of patents from the 1800s. Often the butt was ash, hickory or maple for strength and stiffness, but many different woods were used. The middle section or sections were often more flexible, of lancewood, greenheart or similar exotic woods. The uppermost sections were often bamboo (Calcutta cane or bamboo was imported as early as 1850; split bamboo came later in the 1800s) for even more flexibility, and the rod sometimes ended with a short section of whalebone or whale baleen at the very tip end. These very flexible ends were not unlike the very soft and flexible tip sections used in modern ice fishing rods and designed today in ice rods for sensitivity and to signal a strike or nibble.

ABOVE: Early fishing rods. Left, a 1906 saltwater boat rod of Tonkin cane, wrapped handle, two-piece, ferruled and with patented screw sliding band reel seat. Center, a 14 foot long English style punt rod with metal sleeve wood ferrules and sliding ring reel seat. Right, ca 1820 ash wood rod, tapered to eight feet long, metal sleeves for protecting the ferrules, no guides, and only a ring at the tip (for tying line).

Rods 147

Early Rod Design

Rods were long, and that together with the primitive manufacturing methods and limited natural materials, required ferruling or splicing. Brown notes that rods for salmon fishing were often 18 to 20 feet long, with a butt of maple, second and third sections of ash or bamboo and a tip of lancewood. Striped and black bass rods were often 12 to 15 feet and varied otherwise from the above only with a butt of ash. Other sections were of the same woods. Trout rods of 12 to 16 feet were constructed with maple butts, ash or lancewood second and third sections and a lancewood top section.

Long rods are also mentioned in *A Book on Angling*, by Francis Francis (1867), who noted that bank or shore fishing rods should be 15 to 16 feet long, though some were as long as 23 feet, and that punt (boat) fishing rods could be as short as 10 to 12 feet. Part of the reason is explained by the then prevalent idea that the point or tip end of a rod should be right over a float, and that no more than one to two feet of line should be between the rod tip and float.

IMPORTED TACKLE THE BEST?

While early colonists had to either make or import all their tackle, in time, American manufacturers of rods, reels, lines and flies also appeared. It was thought up through the 1830s, however, that the best tackle was to be obtained from England.

Paul Schullery, in his 1987 book, *American Fly Fishing*, notes that William Penn, who received from the king the tract of land that became Pennsylvania, apparently also enjoyed fishing, as did his daughter. When writing to her brother in England in 1737, she asked him to obtain for her some tackle that it seems was not available, or of sufficient quantity or quality, in the colonies. "My chief amusement this summer has been fishing," she wrote to her brother. "I therefore request the favour of you when Laisure Hour will admit, you will buy for me a four joynted strong fishing Rod and Real with strong good Lines and asortment of hooks the best sort..."

Even much later, in 1833 Jerome V. C. Smith, M.D., wrote about the same problem in his book, *Natural History of the Fishes of Massachusetts*. In writing about the pleasure and science of fishing and fly fishing, he writes: "There are not only the individuals of whom we speak, but others, who, availing themselves of all the information to be acquired from books and experience, are fully aware that fly-fishing is the perfection in angling."

"They import the best tackle from England, for it is not to be bought in all its variety in this country, including a stock of artificial flies, ..."

Much importing has continued as anglers have continued to import reels (Hardy fly reels) from England, spinning reels (such as the French Mitchell imported in the 1950s), lures (Rapala) and other recent gear brought in by American importers such as Daiwa, Shimano, Berkley, Johnson Worldwide Associates. Rods and reels imported are imported from Korea, Sri Lanka, Bangladesh, China, Thailand, Japan and other countries, mostly in the Pacific Rim area.

All commercial rods were sold with soft bags of linen, wool or canvas, though metal and leather cases were not unknown. Rod prices, by today's standard, were steep. Inexpensive rods sold for from $2 to $5, while high-quality rods ranged from $5 to $50. Considering that Charles Hallock wrote in *The Fishing Tourist* in 1873 (and considering the 25 years of inflation after Brown) that a wagon could be hired out for $1.50 per day and that fishing guides were demanding $2.50 a day, that $50 works out to be 20 times the daily fee for a fishing guide—pretty exorbitant by modern standards, even for the most expensive rods and with the least expensive guides of today. Some early tackle shops catered to this upper crust of fishermen who could afford such expensive tackle.

Ferrules and Splices

Since these rods were in sections, they required ferrules or some method of joining them. Metal ferrules, in theory if not design, were just like those used on modern rods up to the self-ferrule (glass-to-glass or graphite-to-graphite) developed 100-plus years later by Fenwick. Splicing and wrapping was also popular and preferred by many since the process less affected the bend or action of the rod.

Splicing involved matching long angularly sliced mating ends to two joining sections, the overlapping splice several inches long. The resulting splice was usually tied or wrapped in place with strong thread or cord. The lack of metal ferrules both allowed field repairs (you could cut a new angled splice) and also lessened the weight of the total rod, which might weigh a pound or more. Metal ferrules were not unlike those of more modern times, except that early ferrules were stepped, the theory being that they would hold better and less hamper the rod action.

Something to Hold a Reel

Reel seats also were developed early, although they were not always popular

Rods 149

or well accepted. Early on, when reels caught up with these rods, they were mounted by clamps, screws or even wrapped onto the long handles using cord and leather strips. Later the foot/reel seat method of today was developed, both with sliding rings and also with screw-down hoods to lock the reel foot to the rod with a fixed hood at the other end. With the development of the true casting rod for use with the multiplying reels in the mid- to late 1800s, the upper ring to hold the reel in place was attached to a finger pull (as it was called then; it's referred to as a trigger today). By pulling on the finger pull with the index finger, the angler was assured that the rod would not be thrown into the water while assuring that the reel would not come off of the rod while casting or fighting a fish.

These finger pulls were straight friction slides; screw locking methods were not used. In some cases, the foot of the reel was just wrapped or tied in place to the swollen handle or grip area of the rod, leaving adjustment for the reel in any position, high or low, on the long rod handle.

Because of the length of these early rods, and because weight was a concern even without the casting methods of fishing today, some rods were equipped in the handle or butt section with spikes to stick the rod into the ground. Other additions to handles also abounded, with patents on the subject beginning in

ABOVE: *Sliding rings were used to hold early reels on rods such as this early Gep rod from Heddon.*

the late 1800s. These included built-in gaffs for landing fish, compartments to hold plugs and hooks, hollow handles to hold extra tips, with built-in air chambers to float the rod if dropped in the water, storage for batteries used to light a float for night fishing, handles that contained a firearm and handles storing a ruler for measuring fish or a scale to weigh the catch.

These additions came later, however, because the method of fishing before reels was to tie the line to the rod, thus restricting the line to the length of the rod for easy flipping of a bait and to prevent the line from becoming unmanageable.

In the case of a heavy or exceptionally strong fish that could not be held, it was not uncommon to throw the rod into the water to allow the fish (often big trout or pike) to tow the rod around for a while and tire itself out before the rod was retrieved and the fish landed. This was mentioned in the first edition of Izaak Walton's *Compleat Angler* (1653) and continued for next 200 years or so as a fishing method or option.

Once reels started to appear in the late 1700s, it became apparent that more line (more than the length of the rod) could be used. Line could be paid out to drift a bait with the current and to allow a fish to run if it was too heavy to land by simply cranking it in or levering it into the boat.

Rods Get Shorter

Reels then also started to develop, while rods continued to change. The long rods that existed through the 1700s and into the early 1800s started to get shorter and to change in material. Gradually rods were being built of 10 feet, then the even-shorter eight-foot three-inch black bass model advocated in the late 1800s by Dr. James Henshall for bass fishing and produced by The Orvis Company. Some even worked their way down into the seven- and even six-foot range, with the concept then (will this sound familiar?) that short and light is more sporting and thus more fun. In fact, one method of fighting and landing fish when the long rods were prevalent was to make changes in the rod

ABOVE: *Some rods had female ferrules on both ends of the handle/reel seat. This way, you could use the rod with the reel above the handle as a casting reel, or below the handle as a fly reel.*

during the fight by removing first the bottom section, then upper sections so as to finally be able to land the fish with a shorter, lighter and more manageable rod than the 12- to 20-foot-length sticks then in vogue. But by 1900, long rods were no longer popular. The "Chicago" rod of about six-foot length was popular in the upper Midwest for bass fishing before the turn of the century.

By 1911, Samuel Camp in his book, *The Fine Art of Fishing,* wrote about rods of 5½ to six feet, and O. W. Smith, in his 1920 book, *Casting Tackle and Methods,* wrote, "To all lovers of the short rod and multiplying reel, this book is affectionately dedicated."

Short rods came about long before this; in fact, soon after the development of the "short" 8-foot 3-inch model suggested by Henshall. An inquiry from O. W. Smith to a J. M. Clark about the development of the short rod (the concept of which began in the Midwest, especially the Chicago area) resulted in this response. "The first conception of a Short Bait Casting rod was made for me in 1885 by Fred D. Divine, now of the Fred D. Divine Company of Utica, New York," writes Clark. "The rod is made out of lancewood, 6 feet, 3 inches long. The rod was a revelation in those days, as the usual lengths of rods was 10½ feet. I fought the point and won out. Today, my banner rod is 5 feet, 6 inches."

Also, different retail outlets promoted different types of rods. A. B. Shipley of Philadelphia was known for promoting, pushing and selling rods of bethabara, also called wasahba wood. Whether the raw wood (for locally making the rods) or the finished rods were imported is not clear. Andrew Clerke (also sometimes spelled Clerk) and its successor, Abbey and Imbrie, were advocates of the split bamboo rods.

ABOVE: *Relatively modern and older styles of "pocket" rods. Top, a 1970s Popeil Pocket Fisherman in which the mini-rod would fold up on the handle. This model also included a mini tackle box in the handle. Bottom, a 1940s stub caster with a coiled spring in the steel blank. The spring helped propel the cast from this short rod that would break down to 14 inches when removed from its handle.*

New Rod Materials

Most of these shorter, lighter rods were made in two sections. This advance brought about the next change of trying to go even lighter with better materials, making the butt of wood and the tip section of Calcutta bamboo, as did Samuel Phillippe (spelled Phillippi by Dr. James Henshall in his 1881 *Book of the Black Bass*) of Philadelphia. This was before Phillippe developed the split-bamboo rod that radically changed rods and led to lighter, more responsive rods for everything from fly fishing to casting to trolling to "big" game. (The definition of big game is relative to the time period, and then may have referred to a 50-pound fish.)

Cane was even mentioned as a part of a rod in the long rods used at the time in the *The Art of Angling*, by Richard Brookes, originally published in 1720. He refers to building a rod with a 10-foot-long butt section of ash or a top of about seven feet "of the best cane or yellow hickory, but not too slender." This considerably predates any other mention of using cane for a rod.

The history of the split-bamboo rod is complex, with the use of split-bamboo in the first section (not the complete rod) perhaps developed in England, judging by an entry in *The Young Angler's Companion*, an English publication from the early 1800s. It referred to fly rods made of hickory with a top section made of several pieces of bamboo joined together after having been cut from the solid part of bamboo. This would seem to preclude interpretation as several sections joined by ferrules or splices and instead indicates sections joined (glued), as were later rods.

Rods 153

sections, including the butt, and later of six strips; the enamel was always on the outside. These rods were for his own use, but afterward he made some for his friends, one of the first being for Colonel T. R. Sitgreaves, with ash butt and joints of four section split-bamboo."

This is also subject to debate, because Henshall also noted in his book that Phillippe made rods with only the top two sections of split-bamboo, and that his rods were crude affairs. This is probably unlikely, considering that Phillippe made his living as a gunsmith and violin maker, as well as making fishing rods. Also, Henshall states that "The first complete split bamboo rod, that is, all of the joints being of this material, seems to have been made by Mr. E. A. Green, of Newark, New Jersey, about 1860, though some claim that the late Thaddeus Norris, of Philadelphia, is entitled to this honor …"

He goes on to state that "The first perfect split bamboo rods for the trade were made by Mr. Charles F. Murphy, of Newark, who, after seeing Mr. Green's rods, saw a chance for still greater improvement…" These were noted as being available to the public and

Phillippe and Split-Bamboo

Samuel Phillippe of Easton, PA, is widely credited as the maker of the first complete split-bamboo rod of four and six strips, although his first efforts were also only sections. Phillippe learned the trade of gunsmithing at about 16, but he also was skilled in general wood and metalworking and in making violins. He also made fish hooks (see Chapter One). "In his first experiments," his son Solon Phillippe is attributed as writing to Dr. James Henshall, "Phillippe made tips and second joints of two, and then three sections of split-bamboo, enamel outside, with butts of solid cane or ash. But these rods would not cast the fly true. He then made the joints of four sections, and found that they would cast perfectly in any direction. He then made complete rods of four

154 Our Fishing Heritage: Tackle & Equipment

ABOVE: *Three split bamboo fly rods from three different periods. Top, a Fred Divine fly rod from 1885. Center, a South Bend Cross Double-built fly rod in which two layers of bamboo were used in construction. Bottom, a Montague split bamboo rod from 1948. Also note the different grip designs.*

being made around 1863 or 1864, almost 20 years after the acknowledged first development by Phillippe. Murphy is credited, without argument, as making the first split-bamboo rods specifically for salmon and black bass fishing.

How Many Strips?

Business records of Phillippe showed that the first split-bamboo rod sold was in 1848, and it was a four-section rod in three pieces. It was all split-bamboo, including the butt. Split-bamboo rods by Samuel Phillippe are thought to have been made as early as 1845, and in 1859 his son Solon was making complete rods of six sections with an 18-inch-long grip of wood. In 1876 he made an eight-strip rod with alternating strips, four of bamboo and four of

EARLY BC ROD MATERIALS
(BEFORE COMPOSITES, SUCH AS GRAPHITE AND FIBERGLASS)

Materials used in early rods up to the development of composite rods of fiberglass, graphite and similar synthetics included: Tonkin cane (used for split-bamboo rods; from Tonkin province of China); Calcutta cane (used for tips on early rods and as early surf rods, rarely split as was Tonkin); ash (butt sections); lancewood (middle sections and also called lemonwood); greenheart (also spelled greenhart); mahoe (from Cuba); hickory; ironwood; bethabara; snakewood; osage orange; yew; beefwood (from Australia); maple; hornbeam; noibwood (selected bethabara); juniper; and willow.

Rods 155

ABOVE: *Raw clums of Tonkin cane bamboo, such as these from the Leonard rod factory ca 1970s, were split and then milled into the strips used to make split bamboo rods.*

TOP RIGHT: *Completed split bamboo blanks with handles and reel seats attached are finished by having guides wrapped in place as with this example from the Leonard rod factor ca 1970s.*

ABOVE: *Completed Leonard split bamboo rod with case and bag, ca 1970s.*

snakewood. Other craftsmen soon followed, along with developing many other variations of split-bamboo construction. Bamboo rods were made with four strips (Edwards), five strips (later on, by Uslan), six strips (almost everybody) and eight strips and ten strips (Krider). Some companies, such as Divine, made both six- and eight-strip rods, and some makers used eight strips for the butt sections and six strips for the finer tips. It was found in trials with the eight-strip tips that the individual bamboo strips were too fine for proper gluing, with the result that many tips contained as much glue as bamboo.

In 1870 Hiram L. Leonard of Bangor, ME, brought out a six-strip bamboo rod, later (1877) joining with William Mills and Sons in partnership and moving the rod-making operation to Central Valley, NY. Though the Tonkin cane used in bamboo rods of today was widely used, early on there were also split-bamboo rods made of Calcutta bamboo.

Bamboo Rod Construction

Large, heavy, detailed books extensively cover split-bamboo rod construction, but the basic concept is simple. First, the skin or outer enamel surface of the bamboo has the strength and resiliency to be bent repeatedly and recover without damage, thus making it ideal for rods. Making rods then or now involves buying cured, undamaged culms (large straight lengths), splitting them, then milling the resulting split strips in frames to get the triangular size and desired taper to fit together as a rod. The taper and angles would vary with the number of strips used in

156   Our Fishing Heritage: Tackle & Equipment

each rod. In making a six-strip rod, for example, each angle would be 60 degrees. For a four-strip rod, the inner angle would be 90 degrees, the outer angles each 45 degrees; for an eight-strip rod, the inner angle is 42.5 degrees and the outer angles 68.75 degrees. Depending upon how the "V" blocks were made, the strips could be made thinner or thicker as to taper throughout the length, to make very tippy rods (like our worm-action casting and spinning rods of today) to very parabolic rods that would bend well down into the handle.

The strips have the nodes removed and are usually arranged so that they are staggered on the finished rod to avoid a single weak area. They are glued, and then immediately spiral- and criss-cross-wrapped for the whole length to assure a good glue bond. Often this is a baked bond, with the rod sections cured in an oven. The wraps are removed, the excess glue on the surface removed and the rod straightened (if need be) by heat or steam. Once finished as a "blank," the rod section is trimmed, then fitted with metal ferrules. A reel seat, grip and tip top are added, and the guides and hook keeper are wrapped in place and varnished. This basic methodology applies to trout fly rods (which this method was originated for) or for the later salmon and bass fly rods, casting rods, trolling rods and, even later, some spinning rods and certainly some early saltwater boat and surf-fishing rods.

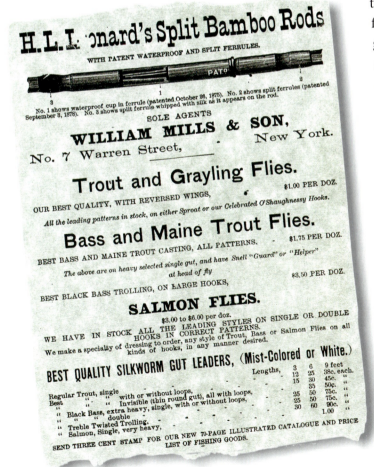

ABOVE: *Some rods were made of two or three layers of split bamboo for maximum strength. This South Bend Cross Doublebuilt rod is an example of a rod with two inner layers of bamboo.*

Rods   157

LEFT: *Close-up of spiral wrappings and label on an early ca 1885 Fred Divine rod of Utica, NY.*

Even with Tonkin cane, as the best of the 2,000 species of bamboo, which is basically a form of grass, problems still existed. The rod designs shifted from strictly fly to other tackle methods as well, but the material was not as strong as was desired for heavier rods to accommodate the casting reels that were coming on the market. Also, the early glues did not always hold well. Inventors and tackle tinkerers over the years came up with some intriguing methods to cope with these problems and to develop finer rods.

One method to add strength was to get more of the strong exterior enamel and less of the pith used. To do this, six-strip rods were double and even triple built, meaning that an additional one or two layers of bamboo were glued over a thin inner six-strip rod. The outer strip was nothing more than tri-angular strips with the inner pithy part cut away to mate with the outer enamel skin of the inner rod.

Solving Problems

Strength was important, since some bamboo rods, particularly those used for bait fishing or trolling with conventional reels, would take a permanent bend, or set. One way to adjust for this was a system of using a special stirrup type of tip top and guides placed opposite each other on the rod (usually a separate upper section only), so that the rod could be reversed 180 degrees after each trip or when needed to work against the set created by a previous fishing expedition.

This did not mean that other woods had been eclipsed at this time. In fact, up through the turn of the century, rods of hickory, greenheart and other woods were used in England to make fly rods for salmon, trout, and tarpon. A gradual evolution of more use of split-bamboo rods, coupled with less use of the then-traditional wood rods, however, did occur. One interesting trend designed to copy the look of the traditional round cross section wood rods was the technique of making a split-bamboo rod (often hexagonal shape), then rounding it off to make it appear as a wood rod, but in the process cutting away much of the enamel skin and removing much of the rod strength.

The wood fly rods for tarpon, as Florida tarpon fishing was just starting to become popular, indicate that English tackle was still being exported to the U.S. There were also ads for "spinning rods," but this did not mean what it first seemed. Spinning, as described at the turn of the century, was fishing with

158 *Our Fishing Heritage: Tackle & Equipment*

lures that spun around, such as the torpedo-shaped, twin opposing-fin Devons, Phantoms, Caledonias and similar lures.

But Tonkin bamboo continued to make inroads against the tradition of other woods. In the 1890s Fred Divine developed a method of making six-strip bamboo rods, but before the glue cured on the strips, twisting the rod end-to-end and holding it in place as the glue cured to make a spiral section rod. This reportedly added stiffness, but made rod construction more difficult and thus never became popular. Dr. George Parker Holden later developed a method of making a five-strip, six-section bamboo rod, also for added stiffness while others used four-strip rods with the enamel on the inside, the pith outside.

Ideas and Patents

To make the butt section lighter, rods were hollowed out, for the entire or partial length of the rod. Later developments in the 1930s by Edwin C. Powell were for rods with scalloped or cut-out hollow sections on each pithy center of the rod to combine some strength and lightness. Rod maker Lew Stoner developed a method of making fluted hollow rods; the fluting added more surface area for gluing. This innovation later developed into the Winston line of rods.

Bamboo rods were also made with wire running through the center and with wire ribs between the joined strips of bamboo (both presumably for stiffness, although it does increase tensile strength

ABOVE: *Split bamboo fly rod showing the tip section and also the shouldered ferrule on a middle section. Note that the ends of the ferrule are wrapped with thread for sealing and strength.*

"THREAD" OUTFITS

Rod weight, rod length and the size of line for which the rod was designed all entered into a designation as to the type of saltwater tackle being used from about 1906 through the '40s. A "3-6" outfit consisted of a rod which is no longer than six feet, with a tip end weighing no more than six ounces, and in which six-thread line was used. These were the days in which the rod tip separated from the handle and reel seat at the forward part of the reel seat, thus the weight was of the blank, not including the handle part.

The lines then were made of twisted linen of Cuttyhunk, and the "six thread" referred to the six strands used to make the twisted line, each strand testing about three pounds, thus an 18-pound-test line. During this period, the lines often tested only about 12 pounds, or about two pounds per thread of the line.

Rods 159

  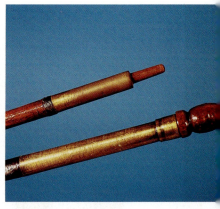

LEFT: *Early style female ferrule with stopper to protect the opening from dirt during transport or storage.*

CENTER: *Two early step-style male ferrules on an early rod. The steps were made for better seating and also supposedly for greater strength.*

RIGHT: *Ferrules, showing the protective stopper in place on the female end of the ferrules and the male step-style ferrule.*

and, at the same time, makes the rod heavy and slow). They were also laminated into round, oval or heart-shaped cross sections instead of the strip method, and impregnated with Bakelite (one of the early plastics) resins, as per the Orvis rods, externally spiral wrapped with metal ribbon, then wrapped between the guides, or every few inches, with thread wraps for strength. The extreme of this was the 1897 patent by John M. Kenyon of Toledo, OH, for wrapping a rod completely—end to end!—with thread, using white silk that would become translucent when varnished.

The "new" rods of today (some by Daiwa) in which the line runs through the center of the tubular blank with no guides used goes back almost 125 years to an 1875 patent and a method for stringing line through the center of bamboo rods. Later patents in 1887 to Everett Horton (of the Bristol, CT, rod company, Horton Manufacturing Company) dealt with

WHEN IS A 12 MM GUIDE NOT A 12 MM GUIDE?

Early ring guides were an offshoot of the jewelry trade, and the steel wire rings used were measured in millimeters by the inside or outside ring size. No one is sure on the exact sizing method, and it might have been a little sloppy in this regard. Nevertheless, it was still accurate enough for fishing purposes and to determine the right ring size for the rod and line usage.

With the development of ceramic guides of aluminum oxide, Hardloy, and such, this went out the window, because the guides were still sized by the outside ring. With the addition of a nylon shock ring inside of the steel or aluminum frame and a ceramic ring inside of the shock ring, the traditional size was no longer even close to the true inside diameter of the ring through which the line runs. In many cases, a size 12 guide had a true ID of about 8 mm, about two-thirds of the stated size. This was less pronounced with the larger ring sizes, since the shock and ceramic rings did not get proportionately larger. It also has become less of a problem recently, as shock rings were found to be unnecessary on some guides or reduced in size, or the inner ceramics reduced in size also. Naturally, this does not affect those buying finished rods, but does still affect those making or refinishing tackle.

the same concept in hollow metal rods. His patent involved using a reel in which the line would come off the rear of the reel, go through a hole in the butt end of the rod and thread out through the tip, avoiding cutting into the rod blank to feed the line.

Naturally, methods of holding the rod, securing the reel seat, and running the line through the guides also had to be addressed with rods that had progressed to reel use and beyond the tie-the-reel-to-the-rod system. Reels were variously wrapped on with cord or leather strips, clamped with special clamps that were a part of the reel or screwed onto the rod with later development of slip rings (such as are still found on many light or ultralight spinning rods). Then came the threaded reel seat with fixed hood, and sliding hood held in place with knurled threaded ring or collet nuts.

Ferrules gained popularity rapidly over the more cumbersome method of the wrapped splices, with ferrules originally two-step or "doweled" style, the step-like male part fitting into a mated female ferrule. Some Irish rods were screwed together. Later, special ferrules were developed. Popular brands were the Super Z ferrules of nickel silver (although black and brass were also available), and the Featherweight brand that assured proper fitting through tiny O-rings around the end of each male ferrule.

Guides

Guides to literally guide the line from the reel and out the end of the rod started as small free-swinging rings on a bracket, identical to the hook keepers used on some rods even today. Both small and floppy, they would be the worst possible thing to use as a guide for anyone wanting line to flow off of a reel and through the guides of the rod. Later guides were developed into the snake guides for fly fishing and still used

TOP: *Early wood and split bamboo rods were often made with guides on both sides to allow switching the strain on the rod on alternate fishing days. These heavy agate guides are on an early wood boat rod.*

ABOVE: *Rods in which the guides were placed on both sides to even out strain required special tip tops. This stirrup-style tip top allowed the line to run through the guide rings no matter which side of the rod it came from.*

Rods   161

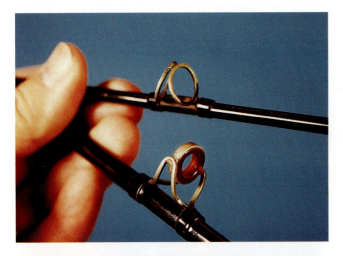

TOP: *Examples of early guides from the 1910s and 1920s include a double ring guide (top) and an agate guide (bottom).*

ABOVE: *Early trumpet guides were funnel shaped and would be used on both sides of a rod where is allowed distribution of strain (top) or on only one side of the rod (bottom).*

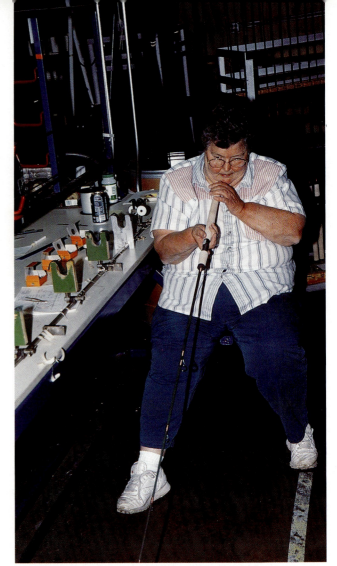

ABOVE: *Factory worker in a rod plant sighting rod guides while wrapping them in place to be sure of proper straight alignment in the finished rod. Note the rod wrapping jig to the left.*

today, and framed ring guides for casting, still-fishing, trolling, bait fishing, and other non-fly methods. (Although some fly rods also had very small and very light wire framed guides all the way up the rod.) Fly rod guides went from these floppy rings to the snake guides to the single- or double-foot ceramic guides used on some rods today.

Although we think these floppy guides are from the 1800s, there are actually earlier mentions. In Richard Brookes' *The Art of Angling* (1720), you can find the following: "It is found very useful to have rings, or eyes made of fine Wire, and placed upon your Rod from one End to the other, in such a manner as that when you lay your Eye to one, you may see through all the rest. Through these Rings your Line must run, which will be kept in a due posture by that Mans; and you must have a Winch, or Wheel, affixed to your rod, about a Foot above the End, by which you may, if it should be proper, give Liberty to the Fish."

Thus, it seems that ring guides are described, along with the rod builder's standard method of positioning guides by sighting through them to check for proper alignment.

The floppy ring guides soon changed to tubular or trumpet guides (usually called bell guides), looking almost like a small trumpet, flared at each end to receive the line. The framed ring guides varied from those of wire to chromed wire to agate (very hard and a natural precursor and similar design to the

ABOVE: *The evolution and examples of some rod guides can be seen in these, left to right; snake guide, metal tunnel guide, agate guide, chromes stainless guide, Aetna (flexible ring) guide, early Perfection Tip guide and modern Fuji single foot high frame guide.*

hard ceramics of today) and Carboloy. Both agate and Carboloy were subject to problems. Carboloy was a somewhat rough, heavy and very brittle guide ring material; agate was a good material but one subject to fine hairline cracks that would not be noticeable but would quickly wear line.

Guides for saltwater rods were often of the ringed, double-sided type (two guides opposite each other on the rod) to help straighten out the sets that occurred with the early wood and then split-bamboo rods. The next innovation was the "Belmar" guides, which had side braces for guide feet that fit onto the side of the rod rather than on top.

Roller guides by Mildrum, Fin-Nor and AFTCO followed. These heavy frames featured a roller and bearing system by which the line would run on and over a pulley-like roller to lessen friction, wear and heat buildup.

The popular chromed steel guides by Varmac and Allen and the flexible spiral Foul Proof guides by Aetna, and the hard but brittle Carboloy guides were less used and losing favor. These ring guides of chromed steel were gradually replaced by Fuji ceramic guides first brought into the country by Lew Childre in the 1970s. Perfection Tip, Varmac and Mildrum made similar guides. The first of these were gray-colored aluminum oxide, (from Fuji,

Rods   163

ABOVE: *Original wrap (mostly coming off) holding wire spring guide on an early 14-foot English punt rod.*

ABOVE: *Agate guide on early steel rod. Note that there is no thread wrap and that the guide is incorporated into a metal sleeve fitting onto the rod.*

Varmac and Perfection Tip; Mildrum guide rings were pink), although at the same time some rod companies were using low-grade white ceramics. The difference was and is that the white guides may ultimately groove with the line; the hard ceramics will not. These ceramic rings were cushioned by a nylon outer ring that in turn was force fit into the aluminum guide frame. Thus, the guide ring looked thicker, even though it was light and damage-proof from line. In time, other even harder guides were

GUIDES WEREN'T ALWAYS CONSIDERED GOOD

Modern design concepts realize that guides, properly placed, help to distribute the strain on a rod as a rod flexes when casting or fighting a fish. A new concept of guides by Fuji, used by a number of modern manufacturers, is to use more guides than in the past, with the guides smaller ring diameter and with a higher frame to help clear and avoid contact with the rod blank. The theory calls for optimal distribution of strain and maximum casting distance, with minimal weight of the guides.

That idea is another that was thought of years ago. Guides and anglers in the 1950s and 1960s were experimenting with the same high frame/small ring concept, making guides for their rods when they wanted maximum casting distance.

Guides, and especially lots of guides, weren't always looked at favorably. In the 1920s through the 1950s, it was felt that the more guides on a rod, the less faith the rod manufacturer had in the quality of his rod blank. For surf-fishing rods, it was considered standard to have only a tip top and one guide. A photo of a surf angler on the cover of the 1950 book, *Fishing the Surf*, by Raymond R. Camp, shows an angler with about a 10-foot rod fighting a fish. The rod had a tip top and one double-side guide about 2½ to 3 feet down from the tip. As a result of this lack of line support throughout the length of the conventional (revolving-spool reel) rod, the line bridges below the rod by about four to six inches as the rod bows.

The double-side guides were not without merit, at least with the tackle and thinking of the time. Separate photos from the 1940s of authors Chisie Farrington and husband S. Kip Farrington, Jr. with large bluefin tuna and their tackle show noticeable bends, or sets, in the rods used. It was for these situations that double (back-to-back) guides allowed reversing the strain on the rod.

ABOVE: *Steel and beryllium copper rods used different types of ferrules and seating systems into the rod handles. The upper steel rod has a tapered collet holding the rod shaft into the handle; the lower beryllium copper rod has a more abrupt seating arrangement.*

added, using rings of materials such as Hardloy, aluminum nitride and silicone carbide. These were used for all types of rods, from some boat and offshore rods to surf (where guides with fold-down frames became popular), popping, freshwater casting, spinning and even fly.

In time, specialty guides were developed that lacked the cushion ring for light spinning and fly, along with thick-frame guides for tough fishing and heavy rods. Today, the trend is to small-ring, high-frame guides for maximum stress distribution, light weight and casting distance.

The development of fishing methods such as trolling, bait fishing, bait casting and such led to both shorter rods that did not require the length needed then and now when casting a fly, and also to materials other than the popular, but increasingly expensive, split bamboo. Bamboo did continue to hold forth, particularly in bait casting and also fly rods, until the Communist Chinese crisis of the early 1950s cut off the supply of Tonkin cane and left bamboo rod makers scrambling for supplies and replacements. Some companies, such as Orvis, either lucky or perhaps anticipating such problems, had stocked and warehoused a many years' supply of bamboo.

Tubular Steel for Strength

Steel and other metallic materials for the shorter rods gradually came into play in the 1920s. Homer Circle, angling editor of *Sports Afield* and an outdoor writer for more than 50 years, remembers working in a sporting goods store from 1932 to 1940 when tubular steel and beryllium copper rods were first sold. The beryllium was added to the copper since it was lighter than aluminum but six times stiffer than steel. These looked like later-day golf shafts (which are made the same way today), made of telescoping tubular sections tapering down in size from the butt to the tip and, in the

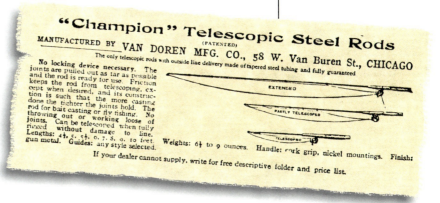

Rods 165

LEFT: Hollow steel multi-section steel casting rod from the teens. It was made with a separate handle, lower agate guide and two-ring guides on the upper part.

process, causing a graduated and increasingly thin flexible shaft with a slow action thought at the time to be similar to that of split bamboo. The 1946 *Fishing Tackle Digest* lists tubular steel (and some beryllium copper) bait casting rods by True Temper (American Fork and Hoe), along with similar construction rods by South Bend, Gephart, Bristol, Montague (with its "Hollosteel" rods, which, presumably, were hollow), Heddon and Shakespeare. The material was tried for long rods, even fly rods, but was immediately considered to be logy and poor for anything long and light.

Ironically, although tubular steel rods did not appear until just prior to the 1920s, the idea was thought of long before that. Under a section entitled "The Rod of the Future" in his 1885 book, *Fly-Rods and Fly-Tackle*, author H. P. Wells notes that a French violin maker had previously made violin bows of tubular steel, and that the same material and construction should be ideal for making fly rods. He noted that he had tried to make such a tubular-steel section for a rod several years prior, but at the time it was a failure. He, however, also gives the name and address for obtaining cold-rolled French steel for anyone interested in trying this. It seemed to take 35 more years, however, before such rods reached the market place.

Heddon manufactured some fly rods, including their "Pal" series described in 1946 as "...drawn from the finest alloy steel tubing with a very thin tube-wall necessary to produce lightness and delicate action." Apparently, these rods had been around a while, since further copy reads, "Severe casting use given these rods prove that they have exceptionally long life—many report rods still giving wonderful service after years of hard, continued use." The cosmetics of these rods were a "rich, brown-tone enamel finish,

166   Our Fishing Heritage: Tackle & Equipment

trimmed in two colors of silk." Was the brown tone to resemble the more expensive and by then traditional split bamboo rods? Gephart and True Temper were among other companies making tubular steel fly rods at the time.

Solid Steel for Durability

Solid-steel rods followed, also tapered for action, but with different cross-sectional configurations. Round and square were the most popular; they were featured in Actionrods, available in 5- and 5½-foot-long, round or square models). Other solid-steel rods were made by Gephart, which had models available with triangular, hexagonal and square shapes. Richardson, Shakespeare, True Temper and Bristol also had solid-steel rapier-like casting rods. Winchester, the arms company, had solid-steel rods in its 1932 catalog, some of the rods as short as 2½ feet.

Some unusual rods were also developed during this steel period, such as the Stubcaster casting rod from Waltco Products of Chicago, IL. The short rod broke down into a 14-inch length when the blank was removed from the collet grip, and it had a double-coil spring in the blank just above the reel seat that supposedly gave "thrilling, live 5 ft. action," according to the ads of 1949. It was $5.95 without the reel.

Grips also changed from wood to cork, a much lighter and more comfortable material. Reel seats changed also on the casting rods from the straight, in-line configuration to an offset reel seat that allowed the revolving-spool reel to sit lower and thus be easier to control when thumbing the reel on a cast. Originally, rods were built straight through the grip and reel seat as one-piece or two-piece rods. Then in the 1920s and 1930s, the in-line reel

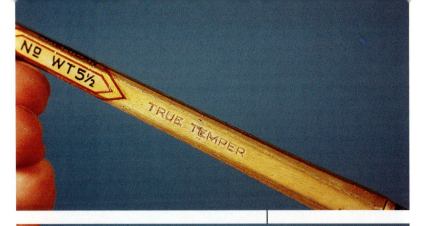

ABOVE: Two views of an American Fork & Hoe (True Temper) square cross section casting rod. Note the stamping of "True Temper" in the upper photo and the decal logo of "Amercian Fork & Hoe" in the lower photo.

Rods 167

LEFT: Eight different bait casting rod handles on tapered hollow steel and solid steel rods. Most are from the 1920s and 1930s. Many style of grips and reel seats are shown, but all the reel seats are of the then-popular offset style.

combination rods that broke down into several parts as a pack rod for travel or camping/back packing and also allowed the angler to switch back and forth between types of tackle. Later, in the 1950s, such multi-use rods of glass were made with fly fishing and spinning reels in mind.

seat/rod blank configuration continued, but with the blank detaching from the handle/reel seat by means of a ferrule.

In some cases, there was a ferrule on each end, and no finger hook, so that the reel could be placed at the end of the rod for fly fishing, or above the grip for bait casting. This was also found in so-called

More New Ideas

Later as glass rods developed, the ferrule system stayed in place with the offset handle or grip. Initially this was with a screw-type lockable collet at the upper end of the grip to fasten the male ferrule of the rod blank into the handle, just as a drill bit gets locked into a drill chuck. Shakespeare developed a

ONE PERSON'S TRASH IS ANOTHER PERSON'S TREASURE

Some years ago, an outdoor writer friend was putting out the trash when he noted some sticks protruding from the trash can of the elderly lady across the street. He investigated, and found that they were fishing rods—split-bamboo fishing rods. Before the garbage men came, he immediately knocked on the door of his neighbor, pointed out that they were fishing rods, perhaps with some value that should be appraised and sold. She didn't care; they were from a distant relative and, yes, he was free to take them if he desired. He did, and ended up with a prime collection of early fly rods from the likes of Edwards, Payne, Leonard and others who were valued and classic pioneers in the art of rod making.

ABOVE: *Examples of early style rods and handles/grips on rods from the 1930s and 1940s. Examples of grips include wood, cork and molded grips.* **Top to bottom:** *solid steel rod (manufacturer unknown), J. C. Higgins (Sears) glass rod, True Temper solid steel rod and unknown glass rod.*

universal casting rod handle that had an adjustable collet to allow it to take any size butt rod ferrule. This was simplified with a slip-in plastic ferruling system in the 1970s introduced by Lew Childre. Several handle designs and grip designs/lengths were available, each taking a slip-in male ferrule that was held securely as a result of an O ring at the end. The male ferrules were made in different inside diameters so that manufacturers, custom-rod builders and hobbyists could match the right size ferrule to any rod blank. Later this got a little more complicated with increasing styles, sizes and types of what was originally a very simple handle-ferruling system for casting rods.

Also, some rod and reel makers made rods with reel seats that would only take their reels, often on purpose to prevent purchase of any but their tackle. In time, both with glass and particularly graphite rods, the trend went back to the straight-through blank rods, the rod blank not ending at the ferrule with the handle and offset reel seat, but extending all the way through the rod to serve as a base for the butt cap, rear grip, reel seat (in-line) and fore grip. One different idea from 1948 was to make a casting rod with a handle on which the line could run through the forward part of the handle and under the rod, with the rod tip upside down in the handle ferrule. This eliminated line/rod friction when playing a fish, and it reduced line wear. This same idea was reinvented some 30 years later in the late 1970s.

As saltwater rods were developed, they had to be different, because the big fish sought were often played from a chair with a gimbal socket in which to place the reel butt. This required a rod handle with a longer rear grip. The first

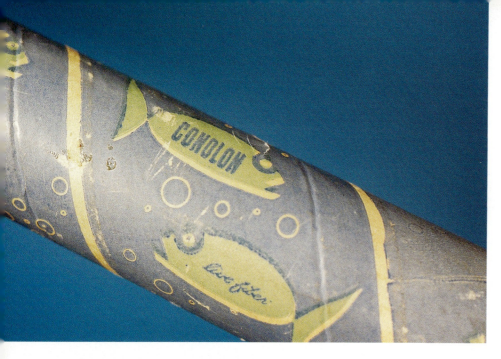

LEFT: *Early rods from the 1920s often came with cases (frequently leather) and cloth bags. Aluminum cases became popular later. This cardboard case with advertising the length of the case and "Live Fiber" to indicate early fiberglass rods is from the late 1940s or early 1950s.*

grips were of wood (often hickory) and later of aluminum with glued-on chrome-plated brass reel seats, and still later with all-aluminum handles and combined reel seats. Foregrips above the reel were initially wood or cork and, later, in the 1970s, were made of cellular foam. Saltwater rods also required different guides for the extreme pressures put on both fish and fisherman. Not all saltwater rods used reel seats, at least not in the 1930s and 1940s. Because of the often massive size of the reels used then for the line capacity required for big game, the reels were high off of the rod, which led to torquing to the side. One solution was the cradle system of holding reels, in which the rod would have a half-round cradle to hold the reel. Of course, the reel would not have a reel seat and was clamped into the cradle. This reduced torquing, made for more comfortable fighting of fish and placed the reel lower on the rod shaft (almost in line with it) for easier reeling and line spooling.

Tubular Glass Gets Going

Tubular-glass rods were developed in the early 1940s and offered the promise of a light, flexible, tough, corrosion-proof rod material. Then, as now, there were two methods of construction, with all companies using the so-called cut-and-roll method. The Shakespeare Company also used their proprietorially developed Howald process. Dr. G. G. Havens of Narmco on the West Coast is credited with developing the first glass rods in the Narmco, later Conolon and then Garcia/Conolon factory. The best guess for a date is 1945.

Shakespeare did similar work. The story goes that Shakespeare was originally making tubular fiberglass lengths for use as tank antennas for World War II, although that can't be confirmed. Supposedly, Henry Shakespeare did make up some early Shakespeare tubular glass rods for his use

170 Our Fishing Heritage: Tackle & Equipment

ABOVE: *Examples of modern graphite rod and early glass rods. Top, a modern Shimano Catana casting rod of graphite with straight-through blank and foam grip. Bottom, an early Shakespeare Wonderod of fiberglass with ferrule/collet blank to handle connection.*

and for some friends. These were made with the hollow cut-and-roll method, but were not hollow, because they had tapered balsa cores around which the glass fabric was wrapped and baked on. The balsa stayed in the hollow rod.

Glass Construction

An early account of these can be found in *Fishing Tackle Digest* of 1946 in an article titled "Shakespeare's New Howald Glastik Wonderod." The article attributed the development to Dr. Arthur M. Howald, technical director for the Plaskon Division of the Libbey-Owens-Ford Glass Company. It states that Dr. Howald reasoned in 1945 that because of the similarity of Plaskon materials to bamboo, it might be possible to make a rod of these new materials that would be stronger and more durable and hence superior to bamboo for fishing rods. The article states: "After preliminary experiments on the strength of glass fiber resin combinations in small diameters, a technique for hand building the new fly rod was developed. A hard, strong surface of parallel glass fibers bonded with synthetic resin was applied over a lightweight non-structural tapered wood core, analogous to the pitch of the bamboo.

"By use of an ingenious method of laying the glass fibers parallel to the core, wrapping with cellophane and then heat treating, a fly rod of this material was made.

"Tests already made indicate that a fly rod constructed as described above, surfaced with resin bonded fibres, is stronger and lighter in weight than a bamboo rod."

The article further states that the same process can be used for making

Rods 171

THE FIRST GRAPHITE ROD?

In books and documents on the subject, Fenwick is given credit as the first manufacturer of a graphite fishing rod, although the Shakespeare trademark on the same name (Graflite) chosen by Fenwick preceded that of Fenwick by two days and caused a controversy in the 1972 American Fishing Tackle Manufacturers Association summer trade show.

In a sense, both companies had the first rods—at least of the tubular design similar to that used for fiberglass. But the year before that, at the same Chicago annual trade show, Abu Garcia had two examples of an early graphite boat/trolling rod. Built in laminated fashion (like plywood, it was not hollow), the guides were precisely placed and line had to be run through the guides for the rod to flex properly and uniformly—and not break.

Ironically, before the show opened and when manufacturers and manufacturers' representatives were setting up their booths, a representative from another company visited the booth to see the new rods and, curious, innocently bent the rod in the middle without the line flexing the rod. The rod shattered, with guides and some graphite going off like shrapnel—and with Abu Garcia losing one of its two expensive prototypes even before the show began! The head honcho at Garcia was not amused. Obviously, this method of construction was never used nor reached the market. The next year, Fenwick and Shakespeare debuted their hollow graphite rods, followed the next year by most other companies.

bait casting rods and that both bait casting and fly casting rods will appear on the market in 1947.

These rods were the precursor of the methods used today in which a tapered steel mandrel is used as the base for wrapping the rod material (glass or graphite), with the mandrel removed after the blank was baked. The core of balsa was used only in early rods.

Glass rods and later the graphite rods are exactly that: glass, graphite or both, as in the case of composites. The glass fibers are very thin and woven into a cloth that in turn is cut to make the rod. The glass fibers of fiberglass (originally Fiberglass and a trade mark for the thin fibers by the Owens Illinois Glass Company) are made by melting glass marbles, which are then strained through holes in a platinum floor of the oven. The fibers are air cooled and run onto a drum, then gathered into threads and run off onto a spool. They are further treated with stretching, baking and a chrome treatment that aids in the resins sticking to the fibers. The resulting threads are then used to make the cloth. The glass cloth is similar to curtains—and curtains are made of glass fiber—and is impregnated with resins. First phenolic resins were used, then polyester resins that allowed adding color to the blanks; today, epoxy resins are used for both glass and graphite rod construction.

There are two types of glass—E-glass and the later-developed S-glass. The E-glass is tougher and more durable and less expensive; the S-glass is used on better rods or on rods that require slightly greater sensitivity. The latter is also the stronger material, so identical rod designs can use less material and weigh less.

Graphite Appears

Graphite, basically a carbon fiber, was developed as part of the space effort and used for high-tech military and industrial applications. Over the years it has developed into higher and higher tensile strength, called modulus, which is the way fishing rod application and quality is often determined. Initially, graphite for fishing rods was only about 20 million (low modu-

lus); today it can range up into 50 to 70 million and often goes by names such as IM6, IM7, IM8, etc., each referring respectively to a higher modulus. Trade, marketing and proprietary names were used by most companies to indicate the same characteristics.

Regardless, the fine graphite fibers are woven into a cloth or fabric that is then used as is glass; cut into a long triangle; tacked to a mandrel; cellophaned; baked; the mandrel removed; and the rod finished and fixed with handle, reel seat and guides.

In addition to these two basic materials, graphite/glass composite rods are also made of cloth in which graphite and glass are mixed in various percentages. Thus, a composite rod might have a very high or low percentage, by weight, of graphite. These are also made in the same tubular material cut-and-roll method.

Of the two methods to make tubular material rods (graphite or glass), the cut-and-roll method is by far most popular. In this, the glass/graphite cloth with fibers running in both directions (warp and woof) is cut into a long, slim triangular shape. Large tables and steel templates make it possible for workers to cut several layers of glass cloth at once. Today, such cuts are often made automatically and computer-controlled to get the maximum use of the material from each bolt of graphite or glass.

MAKING A FIBERGLASS FISHING ROD

1. Steel mandrels like these at a Shakespeare factory are reused to make hollow rods of glass and graphite. Different mandrel lengths, diameters and tapers are used to make different types and actions of rods.

2. This modern computer operated machine used by Berkley, Abu Garcia and Fenwick will cut many layers of graphite or glass. The tapered sections of graphite or glass are then rolled on a blank to make a rod.

3. A hot tacking iron is being used by this Fenwick worker to attach the tapered strips of graphite to the steel mandrel prior to rolling them into a rod and baking.

Rods 173

Once the material is cut, an iron is used to tack the edge of the cloth to the tapered steel mandrel. This tapered steel mandrel is what makes the rod hollow and also determines the diameter and in part the taper of the blank. Once the edge of the material is tacked, rollers on universal joints (required because of the taper of the blank) are lowered to roll the mandrel, in the process rolling the cloth around the shaft.

The result is then put on a separate machine that wraps the blank end-to-end with a clear cellophane-like tape to hold it in place. Bake ovens cure the resins and seal the wrapped cloth into a finished rod. Once removed from the ovens and cooled, the mandrel is pulled out to be used again and the rod blank is ready for finishing.

Finishing requires trimming the ends, adding a reel seat and cork or foam grip, then adding the guides, which are wrapped with thread and sealed. Sealing was initially with varnish, and today is done with epoxy.

Howald, A Different Process

The Howald process of making blanks involves an initial wrapped layer of material around the mandrel, then carefully machine-laid longitudinal layers of material, around which a second wrapping of material is wrapped for hoop strength. Any, or all, of these materials or layers can be glass or graphite. The machinery to accomplish this is complex and creates the blank with a taper determined by the mandrel used and also by cutting and removing some of the longitudinal fibers as the materials are laid down from butt to tip end. The same Howald process is used today by Shakespeare to make graphite and glass composite blanks (such as the Ugly Stik) with a spiral wrapping of graphite, a longitudinal layer of glass and graphite, then a final outer tight spiral wrap of graphite.

The Pultrusion Process

Another method for making glass blanks is the pultrusion method, by which the long strands of fiberglass are fed through a bath of resin, then through a die that compresses the glass/resin bundle into a round uniform blank, the blank continuously pulled by tension through the die. This is credited to a Mr. McGuire of Kansas City whose work led to the development of the Phantom Products Inc. of Kansas City, which advertised in the mid-1950s. Airex, a division of Lionel (the company that made toy and model trains), also had an inexpensive solid-glass rod. The pultrusion process produces a long length of solid fiberglass rod, which is then cut into rod lengths and, with centerless grinding, formed into a tapered rod. Naturally, such rods, which are still made, are heavy and used primarily for heavy saltwater and shark rods. They are less expensive than other rods because of the lower cost of construction. Ironically, while these solid-glass rods were, and are, among the cheapest of the rods available, and because of their weight, best only for heavy fishing or trolling, the same technology is used today to make very light or ultralight spinning rods using a solid graphite tip or blank.

ABOVE: *Examples of modern and old handles of casting rods. Top, a Shimano rod with a straight through blank and skeletal reel seat. Bottom, an old style rod with offset handle, angled grip and separate collet and ferrule for attaching the blank to the handle.*

Graphite and Boron

The method for making standard graphite rods is almost identical to the original method of making fiberglass rods using the cut-and-roll method. Differences are obviously the use of a graphite cloth, modern resins and more modern fittings of grip, reel seat and guides. That's not the end of graphite construction however, since in the early 1980s, boron was introduced as a new rod material that promised even greater sensitivity than the graphite then in use. Many rod companies added this in various ways, most of which were not divulged to the public. Some just added boron in short lengths to the butt end of the rod, thus allowing them to say that the blank included boron, though it had little effect on sensitivity of other vital rod functions. Others had it running all or most of the rod length, but just in one strip that would be on one side of the rod, not uniformly distributed around the blank circumference. Also, the rods with boron were considerably more expensive than those with only graphite, and more than one expert has described the jump from graphite to boron rods in sensitivity as a baby step in contrast to the giant step made in the jump from glass to graphite.

Some Different Graphite Construction

Other ways to make graphite rods do not utilize the cut-and-roll method or the Howald process. In 1993, a patent was granted for making graphite fishing rods using thin linear laminates of graphite, these cut into strips to make a hollow, hexagonal rod that also had reinforcing graphite strips internally. In effect, it is as if long, slim T sections of graphite are tapered to make the external walls and honeycomb structure of the blank. Currently, Cape Fear Rod Company is making rods this way.

Rods

LEFT: *Examples of tip tops used on rods from various periods. Left to right; old style roller tip from Great lakes lake trout rod, large tip top on old wood muskie rod, trumpet or stirrup style tip (two), three ring tip top for double side rod, tip top on solid steel rod, tip top on tubular steel rod, agate tip top and modern ceramic Fuji tip top.*

Prior to that, Walton Powell of Powell Rods developed a method of bonding linear graphite sheets to a closed cell foam. This was then cut into strips and ultimately triangular strips on V blocks, then glued together. This is how Hexagraph rods are made, with the foam on the inside (like the pith of the bamboo) and the graphite fiber on the outside (like the skin of the bamboo) of these hexagonal rods. Naturally, the color is a rich brown, perhaps to remind purchasers of bamboo or to simulate bamboo. Other than using the new materials of graphite on foam, the construction is basically identical to that developed for bamboo 150 years ago.

In addition to graphite and glass, other materials have been used, but more for added strength, durability and toughness than for added sensitivity or to change the action or power. For example, Kevlar, the material for some fishing lines and bullet-proof armor and police vests, has been used in a weave around the outside of graphite blanks, and nickel fibers have been scattered in with graphite for strength.

Modern Designs

Along the way, designs of rods have varied with efforts to improve the tackle. Originally, offshore saltwater boat rods varied in length, but ultimately most were made about seven feet long, including an 18-inch rear grip and reel seat, ferruled at the upper end of the reel seat, the rod sporting five roller guides and a roller tip top. Most of the blanks were even, parabolic action. In time, West Coast fishing in the 1960s changed slightly, with anglers going to slightly longer rods with lighter tips for flinging or casting live bait such as anchovies on West Coast party boats. They also added more guides and sometimes went with standard ring guides. Since these rods were fished standing up, they also required shorter rear grips or butts. In time, the industry responded with short butts for stand-up fishing now available on a number of commercial rods and the butts available for custom-rod builders.

Other innovations also came along in spinning and casting, with one of the most unusual the swelled butt Fightin' Rods from Shimano in which the butt section of the rod was really an extension of the reel seat hoods that were built onto the blank. Thus, it was the first of the skeletal reel seat rods with the design also incorporated by G. Loomis, Zebco and others. In time, these "fat butt" rods lost favor, but the skeletal reel-seat design remained, with reel seats that included hoods on a platform to hold the reel foot, with the rest of the reel seat open to expose the rod for maximum feel and sensitivity. Because the reels are molded of graphite/plastic, this also made them very light. This was not the first of the reels seats in other than metal, however. In 1930, Heddon made plastic reel seats in the traditional threaded hood, tubular style of their proprietary Heddylin (pyralin) plastic.

In freshwater, rods also changed, with one of the notable rods of the early 1970s being the flipping rod developed by Dee Thomas and marketed in a 7½-foot telescoping butt version by Fenwick in 1976. These were stiff rods that were the modern, guided equivalent of the cane pole used 200 years earlier for skittering. This wasn't the first telescopic rod like this though. Earlier, Horrocks-Ibbotson had a glass spinning rod with a hollow cork handle, the blank fitting through the collet to make a rod of anywhere from six to seven feet long.

Fly rods became tougher in the 1960s as fly fishermen enthusiastically embraced not only the trout fishing of the past, but also bass fishing, pike fishing and the "new" frontier of saltwater fishing. Scientific Anglers introduced their complete line of fly rods, weights 4 through 12 and their heavy-duty tarpon-style Great Equalizer in 1968. At about the same time, Fenwick introduced an FF116 model nine-foot, one-inch, two-piece fly rod that also featured a four-foot-long insert section to stiffen the butt section when fighting a fish. The insert was placed in the rod after hook-up. Using it, Stu Apte landed a then-new world record tarpon of 151 pounds, and Lefty Kreh landed a Florida tarpon of 118 pounds. Modern saltwater fly fishing had arrived by the late 1960s.

Guides got lighter and tougher with the various ceramics, allowing another trend of the late 1970s and early 1980s: the so-called "noodle rods" for light tackle fishing. These were longer and lighter than would be normally used for any type of fishing, often about nine to 12 feet long and designed for two- to four-pound-test line. First, fly rod blanks were used, then companies such as Lamiglas, LCI, Fenwick and others began making specific noodle rods. It was almost a trend to the early long rods and light horsehair lines of the colonists. At the same time,

shorter (nine to 11 foot) rods with a tippy action were developed for the new sport of downrigger fishing that started in the mid-1970s. These rods were held in almost vertical holders, the rod tip bent as the line was bowed in the water going straight down to the downrigger release.

ABOVE: *Modern rods with through-blank construction have the reel seat with the blank exposed for maximum feel and sensitivity. Here, the blank can be seen on this skeletal-style spinning reel seat.*

WHAT, NO REEL?

Early in the colonies, and prior to that in England and Europe, fishing with a reel was thought to be unsporting.

Reels—windes, wheels and winches they were called then—were the mark of a poacher, presumably since it was thought that it gave an unfair advantage to the angler by being able to vary line length and thus control the fish.

The standard method of fishing then was with fixed lines, the lines tied to the tip end of the rod. If a large fish—say a pike or large trout—were to take the bait or fly, and prove to be too difficult to control even on heavy 12 (horse) hair line, the simple answer was to throw the rod into the water until the fish tired.

Rods 177

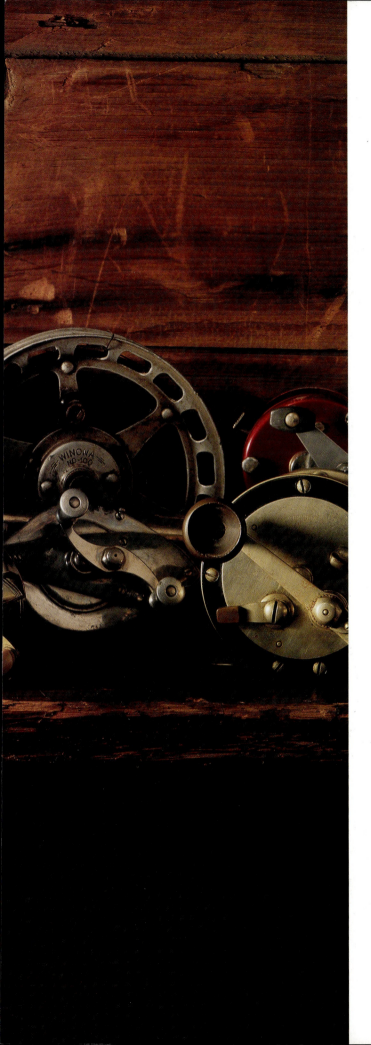

Reels

Introduction

Whether rods or reels first followed a simple coil of line and hook is debatable. In some areas, the idea of wrapping line loosely around a frame or object to throw the line so that the line would coil off (like the basis of spinning) occurred before the rod. Even today, plastic spools with a bar between the rims to serve as a handle are sold as yo-yo reels or Cuban yo-yos for this purpose. This design was prevalent in the South Pacific and elsewhere but does not seem to have originated independently in this country. Rods were used in China at least 800 years ago, and illustrations show some sort of reel attached to the rod.

Conversely, rods without reels—the line tied to the end of the rod—are shown and described as having been used by the Egyptians, Romans, Macedonians and others. The first appearance of a reel on a rod appears to be about the 13th century, based on a Chinese painting of the time that shows an angler holding a short rod, a guide near the reel and a tip top on the end, with a side-mounted reel holding line. The reel looks as if it might be large diameter and narrow, seeming like a wire cage, and almost like the Billinghurst reel from Rochester, NY, that would come along six centuries later in the early 1800s.

The first mention in text of a revolving-spool reel appears to be in Thomas Barker's *Art of Angling* of 1651, two years before the first edition of Izaak Walton's *The Compleat Angler.* Barker describes reels and reel use in several ways and several places in his book. For trolling for pike he states: "within two foot of the bottom of the rod there was a hole made to put in a winder to turn with a barrel, to gather up his line and loose it at his pleasure." He also states that

his 12-foot rod shall have "a ring of wire in the top of the rod for his line to run through," further indicating that the reel was used to play out and reel in line through this guide on the rod.

For salmon fishing he recommends the following: "The first thing you must gain must be a rod of some ten foot in the stock, that will carry a top of six foot pretty stiff and strong, the reason is, because there must be a little wire ring at the upper end of the top for the line to run through, that you may take up and loose at your pleasure; you must have your winder within two foot of the bottom to go on your rod made in this manner, with a spring, that you may put it on as low as you please." The accompanying illustration is poor at best, but seems to indicate a spring that would fit around the rod and clamp it in place, and in essence, a simpler version of the thumb screw clamps for holding reels that would follow later.

Reels Without Rods

Both before and after reels were developed to store line (you could not cast with them yet), some reels were used without rods or at least separate from the rod. This existed in many parts of the world. An example is the Cuban yo-yo system of throwing line off of a spool, the face of the spool allowing the line to come off as line flows off of a spinning reel. Frames of wood were used similarly by the Siwash Indians of the Pacific Northwest. Similar frames were used in Spain, France, Italy and Switzerland. These frames supposedly measured about 14 inches by 18 inches, according to A. J. McClane in his book *Spinning for Fresh and Salt Water Fish of North America*. This

ABOVE: *Early reels from the 1890s include the Yawman & Erbe Automatic Combination reel that was side mounted with a key-wound automatic feature (left) and an early Meisselbach side mounted casting reel.*

evolved in the early 1700s into a round frame, almost like a modern wood line drier, that was held in the left hand while using a rod in the right hand, a ring or tip top in the end of the rod, to lever or throw the line out even farther.

The Scots, in the 1700s, developed the idea of coiling the line on a basket, or platform (almost like the stripping basket of the fly fisherman) and casting by using the separate rod as a lever. At the same time, some fishermen with reels on rods stripped line off of the reels to form loops or coils held in the hand, then cast by using the rod as a lever and allowing the coiled line to flow through the guides. The Swiss in the late 1700s invented the idea of coiling the line on a large wire-frame spool or "bird cage," strapping this to a belt and using it with the separate rod. The line, however, had to be coiled by hand. This idea was revisited in 1949 by the Yakima Bait Co., of Yakima, WA, which then announced their new belly winder that used the same idea, but with a metal drum, crank handle, roller line pickup and drag for fishing Western rivers for salmon and steelhead. Fiberglass rods were used with this rig.

In earlier days in this country, and continuing until recently, automatic reels (not automatic fly reels), without a rod, that clamped to the gunwale of a boat were used in the New York Finger Lake region when trolling wire for lake trout.

FISHING BEFORE REELS

Fishing before reels were developed or accepted (in their early years reels were considered to be the tool of the poacher), other methods of angling were used in addition to throwing the rod into the water. Some early angling was done with the primitive equivalent of long lines, really trot lines (not trout lines, as they have been sometimes pronounced) that were nothing more than a series of hooks on short leaders, all attached to a long line, which often extended across a river, tied to trees on the banks.

Another method was to use reels or line-storage devices that were fitted onto floats, the line hanging down a few feet in the water with a hook and bait. They were the little-known early equivalent of jug fishing, not legal in all states or situations, whereby line is hung from a jug (often a plastic gallon Clorox jug); the jug is retrieved by a nearby boat of anglers when the jug starts to dance as a fish takes the bait.

Dame Juliana Berners in her 1496 writings mentions having some real fun by using geese. "And if you would have some good sport," she wrote of pike fishing, "tie the line to a goose's foot and you will see some good tugging before you can decide whether the goose or the pike will have the better of it." Today, animal abuse laws, fishing regulations or at least public outcry would prohibit such "sport."

A more modern variation of this could be found in the outdoor magazines in the 1940s and 1950s, which suggested tying a short line and worm-baited hook to a duck or goose decoy, where upon a catfish would grab it and make the decoy move naturally. Naturally, this could only be done where legal and with both a hunting and fishing license.

Winches and Windes

Early revolving-spool reels were, at the time, called winches and windes and were little more than simple spools held in a frame; the spool turned with a handle and with a simple click to prevent the spool from overrunning. They were not used for casting, but for storing line to pay out or retrieve while bank fishing or trolling.

In addition to the first recorded mention of a reel by Bowlker (in text, not counting the earlier Chinese illustrations), other mentions of winds and winches occurred in Walton's *The Compleat Angler* (second edition, 1655) and Venables' *The Experienced Angler* (1662). Walton does not mention much about it, however, remarking only that the reel fitted near the hand or somewhere in the middle of the rod. Venables refers to using the winch to wind up line, indicating a method by which more line might be used than that tied to the end of the rod.

Sales of reels were recorded in the late 1700s. Reels were being sold in London by Onesimus Ustonson, tackle maker, who described his wares in ads as "the best sort of Multiplying Brass Winches, both stop and plain." Wood reels were also available. The reference to stop and plain seems to indicate either a click or locking mechanism to prevent spool rotation.

Early U.S. references come from Philadelphia, as seen in a receipt from Edward Pole who on May 27, 1784, sold to a General Cadwalader two "small lines on reels." Ads by Pole from 1774 through 1783 in Dunlap's *Pennsylvania Packet* show him offering from his shop "6, 8, 10, and 12, stave pocket reels, furnished with lines, &c. Trolling wheels for rock, trout or perch, with or without multipliers."

The earliest of these were from England, no doubt imported to the Colonies along with other goods, including hooks, rods and other fishing gear.

Early Simple Reels

Not everyone agreed about the need for a reel, even well after they had been developed and were gaining some popularity. Brown, in his *American Angler's Guide,* notes that reels were in a state of transition even in 1849 when his book was published, although he clearly lands on the side of reel use for sport fishing.

"Many old-fashioned Anglers think that this is a superfluous

article in the equipment of a sportsman; but to any one who has used it, it is almost as indispensable as the rod itself. The main object of the reel is to give the fish a sufficient quantity of line to tire itself, and consequently affords more sport than could be obtained by the rod alone. By means also of this valuable accessory, fish of almost incredible weight, may be captured where the rod would prove utterly useless."

Also, it was not always clear what type of reel to use for which type of fishing. Multipliers were used for fly fishing and simple click reels used for trolling, and vice versa. "A reel or winch is indispensable; it should be such as is called multiplying, with which advantage is take in exhausting the fish, by winding up the line with greater rapidity, whenever it becomes relaxed," said Jerome V. C. Smith in his 1833 book, *Natural History of the Fishes of Massachusetts*. This was in a description of the rods, reels, lines, flies and accessories used for trout fly fishing.

"Whether it be a multiplier or simple reel, in fly-fishing for Trout, it should be small; for a greater length than twenty yards of line is seldom if ever required," noted Thaddeus Norris in his 1864 *American Angler's Book*.

The same blurring that existed between direct-drive and multiplying reels also existed when it came to spool width. Spools could be narrow or wide in either click or multiplying reels, and the upright-frame narrow-spool reel that we think of today as a fly reel did not come into existence until 1874. (The basic fly reel, side-mounted, wire frame, large diameter and narrow spool, was introduced August 9, 1859, with the Billinghurst.) Reels and rods still had to catch up with each other. Because many early rods did not have reel

ABOVE: *Examples and different views of three types and sizes of the early wood single action Nottingham reels.* **Left to right:** *a small wood Nottingham with the typical brass four point star brace, a larger Nottingham and a small double handle Nottingham. Reels similar to these are still available today.*

BELOW: *Billinghurst "cage reel," a narrow-spool reel that presaged the modern fly reel.*

Reels

seats, many reels were tied in place on the rod, fastened with a split circular clamp held by a wing nut, or fitted with a screw or bolt that went into or through the rod handle.

Early Multipliers

In Charles Goodspeed's book, *Angling in America*, mention is made of a 1772 English manuscript that refers to reels vastly improved since Barker's time (1651), and that they are very common, including two sizes, with a brass screw to fasten to a rod. It also states that "Some made with a multiplying reel to wind up three times as much in one turn and are well worth double the Price of the Plain ones."

Writers such as Richard Brookes (1781, *The Art of Angling*) still eschewed reels and suggested wrapping the line to the rod, but the trend was steadily going toward the reel, even if not yet a casting device.

LEFT: *Early rods often lacked reel seats so that early reels were sometimes made with ring-type clamps that encircled the rod and were tightened in place as with this ca 1850 brass British multiplying reel.*

WOOD IN REELS, THEN AND NOW

When mechanics, machinery and metal working were not perfected, reels were made of wood also. The earliest of these were the English Nottingham reels that had large wood spools, often a metal star- or spider-shaped back bracket for reinforcement, a simple line guide and a reel foot for attachment to a rod. Naturally, these were single-action reels, with the handle on the reel spool, just like fly reels.

The first of these were made around the mid-1800s in the suburbs of Nottingham, thus the name Nottingham reel. There were many designs, depending upon the maker, with some even featuring a wood drum into which the wood spool fit. Popularity of these reels continued into the mid-1900s, particularly in England, although they did have an influence on reel production in Canada.

The Peetz reel is a Canadian wood reel of the same basic design as the earlier Nottinghams and designed for Northwest fishing for salmon. Boris Peetz, a Russian silversmith and immigrant to Canada, built the first of his reels in the early 1920s, following the success of an angler who switched from hand-lining salmon to using an imported wood reel on a rod.

Peetz ultimately produced the varnished wood reels in four-, five-, six- and 6¾-inch sizes (diameters). The reason for the larger diameter is simple—the large 6¾-inch-diameter reel would retrieve more than 21 inches of line when full—as much or more than some multipliers.

The family sold the business in 1977, but today Peetz reels are still made and sold, primarily in Canada, but also to devotees throughout the world.

ABOVE: *Meisselbach & Bro. "Good Luck" reel with patented ball bearings, ca 1900. Such reels were immensely popular for still-fishing for decades.*

The multiplying feature allowed retrieving line more rapidly to fight a fish and to allow a fish to run until it was exhausted, rather than having to throw the rod with the line tied to it into the water. Both multipliers and single-action reels allowed a form of "casting" without use of the reel, very similar to flipping of today. This method, practiced in the mid-1700s, required guides on the rod to allow the line to flow out. Called the looper, it involved stripping line off of the reel, coiling it in the hand and casting by using the rod as a lever. Hopefully, the line would flow off of the fingers, one coil at a time. This enabled the angler to make a cast longer than double the length of the rod (the only method possible with the line tied to the rod tip) and to retrieve and play fish with the reel.

There was also debate, long after the developments of the Kentucky reel makers, about the need for some of the improvements in reels. "Many innovations have been made on the old English Reel by American anglers and mechanics; some of these, it is contended, are not improvements," said Thaddeus Norris in his 1864 book.

Multipliers were even used for saltwater fishing then, casting menhaden bait from the beach or rocks for striped bass, a principle species sought along the Northeast and mid-Atlantic coasts. But the developments and features that we

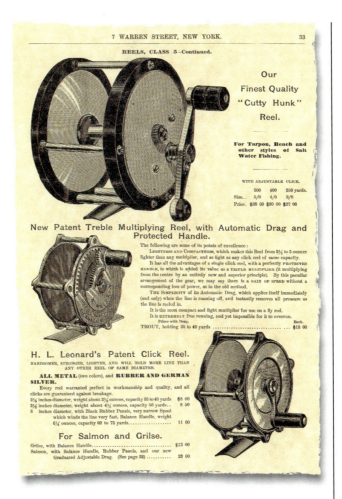

take for granted today were not so standard or obvious 100 or more years ago.

It wasn't easy being a manufacturer of saltwater reels in the mid-1800s, at

BELOW: **Top row (left to right):** Early raised pillar Julius Vom Hofe casting reel, late 1880s; larger size Hendricks raised pillar reel; Gayle casting reel by George W. Gayle and Son–this is a rare aluminum model weighing 3½ ounces with a cork arbor. **Middle row:** 1905 Meisselbach take-apart reel; Meek-Horton 2MJ model baitcasting reel with jeweled bearings from the late 1930s (the tournament model has a wider spool); Blue Grass Simplex Meek-Horton free spool bait-casting reel. **Bottom row:** Shakespeare Criteria model, rare left hand model; Pflueger Alpine model casting reel with leather pad for brake; South Bend with special anti-backlash bar control.

Reels 185

least according to Genio Scott in his 1869 book, *Fishing in American Waters.* Saltwater created its own problems for reel makers and fishermen, namely the corrosion of parts and the need to have a durable, reliable reel for landing the usually larger fish caught in the sea.

"Reels for this kind of fishing," Scott writes of fishing and casting bait for striped bass, "have taxed the ingenuity of the best fishing-tackle makers in the Union. The balance crank should be designed with the greatest nicety of proportions, to prevent a momentum hard to check with the thumb, and still the crank should not be so short as to be difficult in reeling. The crank should also be placed so far back and low on the end of the reel as to not endanger the fingers of the angler

ABOVE: *Some early reels came apart without screws. This early (ca 1920s) Meisselbach Tri-Part reels had side plates that unscrewed as shown to expose the mechanism for care and repair.*

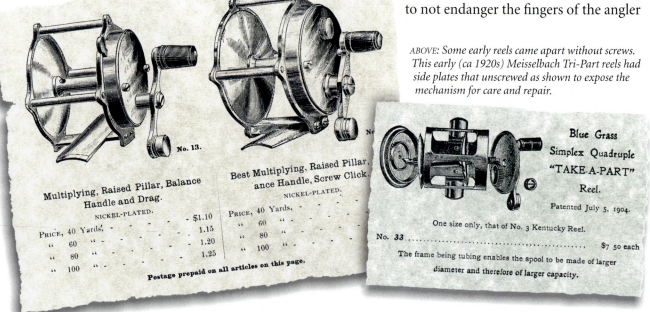

ABOVE: *Early reels. Left, a Meisselbach BakeLite reel from ca 1900. Right, a B. F. Meek & Sons Blue Grass #4 casting reel from ca 1890s.*

by a sudden strike of a heavy fish, for a bass does not, like the salmon, stop to study the cause of a pain in the jaw, but straightaway makes a run without hesitation. The best materials for reels are supposed to be German silver, brass or bell-metal. The wheels should run on jewels, and be so covered with an inner case as to protect them from saltwater. The reel should not be too long; the one represented on the plate of bassing implements indicates the shape. It should be a triple multiplier, without check or drag, and large enough to carry from two to three hundred yards of fine linen line." The jewels used were either agate or industrial rubies, with agate more expensive, yet preferred.

The above is a pretty good description of the requirements of a modern reel in some factors, woefully lacking in others. The 3:1 gear ratio is pretty good for most saltwater fishing, the line capacity good and the small crank or handle adequate. Today, the jeweled bearings would be improved and replaced by ball bearings. The lack of a check, anti-reverse and drag would be considered serious lapses today. The original drag seems to have been friction burns on the thumb!

Kentucky Reels from Snyder and Others

Seventeen towns in southwest and northcentral Kentucky proved to be the birth place of what we might call the modern casting multipliers—the highly collectible Kentucky reels. It was in Paris, KY, where silversmith and watchmaker George Snyder built the first multiplying reel made in the U.S. He made it for his own use, sometime between 1813 and 1820, for fishing in nearby Stoner Creek. He ultimately made about a dozen reels, with his sons

Reels 187

LEFT: Rows of reels show the differences in arbors over the years. Early reels had small arbors such as in the lower left, but gradually reels were changed to reduce the weight of the line that would cause inertial casting problems. Possibilities included cork arbors, hollow aluminum arbors and perforated hollow aluminum arbors such as on the Langley Target (upper row, second from left) and the modern Quantum Professional (upper right).

making a few more. There is confusion to this day over these few reels crafted by George and his sons John and Charles.

Some of the reels have markings (J & C Snyder) that indicate manufacture by the two sons. Census records of the time are not precise as to the names or numbers of Snyders in the area. There is also an indication from an English multiplier found in the area that Snyder might have used this English reel to make his refined model, although this in no way detracts from his accomplishment. His innovations included bushings and sometimes jewels for the bearings in the tail plate and head plate, where previously only holes in these plates held the spool axle. These bushings were also adjustable by screws to allow for wear and to reduce side-to-side play. He also used steel pinion gears and brass or steel main gears.

RIGHT: New York-style brass reel with a ball-handle made by John Conroy, ca 1845.

Although he started with gear ratios that were simple multipliers of each other (3:1 with 21 teeth on the main gear, and seven on the pinion), he ultimately realized that this would cause excessive wear on the teeth and went to odd-number gearing teeth such as 30 teeth in the main gear to seven teeth in the pinion (4.3:1 gear ratio) to allow for a "hunting tooth" to create more even gear wear as all teeth on one gear ultimately engage all teeth on the second gear.

Steven Vernon and Frank Stewart in their book, *Fishing Reel Makers of Kentucky,* list a total of 10 salient features for these reels, in addition to some favorable comments by James Henshall. These included, in addition to the above, positioning of the pillars to leave thumb space for line control, two-part head plates to hold the gearing, wide spool reels not unlike those of today and on/off push-button click spring controls.

Admittedly, because other reels were being made commercially in

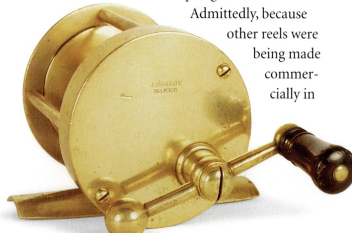

188   Our Fishing Heritage: Tackle & Equipment

New York by John Conroy and in Kentucky by Meeks, not all of these innovations can be traced directly to Snyder, but he did lay the foundation for American reels and innovations to follow.

Jonathan F. Meek and his brother Benjamin F. Meek, watch-repairmen and jewelers, made their first reel in their shop in Frankfort, KY, about 1836. They were joined a year later by 16-year-old apprentice Benjamin C. Milam. The first reel was a result of the insistence of a Judge John Brown that the Meeks make him a reel, for he was dissatisfied with currently available reels and had employed the Meeks for previous reel repair. The Meeks cut the gears on a cutting engine in Danville, and the resultant reel prompted so many requests from other fishermen that the Meeks sent to Switzerland for the appropriate tools for making reels.

By 1849 Milam had become a partner with the two brothers, but in 1852 the reel-making business failed. It had an output of about 75 reels from 1836 to the demise of the company 16 years later. These reels were similar in casual appearance to the Snyder reels, all with single (no counterbalance weight) crank, axle bushing, no level wind and wide, low spool.

In time, reels were offered of German silver or brass with brass and steel gears, polished (lapped) gears, buffalo horn or ivory grips. They were better and fancier than the original Snyders. An 1883 catalog shows that the German silver reels sold from $18 to $30, depending upon size; the brass reels sold for only a few dollars less. Meek Reels was eventually sold to William Carter and James

BELOW: *New York-style German silver reel with a serpentine crank made by Conroy, Bissett, & Malleson, 1876.*

LEFT: *This early and rare Kentucky Gayle reel was made of aluminum with the exception of the ivory handles. The arbor is very hard cork. On the inside of the frame are the engraved notations, "Hand made."*

O'Conner, who continued the company, retaining the high quality but slightly reducing the prices.

Gayle reels, built in Frankfort, KY, by George W. Gayle and his son Clarence, were supposedly made as early as 1882 or 1883, although no reels for these dates have been found. By 1889, they were advertised in Philadelphia tackle shops. These reels were similar to the earlier casting reels, with single, counterbalanced handles or double handles, improved gearing and the use of red, hard rubber for both the plates in some reels and also the grip. Because the reels continued into the 1930s, they also experimented with the then-new plastic Bakelite. They also made a few of aluminum, then a relatively new material for manufacturing. A circa 1890 to 1900 aluminum Gayle reel weighed only 3½ ounces. Other minor Kentucky reel makers such as Conery, Conroy, Dalton, Fullilove, Deally, Sage, Medley and others abounded in the area and continued to make reels well into the new century. At the same time, Julius and Edward Vom Hofe were making larger reels, primarily for saltwater fishing.

LEFT: *German silver and hard rubber saltwater reel made by Julius vom Hofe and incorporating a clutch patented in 1895 by Frederick Wilkie.*

190   *Our Fishing Heritage: Tackle & Equipment*

The Golden Age of Early Casting Reels

Around and after the turn of the century, along with the continuation of some of the classic Kentucky reels, other companies—Heddon, South Bend, Shakespeare, Pflueger and others—got into the business. These reels were built along the lines set by the earlier Kentucky reel makers, but now were concerned more with assembly-line production for the mass market along with improvements in drags, anti-backlash or control devices and similar mechanisms.

Because reels were now used for casting bait and, later, lures, early attempts were made to control the over-running of line, that is, backlash. One of the earliest of these was a centrifugal brake from 1892 in a Bean level-wind reel, in which a brake block on the spool was thrown against a flange to cause friction and slowing of the spool. The principle, although not the mechanism, was the same as that used with the radial arms containing brake blocks featured on modern centrifugal cast-control reels.

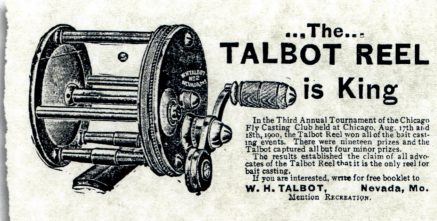

WHERE HAVE ALL THE REELS GONE? (RODS AND LURES TOO!)

When the author visited the Shakespeare plant in Columbia, SC, some years ago, the company had been bought by the Anthony Company, a manufacturer, then and now, of swimming pools. During a conversation with one of the executives, it was revealed that Shakespeare had kept early models, prototypes, examples of different reels, rods and lures, storing them for safe keeping in the plant in four large wood boxes on four wood pallets. They were stored on high shelves to prevent their misuse or any misunderstanding of their importance.

During one of the changes that take place in all companies and manufacturing plants periodically, an Anthony executive decided that the wood boxes took up space that could be better used for manufacturing and inventory purposes. As a result, most of this historical treasure trove—reels, early bamboo and fiberglass rods, early Henry Shakespeare rods built with the first balsa cores, presentation rods with gold fittings and guides, prototypes of early reels, original lures in their boxes with spec sheets and instructions, patents, notes and history—was taken to the trash compactor outside the plant. Some few reels were saved, along with some lures, but most were irretrievably lost. So much for history and an appreciation of the past, according to verification by two Shakespeare executives, neither of whom was around when the carnage took place.

Reels

ATTACHMENTS FOR REELS

Throughout history, inventors have always come up with after-market ideas to add to reels that would presumably make them better. One of the earliest of these was the leather thumb brake that through clips would fasten onto the horizontal bar of any reel to provide thumb protection when casting and when fighting fish. Not a reel accessory, but for the same purpose, thumb stalls or guards that were like a leather glove for the thumb, with a wrist strap to keep from losing it, were also popular, particularly with surf casters of the 1940s using revolving wide-spool reels.

With the advent of the level-wind reel came the additions that would convert any reel into a level-winding model. In 1905 the A. W. Bishop & Son sold a separate spooling device that could be attached to any reel and used a worm gear to move a line guide back and forth in front of the spool. The $1 1908 Ross Thumb Spooler spooled line by means of a thumb-operated lever, the whole device easily adjusted to any reel and attached to any rod, so said the ad. The 1909 Sportsman's Supply Co. Frictionless Spooler appears to have been attached to the reels under the reel foot and would flip down and out of the way for frictionless casting. In the up position, the line would run over a pulley, which would spool back and forth through a worm gear.

Replacement handles from companies other than the reel manufacturers were sometimes available. The Gator Grip Company made replacement handles of several styles (including a short-lived four-handled model) for the popular reels of the time, including Abu Garcia Ambassadeurs, Daiwa Millionaires and others. One different type of handle was the "cub" handle, in which the drag was adjusted to a prescribed setting by means of screws that controlled pressure on the handle-mounted drag plates.

Gator Grip also manufactured a clip-on thumb bar that would work like a factory model, through an extension that would depress the side-mounted push button. Berkley made a similar item for a short period. Caps to cover the left side plate of casting reels for more comfortable palming (before the days of the smooth, left side plates) were manufactured by Bumble Bee. They also made a V groove line cutter that would attach to the right side plate by means of the thumb screw. Some reel companies made different handle designs for their reels, such as the three that were available for the 1949 Aero Cast casting reel. Currently, some after-market handles—often larger and longer than the factory handles and called power handles—are sold for casting reels.

Line counters (both analog and digital) are included in some trolling reels, but there have always been a few that could be added to the rod or reel after purchase to count line. They work by the line going around a pulley, the revolutions of the pulley counting the line yardage.

Both original equipment manufacturers and after-market companies have made separate gear kits for higher-speed reeling (speed gears), V spools for easier casting, drag kits for better drag control and manual conversion kits to switch spinning reels from a full bail to manual (often for surf casting).

Some companies, such as Accurate, supply special anodized aluminum frames as replacement for standard reels (usually saltwater), and others, such as Electric Fishing Reels Systems and Fish-Ng, make electric attachments to fit reels (often Penn, for saltwater fishing).

Perhaps the first level-wind mechanism was found on the Milwaukee reel, invented by Nelson McGregor and his partner Cornelius Wheeler and patented in 1894. Later patents by this same team improved the device with a gear train to move the level wind more efficiently.

Another feature, developed in 1907 and used mostly on South Bend reels, was patented by the inventor, Henry Baumgartel. It consisted of a free-swinging bar on the front (forward) part of the reel, under which the line ran. During a cast, the tension of the weight on the line raised the bar, but slack line or at end of the cast would drop the bar to allow a brake block to rub against the spool flange to slow the reel. This concept could be found on South Bend reels in their 1912 catalog, and it continued on reels well into the 1950s.

Ironically, level-wind mechanisms were not found on the popular and classic Kentucky reels, despite the fact that the method for accomplishing this was known. In 1860, Mark Palmer was issued a patent for a level-wind mechanism that would be right at home on the most modern of reels. It has the endless groove worm gear, a slotted bar or pawl that rode in the groove of the gear and the sloping vertical line guides to tack the line continuously back and forth. However, this did not seem to gain wide popularity until the 1910s, along with the friction spool control, which South Bend introduced then. Naturally, this could create problems in slowing the line during a cast when long casts were desired, but patents took care of that also.

A 1906 patent used the basic level-wind system but had a line guide that flared into a wide ring at the top (the two arms flared out to make a ring), so that when the level wind was flipped forward, the line would have a large ring through which to travel, rather than the close-

ABOVE: Wm. Shakespeare, Jr., Co. Model C, with the level wind patented by Shakespeare.

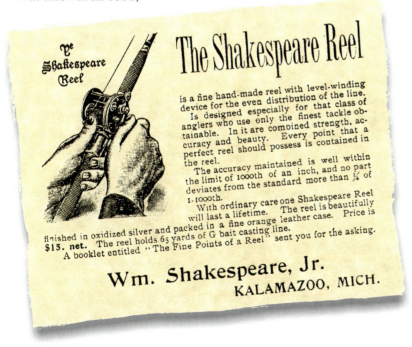

Reels 193

ABOVE: *Shown in both a photo (reel ca 1918) and an ad (from 1926) is the Pflueger "Supreme," one of the most successful baitcasting reels ever made. The unusual level wind automatically lifts the line into the guide after a cast.*

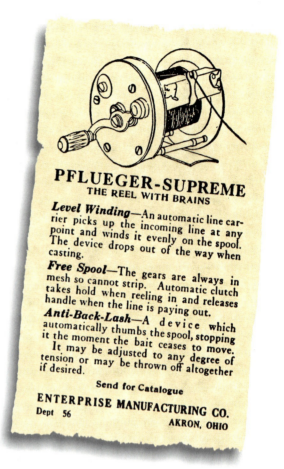

positioned bars of the line guide. This was used on American Co. reels; Shakespeare made a prototype using this concept; and Ocean City used it on their surf-casting Inductor and Farcaster models in the 1940s.

Although the Kentucky period of reel making was over, the new models made it possible for more anglers to afford a reel and, thanks to mass production, to easily obtain one. The popular tackle companies of above, along with Coxe, Bronson, later Langley, Horrocks-Ibbotson and others, did produce some top-of-the-line reels. Horton Manufacturing Co, purchased Meek in 1916. One of the best known was the Pflueger Supreme, with a well chosen name, since it reigned supreme in the minds of many anglers from its debut in 1918 and a more modern version developed in 1927.

194   *Our Fishing Heritage: Tackle & Equipment*

Fly Reels Defined and Described

Though fly reels had been around since there were any reels, according to most accounts, they varied widely in type, spool width and retrieve method (multiplying vs. single action). Generally, Charles F. Orvis is given credit for creating in 1874 the narrow spool, upright model that we see as the true roots of the fly reels of today. Prior to that, fly reels were often of the side-mounted Billinghurst style, followed by the hard-rubber side-mounted Gem reels. But Orvis might be receiving too much credit. Some prior fly reels were side-mounted and wide-spooled, but there were also single-action upright models that, though not narrow spooled, would not be that much different from some of the wide-spool models required for greater line capacity and, until recently, used for Atlantic salmon fishing. Popular wide-spool fly reels included those by Leonard, Chubb, Pflueger and Vom Hofe. Even then there were debates about single action vs. multipliers for fly fishing, with Theophilus South writing in 1841 (*Fly Fisher's Text Book*) that multipliers were fine for trout, not so good for salmon. William Scrope in his book, *Days and Nights of Salmon Fishing,* 1843, echoes that second statement by noting his multipliers getting jerky and unable to wind in line when inadvertently hooking a salmon while fishing for trout.

So-called "contracted" reels—those being high and narrow, as opposed to

ABOVE: *Single-action fly reels have stayed very similar over the years. Left, an early Shakespeare Russell reel, model 1884 GA, from ca 1915. Center, an unidentified fly reel with raised pillars and on/off click. Right, a modern Scientific Anglers Mastery Series reel, model 45, from the late 1990s.*

Reels 195

BELOW: *Orvis fly reel with a narrow, perforated frame, patented in 1874. This was the immediate forerunner of the modern fly reel.*

more standard reels that were low and wide—were well established in England by the 1830s. South refers to upright single-action reels "very narrow between the plates," and large diameter to take up as much line as a single-action reel will allow.

Scrope even notes that after his experience with multipliers on salmon, he ordered some contracted reels, insisting that "the cylinders should be of a very ample circumference, which gives the same advantage that a multiplying reel has with the usual cylinder."

This was obviously thought of and done prior to the publication dates of 1841 and 1843 respectively, indicating that the English thought of the narrow, upright single-action reel for fly fishing first. At the very least, similar ideas were offered from both sides of the pond, albeit Orvis' being 30 years later. This also points out the advantages of a large circumference reel, recognized again just recently with the large arbor concept.

With the upright reel came the standard pawl/click mechanism. Some were fixed, some adjustable to use as a light, though jerky drag.

Spinning Developed Earlier Than We Thought

Though we might think of spinning as entering the U.S. after WWII, in reality, the earliest imports were in 1935. The Luxor reel was imported from France then by Bache Brown. Even earlier, the first reels with the open-face spinning concept were made about the turn of the century. Yet, even earlier, the truly first reel to use the spinning concept was designed in the U.S. in Baltimore, MD, as a closed-face spinning reel that allowed casting off of the end of the spool and retrieving by rotating the spool as you would a revolving-spool baitcasting reel. The Winans & Whistler rod and reel (it was a combined deal) was patented on March 23, 1875, and designed to prevent the then-current problem of backlash in the developing sport of casting. The patent exists, although no rod/reel combo has been found. The patent shows a reel that looks remarkably like the side-casting flat-cased close-face spinning reels that would be widely marketed in the early- to mid-1950s.

Because this patent presumably went nowhere, the scene shifts to England with the early Holding, patented on November 28, 1878. The reel was an open-face spinning reel, but one that, unlike modern reels, mounted on the top of the rod. It was a simple spool on a reel foot that allowed a 90-degree pivot to present the face forward when casting. It allowed the line to come off in coils, the reel turning on the foot for retrieving by turning a handle on the revolving spool. It was, in essence, a wood reel (wood reels were called Nottinghams) with the above modifications. This was followed by the Perth, Scotland, Malloch reel of 1884 that pivoted like the Holding, but had a large ring (like a guide ring) on an arm that extended a few inches in front of the spool when casting.

The first reel to hang under the rod, as with modern spinning tackle, was the "rustic" reel of Viscount Henry de France. The spool remained in one position during both cast and retrieve, but retrieve required a large hook, like a crocheting needle, to spool the line back on the reel. Although crocheting in a hooked fish was an awful nuisance, the hooked needle was the precursor of the pick-up arm/bail and the line roller.

The Illingworth reel was next, ironically called in patent applications a "baitcasting reel." The patent was granted on January 4, 1906. The origi-

ABOVE: *The 1960's Italian Holliday reel had only a manual pick up, but the screw-off removable rotors allowed spools to be changed and interchanged. Here, both reel sizes are shown.*

BELOW LEFT: *Wooden British "Nottingham" reel, ca 1885.*

BELOW RIGHT: *Early "Sidecaster" by Peter Malloch, a Scot who popularized the spinning reel. The spool swiveled 90° between casting and retrieving positions. Malloch began his work in 1884.*

Reels 197

nal evolved through several models, but it basically looked and almost worked like the hand drills of years ago. A large wheel was turned with a handle, and bevel gears then rotated a primitive bail to pick up the line that went around the forward-facing stationary spool. The spool also went back and forth in a reciprocating action, much like modern reels. Later Illingworths looked very much like modern reels, with large spools, small gear housing, and a foot and post that allowed mounting under the reel. The half bail (pick-up arm) was introduced with the 1919 Illingsworth; the first full bail on a spinning reel was featured on the 1934/35 Hardy.

Not everyone was enthused about the new method of being able to cast light lures, particularly in those early days when skill, ethics and sportsmanship were considered paramount over simple buy-it-and-use-it technology. "The Illingworth reel seems to put the trout at the mercy of the man who is out to kill and is not keen enough on the sport to take the trouble to learn the difficult part of the game," wrote Eric Taverner in his 1929 English book, *Trout Fishing From All Angles*. "'Minnow-gun' it was aptly called by an angler of my acquaintance and not without reason! It puts the minnow anywhere it is asked and anyone after half an hour's practice can do it. He simply pulls the trigger; the minnow goes in and the trout comes out! It is a useful method of removing trout undesirably large for the river, but it is liable to misuse in unscrupulous hands," Taverner concludes. Naturally, that same simplicity of modern spinning and spincast reels is often what keeps more people trying and enjoying the sport, although concerns about conservation and sportsmanship still exist.

From the Illingworth, it was a short jump to the reels that were improved, modified and advanced through the early part of the century. Reels shifted from on top of the rod to underneath, hanging there as do modern open-face reels. The manual roller (you had to pick up the line to place it on or remove it from the roller for retrieving or casting), the pick-up arm and the full bail were debated for years, with the full bail ultimately gaining total support only after the 1950s.

Ultralight Spinning

Ultralight spinning might seem to be a redundancy, since spinning was designed to cast small lures impossible to throw with baitcasting tackle, yet too heavy for fly gear. The first UL reel might have been the #3 Illingworth, weighing 6½ ounces. The first

ABOVE: *Spinning reels from different periods include clockwise from upper right; the Fix reel with full bail, the Ashaway Slip Cast spinning reel that mounted on top of the rod, Ocean City 350 with metal half bail on front of spool and Luxor spinning reel with full bail. Center, a large Shakespeare saltwater Sea Wonder spinning reel.*

BELOW: *German silver and hard rubber trolling reel made by Edward vom Hofe, ca 1900.*

modern UL reel was the Italian-made UL Cargem Mignon 33, which also had a skirted spool, long before others. This was followed by the popular Alcedo Micron. Other reels followed, but eventually the UL fell slightly out of favor. It came back into popularity recently, however, with tiny reels from most of the major companies debuting in the 1990s. The smallest of these currently are the 4.8 ounce Silstar TF-20 and the Pinnacle T-2. Both hold 90 yards of four-pound-test line. The Silstar model features three ball bearings; the Pinnacle has three shielded ball bearings and a titanium spool lip.

Early Trolling Reels: No Drag, Lots of Muscle

Early trolling and still-fishing conventional reels for saltwater were simply oversize winches or multipliers with more line capacity. They were often larger reels, wide-spooled for greater line capacity, geared and frequently featuring a click. They also often offered a leather brake drag. It had become obvious that large fish would not easily come to gaff, and that one of the main purposes of the reel was for line capacity that allowed the fish to run and tire itself. So, some sort of drag was imperative. At first, this was often nothing more than a fitted (or aftermarket attached) strip of leather on clips that fitted to the rear reel pillar. The patent for this was 1905 and was initially used by Pflueger on its reels, later by other companies. This allowed thumb pressure on the spool as the fish took line. These were also used on some freshwater reels.

Reels 199

Trolling Reel Developments

The concept of a drag to slow fish took on greater importance with saltwater fishermen fishing out of places such as the California Catalina Tuna Club. Earlier attempts (from 1864 on) of making a drag with a couple of frictional washers or the Wm. Mills used ratchet and pawl or drag washers between the handle and crankshaft (which later became popular as the Pflueger "Cub" handle and also used on an Ocean City reel) were all tried and used on some early reels. Centrifugal force brakes, spider arms with brake pads and other devices were invented, each with advantages, all with a method of disengaging when line was being retrieved and most with an anti-reverse mechanism to keep the handle from turning when line was being taken out.

In 1902 Vom Hofe patented his "Adjustable Friction Drag" that did not at first include the now-ubiquitous star-shaped adjustment wheel. It did, however, have the main gear sandwiched between the drag plates. Reels with these early drags used a key that was inserted into a hole in the sideplate to adjust the drag friction. Accounts of the star-drag system vary widely, as detailed in *Antique Fishing Reels,* by Steven K. Vernon. The accounts all basically note that the design came from big-game angler William Boschen and that, over the years, there were features from patents of Julius Vom Hofe, J. A. Coxe, George Farnsworth (boat captain and fishing companion of Boschen) and others that helped develop the standard drag that made it possi-

ABOVE: *Star drag on Pflueger model #1995 Summit casting reel, in which the free spool button is in the center of the star drag mechanism and which also has a small compartment (upper screw on sideplate) to hold a spare level wind pawl.*

LEFT: *A B. C. Milam & Son reel, Model #3, ca 1900. It is also marked "The Frankfort Kentucky Reel" in an arc above the name.*

ble to land large fish in saltwater and is a basic of most freshwater casting reels today. Some early saltwater big-game reels, such as the expensive but excellent Kovalovsky from the late 1930s, were huge. They featured massive drags, and some fit into a cradle system on special rods, instead of using reel feet that fastened to reel seats.

In the early part of the century, more companies (such as Ocean City, Penn and, in 1933, Fin-Nor) got into the saltwater market. Otto Henze of Penn developed the concept of four bridge screws to hold the reel together, making cleaning, maintenance and disassembly easy, thus revolutionizing reel servicing. This went even further in the late 1930s with the popular surf-casting Penn Squidder that featured a one-screw take-apart system for instant repairs or spool changes. The Penn Senators came into being in the 1940s with star drags, offering a range of sizes for any saltwater fishing. The popular Fin-Nor trolling reels of the 1930s included sizes up to a huge 15/0 model. These were followed by the lever-drag Penn Internationals of the mid-1960s. They were followed by two-speed reels with different gearing for different fishing. Other companies featured this also, including Fin-Nor and Shimano, which today also have two-speed (geared) trolling reels. In any of these, the high-speed gearing makes it possible to gain line rapidly, while the low speed gearing makes it possible to retrieve line against resistance.

Most of these reels, particularly in large sizes, had no level-wind mechanism, although one Penn model did have a unique spiraled flat bar as a level wind. The line ran over and contacted with the chromed spiral bar that was geared to turn so that it pushed the line alternately back and forth, side to side. There were no vertical line guides as on freshwater reels.

Fly Reels Stay Simple

You could almost say that there were no changes in fly reels from the 1874 upright narrow-spool model of Charles Orvis to those of today. The simple, narrow, upright direct-drive reel with one or two click drives is still available from a few-dozen manufacturers for light panfish and trout. The only additions to some modern reels may be a modern drag of disc, drum, caliper or arbor style. In fact through about the 1960s, fly reels, other than those for saltwater and big game, continued with the pillar and post method of construction. Only in the last several decades can we find reels of cast aluminum with the frame molded into one piece for both strength, durability and assembly cost savings. It was also in the 1960s that the rim control fly reels came into being with the most popular reels of the time, the new (Hardy made) Scientific Anglers System reels. Soon after, almost all reel companies were making at least some reel models with a palming rim.

During this period, there were some changes in fly reels, such as the multipliers of Martin, the magnetic Johnson that was widely used by Joe Brooks in the 1960s and the evolution of the anti-reverse reel.

ABOVE: *Fly reels.* **Top row (left to right):** *Martin automatic fly reel 1905, raised pillar; St. Joe by South Bend; Vernley by Horrocks-Ibbotson reel made of Bakelite; Hawthorne single action reel with drag system.* **Second row:** *Shakespeare Tru-Art automatic fly reel; Pflueger 1495 Medalist; wedding-cake style Fin-Nor; Pflueger 578 Supreme saltwater fly reel.* **Third row:** *Multiplier by Daiwa (made by English J.W. Young); Abel #1; anti-reverse big game Penn International.*

LEFT: *Brass fly reel made by the Terry Clock Company, ca 1880.*

ABOVE: *Automatic fly reels came in both vertical and horizontal styles. Left, a vertical mount Ocean model #90 automatic fly reel in black finish, ca 1940s. Right, horizontal mount Martin model #28 automatic fly reel in silver finish, ca 1930s.*

The last had a handle separate from the reel spool and drag, enabling a fish to take line without the grip turning wildly and busting knuckles. Multipliers continued to be made by Martin, and some few were manufactured or imported by other companies. In the 1980s, Daiwa had a very nice multiplier that was made by J. W. Young of England. Then there were the automatics!

Automatic Fly Reels

Automatic fly reels are just that: reels with a built-in spring that will retrieve line when activated by a lever arm. One of the first of these was made by Yawman & Erbe Company of Rochester, NY, with its Y&E reels, patented in 1880. The basic design then is not unlike those of today. The earliest, however, used a key to wind up the spring. Today, automatic reels, mostly by Martin, have the spring wound by turning the outside casing. All of the reels have the spring activated by use of a lever

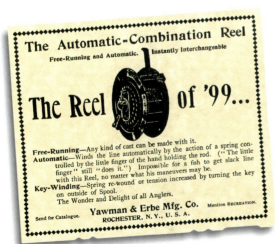

Reels 203

arm controlled by the little finger. Y&E reels eventually were marketed by Horrocks-Ibbotson in 1920. Kelso, Smith, Carlton, Meisselbach and others produced automatic fly reels in this early period. The most popular automatic fly reels were made by the Martin Fishing Reel Company, which also made single-action and multiplying fly reels. Their patents on these reels began in 1892, and they made their reels in several sizes and shapes. In the 1940s, most of the automatic fly reels were still "flat"—not upright—and were made by not only Martin but also Perrine, Shakespeare, South Bend, Heddon, Horrocks-Ibbotson, Utica, Wolverine, Ocean City and others.

One variation of the above during the 1940s and continuing into recent times was the P&K Re-Treeve-It reel that used a lever to spin the spool to retrieve line, rather than a spring. It was a simple concept, yet the reel was not so easy to use, because activating the lever to spin in enough line with the little finger was awkward at best. The Fly Champ of the same 1940 period looked and worked similarly.

In the late 1980s and early 1990s an automatic fly reel from France featured a motor-operated system for retrieving line that used two AA batteries.

Spinning Captures Anglers' Fancy Around WWII

Spinning did not really become popular in the U.S. until after the Second World War, but there were early inroads of the tackle before the war years. Perhaps the first spinning reels reached this country in 1935 with the Luxor, and the first small books mentioning it were published in 1941. *Bait Casting for the Novice and the Expert* was a small, 92-page bound book published by *Outdoor Life* magazine in 1941. Despite the name, it had several pages on spin-

ABOVE: *Line pick up on spinning reels varied, particularly in the post World War II "early days" of the sport. Left, a full bail pick up (as used on most modern reels) on a French Pezon & Michel Luxor reel. Center, a pick up arm (sometimes called a half-bail) on a French Depose Ru-Sport. Right, a manual pick up (no bail or arm and not automatic) on a Spanish Sangarra spinning reel.*

204 *Our Fishing Heritage: Tackle & Equipment*

ning, then called "thread-line spinning." The reel is the basis of spinning (you can spin, awkwardly with a spinning reel and casting rod, but not with a casting reel and spinning rod), but the five brief pages devoted to this aspect of the sport (and not really baitcasting) make it a little confusing. "The spool of this reel is fixed and does not revolve," it states. "This spool is placed at right angles to the rod, and the line flows off of it smoothly and evenly. An ingenious pickup is thrown on for the cast, and with the completion of the cast automatically picks up the line directly the angler begins to wind in the retrieve. A metal finger automatically spools the line in such a manner that it will flow out easily again with the next cast. This reel is very light and is multiplying. The whole operation of the reel is simpler than can be described." Well, I guess so, since I would hate to learn spinning from these directions alone. A single photo in the back of the book shows a Luxor reel, but not any step-by-step or close-up casting instructions.

Spinning, another small 1941 book (31 pages), by Bache Brown, may be the first published here devoted exclusively to the sport. It does have casting photos (ironically courtesy of *Outdoor Life*) and does have step-by-step photos of the reel operation during casting and retrieving. It again uses a half-bail Luxor reel. So new was this method to the American angler that the book describes the function as being similar to that of firing a harpoon or breeches buoy line, which flows off the end of a drum to reduce friction and backlash. Features desirable then were the star drag for line control and a gear ratio of at least 3.5:1.

Reels immediately after WWII included those by Bache Brown, Airex, Mitchell, Luxor and others. Ironically, the 1946 *Fishing Tackle Digest* only included spinning reels, although it did

TOP: *Spinning reels showing different sizes of spools and types of bails.* **Clockwise from lower left-hand corner:** *Garcia Cap, Airex Vic, Ocean City 300, Staro, Pecos Luxe, Fix-Reel, Ashaway Slip Cast and Johnson spinning reel.*

ABOVE: *Some reels, like these Daiwas from the 1970s, featured reels that could only be fitted onto special rods that would take the through-bolt feature as shown.*

include listings of baitcasting, fly and automatic fly fishing tackle along with a brief article on spinning. The third edition of 1952 did include reels by the above companies, along with those by Alcedo, Bradco, Fix, Cap, Bristol, Pelican, Record, Ru and others in open-face spinning style. It also featured closed-face reels from Johnson, Humphreys, Fre-Line, Good-All, and an Ashaway Slip Cast and others. These closed-face reels were often used on top of baitcast rods and underneath fly rods.

The open-face spinning reels were best characterized by the Mitchell 300 (from France) that first was available with a pick-up arm (half bail), then later with a full bail. Reels of the time were also made without any pick-up mechanism and with a manual roller that required removing the line from the roller for casting and replacing it there for line retrieval.

More reels followed, including a mix of those made in this country and imported from abroad. Reels by Airex, Martin, Langley, Ocean City, Orvis, Record, Fix, Heddon, Garcia, Centaure, Shakespeare, Waltco and others became popular. There were innovations tried, such as the Waltco of all Dupont nylon to prevent any rust or corrosion. Unfortunately the nylon gears did not hold up for the long haul, and the metal screws and bail did eventually rust.

ABOVE: Spinning reels. **Clockwise from top left:** 2062 Shakespeare, Shakespeare Norris, Pflueger Pelican, 2068 Shakespeare spinning reel and 301 Mitchell.

Spincast Makes It Easy and Makes New Anglers

Closed-face spinning reels in which the line came off the face of the spool, the spool contained in a shield or cone, were initially not unlike the Winans & Whistler of 1875. Most of these were narrow, side mounted, advertised for both baitcasting and spinning and fitted on top of a standard baitcasting rod. Models available in the mid-1940s included the Wright & McGill Fre-Line, the Humphreys, Good-All, Johnson and others.

The big innovation and change in the industry came about when R. D. Hull walked into the Zero Hour Bomb Company (which became Zebco) with an idea for a forward-facing spool in a nose cone that would work like spinning, but without the problems of open-face reels and yet would solve the baitcasters backlash problem.

Actually, Shakespeare had a spinning reel prior to Zebco, made in Canada, but the thought by the executives was that it was too different and would not be popular.

The Zero Hour Bomb Company had been making time bombs for use with

dynamite in oil well "shooting," but it also had some government military contracts. With the combination of the war ending and its patents expiring, the company looked for new products. Hull convinced the company of the merits of the idea, signed a contract and worked for the next year on a prototype. Five of the first "Standard" reels came off the production line on May 7, 1949. (The tale is that they kept the company name, until a salesman had the company send one to President Eisenhower, upon which alert Secret Service agents dumped the package from the "bomb" company into a bucket of water to wait for the bomb disposal unit. Eisenhower did eventually get his reel. In 1950 the product name was shortened to Zebco, and in 1958 the corporate name was changed to this also.)

The idea was that the new spincast reel was so easy to use (Taverner would not be pleased!) that anyone could

ABOVE LEFT: *The first three Zebco spincasting models had a "ball" on the back for thumb control as the reel's anti-reverse.*

ABOVE: *The Zebco 33 was introduced in 1954. It was still called a "spinning reel" and sold for $19.50.*

Reels 207

ROD/REEL COMBINATIONS

Rods with built in reels also surfaced in the late 1930s and through the early 1950s. One of the most popular was the Hurd Super Caster, which featured a magnesium/aluminum alloy frame, checkered handle pistol grip on the rod, and interchangeable spring steel tips. The reel was a level-wind baitcasting model, with thumb-levered casting control. The similar, but less expensive, Hurd Caster, did not have the thumb-activated casting control. Other companies of the same period with the same idea and one piece casting reel/rod combos included Kerr, Stream Liner, Benson and Premax.

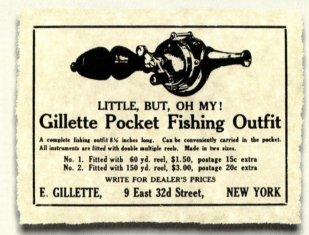

Earlier tackle makers used the same concept. The first spinning or spincast reel was an all-in-one rod and reel combination—the 1875 Winans and Whistler. George Hancock in 1880 patented a reel built into a rod handle, while the same idea but different design was patented in 1865 by a William M. Stewart. The Whirlaway from Great Lakes Products in 1950 was a rod/reel combo in which the closed-face spinning reel was at the end of the rod (like fly tackle), with the line coming out the front and through a line guide on the rod.

LEFT: *Popeil Pocket Fisherman was never embraced by serious anglers, but was a popular merchandising item that incorporates a rod and reel. Many rod and reel combinations, both standard length and collapsible, have existed over the years.*

master it immediately. Astute salesmen and manufacturers' representatives immediately used this to their advantage, by casting it while wearing boxing gloves, having a monkey cast it, casting it with a slingshot and establishing a world record for the number of consecutive casts without a backlash.

Other companies hastened to get into the market, many sticking to the basic design, but some making under-rod-models that could be used with a spinning rather than a casting rod. One example was the 1951 South Bend Spin Cast with Carboloy line pick-up pin and easy takedown. Garcia later made a similar under-rod closed-face spinning reel. The Zebco model 33 was introduced in 1954 and, with improvements, continues to be made today. Along the way, heavier models have been made, some for light saltwater, and many with a star-drag system for improved control of fish.

Spinning in the Surf and Saltwater

With the realization that spinning prevented backlashes, some of the biggest reels were produced for surf and saltwater fishing. These were not really different from the smaller freshwater and light saltwater reels, other than for some considerations for corrosion and rust, larger spool size for greater line capacity of the heavier lines used and better drags. One problem with the surf reels was that the sharp snap of the long cast would snap close the bail, ruining the cast, if the bail operated on a simple

ABOVE: *Some spincast reels were made to fit under the rod for use with a standard spinning rod, instead of on top of the rod for use with a baitcast-style rod. These examples include, left to right, a South Bend Spin Cast #1600, Quantum MT1 Micro, Bronson 63L and Shakespeare 35U.*

LEFT: *Over the years, spinning reels have used both front (in spool) and rear (in reel housing) drag systems. Here, a front drag is shown on a 1960s Herter's reel (top) and a rear drag on a Zebco Cardinal #3, manufactured by Ambassadeur in Sweden.*

rollers only (no bail or pick-up arm) to prevent possible problems.

Bigger and bigger catches, mostly in saltwater, were being made with spinning tackle. A. J. McClane caught a 44 pound barracuda in 1951 on an Alcedo 2C/S, using a ⅜-ounce plug. Other notable early catches include the 1955 catch by Costa Aronis of a 65-pound California sea bass and a 61-pound 10-ounce striped bass caught in 1956 by Leo Garceau. Today, of course, spinning tackle is used on offshore boats when trolling for marlin, shark, wahoo and dolphin.

In time, by the late 1960s and early 1970s, big spinning reels were being used for offshore trolling for big game, often with 20-pound-test and heavier monofilament, and stiff, seven-foot spinning rods. On long casts, it was felt that some friction might occur against the cup of the rotor as the line flowed off the spool, so in 1970, Daiwa introduced the skirted-spool concept to spinning reels. This eliminated the cup, and a rear-facing covering protected the rotor and reciprocating spool shaft.

rocker-type spring mechanism. This was also a problem with some of the smaller reels. Consequently, early reels were made so that by opening the bail, you would lock the bail open. You could not snap it closed until you turned the handle, releasing the bail. This also led to some anglers using reels with manual

210 *Our Fishing Heritage: Tackle & Equipment*

Another improvement occurred in 1980 with the development of the graphite spinning reel, often with complete graphite housing and sometimes graphite spool as well. By the late 1990s some spools were being made of tough ABS plastic, instead of aluminum or graphite. Ironically, these graphite reels were best suited for the larger reels, since the graphite, being weaker than cast aluminum previously used, required more material for equivalent strength. In small reels, this just made the housing, posts and reel feet too bulky, so that small reels, even in a given series of "graphite" reels, were often still metal.

Spinning Changes Over the Decades

Shimano, Daiwa, Penn, Quantum, Abu Garcia, Shakespeare, Silstar, Pinnacle, South Bend and, more recently, Marado, Van Staal, Fin-Nor and others all made small but vitally important changes and improvements over the last several decades. In the 1970s, the drag, previously in the front with stacked drag washers in the spool, was shifted to a similar system on the spool shaft in the rear of the gear housing. This continued, along with some reels with front drag, for the next two decades. A new trend is with an Abu Garcia center-positioned (rotor) drag system.

The rear drag also made it easier to develop the pop-off spools that allowed instant easy change of a spool for new line or another pound-test line, without changing the drag setting (in the rear).

Shimano developed the BaitRunner reel, shortly copied by Ryobi, Zebco, and Abu Garcia in some of their reels. This innovation incorporated both a rear and front drag, with the front drag the "main" drag, and preset to fight the

ABOVE: *Dual drag reels for bait fishing were made by Shimano, Abu Garcia and Zebco. This Shimano 3500 BaitRunner shows the light-tension rear drag for controlling line while bait fishing. A front drag for fighting fish was located in the spool, as with most front drag reels.*

Reels 211

fish; the rear drag a very light drag (which could also be adjusted) to allow a fish to take out line when picking up a bait. The rear bait drag allowed bait or still-fishing with the bail closed, and the drag was light enough to not alarm the fish. Switching the rear bait drag off shifted the action to the front drag to strike and fight the fish.

The automatic casting feature came into being in the 1970s and consisted of an arm that when lifted by the finger would open the bail. The arm was positioned to allow lifting the line with the index finger at the same time as lifting the arm to permit one-hand casting. No longer did you have to use the other hand to open the bail. It was a feature equivalent to the thumb bar of casting, which also allowed one-hand casting. This reached culmination with the Quantum Hypercast of 1993 that incorporated a pin to pick up the line as the arm lifted the bail open—eliminating the necessity of engaging the line with the index finger.

By the mid-1980s, companies were switching from the shallow, large-diameter spool to those that were deeper front to back and smaller diameter—the so-called long-casting spools. Most companies went to this design and are still using it. In the 1980s, more and more ball bearings were being used in reels of all types, especially spinning reels, with ball bearing races used on the line roller, handle shaft supports, reciprocating shaft supports, bails, etc. Better reels today also have recently (mid-1990s) introduced

AUSTRALIAN AND ALVEY REELS

Side-casting reels, like the early Holding and Malloch, retained popularity in some areas. The Australian Alvey uses the same principle, that of turning the reel so that the face of the spool is forward for casting, as a spinning reel, and rotating the spool 90 degrees to retrieve it like a bait caster. It was developed with large diameter spools for the long casts necessary from Australian beaches.

From the 1960s through the present, they have also been imported to the U.S., where they have a small, but devoted, following. The problem with this basic design is that the repeated shift from spinning to revolving-spool mode will rapidly twist the line.

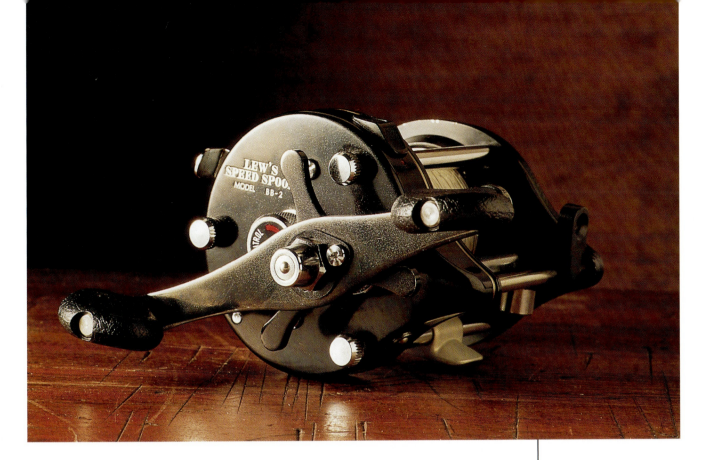

TOP: The Lew's Speed Spool BB-1 was a radical departure from the basically round-sideplate reels of the 1950s and 1960s. It heralded the way for the low-profile tear-drop-shape reels many companies made from the 1970s through the 1990s. (This photo shows a similar BB-2 model.)

infinite or constant anti-reverse, in place of the previous system of using a pawl and gear teeth to which the reel spool would back up on a strike. The result is less strain on the reel and gearing.

Casting Reels Change After WWII

Casting reels stayed basically the same through the mid-century, although constant improvements were being made. Around 1950, Langley introduced lightweight aluminum casting reels that had a wide, hollow, perforated aluminum arbor that made casting easier both through the reduced weight of the line and the reduced weight of the arbor.

In the 1950s the Swedish Ambassadeur 5000 was introduced and might have saved casting from the continuing onslaught of spinning popularity and advances. The invention by Goth Gorgstrom of Garcia of the radial arms with the removable and interchangeable brake blocks for centrifugal cast control was a practical, easy-to-use casting reel system that did much to eliminate the backlash problem. Other models followed the bushing-model 5000, including the ball bearing Ambassadeur 5000C and the wide-spool 6000, along with even larger models for saltwater. These wider-spool models were popular for light trolling, saltwater popping applications and heavy freshwater casting for pike and muskie. Shakespeare had its President model and Pflueger its popular Supreme.

In the early 1970s, Lew Childre, a cane pole tackle salesman from Alabama, introduced the reel that was to change casting for the next two decades—the Lew Childre Speed Spool, model BB-1. This was a radical departure from the round side plate reels of Garcia, Heddon, Pflueger, Shakespeare and others in that it had the now-common teardrop shape with a small ring line guide (rather than the two vertical bars), and a recessed reel foot to allow it to sit low on a casting rod for easy cast-

Reels 213

LEFT: Two baitcasting reels—the original Ambassadeur 5000C and the original Ambassadeur 5000. The 5000 has shims and bushings, while the 5000C has bearings.

ing and palming. They followed with other models, and soon the industry was making teardrop-shape reels for all freshwater and even some saltwater fishing.

At about the same time, flipping became popular with the Dee Thomas flipping rod from Fenwick. Specific flipping reels with small line capacity but with the controls for flipping only were introduced by Shimano and others. Other reel models and reel companies made standard casting reels with a "flipping switch" that allowed switching to a flipping mode. The difference was that in normal use, the thumb bar would place the reel in free spool for casting, and you would engage the drag only upon turning the handle, but for flipping, pushing the thumb bar would place the reel in free spool for paying out line while flipping, but releasing the pressure would instantly place the reel in a drag mode again.

Another major change occurred in 1981 when Daiwa introduced its Magforce magnetic anti-backlash reel, shortly followed by Shimano and Garcia. This utilized a system previously developed by Ocean City with its Inductor reel. Casting set up a magnetic field between the magnets and the spinning spool to slow the spool and control the cast. The magnets never touched the spool, but adjustments allowed for a force strong enough that a cast could be begun, the rod/reel

MAGNETICS IN REELS

The current interest in magnetics as cast control in casting reels started in 1981 when Daiwa debuted their Magforce magnetic anti-backlash control. Shimano and Abu Garcia followed with the same idea almost immediately, with all the other reel companies using the same concept in reels shortly after. Magnetic cast control continues to this day, even with current trends back to the round side plate, centrifugal control casting reel as begun by the Shimano Calcutta.

But this was not the first or only use of magnetics in reels. In the 1950s and 1960s, the Johnson Reel Co. manufactured a magnetic fly reel, although the magnetic feature was to hold the spool on the reel. It did exert a slight but very smooth drag on a fish taking out line. No cast control is used in fly reels, so the later concept of Daiwa and others did not apply. Even earlier, Ocean City manufactured an Inductor reel, which did use magnetics as did the later Daiwa design. The Inductor, listed under saltwater and surf-casting reels in the 1954 Fishing Tackle Digest, is described as: "Sliding button on rim actuates a simple cam which controls gap between magnets and copper disc, thus increasing or decreasing braking effect for lures of any weight." Several models were available, both with and without level wind.

placed on the ground with the lure in the air, and the reel would not backlash.

A switch to tougher unitized frames in casting reels and a return to the round, centrifugal force reel was started by Shimano with its Calcutta model in 1991. This made for a tougher reel and one that again worked well, albeit with the old standard brake blocks rather than the magnetic field system of cast control.

Drags continued to improve also, with cork and felt giving way to impregnated woven graphite discs, Teflon and other high-tech materials that promised long wear and even brake control.

Fly Reels Start to Go High Tech and Big Game

A few years ago, the author compiled a listing of fly reels currently made then, ranging from the simplest $7 retail all-graphite J. T. fly reel to the $5,000 special-order titanium Charlton saltwater machined reel. The result was over 80 manufacturers or importers, with more coming all the time. Today, that number might approach 100. The big trend has been in the high-tech fly reels of machined aluminum, often using an aircraft-grade 6061 T6 alloy and anodizing the finished parts to protect them from corrosion and especially saltwater damage.

Once fly fishing started to dip seriously into saltwater in the late 1950s and early 1960s, a few reels were developed just for the sport of capturing bonefish, tarpon, snook, sharks, barracuda and other inshore and offshore species. Seamaster, founded and owned by Bob "Mac" McChristian, began making spinning reels in 1947, including some early and rare manual pick-up style before switching to full-bail reels. Then they shortly shifted over to making high-quality, bar-stock fly reels in 1950 or 1951.

Fin-Nor had started as the Finley-Norwood Machine Shop of Miami in 1933, begun for the purpose of making trolling reels. Their first reel was a giant 12/0 ocean trolling reel, later making a 13/0 and 15/0 sizes. In the late 1940s or early 1950s, they combined with the rod maker, Tycoon Tackle, to become Tycoon/Fin-Nor and carried both rods and reels. The first fly and spinning reels were made in the late 1950s or early 1960s, with the Gar Wood design "wedding cake" style of fly reel. The

ABOVE: *Reels are often made using a variety of processes from injection molding to casting to machining. These are machined fly reels ready for assembly in the Abel plant (Steve Abel in photo).*

company later switched from the wedding cake design (which had a side plate in layers, like a wedding cake) to a smooth, rounded side plate, also making big-game fly reels and anti-reverse fly reels.

Initially, all early fly reels were direct drive, that is, the handle was attached to the spool so that the handle would turn around as the spool turned when a fish took line. In time, some anti-reverse reels were developed with the handle attached to a plate separate from the spool; the handle did not turn when a fish took line.

The big explosion and expansion in fly reels came when Steve Abel decided to get into fly reel manufacture in 1987. Prior to that, Abel had a machine shop making airplane, gun and aerospace parts, then medical pacemaker parts. He made a few reels for friends and acquaintances for the 1987 San Mateo fly fishing show, at a time when only Fin-Nor, Seamaster and Ted Juracik, with his Billy Pate reel, were making saltwater fly reels. Abel provided some to manufacturers' representatives and fishermen in Florida—and, subsequently, the interest in saltwater fly fishing exploded. Dozens of companies have gotten into manufacturing high-quality saltwater fly reels.

Less expensive reels of the late 1950s and early 1960s included the Pflueger Supreme 577 and 578 models of fly reel and the saltwater model Shakespeare.

Today, however, names such as Aaron, Ryall, Islander, Charlton, Bauer, Ascent, Bellan, Henschel, Lamson, Pate, Tibor, Steel Fin, Teton, Penn and many others all make machined fly reels, often with modern CAD-CAM technology. The big advantage of all such reels is not only the greater strength and durability of the tough frame and spool for dealing with large fish, but also the improved and larger drag surface area in disk, caliper, drum and similar drag systems that are capable of stopping big fish and holding up through a long fight again and again.

Excellent cast and machined reels are made by Scientific Anglers, Cortland, Shakespeare, Pflueger, Ross, Orvis and others. Though not as strong as a machined reel, they still incorporate the unitized one-piece frame of the machined reels and, thus, are stronger and more durable than the previous reels of pillar-or-post construction that utilized small screws to hold the frame plates to the horizontal posts.

LARGE ARBOR, LARGE DIAMETER FLY REELS

One current trend from about 1995-on is that of larger arbor fly reels. These reels have a larger diameter with a larger arbor to maintain the same line capacity, but to retrieve more line with each turn of the handle. This is particularly important for any single-action reel. Thus, a reel with a three-inch diameter spool will only retrieve at best about 9½ inches of line per handle turn, where as a reel with a five-inch-diameter spool will retrieve almost 16 inches of line per handle turn. The key is to make sure that the reel has a larger outside diameter than one normally used for the same fishing and line size. In the haste to market the current craze to large arbor fly reels, some manufacturers have forgotten that basic fact and keyed in only on arbor size to in effect make "reduced capacity reels."

Ironically, the trend to the large arbor in fly reels is not new at all. Some of the earliest reels including the side-mounted Billinghurst, Gem, Winona by Heddon, inexpensive Wawasee and the more standard Diamond, Meisselbach, Pflueger Progress, Hardy Barton and many others, all had large arbors, even if not with the overall circumference of modern reels of this design. The early wood Nottinghams were all larger diameter.

ABOVE: *Many different cast control systems have been tried and used by manufacturers over the years. Some of these include, clockwise from upper right, Shimano Bantam Chronarch with six pin centrifugal brake system, South Bend #550 B with bar style anti-backlash device from the 1940s, Meisselbach Symplo reel with bar-type of anti-backlash device and Abu Garcia Ambassadeur 6500 C3 with two pin centrifugal brake system.*

Current Reel Trends and Advances

Currently, the trend continues with the round reel begun by Shimano. Reels today can have two, four and six radial arms for the brake blocks that control the cast and eliminate backlash. In 1999 Quantum introduced the first adjustable centrifugal cast control system. Other companies have also joined the market of reels, rods and accessories. Marado, Silstar, Pinnacle and JWA with its Mitchell are making advances not only in design, but also in keeping prices down.

On all reels, we find the infinite or constant anti-reverse that eliminates strike shock to the gears and pawls and hardened lips (often titanium) on spinning reel spools to lessen line wear and reduce friction. Some reels have cross winding to accommodate the new braided lines and to prevent them from cutting into the line. Smoother drags, fewer spinning reels with rear bait drags, no fault bails and bail spring are today common on most spinning reels. Fly reels have gotten better with die cast or machined frames, and spincast reels continue to perform well and remain low cost.

The one trend in all reels—casting and spinning—is that we have come full cycle from the 1700s when most of the tackle was imported. The only difference is that in place of imports from England, today's imports are from Sweden, for example, and Pacific rim countries, such as Sri Lanka, Korea, Bangladesh, Thailand and Japan, which can offer lower prices.

Reels

 # Accessories

The accessories of the past were as important to the angler as his basic rod, reel, line and lures. They were no match, however, for the vast variety of accessories available today that even includes GPS (global positioning system) to pinpoint fishing hot spots and side-scanning Sonar that can find fish in open water or track a shoreline to maintain a certain position from the bank.

Accessories evolved, as did fishing, when their need was identified. Bigger fish required nets or gaffs to land them. Big fish brought with them a sense of pride by the angler and the desire to weigh or measure the catch. Pliers are a staple with many fishermen to adjust tackle, remove hooks from fish, even clip off hooks or bend down barbs when hooks become caught in clothing or people. Catch-and-release is a relatively recent concept, so the idea of special ways to preserve the catch led to stringers, creels and fish baskets. And if you weren't releasing your fish, you had to fillet or clean them, thus the special thin, flexible-blade fillet knives.

Lures and tackle get snagged, leading to the development of some way to unsnag them from the bottom without getting wet. Trolling from boats led to fishing rod holders to allow more freedom while fishing. A desire to get into shallow water led to the development of fishing waders and hip boots, originally called fishing pants. Some accessories change as the tackle changes. The need to wash and dry linen and silk lines to prevent rot disappeared with the development of long-lasting synthetic lines of nylon, Dacron, monofilament and gel-spun polyethylene. Fly anglers still use line winders through, not so much for drying lines (the silk fly lines of the past would also rot), but to change lines—shooting head,

ABOVE: Accessories include: Fish grips with a scaler; brass fish stringer; fish-shaped scaler and knife; fishing soap; plug knocker; Depth-O-Therm thermometer; bait box; and hemostats. At the left of the photo is a worm box designed so that a worm will move into each of the tubes, which can then be removed by taking the cap off of the tube.

sinking, sinking tip and floating—as fishing conditions or areas change. A way to carry the lures, fillet knives, disgorgers, spare reels, pliers and other gear necessitated a tackle box or bag.

Here are a variety of stories on the evolution of many fishing accessories.

Clearing Ring/Lure Retriever

Even back in the 1600s, anglers would get their gear caught on a snag or piece of bottom structure. To keep from breaking the line and losing the fly or bait and hook, clearing rings were used. These first "lure retrievers" were nothing more than a large, hinged ring that could be fitted around the line. A heavy line was attached to the ring, so the ring could be dropped to the bottom to follow the fishing line to the snag and hopefully dislodge the hook for retrieval. Brown, in his 1849 book, describes these very well. They were made of iron or lead, from four- to six-ounces in weight, about three inches in diameter and with a hinge or joint that allowed placing the ring around a line. It was attached to a 12- to 15-yard length of stout line, placed around the fishing line "and sent down as a messenger."

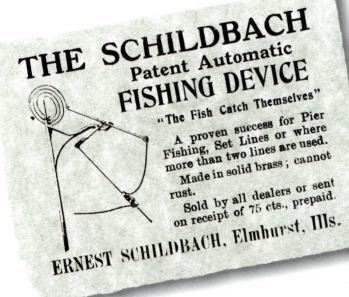

Lure retrievers of recent times usually have open spiral springs or clips for easily fastening to the fishing line. They also rely on weight to help dislodge the lure. Some have rings or chains to help catch the hooks on lures to aid in pulling them free. A few lure retrievers of today work completely differently and consist of an open-spiral spring on the end of a telescoping pole, almost like an extended boat hook. They can extend up to 20 feet. This allows placing the spring around the fishing line and following it to the lure, using the pole to push the snagged lure free. These can only be used in shallow water. The line-operated retrievers can be used in any depth of water, provided that currents and winds don't prevent you from staying directly over the lure when dropping the retriever. The greater the angle under which these are used, the more the problems and the less likely they will be successfully resolved.

Another type of retriever was used not underwater, but in trees to retrieve flies caught by fly fishermen where the cast got away from them or when they were not watching their backcast. These

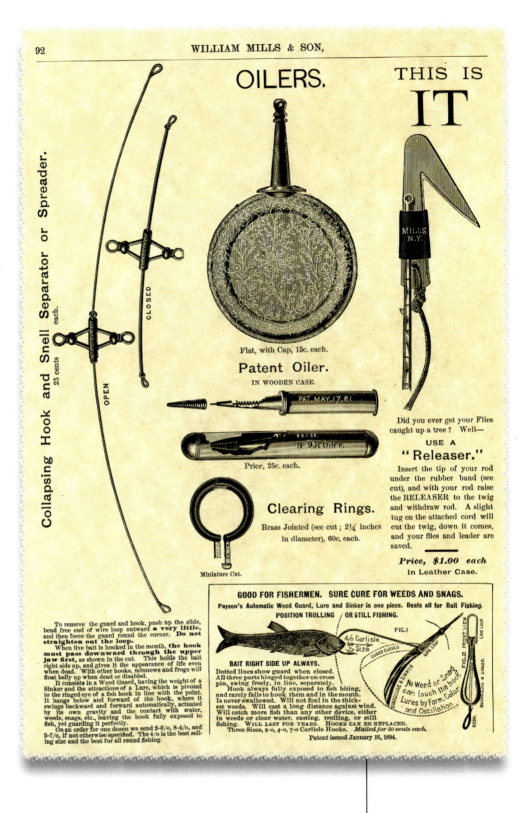

are nothing more than inverted J-shaped cutters, with a point that fitted into the rod tip top and were designed to catch and cut the offending twig. A line that was attached to the retriever allowed pulling or cutting the tree branch without damaging the rod tip, which was only used to position the cutter above the angler's reach. In the 1830s, landing nets often had a detachable handle to which a hook could be fastened to pull down a limb to retrieve a fly or lure.

Tackle Boxes

Tackle boxes probably were invented as anglers began to use more accessories, snells, hooks, sinkers, floats, bait and, ultimately, more lures. This required some way to carry them, thus the box and later the tackle bag. Initially, tackle boxes, which were sometimes called kits or tackle kits, were wood boxes, opening along the top, and sometimes with a separate, removable wood tray that held lures and other equipment. Tackle boxes have probably been around since the mid-1700s. Edward Pole advertised in 1774 that his Philadelphia shop carried, "Small portable boxes, completely furnished with a variety of fishing tackle." Sounds like a filled tackle box.

Unlike modern boxes, which usually have uniform compartments for lures, these early boxes often had trays with random size compartments that suggested the use of assorted sinkers, bobbers, hooks,

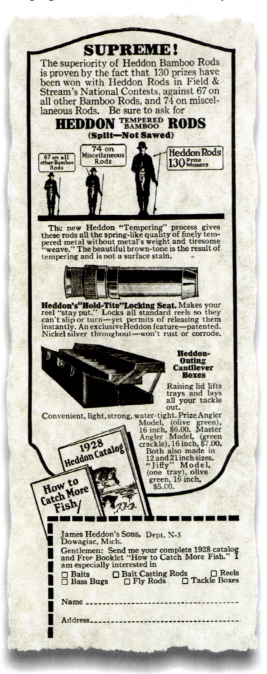

snells and the like rather than the lures that would come later. Most of these wood tackle boxes had dovetail construction for durability. Wood boxes were generally gone by the 1950s.

Gradually, boxes were made more with fishing in mind. Up through and past the war years, the Kennedy steel boxes were popular. These were originally made as boxes to hold mechanic's tools, but styles for fishing, including the basic and one-, two- or three-cantilevered trays, became standard. A big feature of these early boxes was the cork-lined trays that were said to protect the box from rust while also allowing the lure to dry out without damage or rusted hooks. But tackle boxes remained a novelty item, not really required, through much of the twentieth century. In the 1952 *Fishing Tackle Digest*, under a section for accessories, there is no category for tackle boxes, even though landing nets, creels, live nets, stringers, reel and rod cases and chemicals and lubricants are listed. Boxes were not listed in the 1954 edition either, although a photo section on loading a boat does show an early metal tackle box.

Aluminum boxes by Umco and others were also popular, overlapping and ultimately eclipsing the heavier steel boxes. Umco later produced a vacuum-processed plastic tackle box, and the Texas company, Whopper Stopper (also manufacturer of lures), produced a small box for lures.

ABOVE: Tackle boxes have changed over the years and have been made of wood, steel, aluminum, fabric and leather. **Back row, left to right:** Plano Soft Side tackle box, Tronick Treink Co. Tronick Tackler and Plano hard plastic tackle box with see-through lid. **Front row, left to right:** Standard tackle Box from Standing Stamping Co. and leather tackle box from Knickerbocker Case Co.

With the search always for better and more modern materials for tackle, the next step was a sturdy, larger plastic tackle box, ultimately the idea of Plano. The Plano Molding Company in Plano, Il, started as a general plastics molding company in 1932, making things such as float balls for toilets, molded radio aerials, push buttons, electric insulators and radio tube sockets. It bought its first injection molding machine in 1938, started molding photographic developing tanks for Sears Roebuck, and during the 1940s had government contracts for war products. Plano continued parts modeling after the war and produced its first tackle box in 1952, shortly thereafter producing the plastic boxes for Sears under the private Sears J. C. Higgins label.

Despite some early tackle box problems with the brittle styrene plastic it used, Plano continued, changing materials as new and better plastics were developed. The company also had to solve the problem of the chemical reaction of soft-plastic worms with the plastic tackle boxes by going to non-

Accessories 223

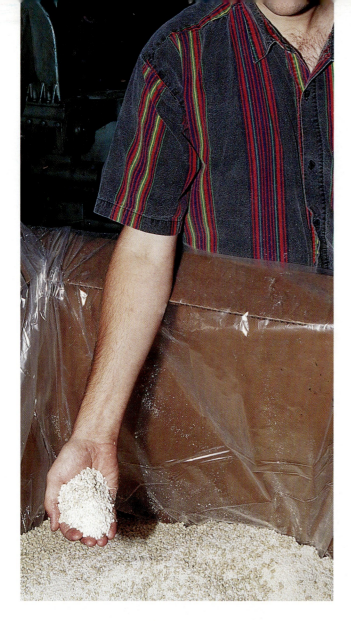

LEFT: *Plastic tackle boxes start as a granular plastic before the plastic is melted and injection molded. Here, granular plastic is shown by a worker in the Plano factory.*

reactive plastics and advertising their boxes as "worm proof." It was not until 1961 that the name was changed from the original Plas-Tak to Plano, dropping the association with Sears and selling boxes under its own name.

The standard lid models were joined by those with a double-lid or hip-roof style in the 8600 series boxes in 1964, followed by separate individual containers designed to fit into the 6300 series box. In the early 1970s the 747 box was born, named for the big Boeing plane. It featured a combination lift-lid and sliding two-tray system for lures, but it retained a large bottom compartment. It was the largest box available and primarily designed for saltwater fishing. The 777, a complete sliding-tray unit for the bass fisherman, followed, along with a host of other boxes and styles. Satchel boxes, both single and double sided, came along, as did more specialty separate lure boxes in a half-dozen different sizes for everything from flies to lures. Companies such as Flambeau, Woodstream and others made similar boxes during the same periods. Rubbermaid, the plastic housewares company, has started producing tackle containers too.

Tackle Bags

Tackle bags have always been around. Probably evolving from a sack in which to hold fishing stuff, they changed into combination bags and creels (with pockets on the fronts and tops of wicker fishing creels), and bags such as the Orvis kit bag (and others). These were originally about the size of a loaf of bread and made of leather-trimmed canvas, with internal dividers, flip-over lid, end pockets and shoulder strap. They were designed to hold anything you wanted to store—reels, lure and fly boxes, pliers, sunglasses, fishing maps … anything! Other manufacturers got into the act to make similar bags. These bags have evolved into different sizes and models, have changed from canvas to Cordura and other nylons and have switched from leather straps to hook-and-loop fasteners. They have been made by companies such as Cabela's, Bass Pro Shops, Offshore Angler, Abel, Loomis, Orvis and many others. One different bag currently available is made of Neoprene and produced by Mangrove. It is not waterproof to the extent that you can place it underwater, but it will keep contents dry even if floating in water or soaked with boat spray.

Along the way, other companies got into the manufacture of so-called soft-side tackle boxes. Often these were foldout-type bags with clear-face zippered compartments to hold assorted lures, but with principle emphasis on spinnerbaits, buzzbaits, worms and jigs. Other soft-side containers were like a soft-sided ring notebook, with zipper lock plastic

ABOVE: *Fly fishermen use a wide variety of boxes made of cloth, leather, hard plastic, aluminum and foam.*

bags attached to the rings, the bags holding and separating lures and lure types. Some of these companies were ultimately absorbed into others, such as the Tackle Logic bags and cases. That company was bought by Plano. Flambeau and other tackle box companies also have soft-side tackle bag divisions.

Fly Boxes and Books

Fly books in the early- and mid-1800s were often wallet types, sometimes with separate pockets for individual snelled flies and leaders. These predated more modern fly boxes, when flies were made with permanently attached snells of gut. Such rigs would not have fit into a modern fly box.

By the 1920s, a variety of fly boxes were available, including separate boxes and styles for wet and dry flies. Several types of fly boxes were available. The dry fly boxes featured individual compartments to prevent crushing the hackle. The Perrine-style, instead of compartments, had individual clips to hold the flies flat by the bend of the hook. As a result, some writers of the period noted that the clip-style hook-holder would tend to crush the hackle and wings of dry flies. A spring-type also developed by Perrine was much

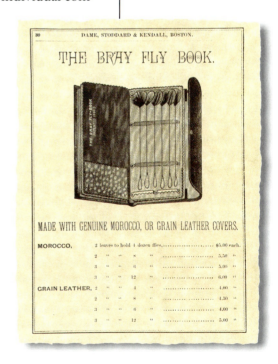

Accessories

better for drys because it held the fly upright by the hook to prevent damage to the wings and hackle. Snelled flies were still used in the 1920s, so some boxes had felt leaves with a metal attachment at the top end for holding the fly hook and springs for securing the leader. Usually each fly book had a half-dozen or more felt leaves like this, sometimes in combination with the celluloid-lid dry fly compartment boxes. Boxes with cork strips were also available for holding larger streamer flies and bass bugs. Those with a leather outer covering and sheepskin inner lining for holding fly hooks were also very popular.

In the 1940s, magnets were the big thing, with Orvis making several boxes that incorporated magnets to hold flies. Some just had several magnets in an otherwise single compartment box, while another from Orvis featured molded plastic slots into which the hook of a streamer fly would fit, held in place by an underlying magnet. Similar magnetic boxes are still available today.

Gaffs

One early patent from 1919 describes the butt end of a fishing rod with a gaff attached, although how this would be used while landing a fish remains to be seen. Gaffs, of course, were far older than this.

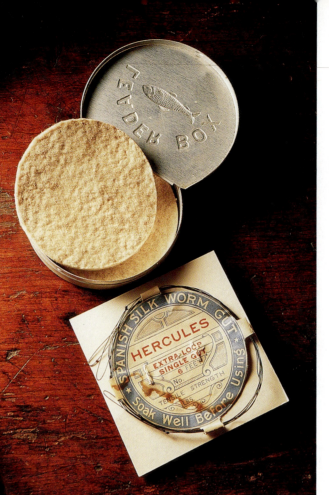

LEFT: *Early leaders of silkworm gut (and also early nylons) required moistening before use, particularly when tying knots. For this, special leader boxes were used. The felt pads from this round aluminum box were moistened and then rubbed on the leader to keep it soft and flexible.*

They were mentioned in John Brown's book *The American Angler's Guide* (1849) and earlier. Hooks on gaffs were often described as being about four inches in length, with or without a barb and featuring a hickory or ash handle about five to six feet in length. These gradually evolved into various sizes of gaffs and eventually into the aluminum handled gaffs of the present, most without a barb and also of varying handle lengths and hook sizes.

The transition from those early gaffs of over 100 years ago to the modern, mostly aluminum-handled gaffs of today included many changes and ideas. In 1902, a Warren Fish Gaff was advertised that had two hooks—one was to grab the fish and the second was to slide down and over the first to impale the fish. In short, this made the two hooks into a ring to prevent loss of a fish, and utilized the same idea, if not the same working mechanism, of the early spring-loaded hooks. The design was probably influenced by those hooks. Does anybody, however, need a two-hook gaff?

226 *Our Fishing Heritage: Tackle & Equipment*

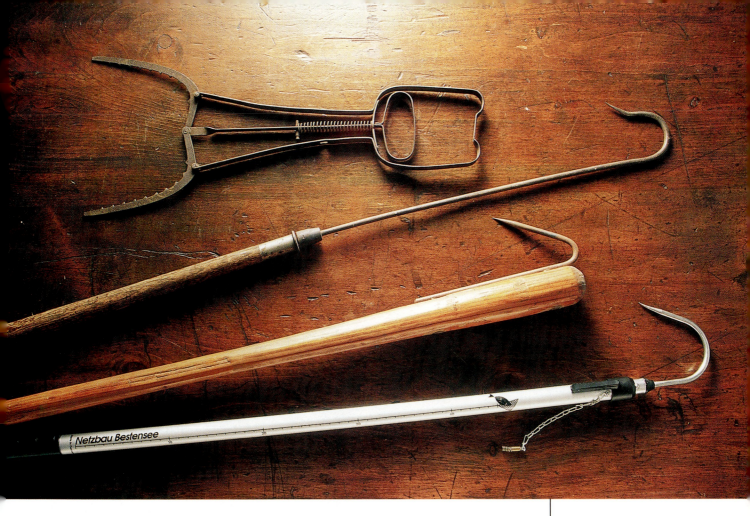

ABOVE: *Fish landing devices of many types have been used over the years. Top to bottom, a grip-activated fish grabber, two wood handled gaffs and a modern telescoping aluminum handled gaff.*

The idea of package gaffs could be found in the 1905 Ideal Gaff Hook, which was a hook on a steel rod, with a handle at the end, but which broke down into three sections by means of threaded connectors, like screwing a bolt into a nut. The 21-inch gaff broke down into seven-inch sections to fit into a tackle box.

The switch from wood handles to metal could be found in the 1911 gaff from Wulff Manufacturing Company of Minneapolis, MN. Its cork-gripped, telescoping gaff made of nickel-plated brass tubing was constructed much like some later telescoping rods. The fixed (not telescoping) stepped tubular-steel rods allowed the 42-inch gaff to collapse into a nine-inch package. During the same period, Hardy's sold several unusual styles of gaffs, including a "New Zealand" style that collapsed into the handle with the weighted end of the handle serving as a club, or priest; and a combination gaff and wading staff, measuring 57 inches long.

Some "gaffs" operated on a completely different principle, more along the lines of the "fish grabbers" available today that work by compressing a handle to grab a fish from both sides. The 1925 Lion Gaff from the O. A. Norland Co. had two toothed jaws, each on a separate spring handle, that were activated to grab

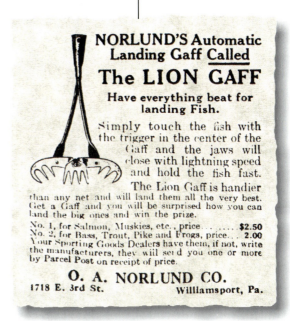

Accessories 227

LEFT: Stringer over the years have included various styles from (left to right) the simple cord, two metal clip styles and plastic clip non-rusting style.

7½ inches when closed to 19½ inches open. Closed, it could be carried in a pocket, because the spring release also shielded the hook point. In 1935, anglers interested in a packable gaff could buy the Biek's Jack-Knife Gaff Hook that folded like a jackknife to fit into a tackle box or pocket, with the handle shielding the hook when closed.

Special short-handled gaffs with two-inch hooks, developed as release gaffs, became popular along with the rise of catch-and-release fishing. These are still popular and often used in light-tackle boat fishing as release gaffs. They allow lip-gaffing a fish to immobilize it, removing a fish by touching the fish with a center spring trigger of the open jaws. This actually followed the Marble's Clincher Gaff that worked the same way as modern fish grabbers, that is, the angler squeezes two handles together to move the jaws, like the jaws of pliers, to grab a fish. This was advertised in *Field & Stream* in its 1915 issues, although Marble became more famous later for its sheath knives.

In 1928 the F. C. Woods & Company sold its Expert Telescoping Pocket Gaff Hook that went from the hook or lure without danger to the angler and then releasing the fish without harm.

Very large gaffs were developed as big-game angling became increasingly popular in the early and middle part of the twentieth century. Most had long handles of eight feet or more, some with a rope attached to a removable barbed hook (a flying gaff). As a result, gaffs range from about one-foot long with a 1½-inch hook to monsters eight-feet long with 10- and 12-inch barbed hooks. Other special-

228   *Our Fishing Heritage: Tackle & Equipment*

ized gaffs are the short and light (usually about two- to three-inch hook and a two- to three-foot handle) surf gaffs used by surf fishermen. These differ only in that they are often supplied with a sheath to hold the gaff on a surf belt and a coiled plastic strap to prevent its loss.

Other landing tools included the big-game harpoon with a detachable point that was thrust through the fish, the handle coming off and the harpoon point twisting at right angles to the line to prevent loss. The fish-friendlier tailer allowed lassoing a fish by the tail, to lift it for photos and to remove the hook. These were typically used for Atlantic salmon.

ABOVE: *Anglers have devised various ways to get lures to fish, one of which is the side planer that planes a line to the side of the boat while holding the fishing line in a release clip. Planers include these two (one for the right side of the boat, one for the left) from Off Shore.*

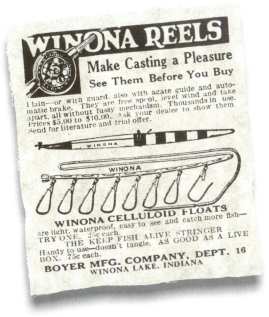

Landing Nets

Landing nets today are made of knotted twine, woven mesh, rubberized fabric and rubber (stretches with the weight of the fish). They are short handled for the stream fisherman, long handled for boat or bank fishing, even slim and with shallow bags for easy catch and release of fish. They come small, medium, big and huge, some with upturned lips on the frame to prevent the loss of large fish.

Older nets were more simplistic, with fewer choices. A 150-year-old description notes that nets then were about 16 inches in diameter, with the mesh made of linen twine or fish line (the same thing), about two feet deep, with a mesh of about ⅜ inch and the bag on an iron or brass ring, with a handle of ash or hickory, not less than five feet in length. Apparently, anglers wanted to be able to reach out,

ABOVE: Nets have varied widely in sizes and styles for different types of fishing. Left to right are long handled aluminum frame net, wire mesh bag net, wood frame stream net, steel frame net, wood frame net and aluminum tubing frame net.

lest they lose the catch. A brass ring was noted as best, because it would not corrode and damage the net as would iron.

Advances were being made, however, even back then. At the same period, collapsible nets were also available, in which the ring was hinged to fold into three curved sections, one end fitting through a ring in the other end, the protruding end screwing into a socket in the handle. Some allowed the ring to fit into a hollow handle for further convenience.

But there were always efforts to come up with something more convenient, thus the Smith Brothers "Angler's Friend." A 1908 ad shows a net without a handle that could be stored in a pocket and assembled on the water to land a fish.

Later collapsible nets such as the 1913 net from the Eagle Folding Net Company of East Orange, NJ, consisted of a handle with a hinged flip-out phosphorbronze net frame attached to a wood handle. The net spread was 11 inches, with an 18-inch depth. Hardy's sold a similar net style right after the turn of the century.

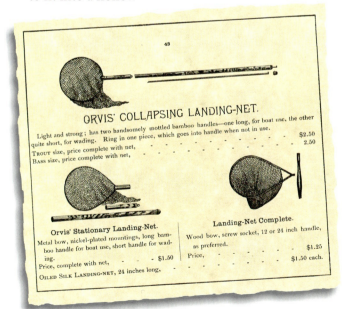

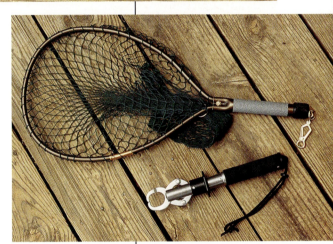

TOP: Nets and creels. **Left to right:** Ideal trout net with wood handle and metal frame; fishing pannier; South Bend Oreno net; cloth creel; wood handle net; wicker fishing creel with shoulder strap; Pompano gaff; modern folding net.

ABOVE: Some early tools were designed to weigh the catch. These modern tools include: a net with a built-in scale from McLean and imported to the U.S. from New Zealand; and the Boga Grip that grips both the upper and lower lip of the fish for holding it when weighing.

Accessories

WHAT YOU NEEDED 50 YEARS AGO

Jason Lucas, angling editor of *Sports Afield* magazine 50 years ago, wrote an article titled "Your Tackle Box And What To Put In It," in 1946 in the first annual edition of the Fishing Tackle Digest. At the end of the article, Lucas listed those accessories needed by anglers. List A includes those things absolutely necessary for all anglers, list B those items not always necessary, but possibly needed under some fishing conditions. Modern anglers, with more knowledge today about fishing and environmental conditions, would no doubt change these lists to make the sunglasses and sun screen a must for list A. They also might leave out the priest in favor of releasing fish and also the line drier now that lines no longer rot when not washed and dried after a trip.

<u>**LIST A**</u>

Air cushion (to sit on)

Cutting pliers

Landing net

Stringer and/or live net

Reel oil, gear grease, spare pawl
(for casting reel) and reel wrench

Assorted sinkers

Spare hooks

Waterproof matches

Snaps, hook hone, knife
and mosquito dope

<u>**LIST B**</u>

Priest (club for killing fish)

Spare rod

Flashlight

Spring scale

Line drier

Stream thermometer

Fishing barometer

Wire leaders

Nylon leaders

Magnifier

Sunglasses

  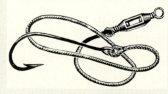 

Pliers

"Plyers," as pliers were known through the 1800s, are an essential part of fishing gear. They allow removing hooks, tightening reel parts, fixing tackle, bending down barbs and the like, and were as important then as they are for many anglers today. Most were simple pliers not different from those used in the workshop, unlike some of the very long-jawed or specialized plier/wire cutter models specifically made for angling today.

Creels, Fish Baskets, Fish Panniers

Since the concept of catch-and-release is relatively new, some method to keep fish for later consumption was required. Particularly for wading or bank fishermen, this was often a container of some sort, variously called a fish pannier, basket or creel. Containers for fish go back a long way. In fact, early wood cuts in some fishing books show a bank-fishing angler with a long rod, the line tied or fixed to the rod, landing a fish (likely a trout) with an open basket alongside him, the basket containing trout. Also, the woodcut shows it as an oblong basket, much as a poaching pan for fish is oblong. If the basket were not designed specifically for fishing, the angler at least chose one that would work best to hold the catch. Izaak Walton later referred to fish baskets, or panniers, as well. Because there was no refrigeration or polyfoam insulation then, wet grass was added to the gutted fish to help keep them fresh.

According to Webster, the word creel dates to about 1250 and means a wickerwork receptacle, although not specifically for fish. An English book, *The Experienced Angler*, published in 1665, shows a wicker or willow creel, very much like those still available today, as a

ABOVE: *The first "green box" portable depth finder by Lowrance (1960s) paved the way for modern electronics which today include GPS (global positioning system) such as the Lowrance Global Map 100 shown.*

part of the frontis illustration that also shows rods, floats, sinkers, hooks and even a reel or winch.

Early fish panniers were basically square-cornered baskets, often with feet, and sometimes large enough and sturdy enough for a bank angler to sit on while fishing. Some would have separate compartments to hold tackle, almost the early equivalent of the ice anglers or bank fisherman's five-gallon plastic bucket for carrying miscellaneous gear to the fishing site.

It is likely that in the U.S., early fish containers, prior to the 1850s, could be something as pedestrian as a gunnysack or a small barrel, because coopering (barrel making) was a principle occupation and barrels were used for transporting many goods. Wicker creels were probably used in the 1600s; leather creels became popular late in that century, although they fell out of popularity by the mid-1800s when much tackle was being imported from England, as well as being made here by fledgling manufacturers. Other materials for making the classic kidney-shaped creel and its variations included wood slats formed in a creel shape, woven or checkerwork birchbark, split bamboo, rattan, palm fronds and split wood such as oak, ash and basswood.

In addition, Hugh Chatham and Dan McClain in their beautiful book, *The Art of the Creel*, note that there were many different methods of construction, including creels that were twined, twilled, webbed,

ABOVE: *Early wicker creel from the 1890s with leather strap and hole through which to add the catch (usually trout).*

wickerworked or checkerworked. Some built as early as 1925 by Chas. Forsburg & Sons of Williamsport, PA, were made with the wickering technique, using aluminum instead of wicker. They also included a removable bait box. Other standard creels of wicker also included leather pockets on the front, rarely on the sides or back. Some were made of canvas as tackle bags with a large mesh pocket on the front for carrying fish, while others had inside compartments along with the bait canteens and separate compartments for snells and terminal tackle. Montgomery Ward in 1949 advertised three canvas creels.

Many sold between World War I and World War II were made in the Orient (one 1939 article in *Western Sportsman* noted that "99 percent of the creels came from Japan") and were modified after import by U.S. companies. These modifications involved removing the buckles and hardware and replacing them with leather straps as well as leathering parts of the top, corners, bottoms and pockets. Names such as Lawrence, Handitop by Eaton and Glenn (1922), Farlow, Hardy (both the former were English but imported here), Cummings, Frisbee, A. E. Nelson, Peters and W. H. McManies were among some of the common names of creels in the first two-thirds of the twentieth century.

Cloth creels or fish containers also were popular and perhaps evolved from a simple sack by which to carry fish home. In the 1940s, a cloth combination creel and fishing kit was widely sold and copied. It consisted of a spring-wire closure mechanism for the main bag for the fish, the front containing several pockets for holding leader wallets, fly and bait boxes and other fishing

ABOVE: *Fish containers.* **Left to right:** *Early fish basket or pannier; cloth creel with metal snap lid from the 1940s and 1950s; wicker creel.*

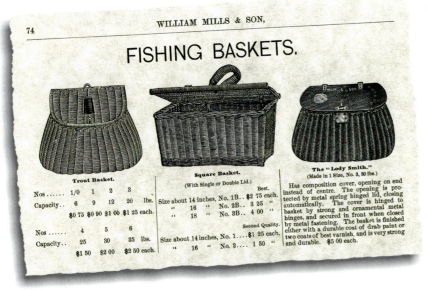

Accessories 235

paraphernalia. About the same time, bags that were designed to keep fish fresh by cooling through evaporation of the wetted bag were introduced.

Disgorgers

Disgorgers have also been around a long time, perhaps developing from a forked stick that could be used to push a hook backward out of a fish's mouth. Today, they are mostly made of plastic, but have also been challenged by a variety of other tools including long-nose pliers, hemostats, J-hook disgorgers (designed to catch the bend of the hook and allow the fish to pull free), Q-type (that work like a J style, but don't require pulling the fish from the water) and specialized devices such as the Ketchum Release designed for removing flies. A brass disgorger being sold today is a reproduction of one from the 1890s. Jason Lucas recommended hemostats for removing hooks; he was perhaps the first fishing writer to do so.

ABOVE: *Decoys were used by the Indians before becoming popular in the north country for spearing fish through the ice in the winter. Decoys such as these could resemble any species of bait fish or even be carved to resemble crayfish, such as the one in the rear of this photo.*

236 *Our Fishing Heritage: Tackle & Equipment*

Minnow Traps

Today minnow traps are often of wire or plastic, made or molded with mesh sides so that the water will flow through them. They're often shaped like a cylinder with a recessed mesh funnel entrance at one or both ends. Bait placed in the center (they usually open in two halves at the middle) attracts minnows, which, once having entered, can't find their way out again. The traps are placed where minnows are likely to congregate, often in the shallows and secured by a stout line attached to a float or a branch on the bank.

Traps for the same purpose were designed years ago, but made of glass, almost like a large Mason jar, but with a special inverted funnel cap that would allow the minnows in, but not out. Obviously, being made of glass, these had to be handled with extreme care.

Minnow Pails

Minnow pails were probably just that initially: a pail from the farm yard. In time, or perhaps from loss of bait minnows from an open pail, tops were added first, then special straight-side containers with a lift-out mesh liner. These liners allowed getting the minnows without having to chase them around the pail. Some of these were designed to be used over the side of the boat, the bait swimming in the container that lay in the water. Plastics ultimately replaced the galvanized tin containers. Some today are designed almost like a small boat that will track along behind a slow-moving boat without the necessity of removing it from the water. In the 1950s, canvas sacks to hold minnows were sold for stream fishing; the sack would hang in the water from a belt.

Accessories   237

LEFT: Ads for waders often emphasized their flexibility, as shown in this ad in a Point Sporting Goods catalog.

were in common usage then, both in boot-foot and stocking-foot styles.

The illustrations from 1883 show hip boots that come up to the crotch and are held in place with belt straps, in both stocking-foot and a cleated-boot style, along with a separate illustration for their "Baxter" Brogue, a wading shoe with straps to make it easy to put on and a fold-out tongue to make them sandproof—pretty well thought out for over 100 years ago!

Some problems existed with waders in those days, however, because partially vulcanized rubber waders had to be warmed before being opened, either by the dealer showing the goods or by the fishermen preparing to go fishing, according to an 1895 ad for chest-high waders from North British Rubber Company, Ltd. The company's thoroughly vulcanized waders did not require that, again according to their ad, and remained soft and pliable. These were stocking-foot waders, custom fitted through a measurement chart and available in shops in seven British cities. Presumably such waders would have been exported to the U.S. as well, for use by anglers here.

Wading Pants and Stockings

These early names are the waders and hip boots that we use today, and from their inception, they have been available in both the current types of stocking foot, where a separate shoe or brogue is required, and boot foot, with the boot shoe built onto the wader. Ads in Kelson's 1895 book, *The Salmon Fly,* show both styles from several different companies. An ad for Abbotts' Waders (London) also indicates that its waders received a gold medal at an 1883 Fisheries' Exposition. Other ads and references from 1865 indicate that they

Rod and Reel Cases

Rod cases and bags have been around for a while. Brown in 1849 described metal cases for heavy rods. Other books from 100 years ago described how to sew a simple rod bag, folding over a long strip of cloth, sewing along the edge and securing some straps to tie the handle into the bag. Leather cases became popular for fly rods, particularly travel rods. Screw-top alu-

238   *Our Fishing Heritage: Tackle & Equipment*

minum cases gained popularity for fly rods, but did not work well for spinning with the larger guides of the rods. Plastic tubing in round cases was used by a number of manufacturers. Some companies such as Fenwick made plastic cases that had a triangular cross section for strength and to prevent rolling.

Fishing Knives

Fishing knives evolved over time from simple pocket knives to those with specialized purposes including: the modern tools that are pliers and knives; fillet knives of many styles; and tougher, stiff and wide-blade bait knives. One early knife from the late 1800s looked like a typical pocket knife, but had some Swiss Army Knife features, including a large blade, small blade, disgorger, button hook (to fasten shoes, naturally!), corkscrew, leather borer and awl (to unfasten loops) and separately had slide-out tools including a broken-eye needle for threading bait, a scissors and "pliers" that looked more like hackle pliers than workbench pliers.

Fishing knives of the 1930s, 1940s and 1950s were often made with two blades, one a long clip blade, the other a scaler (serrated) with a forked-shape disgorger on the end. These were heavily advertised and sold at the time. A KaBar knife advertised by early fishing personality Gadabout Gaddis included features as above, along with a bottle opener and hook-sharpening stone and also had a magnetized tip in the disgorger for picking up hooks.

Perhaps the most popular fillet knife was the Normark Rapala knife with the simple wood handle and slip-in leather sheath. It was introduced into this country by the Normark Company, importers of the Rapala fishing lures. During trips to Finland to check on production of the Rapala lures, Ron Weber of Normark learned of Marttiini knives that had an excellent reputation in their native Finland. Weber wanted

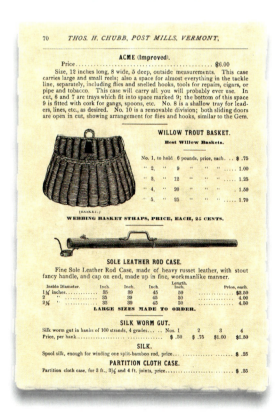

ABOVE: *Examples of early fishing knives include, left to right: Combination gaff, scaler, disgorger and blade; small Rapala Fish 'N Fillet knife with sheath; and Kabar fisherman's knife with blade, scaler, bottle opener, disgorger, sharpening stone and magnetized tip for picking up hooks.*

Accessories

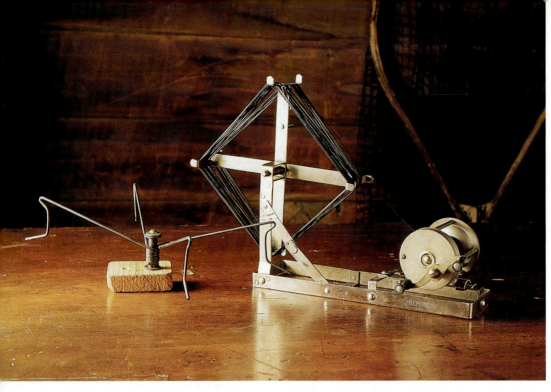

LEFT: *Line winders were necessary in early fishing, to wash and dry lines between trips to prevent rot. Line winders could be simple as the one shown on the left, or more complex and designed to hold the reel for removal and later re-spooling of the line (right).*

the small family-run company to make a fillet knife with a thin blade similar to those he had worn down and which butchers liked for filleting. At first the family refused until Weber gave them an initial order for 20,000 knives. After experiments and prototypes, the first of the order reached the U.S. in 1967 as the Normark Fish 'N Fillet knife. It was a huge success, and at one time knives and their accessories accounted for 40 percent of the Normark business. Other sizes of knives followed, along with cutting and filleting boards, videos on how to fillet and clean fish and booklets on filleting. By 1995, 25 million Fish 'N Fillet knives had been sold.

Fly Tying Vises and Tools

Originally, flies were tied by hand, even more literally than today. There were no vises other than standard tool vises to hold the hook while tying, and early vises described in books resemble nothing more than a small version of an old-time machinist's vise. These were upright vises, with large jaws, not the specialized small-jawed angled vises used today. In time, jeweler's vises were used, because they are small versions of the machinist's vise, placed on an upright post, similar to the system used today. Some strange vises included the turn-of-the-century model that was fastened to a base plate which was held in the mouth by G. E. M. Skues, adversary of Halford and "father" of the nymph, and the thumb-mounted vise available at the same time. But in time, the tools of the trade resembled the tools of today.

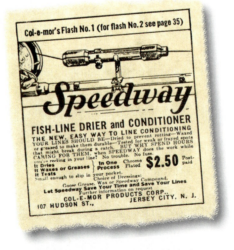

An article by John Harrington Keene in *American Field* in 1887 had an illustration of fly tying tools that included a straight upright vise that clamped to the table (just like vises of today) and used a thumb screw to tighten the hook in the vise jaws. Also included were hackle pliers, a bodkin (like an awl), scissors and a small hook (the hook's purpose is now unknown). All, other than the vise, are almost identical to tools used today and are basic for all fly tying.

By 1897, D. H. Thompson made the first vise of the modern ilk with a lever-and-cam closing style that is still widely used, and the basic design of which is still made by the D. H. Thompson Co.

Line Winder or Dryer

A few years ago, Angler's Image manufactured a line winder for fly fishers. It worked like a series of scissors, the bars making up the scissors part that was adjustable by means of a thumb screw on a central axis. It is great for changing lines, shooting heads and spooling backing on fly reels, and it has been well received. In 1869, Genio Scott (*Fishing in American Waters*) described and illustrated a line dryer that was almost identical in appearance and certainly identical in function. It clamped to a table and could be scissored in or out to arrange the line drying rack, just as with the 1990's version.

Fishing Suits/Fishing Jackets/Fishing Vests

Lee Wulff is credited with making the first fishing vest in the 1930s, and photos of him Atlantic salmon fishing during that period show him wearing a slim vest of his design. Fishing vests and fishing jackets did exist before this, however. A Dame, Stoddard and Kendall catalog from before 1890 describes an "Isaac (sic) Walton Fishing Suit" with separately-sold pants, coat and vest. The coat is shown and has large cargo pockets along with pockets on each sleeve. By at least 1895, George Kelson, author of *The Salmon Fly,* had developed a fishing jacket with four breast pockets and two sleeve pockets that seems to be at least one forerunner of the 1930's fishing vest. Thaddeus Norris in his 1864 book wrote of fishing jackets of hip length, inside and outside breast pockets and skirt pockets, each large enough to hold a fly book. 🪶

ABOVE: *Fishing accessories, then and now, can include vests, landing nets and fly boxes.*

Accessories

ABOVE: *Examples of some of the 450-plus editions of Izaak Walton's* The Compleat Angler. *Left, a two-volume set from 1880 (the red volume is the smaller miniature edition); center, the LeGallienne edi-* *tion from 1897, foreground, a small 1825 version; right rear, a 1901 edition; and right foreground, an 1887 edition.*

English Books and the English Influence

Long before publishers were established in this country, or before early publishers started publishing books on fishing, imported English books were the only references available. The first well known book was the *Treatyse On Fishing With an Angle,* credited to Dame Juliana Berners and published as part of the *Boke of St. Albans,* a book treating fishing, hawking and riding to the hounds. It was both a fishing manual and a tackle how-to-do-it instruction guide to everything from making lines to rods to flies.

Perhaps the most famous book (now published in over 400 editions) was Izaak Walton's *The Compleat Angler,* first published in 1653 and subsequently republished in 1655, 1661, 1664 (a reissue of the 1661 edition), 1668 and 1676. It was the fifth, or 1676, edition (the last published in Walton's lifetime) that included the works of Charles Cotton ("Being Instructions How to Angle for a Trout or Grayling in a Clear Stream") on fly fishing as part II and a fourth reprinting of Col. Robert Venables' *The Experienced Angler* (1662) as part III of a book entitled *The Universal Angler.* Venables has almost been forgotten, but Cotton lives in the hundreds of editions of *The Compleat Angler,* most taken from the fifth edition, that have since been published over the ensuing 325 years.

It was this book that instructed about fishing with bait and flies, methods of making lines and rods, natural history and seasons and habits and habitat of the fish sought. That the British fish emphasized in the text—trout and pike—were also native to the colonies helped. The mention of other British species such as roach, tench, chubb and others did not seem to detract.

244   *Our Fishing Heritage: Tackle & Equipment*

Books & Periodicals

Introduction

A knowledge of history often depends as much on the literature of the period as it does on the items and recollections of the times. People die and, if their recollections are not recorded on paper (or nowadays on audio tapes, film or video), that history is lost. Furthermore, any detective or district attorney will tell you that personal recollections are often not the best evidence of what really happened, of what something or someone really looked like or when it occurred. In fishing, the early rods, lines, nets, creels, and other paraphernalia can, and will, disintegrate and decompose in time unless carefully preserved under museum conditions. Fortunately, increasing interest in tackle and tackle history has collectors in this and other countries scouring attics, shops and basements for examples of early tackle and for the catalogs, magazines, ads and books that provide us with the evolution of tackle development.

Books, magazines, catalogs and such are often more prevalent and easier to collect and check than individual angling equipment.

A book might contain a few references to types of tackle or be filled with photos and drawings of tackle use. Some fishing annuals published over the years by magazine publishers and some tackle companies even today provide a wealth of information about tackle. The period from the mid-1940s through the 1960s were the main period of these annuals, which are still sought by collectors today.

But angling history—true history of the several-hundred years of angling practiced in this country—is best found through a look at all the literature available from the time periods studied.

Richard Brookes in his *Art of Fishing* (1720) covers early use of the reel (windes and winches) and also touches on saltwater fly fishing. The English influence continued in books, even up to and including John Brown's 1849 *The American Angler's Guide.* The subtitle states, *Containing the Opinions and Practice of the Best English and American Anglers, with the Modes Usually Adopted in all Descriptions of Fishing, Method of Making Artificial Flies, etc.*

Early American Books

An 1835 English book, *The Angler's Souvenir,* made fun of the paucity of literature on fishing in the U.S., noting that we were "not yet sufficiently civilized to produce anything original on the gentle art..." That there were no important books written about fishing prior to 1800 is without question. There might have been occasional references to fishing, some casual comment and some literature in the many publications that cropped up and often died in the period. Bartram, in the 1791 book, *The Travels of William Bartram,* mentioned fishing with a "bob" that would roughly resemble hair-bodied bass bugs of today and also wrote of fishing experiences in his travels. Other references to fish and game were by Mark Catesby on fish of the Carolinas, Florida and the Bahamas; Pehr Kalm, whose 1770 English book, *Travels into North America,* also described the fish. Louis Hennepin's 1698 book, *A New Discovery of a Vast Country in America,* and others were the first timid acknowledgment that there might be something here for sport.

ABOVE: *Early fishing books published in the U.S. or about it include works such as these by Thaddeus Norris, Robert Barnwell Roosevelt, John Brown, Charles Hallock and others.*

Fish and Fishing Go Hand In Hand

Early books were less on the subject of fishing than they were narratives, along with often detailed discourses on the fish of the area. Today, that might seem to be useless, but, then, with a new country and new science still paving the way for a more modern society and the thirst for knowledge, perhaps this is understandable. It was noted in the early 1800s that ichthyology had received little attention in the pursuit of science, despite the fact that the New York fish markets contained all manner of edible fish. That might explain the marriage of often scientific accounts of fishing along with sporting methods to catch them.

Books & Periodicals

SOME FORGOTTEN GIANTS

As with most things in culture and society, worth and value do not always go hand-in-hand with popularity, recognition and fame. The same applies to angling writers. Though writers are often a reflection of the age in which they live and their works mostly popular while they are living, some do span the ages. Theodore Gordon is revered as the father of American dry fly fishing; Dr. James Henshall, because of his *Book of the Black Bass,* still commands some respect even 120 years after his book was published. Books by Joseph D. Bates on spinning and fly fishing continue to have some popularity, particularly with a recent retrospective of his work. Also, it would be hard to forget the work of A. J. McClane, who wrote incisive fishing columns for *Field & Stream* for many years and who wrote several books before writing and editing the massive *McClane's New Standard Fishing Encyclopedia and International Angling Guide* in 1974. Within that tome's 1,156 pages, all of fishing was covered, literally, from A to Z.

An example of those who never gained recognition or rapidly lost fame include John Harrington Keene, who in 1885 wrote about dry fly fishing in America, predating Theodore Gordon by 20 years (who wrote about it after the turn of the century and is credited as the father of fly fishing in America). His writing even predated Englishman Frederic Halford, who, due to his 1886 book on the subject, has been credited as the father of the dry fly. Keene wrote two books (*Fly-Fishing and Fly-Making* and *Fishing Tackle, Its Materials and Manufacture*) and wrote many magazine articles about cork-bodied flies, terrestrials, dry flies, midges, detached-body flies, flies with interchangeable parts, double-insect patterns and a host of other things, along with explicit directions on how to tie his designs.

He gained little recognition at the time, and was later ignored by other book and magazine writers, likely due to a falling out with Charles Orvis, with whom he had some business dealings. He remains a small footnote in the history of fly fishing, rather than the full chapter he deserves to be.

George Leonard Herter was by all descriptions, through his catalogs and books of the 1940s and '50s, a bombastic, self-aggrandizing, conceited, pompous man who in his later catalogs described most of his goods as being invented by him, certainly the best in the world and definitely not to be confused with inferior imitations. Nevertheless, several of his books were complete, thorough and excellent for the time period in which they were published. His *Professional Glass and Split-Bamboo Manual and Manufacturer's Guide* (1949 and 1953) remains an excellent tome on the development and history of rods in general and the manufacturing processes. His *Professional Fly Tying and Tackle Making Manual and Manufacturers' Guide* (1941 and printings through the 1960s) was, and still is, an excellent discussion of all aspects of fly tying.

Jason Lucas was angling editor of *Sports Afield* until his retirement in 1964. Lucas' book, *Lucas on Bass Fishing,* published in 1947, contained perhaps the most complete description of deep-water fishing for bass, structure fishing, patterns, seasons, lure color, color recognition by fish, retrieves and much more—information that was not widely recognized until 20 or more years later with the influx of specialized bass magazines and bass tournaments. It was definitely before its time. If Henshall is thought of as the father of bass fishing, then Lucas might be thought of as the big brother to the modern sport.

Natural History of the Fishes of Massachusetts (1833), by Jerome Van Crowinshield Smith, M.D., is considered the first book on fishing published in this country. It is as much or more about fish than about fishing. Early chapters cover general descriptions of fish and fish anatomy, from eyes to air bladders; the rest of the book describes the individual fish species known then, sometimes along with a little information on fishing. Only the last 76 pages of this 399-page volume are exclusively devoted to angling in a section entitled, "On Trout, Interspersed with Remarks on the Theory and Practice of Angling."

In this, he wrote about lines, rods, reels, flies, fly fishing, leaders, methods of angling, trout and some other forms of angling. The change to fishing can be found in John Brown's *The American Angler's Guide* of 1849, which discusses, almost completely, fishing for the species listed, rather than their biology, anatomy or taxonomy. Frank Forester (Henry William Herbert), in his mid-1800s books, *Fishing With Hook and Line* and *Frank Forester's Fishing of the United States and British Provinces* set the stage for future writings on the sport. Both were excellent classic works of the time, discussing not only the common practices of trout fishing, but also dipping into coastal striped bass fishing and shad fishing on the fly. There was a mix of both biology and fishing skills in books for quite a while, just as books today can be found with a great deal on the quarry in addition to the methods to catch it. Thaddeus Norris in 1864 published his *The American Angler's Book,* which, though covering enough of biology and habitat to be helpful, was mostly on the sport of fishing. The same applied to Henshall's 1881 *Book of the Black Bass,* in which the three parts were on the biology of the bass (191 pages), tackle and angling implements (150 pages) and angling and fly fishing (106 pages). Thus, though an ideal book for the time and full of tackle history and equipment, the largest of the three parts was on the fish themselves.

The same argument could apply to Genio Scott with his 1888 *Fishing in American Waters* in which three of the seven parts of the book dealt with commercial fishing, fish culture and basic ichthyology, subjects not always of interest to anglers.

Early References to Tackle

In some early books, tackle was little mentioned. Some of this might be a result of the author considering that all readers would know about the subject, or the author not knowing as much as

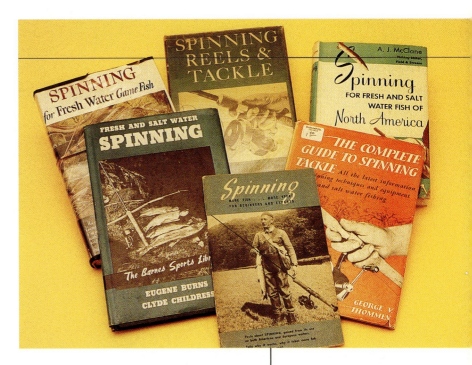

ABOVE: *Early books on spinning from the 1940s and later. The earliest of these is the smallest booklet in the front center, published in 1941.*

Books & Periodicals

he should, or the subject being simple and not requiring much explanation. For example, Smith in 1833 noted only that reels should be single action or multiplying, describing the use of each type, but nothing more about these then relatively new devices. Brown, in 1849 had 2½ pages on rods, one page on reels and three-quarters of a page on lines. And these were small pages!

That gradually improved however, with Norris in 1864 not only including descriptions of the fish tackle required for each type of fish covered (trout, pike, carp, herring, catfish, eels, salmon and saltwater species) but also having a chapter on tackle (including "hooks, sinkers, swivels, gut, leaders, snoods, lines, reels, rods and bow dipsys [spreaders]"), chapters on fishing outfits ("wading jacket, trousers, boots, creel or basket, landing-net, rods, reels, lines, leaders, flies, the whip [leader with flies attached]") and chapters on "repairs, knots, loops and receipts [recipes for dying guts, etc.]", along with separate chapters on fly making, rod making and fish breeding!

Early fishermen had to be more tackle makers, when it was a necessity, than today, when it is an interesting hobby. In the 1700s fishermen were almost required to make their own hooks, lines and rods, prepare their own leaders and tie their own flies.

Gradually, lines were taken care of by fledgling companies and hooks imported or made by some shops; rod making and fly tying, however, continued well into the late 1800s. Even earlier, rods were manufactured both in England (imported) and in

ABOVE: *Early fishing books shown here include the* American Angler's Book *by Thaddeus Norris,* Fishing in American Waters *by Genio Scott,* Just Fishing *by Ray Bergman,* Fisherman's Luck *by Henry Van Dyke, and* Dry Fly Fishing in Theory and Practice *by Frederick Halford.*

248   *Our Fishing Heritage: Tackle & Equipment*

the U.S., but by modern standards they were often terribly expensive. Many anglers made their own rods, which ranged from crude to sophisticated.

Excellent descriptions were to be found in some books, such as the 1881 *Book of the Black Bass,* by Henshall. Henshall described the history of tackle at that time: particularly rods, with references to Sam Phillippe and the split bamboo of the time; early lures and flies of the period; reels, including the fly fishing "click reel" and the bait fishing "multiplying reel"; lines and how they were used and made; and angling accessories. Were all books as full of angling tackle information as was Henshall's, there would be fewer gaps in our angling knowledge today.

As the evolution of angling books continued, so did the descriptions of tackle in these books. Often they became more detailed about the equipment to use and what was available and devoted less attention to how to make the lines and rods. Often flies and fly tying became a separate subject, perhaps first epitomized by Charles F. Orvis and A. Nelson Chaney's *Fishing With the Fly* (1883), which included 15 colored plates of flies in five categories—trout, salmon, bass, lake and hackle flies. English books such as Frederic M. Halford's *Floating Flies and How to Dress Them,* published in 1886, then followed by many others such as *The Salmon Fly,* by George M. Kelson (1895), also were popular here. There were other books on general tackle over the years. Herter's *Professional Fly Tying and Tackle Making and Manufacturer's Guide* (1941) comes to mind, along with Harlon Major's *Salt Water Fishing*

Tackle (1939, 1948 and 1955), Vlad Evanoff's *Modern Fishing Tackle* (1961) and Gary Soucie's *Hook, Line, and Sinker* (1982), the last an excellent book devoted to terminal tackle.

There was also an increasing saltwater influence in the 1910s and '20s, with famed Western writer Zane Grey's *Tales of Swordfish and Tuna, Fishing Virgin Seas, Tales of Fishes, Tales of the Angler's Eldorado, New Zealand, Tales of Tahitian Waters* and *An American Angler in Australia.* He also wrote several books on freshwater fishing. Books in the 1930s included *American Big Game Fishing,* by Eugene Connett, published by Derrydale Press, a premier publisher of hunting and fishing books of the

ABOVE: *Bass fishing became popular with the turn of the century and the development of bass lures and tackle. Popular books during that period included* Book of the Black Bass *and* More About the Black Bass, *both written by Dr. James Henshall in the 1880s, and* Lucas on Bass Fishing *by Jason Lucas from 1947.*

time that offered both trade and expensive limited edition volumes. S. Kip Farrington Jr. wrote *Fishing the Atlantic, Fishing the Pacific* and *Atlantic Game Fishing* in the 1930s.

The Fly Fishing Influence

Early angling was by fly fishing or various methods of fishing with bait. As a result, books extolled these facets of the sport. Many early books, beginning with Dame Juliana Berners' 1496 work, also described tying flies, along with fishing techniques. That continued in books through the 1800s, although some books from the latter third of the 1800s and on through the first third of the 1900s picked up on the relatively new sport of baitcasting, first used with bait and then, at the turn of the century, with lures.

Early books always included some fly fishing, and by the early part of the century there were specialty books such as the 1914 *Dry Fly and Fast Water* and the 1924 *The Salmon and the Dry Fly*, both by George M. L. LaBranche. The salmon fishing of the time was often reserved for the wealthy, as noted by Henry Van Dyke, who, in his *Travel Diary of an Angler* notes that a catch of eight salmon in a week represented a cost of well over $100 per salmon (that was in 1929 dollars!). During this same period, average farmer wages were $401 annually; some salaries in other fields averaged $15 per month! Later, Ray Bergman's massive 1938 book, *Trout,* educated thousands of anglers over the next two decades.

Fly fishing continued to hold its own, with many books incorporating techniques for both baitcasting and fly fishing. After World War II, the general books might cover fly fishing, baitcasting and the new sport of spinning. Books only on fly fishing or trout or on a combination of fly fishing and baitcasting by authors such as Ray Bergman, John Alden Knight, Ray Ovington, Robert Page Lincoln, Joe Brooks and others began to appear in the 1940s and 1950s

In the 1950s, the "new" sport of saltwater fly fishing was "discovered." That was the year that the small book, *Salt Water Fly Fishing*, by Joe Brooks was published, heralding the spate of books on the subject that continues to increase to this day. George X. Sand's *Salt-Water Fly Fishing* (1970) was followed by Lefty Kreh's *Fly Fishing in Salt Water* (1974, 1986 and 1997). Today you can fill a wide bookshelf with books on bonefish, permit, tarpon, billfish, redfish, inshore saltwater fly fishing and offshore saltwater fly fishing, along with fly tying volumes on saltwater flies.

There was also increasing interest in warmwater fly fishing for smallmouth, largemouth, panfish, pike, and even carp, with fly fishing books on the last two just recently appearing.

The Rise of Baitcasting and Baitcasting Books

Baitcasting, as a way to get bait out to fishable waters, developed in the mid-1800s and, by the latter part of the century, had developed into an important new fishing tool to accompany trolling and fly fishing. But it also required some knowledge of both the tackle, which was totally different from that of fly fishing and more complex than that needed for trolling, and also of the casting method, which was more like throwing an apple on a stick than it was the gentle false casting of the fly angler.

At the turn of the century, the development of wood plugs, more metal spoons and other lures with which to fish, better reels and rods, and that newfangled thing, the automobile (which started to appear at about the same time as wood lures), brought about a lot more interest in fishing (you could easily get to spots with Henry Ford's invention) and baitcasting. There was no spinning yet, and baitcasting threatened to take a little of the glamour out of fly fishing, just as spinning would also ineffectively threaten fly fishing some 50 years later in the late 1940s and early 1950s.

Books at and after the turn of the century echoed the interest in baitcasting. *Fishing Tackle,* by Perry D. Frazer (1914), *Practical Bait Casting,* by Larry St. John (1918), *Casting Tackle and Methods,* by O. W. Smith (1920), *Fishing Kits and Equipment,* by Samuel G. Camp (1923), *Bait-Casting,* by William C. Vogt

MUSEUMS

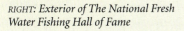

ABOVE: Display cases at The National Fresh Water Fishing Hall of Fame

Museums of old tackle provide additional appreciation of our tackle history. There are some excellent museums devoted exclusively to fishing memorabilia and other museums that have sections devoted to fishing tackle or periodic displays and exhibits of antique tackle. Some of the better dedicated museums are:

AMERICAN MUSEUM OF FLY FISHING, P.O. Box 42, Manchester, VT 05254, telephone 802-362-3300 (museum of fly fishing tackle and history)

CATSKILL FLY FISHING CENTER AND MUSEUM, P.O. Box 1295, Livingston Manor, NY 12758, telephone 914-439-4810 (museum of fly fishing tackle and history)

INTERNATIONAL GAME FISH ASSOCIATION, 300 Gulf Stream Way, Dania Beach, FL 33004, 954-927-2628 (museum and collections of both freshwater and saltwater tackle, photos and memorabilia)

NATIONAL FRESH WATER FISHING HALL OF FAME AND MUSEUM, Box 33, Hall of Fame Drive, Hayward, WI 54843, 715-634-4440 (museum of freshwater fishing tackle and memorabilia)

The National Fresh Water Fishing Hall of Fame located in Hayward, Wisconsin is one of the most complete museums on the history of fishing. Whether you are a historian, tackle collector, outboard motor enthusiast or an average fisherman, there is something there for everyone. This unique collection represents our heritage on the waters and a passion for the sport of fishing.

RIGHT: Exterior of The National Fresh Water Fishing Hall of Fame

Books & Periodicals

(1928), *Modern Bait & Fly Casting,* by Ozark Ripley (1928), *Bait Casting,* by Gilmer G. Robinson (1941) and *Advanced Bait Casting,* by Charles K. Fox (1950) were examples of important books and valuable information about the sport of the time. Fox was particularly influential, since his books marked a realization of light lines, light lures, and slightly longer rods (he suggested six-foot six-inch split-bamboo rods). This was a trend that would continue and would counter the heavy lures, lines and short rods (sometimes ridiculously short and only a few feet long) of the 1920s through the '40s.

As bass became more popular, books such as *Lucas on Bass Fishing,* by Jason Lucas (1947), *Black Bass Fishing,* by Robert Page Lincoln (1952) and *Freshwater Bass,* by Ray Bergman (1942) picked up where Henshall left off. The bass trend died for a while, but came back with more books in recent years, much the result of the formation of the Bass Anglers Sportsman Society (B.A.S.S.), formed by Ray Scott in 1968. That noteworthy event led not only to more books on bass fishing, but also to tournaments, the modern bass boat and advanced developments of all phases of the tackle industry. These modern (since the 1960s) books are not always specific to baitcasting, but often with a heavy emphasis in that area, since modern anglers are using the tackle that works, and for bass that is often a mix of spinning and casting.

Fishing Annuals, Catalogs and Magazines

Fishing annuals, catalogs, ads and magazines provide a valuable look at our fishing history and of the tackle used way back when. Catalogs of tackle companies, if there was any universal collection of all the catalogs of all the companies and tackle makers, would be the best possible view of how tackle developed, who bought whom, which lure or reel or rod design preceded another similar design, etc.

ABOVE: *Catalogs are valued sources of information on tackle and techniques of a given time period. Catalogs such as these show products and manufacturers that no longer exist.*

Unfortunately, such complete collections, even of a few companies, are seldom available.

Catalogs, as do magazines, also show the shift of interests, philosophies and mores over the years. Early catalogs were often filled with huge catches of fish. The 1903 Heddon catalog for example, proudly showed and described "a string of 73 bass, two blue pointers, one perch and one sun fish." Magazines also often showed stringers of fish, but both gradually evolved in the 1960s and 1970s into showing fewer fish, often just a single catch that presumably could be released. The shift was more toward environmentally friendly fishing.

Similarly, magazines, both in the articles and in the tackle ads, also provide a look at history, and modern trends at the time of publication. Early magazines were seldom just about fishing or fishing and hunting, as are magazines of today. Then, fishing information was often carried in magazines such as the monthly *American Turf Register and Sporting Magazine*, begun in 1829. A weekly sporting paper, *The Spirit of the Times*, was begun about the same time (1831). It was for the *American Turf Register and Sporting Magazine* that William Henry Herbert, better known by his pseudonym of Frank Forester, wrote. He became the best-known outdoor writer of both fishing and hunting of his time, writing articles and publishing books.

Magazines such as *Field & Stream* (begun in 1896 as *Western Field and Stream*), *Forest and Stream* (1873), *Outdoor Life* (1897), *Sports Afield* (1887) and many others ushered in a golden age of fishing at the turn of the century. Though the ads are interesting from a fishing standpoint, they also tell something about us as a nation at the time. A *Forest and Stream* ad of the 1900 period promoted a "Scalp For Sale—A First Class Comanche Scalp; taken in Texas; ears on; all round cut; extra long hair. Inquire at Office of *Forest and Stream*."

In the 1940s the magazines were proud to run ads from major companies, which, in turn, proudly pro-

ABOVE: *Magazines, annuals and periodically-published fishing digests often have a lot of information on the tackle and fishing methods of different eras.*

Books & Periodicals

claimed their manufacture of items for the war effort, sometimes even boasting about their products going to Russia to help. That was when the U.S.S.R. was one of our allies in the effort to defeat the Germans, and before the Cold War.

Fishing annuals of the time, along with annual fishing digests, fishing almanacs, etc. also provided a look at the newest and latest in fishing gadgetry. Some 1940's publications included the *Sportsman's Year Book* and the *Hunting and Fishing Handbook,* both published by the National Sportsman, publisher of *Hunting and Fishing* magazine. The two yearbooks contained no ads, but lots of information on the tackle and techniques of 50-plus years ago.

In the 1960s Crown Publishers produced several years of the *Fishing Tackle Digest,* a mix of articles and tabular listings of tackle of the times. The large format *Sports Afield Fishing Annual* was eagerly anticipated in the 1950s and 1960s, replete as it was with both articles and often the first look through ads of the new tackle of the year. Also in the 1960s Ridge Press and ABC published the hardback quarterly, *The American Sportsman,* echoing the popular Sunday TV show covering fishing and hunting.

In the mid-1970s, Stoeger produced several annual *Angler's Bible,* large format, thick, cheap-paper volumes with loads of articles and no ads, offering another look at the tackle and techniques of the time. Abu Garcia's fishing annuals, a mix of catalog ads and fishing articles and tips, were popular in the 1970s.

Since then, the major magazines such as the "big three"—*Field & Stream, Outdoor Life* and *Sports Afield*—have continued, along with a host of new general publications, such as *North American Fisherman* and *Gray's Sporting Journal,* and species- or tackle-specific magazines such as *Bassin', Saltwater Sportsman, Sport Fishing, Crappie World, Fly Tyer, Warmwater Fly Fishing, Florida Sportsman* and *Fly Fisherman.*

More Facts and Less Anecdotes

Other than humor books about fishing and hunting, most books today are pretty much straight facts. This is probably reflective of today's society, in which time is a valuable commodity. Article length in magazines has shrunk from about 3,500 to 5,000 words in the 1940s and 1950s to somewhere between 1,500 and 2,000 words today in most magazines. The "me and Joe" stories recounting tales of trips are gone from books and magazine stories in preference to where-to-go, when-to-fish, and how-to-catch articles. In the past, anecdotes and folksy humor was the theme woven through much writing. A prime example would be the books and writings of Ed Zern (*Field & Stream,* "Exit Laughing") in the 1950s and 1960s. Patrick McManus is an example of that genre continuing today.

After the turn of the century, some otherwise practical fishing books ended with poetry, or had poetry or quotes from other famous authors as headings or subheadings in chapters and in articles. Dixie Carroll, the pseudonym for the writer Carroll Blaine Cook, wrote in the preface of his 1919 book, *Fishing Tackle and Kits:* "Fellows of the rod and gun, brothers of the outland trails, men of the quiet camp-fires, hear me now you all who know the teasing whisper of the wind as it soughs through the pines, the

---

HUMOR IN WRITING

Some writers used (or attempted) levity, such as this section from John J. Brown's *The American Angler's Guide* of 1849, immediately after discussing the variety of sinkers used in fishing. "Should this chapter prove rather *heavy* for the patience of the reader, it is to be hoped that the buoyancy of the next may enable him to recover his equilibrium." The italics are Brown's. He then goes on to discuss floats.

laughing voice of the fast-running stream waters, the quiet murmur of the placid lake as the waves kiss the moonbeams sent down from the starlit sky above, the deep silence of the nightlands of the out-o'-doors, you are the chosen children within whose being beats the heart that is true and from within come thoughts that are pure and golden."

The seeming point here, that only outdoorsmen are the pure and perfect, ignores the rest of the world with other interests and might seem somewhat elitist. It also takes a long time wandering around to paint a picture of the outdoors. Ironically, while much of the book follows that rambling and folksy theme, it also has a great deal of practical information about lures, tackle, reels, rods and techniques. Today, any junior editor fresh out of journalism school would have scrapped those lines, broken the thoughts up into several sentences or edited it down to some simple prose.

The Rise of Regional Books

Currently, there are publishers who are devoting all, or a major part, of their publishing efforts to producing regional books. Both major and minor publishers have produced books on both hunting and fishing, often confining themselves to a specific state and a detailed description of the fishing opportunities, tackle, suggested flies or lures, seasons and patterns, either as general information or specific to each water. Waters are then covered in detail, usually with maps, access points, boat and guide availability, regulations, etc. Some also include information on the area including gas stations, motels, bed-and-breakfasts, restaurants, tackle shops and the like that would be helpful to any visiting angler.

ABOVE: *Signed and limited edition numbered books are more valuable than trade editions or unsigned books. This muskie book has a muskie stamp, numbering of the limited edition and author's signature.*

Some can be quite specific. Others cover a state, and still others cover an entire region. Examples of quite specific books would be: *Fishing the Tidal Potomac River,* by Ken Penrod and self-published by PPC Publishing; *Guide to Pennsylvania Limestone Streams,* by A. Joseph Armstrong and published by Stackpole Books; and *Fishing Lake Anna* (a bass lake in Virginia), by Teddy Carr and published by PPC Publishing. Examples of state guides include: *How to Fly Fish Alaska,* by Jim Repine and published by Frank Amato Publications; *Montana Fly Fishing Guides* (East and West volumes), by John Holt and published by Greycliff Publishing Co.; and *Fly Fisher's Guide to Idaho,* by Ken Retallic and Rocky Barker and published by Wilderness Adventures. Regional guides include: *Northeast Guide to Saltwater Fishing & Boating,* edited by Vin T. Sparano and published by McGraw Hill Publishing; *Northeastern Bass Fishing,* by Bob Elliott and published by Stone Wall Press; and *A Fly Fisherman's Blue Ridge,* by Christopher Camuto and published by Henry Holt and Company. The latter covers fishing mountainous regions from Pennsylvania down through the Carolinas.

All such books are valuable less for their pushing the frontiers of fishing knowledge than they are for the valuable information on the region. As anglers move around more, have more disposable income and leisure time or retire to enjoy angling full time, such books provide a shortcut to learning about a lake, river, state or region. They provide valuable advance information that can help on everything from when and where to go, to what to take and what to expect when you get there. They can get you on the water with the right equipment and the knowledge to know when, where and how to catch the fish. In the past, state fish and game departments would supply valuable information through maps, guides, booklets and sometimes even books, but there is less of that material being produced in today's cost-cutting age.

Though there is a plethora of regional books now, the concept is not new. The problem with such books is that while currently valuable for a short time after publication, they can rapidly become dated if too specific. Even without that, some early books mention prices, with one turn of the century volume noting that a good canoe can be bought for $10 to $15.

An example of an early work and such dating is Charles Hallock's *The Fishing Tourist,* published in 1873. It was a guide to fishing with emphasis on the Northeast, but it also included some coverage of the Pacific Coast and Michigan and the north-central states. After writing about the Adirondacks and including the date for ice-out, the railroad from Plattsburgh to Point of Rocks on the Ausable, the availability of stage coaches, how to fish for surface lake trout and where to get boats, he notes: "The necessary expenses of the tourist are about $3 per day, whether he stops at a hotel, camps, or takes a guide. The charge for a boat and guide is $2.50 per diem; hotel fares from $1.50 to $2.50." Try that today. You might get a candy bar and a soft drink, but then again, you might get only the candy bar!

Niche Books for Species, Techniques and Tackle

Books in the 1800s for the most part did not cover specific species and how to catch them. Most covered all fish, all fishing methods of the time and often more than you would really want to know about fish biology. That started to change in the late 1800s with the publication of *Book of the Black Bass,* by Henshall, which was a thorough exploration of the fish and also the tackle and techniques of the time.

Though there are no absolute threshold changes in books, there are trends. Books around the time of Henshall continued to be generally about fish, just as the coverage in many books today. Trends in angling did gradually evolve, however, perhaps echoing the trends of separation of tackle types that began in the late 1800s and early 1900s. Books after the turn of the century could be found on baitcasting, flies and fly fishing, saltwater angling, bass, trout, even pike. Baitcasting required instruction to master well, thus the need for books and articles on the subject.

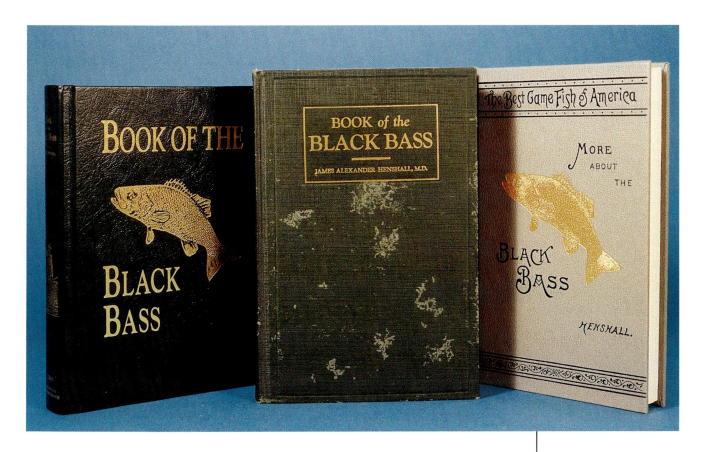

ABOVE: *An early edition of Henshall's* Book of the Black Bass, *with a modern reprint to the left and a reprint of his other book to the right.*

The same applied to the new sport of spinning as we went into the 1940s and 1950s, when books on the subject by Ovington, Thommen, Bates, Burns and others began to appear. With the increased ability to produce high-quality photography, first with black and white and then color, along with the increasing ease of making high-quality closeup photos, more books showed lures, flies and fly tying in the 1970s through the '90s. Better line drawings and detailed illustrations of fishing techniques and tackle also added to the consumer's easy and quick understanding of the sport. Books covering trolling, downrigger fishing, specific species, bait fishing, lure fishing, knots, rigs, lure tricks and modifications, casting, boat fishing, river techniques and other aspects of the sport are today endemic.

The Changing Fishing Book Market

New tackle and fishing techniques and increasingly higher quality books have made it easier than ever to learn about fishing. Publishing higher-quality books, combined with inflation, has caused an increase in prices. The hardback book, *Bait Casting with a Thermometer,* by Frank R. Steel, sold new for $1.50 when it was published in 1947. The 1954 hardcover, *Fresh Water Fishing,* by Larry Koller (with the front and inside cover in color!) sold new for $2.75. Today, paperback fishing books may cost as much as $20; hardcover books without color are priced up to about $30; and hardcover books with a lot of color can range up to $100.

Nick Lyons, patriarch of The Lyons Press and a longtime book publisher, notes that since 1970 there has been an

Books & Periodicals

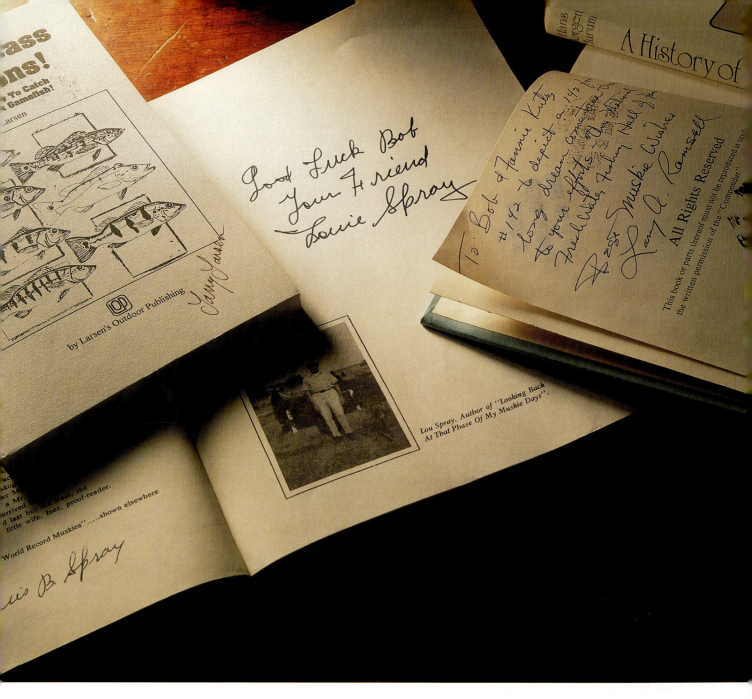

explosion of fishing book titles. From the relatively few books of the 1800s, to a gradual increase in titles in the early 1900s, to the gap of the war years, to the increases that began in the 1950s, fishing books can be found on any subject desired. Today, there are several wholesalers who deal exclusively with fishing. *Angler's Art,* Barry Serviente's national mail-order catalog, deals exclusively with fly fishing books. Used-book dealers in the realm of old, used and rare fishing and hunting books are flourishing. More and more books of all kinds, including fishing books, are being sold on the Internet. Books, along with the many magazines that deal with all aspects of fishing, offer anglers instant information, factual instruction and a shortcut to the tackle and techniques of the sport.

ABOVE: *Examples of signed books from one collection. Some book collectors try to have their books signed by the author whenever possible. These books include signed copies of titles by Larry Larsen* (Peacock Bass Explosions), *Louie Spray* (My Muskie Day), *Larry Ramsell* (Compendium of Muskie Angling History) *and Hans Jorgen Hurum* (History of the Fish Hook).

Bibliography

Collector Books

The following are books for and by collectors of fishing tackle and, as such, are useful in providing detailed information about the title subject and sometimes pricing guidelines for collectible tackle. They may provide information on the history and evolution of tackle and are of most use to those who have or are considering accumulating a tackle collection.

Baron, Frank R. and Carver, Raymond L., *Bud Stewart, Michigan's Legendary Lure Maker,* Hillsdale, MI, Ferguson Communications, 1990

Bourdon, Jim, *South Bend, Their Artificial Baits and Reels,* Grawn, MI, KLR Communications, 1985

Brown, James T. *The Fly Reel,* New York, NY, The Lyons Press, 1999

Brown, Jim, *A Treasury of Reels,* Manchester, VT, American Museum of Fly Fishing, 1990

Bruns, Henry P., *Angling Books of the Americas,* Atlanta, GA, Anglers Press, 1975

Caiati, Carl, *Collecting Fly Fishing,* Brooklyn, NY, Alliance Publishing, Inc., 1997

Calabi, Silvio, *The Collector's Guide to Antique Fishing Tackle,* Edison, NJ, The Wellfleet Press, 1989

Campbell, A. J., *Classic & Antique Fly-Fishing Tackle,* New York, NY, The Lyons Press, 1997

Carbaugh, Gary, and Spurr, Dick, *Colorado Reels and Old Fishing Tackle,* Grand Junction, CO, Centennial Publications, 1994

Chatham, Hugh and McClain, Dan, *The Art of the Creel,* Ennis, MT, Blue Heron Publications, 1997

Clark, Malcolm, Sr., *Introduction to the Kentucky Reel,* Frankfort, KY, The Kentucky Reel Publishing Company, 1987

Clark, Malcolm, Sr., *The Meeks,* Frankfort, KY, The Kentucky Reel Publishing Company, 1988

Dowden, Nigel, *Old Fishing Tackle,* Buckinghamshire, UK, Shire Publications, Ltd., 1995

Dupont, Stephen, *Crafting of a Legend, The Normark Story,* Minnetonka, MN, The Normark Corporation, 1998

E. F. Payne Rod Co., *Reproduction, Corporate Records, 1930-1968,* Grand Junction, CO, Centennial Publications, 1992

Frazier, Jim, *Al Foss,* Hollywood, FL, self-published, 1985

Gabrielson, Ira N. ed., *The Fisherman's Encyclopedia,* Harrisburg, PA, The Stackpole Company, 1950 and 1963

Gingrich, Arnold, *The Fishing in Print,* New York, NY, Winchester Press, 1974

Graham, Jamie Maxtone, *Fishing Tackle of Yesterday,* Lyne Haugh, Scotland, UK, self-published, 1989

Hanyok, Paul M., *Maryland's Conservation Laws, Licenses, and Enforcement Officers,* Mt. Airy, MD, Old Line Press, 1996

Harbin, Clyde, Sr., and Wetzel, Bill, *A Collector's Reference Guide to Heddon Fishing Lures,* Bamberg, SC, 1984

Harbin, Clyde A., Sr., (The Bassman), *James Heddon's Sons Catalogues,* Memphis, TN, CAH Enterprises, 1977

Hillman, Anthony, *Carving Traditional Fish Decoys,* New York, NY, Dover Publications, Inc., 1993

Homel, D. B., *Antique Fly Reels,* Bellingham, WA, Forrest Park Publishers, 1999

Homel, D. B., *Antique & Collectible Fishing Rods,* Bellingham, WA, Forrest Park Publishers, 1997

Homel, D. B., *Old Fishing Tackle and Collectibles,* Bellingham, WA, Forrest Park Publishers, 1995

Homel, D. B., *Classic Fishing Lures and Angling Collectibles,* Bellingham, WA, Forrest Park Publishers, 1998

Horrocks-Ibbotson Co., *Reproduction of Catalog No. 39, 1949,* Grand Junction, CO, Centennial Publications, 1997

Irwin, R. Stephen, M. D., *Sporting Collectibles,* Wayne, NJ, Stoeger Publishing Company, 1997

Jellison, Harold and Homel, D. B., *Antique & Collectible Fishing Reels,* Bellingham, WA, Forrest Park Publishers, 1996

Johnson, Victor R. and Johnson, Victor R., Jr., *Fiberglass Fly Rods,* Grand Junction, CO. Centennial Publications, 1996

FOR COLLECTORS ONLY

There are two organizations involved with tackle collecting. For information on membership and benefits, contact one of the following. The first, the National Fishing Lure Collectors Club, has members involved not only with lures (their principal interest) but also with rods, reels and other tackle. The Old Fishing Reel Collectors Association is involved primarily with fishing reels.

NATIONAL FISHING LURE COLLECTORS CLUB, HCR 3, Box 4012, Reeds Spring, MO 65737

OLD REEL COLLECTORS ASSOCIATION, Arne Solund, Secretary/Treasurer, 849 N.E. 70th, Portland, OR 97213

Although new books are available from, or may be ordered through, any new-book store, old-book stores will sometimes have old fishing books. Some rare-book mail-order dealers specialize in sporting books. A source for new collector books (books by collectors and about specific collector tackle items) is: **Highwood Bookshop,** 10381 E. Shady Lane, Suttons Bay, MI 49682; Telephone 616-271-3898 (Monday-Friday), 24-hour fax 616-271-5013

Keane, Martin J., *Classic Rods and Rodmakers,* New York, NY, Winchester Press, 1976

Kelly, Mary Kefover, *U.S. Fishing Rod Patents and Other Tackle,* Plano, TX, Thomas B. Reel Company, 1990

Kimball, Art and Kimball, Scott, *Early Fishing Plus of the U.S.A.,* Boulder Junction, WI, Aardvark Publications, 1989

Kimball, Art, Kimball, Brad, and Kimball, Scott, *The Fish Decoy,* Boulder Junction, WI, Aardvark, Publications, Inc., 1986

Kimball, Art, Kimball, Brad, and Kimball, Scott, *The Fish Decoy, Volume II,* Boulder Junction, WI, Aardvark Publications, Inc., 1987

Kimball, Art, Kimball, Brad, and Kimball, Scott, *The Fish Decoy, Volume III,* Boulder Junction, WI, Aardvark Publications, Inc., 1993

Kimball, Art, and Kimball, Brad, *Fish Decoys of the Lac Du Flambeau Ojibway,* Boulder Junction, WI, Aardvark Publications, Inc., 1988

Lawson, George S., Jr., *Fishing Tackle Collectibles,* Capitola, CA, Monterey Bay Publishing, 1998

Lawson, George S., Jr., *Lawson's Price Guide to Old Fishing Reels,* Capitola, CA, Monterey Bay Publishing, 1997

Lawson, George S., Jr., *Lawson's Price Guide to Old Fishing Rods & Misc. Tackle,* Capitola, CA, Monterey Bay Publishing, 1997

Lawson, George S., Jr., *Lawson's Price Guide to Old Fishing Lures,* Capitola, CA, Monterey Bay Publishing, 1996

Luckey, Carl F., *Identification and Value Guide, Old Fishing Lures & Tackle, No. 5,* Iola, WI, Krause Publications, 1999

McClane, A. J., ed., *McClane's New Standard Fishing Encyclopedia and International Angling Guide,* New York, NY, Holt, Rinehart and Winston, 1974

Melner, Samuel and Kessler, Hermann, *Great Fishing Tackle Catalogs of the Golden Age,* New York, NY, The Lyons Press, 1989 (softcover 1999)

Minarik, Thomas and Minarik, Thomas, Jr., *Identification Guide to Hooks & Harnesses,* Tinley Park, IL, self-published, 1993

Montague Rods, *Reproduction of Catalog No. 39,* Grand Junction, CO, Centennial Publications

Muma, John R., *Old Flyrod Lures,* Lubbock, TX, Natural Child Publisher, 1991

Muma, John R., *Collecting Old Fishing Tackle,* Lubbock, TX, National Child Publishing Co., undated

Murphy, Dudley and Edmiston, Rick, *Fishing Lure Collectibles,* Paducah, KY, Collector Books, 1995

Murphy, Dean A., *Fishing Tackle Made in Missouri,* Hartsburg, MO, Dammo Publishing Company, 1993

Orrelle, John, *Fly Reels of the Past*, Portland, OR, Frank Amato Publications, 1987

Neff, S.A., Jr., *The Collector as a Bookbinder*, Wilkes Barre, PA, Sardoni Art Gallery, Wilkes University, 1999

Peterson, Donald J., *Folk Art Fish Decoys*, Atglen, PA, Schiffer Publishing, Ltd., 1996

Pollard, Douglas F. W., Peetz, *A Reel For All Time*, Surrey, BC, Canada, Heritage House Publishing Company, Ltd., 1997

Reinard, Ken, *The Colonial Angler's Manual of Flyfishing & Flytying*, Lancaster, PA, Fox Chapel Publishing Co., 1995

Richey, George, *Made in Michigan Fishing Lures*, Honor, MI, self-published, 1995

Robb, James, *Notable Angling Literature*, London, England, Herbert Jenkins Ltd., undated

Salive, Marcel L., *Ice Fishing Spears*, Marjack Publications, 1993

Sinclair, Michael, *Fishing Rods by Divine*, Grand Junction, CO, Centennial Publications, 1993

Sinclair, Michael, *Heddon: The Rod with the Fighting Heart*, Grand Junction, CO, Centennial Publications, 1997

Smith, Harold, *Collector's Guide to Creek Chub Lures & Collectibles*, Paducah, KY, Collector Books, 1997

Smith, Larry M., *Great Tackle Advertisements, 1874-1955*, self-published, 1990

Spurr, Dick, *Classic Bamboo Rodmakers Past and Present*, Grand Junction, CO, Centennial Publications, 1992

Spurr, Dick, and Jordan, Gloria, *Wes Jordan: Profile of a Rodmaker*, Grand Junction, CO, Centennial Publications, 1992

Starkman, Susan B., and Read, Stanley, E., *The Contemplative Man's Recreation*, Vancouver, Canada, The Library of the University of British Columbia, 1970

Stein, Gerald S., M.D., and Schaaf, James W., *Dickerson: The Man and His Rods*, Grand Junction, CO, Centennial Publications, 1991

Stockwell, Glenn, *Fly Reels of the House of Hardy*, London, Adam & Charles Black, 1978

Streater, R.L., with Edminsten, Rick and Murphy, Dudley, *The Fishing Lure Collector's Bible*, Paducah, KY, Collector Books, 1999

Tonelli, Donna, *Top of the Line Fishing Collectibles*, Atglen, PA, Schiffer Publishing, Ltd., 1997

Turner, Jack L., *The Collectors Guide to The Helin Tackle Company*, self-published, 1996

Turner, Graham, *Fishing Tackle: A Collector's Guide*, London, Ward Lock, Ltd., 1990

Turrell, W.J., *Ancient Angling Authors*, London, England, Gurney and Jackson, 1910

Vernon, Steven K., *Antique Fishing Reels*, Mechanicsburg, PA, Stackpole Books, 1985

Vernon, Steven K., and Stewart, Frank M., III, *Fishing Reel Makers of Kentucky*, Plano, TX, Thomas B. Reel Company, 1992

Waller, Phil, *Fishing Reels: Collecting for All*, self-published, 1993

Westwood, T., and Satchell, T., *Bibliotheca Piscatoria*, London, England, Peyton & Co., 1883

Wetzel, Charles M., *American Fishing Books*, Stone Harbor, NJ, Meadow Run Press, 1990 (reprint of privately printed 1950 edition)

White, Karl T., *Fishing Tackle Antiques and Collectibles*, Luther, OK, Holli Enterprises, 1995

White, Phil, *Meisselbach and Meisselbach-Catucci Fishing Reels*, Grand Junction, CO, Centennial Publications, 1995

Wong, Terry, *Collector's Guide to Antique Fishing Lure Colors*, self-published, 1997

Wright, Ben, *The Wright Price Guide for the Reel Man*, LeRoy, NY, MMY Compilations, 1996

Wright, Ben, *The Wright Price Guide for the Reel Man: Reel Through the History and Evolution of the Open-Face Spinning Reel*, LeRoy, NY, MMY Compilations, 1999

Young, Paul H., Co., *More Fishing, Less Fussing: Reproduction of 1956 Catalog of Paul H. Young Co.*, Grand Junction, CO, Centennial Publications, undated

Historical References

You could argue, correctly, that every book on fishing contains some valuable information on the sport, the tackle and fishing or tackle history. After all, the techniques used by, and the books read by our fathers and grandfathers in the 1930s, '40s and '50s, were current then and historical today. The following brief listing is of books that provide information on tackle and fishing methods at various times in American fishing history. There are many others, and there may be different editions or recent reprints of some of the following. Many will be out of print and only available through used- and rare-book dealers or in libraries.

Some relating to fishing history are still available. In addition to these listed, other valuable references to tackle history are the many fishing annuals, fishing digests and infrequent specialty publications periodically published by magazine and book publishers and sometimes even tackle companies. They all provide a varied and valuable look at our fishing past and the tackle used by our parents, grandparents and forefathers.

Bates, Joseph D., Jr., *Spinning for Salt Water Game Fish,* Boston, MA, Little, Brown and Company, 1957

Bates, Joseph D., Jr., *Spinning for Fresh Water Game Fish,* Boston, MA, Little, Brown and Company, 1954

Bates, Joseph D., Jr., *Spinning for American Game Fish,* Boston, MA, Little, Brown and Company, 1947

Bates, Joseph D., Jr., *Streamers and Bucktails, the Big Fish Flies,* New York, NY, Alfred A. Knopf, Inc., 1979

Bergman, Ray, *Fresh-Water Bass,* New York, NY, Alfred A. Knopf, Inc., 1942

Bergman, Ray, *With Fly, Plug, and Bait,* New York, NY, William Morrow & Company, 1947

Bergman, Ray, *Trout,* New York, NY, Alfred A, Knopf, Inc., 1938

Berners, Dame Juliana (attributed to), Sapir, Glenn (new preface), *A Treatise on Fishing With a Hook* (Treatise on Fishing with an Angle), New York, NY, North River Press, Inc., 1979 (translation reprint of 1496 edition)

Bowlker, Charles, *The Art of Angling,* London, England, Procter and Jones, 1829

Brown, John J., *The American Angler's Guide,* New York, NY, H. Long & Brother, 1849

Bueno, Bill, (editor), *The American Fisherman's Guide,* New York, NY, Prentice-Hall, 1952

Burns, Eugene, *The Complete Book of Fresh and Salt Water Spinning,* New York, NY, A. S. Barnes and Company, 1952

Camp, Samuel G., *The Fine Art of Fishing,* New York, NY, Outing Publishing Company, 1911

Camp, Samuel G., *Fishing Kits and Equipment,* New York, NY, The Macmillan Company, 1923

Camp, Samuel G., *The Angler's Handbook,* Columbus, OH, The Hunter-Trader-Trapper Co., 1925

Carroll, Dixie, *Fishing, Tackle and Kits,* Cincinnati, OH, Stewart & Kidd Company, 1919

Coykendall, Ralf, ed., *The Golden Age of Fly-Fishing,* Woodstock, VT, The Countryman Press, 1997

Cheney, A. Nelson (introduction), *American Game Fishes,* Chicago, IL, and New York, NY, Rand, McNally & Company, 1892

Evanoff, Vlad, *Modern Fishing Tackle,* Cranbury, NJ, A. S. Barnes and Co., Inc., 1961

Fox, Charles K., *Advanced Bait Casting,* New York, NY, G. P. Putnam's Sons, 1950

Francis, Francis, *A Book on Angling,* London, England, Longmans, Green & Co., 1867

Frazer, Perry, *Fishing Tackle,* New York, NY, Outing Publishing Company, 1914

Gallaher, Wallace W., *Black Bass Lore,* New York, NY, G. P. Putnam's Sons, 1937

Goodspeed, Charles Eliot, *Angling in America,* Boston, MA, Houghton Mifflin Company, 1939

Hallock, Charles, *The Fishing Tourist,* New York, NY, Harper & Brothers, 1873

Henshall, James Alexander, M.D., *Book of the Black Bass,* Cincinnati, OH, Robert Clarke & Co., 1881

Henshall, James Alexander, M.D., *Bass, Pike, Perch & Others,* Norwood, MA, Norwood Press, 1903

Henshall, James Alexander, M.D., *More About the Black Bass,* Cincinnati, OH, Robert Clerke, & Co., 1889

Herter, George Leonard, *Professional Glass and Split-Bamboo Rod Building Manual and Manufacturer's Guide,* self-published, 1953

Herter, George Leonard, *Professional Fly Tying and Tackle Manual and Manufacturers' Guide,* self-published, 1953

Holberton, Wakeman, *The Art of Angling,* New York, NY, Dick & Fitzgerald, 1887

Knight, John Alden, *Black Bass,* New York, NY, G. P. Putnam's Sons, 1949

Koller, Larry, *The Complete Book of Fresh-Water Fishing,* New York, NY, Bobbs-Merrill Company, Inc., 1954

Koller, Larry, *The Complete Book of Salt-Water Fishing,* New York, NY, Bobbs-Merrill Company, Inc., 1954

Little, G., *Angler's Complete Guide and Companion,* London, England, G. Little, 1881

Lincoln, Robert Page, *Black Bass Fishing,* Harrisburg, PA, The Stackpole Company, 1952

Lucas, Jason, *Lucas on Bass Fishing,* New York, NY, Dodd, Mead and Company, 1949

Lyman, Henry and Woolner, Frank, *Tackle Talk,* Cranbury, NJ, A. S. Barnes and Co., Inc., 1971

Major, Harlan, *Salt Water Fishing Tackle,* New York, NY, Funk & Wagnalls, 1939

McCarthy, Eugene, *Familiar Fish: Their Habits and Capture,* New York, NY, D. Appleton and Company, 1900

McClane, A. J., ed., *The Wise Fishermen's Encyclopedia,* New York, NY, Wm. H. Wise & Co., 1951

Netherton, Cliff, *History of the Sport of Casting, Early Times,* Lakeland, FL, American Casting Education Foundation, 1981

Netherton, Cliff, *History of the Sport of Casting, Golden Years,* Lakeland, FL, American Casting Education Foundation, 1983

Norris, Thaddeus, *The American Angler's Book,* Philadelphia, PA, Porter & Coates, 1864

Oppel, Frank, compiler, *Fishing In North America, 1876-1910,* Seacaucus, NJ, Castle, 1986

Osten, Earl, *Tournament Fly and Bait-Casting,* New York, NY, A. S. Barnes & Company, 1946

Ovington, Ray, *Spinning in America,* Harrisburg, PA, The Stackpole Company, 1954

Radcliffe, William, *Fishing from the Earliest Times,* Chicago, IL, Ares Publishers, 1974

Rau, Charles, *Prehistoric Fishing in Europe and North America,* Washington City, DC, Smithsonian Institution, 1884

Reiger, George, *Profiles in Saltwater Angling,* Englewood Cliffs, NJ, Prentice-Hall, Inc., 1973 (New edition, Camden, ME, Down East Outdoor Group, 1999)

Ripley, Ozark, *Modern Bait and Fly Casting,* New York, NY, D. Appleton & Co., 1928

Robinson, Gilmer, *Bait Casting,* New York, NY, A. S. Barnes & Company, 1941

Roman, Erl, *Fishing for Fun in Salty Waters,* Philadelphia, PA, David McKay Company, 1940

Roosevelt, Robert Barnwell, *Superior Fishing,* New York, NY, Carleton, 1865

Roosevelt, Robert Barnwell, *Game Fish of the Northern States of America,* New York, NY, Carleton, 1862

Schullery, Paul, *American Fly Fishing,* New York, NY, The Lyons Press, 1987

Schultz, Ken, ed., *The Macmillan Fishing Encyclopedia and Worldwide Angling Guide,* New York, NY, the Macmillan Company, 1999

St. John, Larry, *Practical Bait Casting,* New York, NY, The Macmillan Company, 1918

Stewart, Hilary, *Indian Fishing—Early Methods on the Northwest Coast,* Seattle, WA, University of Washington Press, 1982

Smith, O. W., *Casting Tackle and Methods,* Cincinnati, OH, Stewart & Kidd Company, 1920

Thommen, George V., *Spinning Reels & Tackle,* New York, NY, Oliver Durrell, Inc., 1949

Vogt, William C., *Bait-Casting,* New York, NY, Longman's Green and Co., 1928

Venables, Robert, Col., *The Experienced Angler,* London, England, Richard Marriot, 1662

Ward, Rowland, *The English Angler in Florida,* London, England, Rowland Ward, Ltd., 1898

Wells, Henry P., *Fly-Rods and Fly-Tackle,* New York, NY, Harper & Brothers, 1885

Waterman, Charles F., *A History of Angling,* Tulsa, OK, Winchester Press, 1981

Waterman, Charles F., *Fishing in America,* New York, NY, Holt, Rinehart and Winston, 1975

Younger, John, *On River Angling for Salmon & Trout,* New York, NY, Arno Press, 1967 (reprint of the 1840 Edition)

Acknowledgements

Over the years I have had the advantage of good friends willing to share and help, along with friends and acquaintances in the tackle and outdoor publishing industries also always willing to lend a hand for some research project, pet idea, article or book. To these, over all the years, I say thanks, since all of that help and all of that information was instrumental in aiding and abetting my interest in both fishing and tackle, and of ferreting out the best ways to use the best tackle to get in on the best fishing.

I have also gained a lot from the writings of outdoor writers of the past, particularly of books, of which I have a fair collection. These writers who took the time to write about the tackle used, how it was made, who made it and how it was used, provided the base for this or any other history that might be done on tackle. The same applies to writers of magazine articles and those unnamed and unsung copywriters who wrote catalog copy that provides so much information on tackle history, tackle evolution and tackle dating.

My researcher, Vern Kirby, called on some friends, all members of the National Fishing Lure Collectors Club, for help and assistance in checking facts and details. He and I want to thank the following: Tom Minarick, Dick Streater, Paul W. Whitfield, Jim Frazer, Steven K. Vernon, Frank M. Stewart III, John Shoffer, Bill Stuart, Barbara Carver, Bruce Boyden, Ben Wright and Clyde Harbin.

In addition, I separately called on specific people and did receive tremendous help. In some cases, my questions yielded much information. In others, despite the attempts of those asked, there is just not much information available, or easily obtainable at the present time, particularly with the time restrictions and deadlines of this book. After all, a book on this subject could be researched for ten years—or more.

In any case and in all cases, and in no particular order, I greatly appreciate the help of the following: Gary King and Karen Anfinston of Pure Fishing, better known as the parent company of Berkley, Fenwick, Abu Garcia and others, who provided me with information on their respective company histories; Diane Knight of JWA Fishing and Marine, the parent company of Mitchell rods and reels, Johnson rods and reels, Johnson and Bass Buster lures, and SpiderWire line, for help with history of their companies; Leon Chandler of the Cortland Line Company, who took time to talk with me and fill me in on his knowledge of the history of fly lines; Tom Kanalley of Cortland, for information on the history of lines and the Cortland Line Company; David LeGrande of Gudebrod, who loaned me early catalogs representative of the years that Gudebrod has been in the line business, along with copies of letters relating to line and fly line manufacture; Bruce Richards of the Scientific Anglers Co., for information and help with the history of fly lines and a history of Scientific Anglers.

Linda Martin and the Wright and McGill Company, for information on early hook manufacturing and a history of the Wright and McGill Company; Kathryn Crandall and the Ashaway Line & Twine Manufacturing Company, for information on early line manufacturing and the line walks of the early days of twisted linen lines; Ken Chaumont of the Bill Lewis Lures, Sports Design and Development Inc., for information on their Rat-L-Trap and rattle lures; Pradco, for help with the history of their companies (Heddon, Cotton Cordell, Rebel, Arbogast, Whopper Stopper and others); Herb Reed of Lunker City Fishing Specialties, for help with the history of the Slug-Go lures; Mark Hildebrandt of the Hildebrandt Corp., for help with the history of the Hildebrandt Company; Tony Tochterman, a longtime friend and owner of the family-owned (three generations) Baltimore tackle shop, Tochterman's, for answering many questions and for his offer of old tackle from his collection to help illustrate the book; Matthew Mayo and Down East Enterprises, publishers of the now-defunct *Fishing Tackle Trade News*, for their extensive help in giving me histories of many of the tackle companies that had previously been published in their periodical; John Mazurkiewicz of Catalyst Marketing, for information on the history of Shimano; Willi Brown and the O. Mustad and Sons Co. USA, for help with the history of fish hooks; Sharon Andrews of Storm Lures, for help with the history of Storm lures; Gary Dollohan, Jenni Foster and the Brunswick Outdoor Recreation Group, for assistance on the history of Zebco and spincast reels; Ed Mesunas and the Penn Fishing Tackle Co., for information on that company's history; Brian Butts of Sampo, for help with terminal tackle history.

Suzanne Newsom and Mann's Bait Company for information on Mann's history; Wayne Kent of Knight Manufacturing Company, present owner of Creme and Burke, for information on their histories; Martin Bustemante and the Eppinger Company, makers of the Dardevle spoons, for information on spoons and the history of the Eppinger Company and of early spoon manufacturers; Sheldon's Inc., for help with the history of Mepps spinners; Uncle Josh, for information and help with the history of Uncle Josh and pork rind; Sevenstrand, for help with the history of its company; Ken Reinard, author of *The Colonial Angler's Manual of Flyfishing & Flytying,* for his help and advice. Photos of early methods of making tackle would have been impossible without the help of Reinard, a "re-enactor" of Colonial times and the Colonial fisherman; Larry Smith, author of *Great Tackle Advertisements, 1874-1955,* who graciously allowed the use of some ads from his book for inclusion in this work, and thus gives us a better picture of the ads and tackle of a 75-year period; Thomas Minarik, who graciously allowed use of some of the illustrations from his book for inclusion in this work; Nick Lyons of The Lyons Press, who published and graciously allowed the use of catalog pages from *Great Fishing Tackle Catalogs of the Golden Age,* edited by Samuel Mellner and Hermann Kessler; Sean Sonderman and the American Museum of Fly Fishing in Manchester, VT, for their extensive help in researching questions and copying from their files and archives articles and histories of early American tackle and tackle companies; Gail Morchower, librarian, and the International Game Fish Association, for answering questions and researching material on the history of tackle; Lefty Kreh, for general information and advice; Ed Dzialo, executive director of the National Fresh Water Fishing Hall of Fame and Museum, for his help and cooperation and for the Hall's assistance to Phil Aarrestad, who photographed much of the contents of this book at the headquarters of the museum in Hayward, WI; Phil Aarrestad, photographer of the individually commissioned photos in this book, for his help and dedication to not only fine photographic quality, but also historical accuracy of the items included in each of the many photos; Jack Goellner and Barbara Lamb, for their help with references and proper ;isting of bibliographic material; and George Reiger, for help with and use of Zane Grey photos.

Special thanks are due to Vern Kirby of Glen Burnie, MD, who worked for me as a researcher on this project. Vern, a long-time friend, was with me from the start on this, read all of the text, caught my errors, corrected my mistakes, suggested changes to the book (most of which I agreed to), caught my lapses and was with me on this through thick and thin … and we're still talking to each other. Without his help from the start, this book would have been unlikely, definitely impossible with the deadlines required and far less than it has become.

Special thanks are also due to Chuck Edghill, another long-time friend, fishing companion and excellent editor. As he has done previously with some of my books, Chuck agreed to read the final manuscript, along the way correcting my misspellings and grammatical errors and making this tome more readable and understandable.

Special thanks are also due to my editors at North American Outdoor Group, Tom Carpenter, Dan Kennedy, Glenn Sapir and all the staff at NAOG. All gentlemen were cooperative and understanding from the start, granted extensions to the deadline (although a little longer would have been better!), and worked with me as we exchanged ideas and thoughts throughout the gestation period, development and writing of the book. Thanks, Tom, Dan and Glenn.

Obviously, though the book would have been impossible without the help from all the above, I remain responsible for any errors, omissions, misinterpretations or slights that may have occurred, but which hopefully did not.

C. Boyd Pfeiffer

Index

A

A. B. Shipley, 152
A. C. Plug, 101
A. E. Nelson, 235
A. J. Baldwin, 42
A. W. Bishop & Son, 192
Aaron, 216
Abbey & Imbrie Company, 59, 104, 152
Abbotts' Waders, 238
Abel, 224
Abel, Steve, 215, 216
Abu Charmer, 83
Abu Garcia, 78, 89, 92, 172, 206, 209, 211, 213, 214
    Ambassadeur 6500 C3, 217
    Ambassadeurs, 192
    Cap, 205
    Voblex, 83
Abu Reflex, 83
Accurate, 192
Accetta Pet trolling spoon, 95
Actionrods, 167
Adjustable Friction Drag, 200
Advanced Bait Casting (Fox), 252
Advanced Lure Inc., 104
Aelian, Claudius, 47, 145
Aero Cast casting reel, 192
AeroSpin line, 141
Aetna, 163
AirCel Supreme, 142
Airex, 205, 206
Airex lures, 83
Airex Vic, 205
Air Flo, 143
Akron Fishing Tackle Works, 64
Alcedo, 206
Alcedo Micron, 199
Al Foss, 52, 69, 83
    Little Egypt pork rind lure, 68
    Shimmy Wiggler pork rind lure, 68
Allcock
    Cleopatra, 57
    Leight and Westwood, 81
    Paragon Minnow, 57
Allen, 163
Allen, Will R., 30
Alnwick rigs, 40
Al's Goldfish spoon, 83
Alvey reels, 212
American Angler's Book, The (Norris), 25, 27, 29, 36, 56, 112, 183, 247–248
American Angler's Guide, The (Brown), 25, 29–30, 34, 53, 146, 182–183, 226, 245, 247, 254
American Big Game Fishing (Connett), 249
American Co. reels, 194
American Fish Hook Company, 64
American Fishing Tackle Manufacturers Association, 142
American Fly Fishing (Schullery), 53–54, 148

American Fly Fishing Trade Association, 142
American Hendryx spinner, 57
American Museum of Fly Fishing, 251
Amnesia, 132
Ande, 131, 134
Andrew B. Hendryx Company, 59
Angler's Art (Serviente), 258
Angler's double knot, 112
Angler's Engineering, 141
Angler's Friend, 231
Angler's Image, 240–241
Angler's prayer, 72
Angler's Pride, 102
Angler's single knot, 110, 112
Angler's Souvenir, The, 245
Angling in America (Goodspeed), 184
Animated Minnow, 67
Anthony Company, 191
Antique Fishing Reels (Vernon), 200
Apte, Stu, 177
Aquasonic Lures, 93
Arbogast (Fred), 30, 71–73, 77, 84, 93, 104
    Cock-Tail Kicker, 71–72
    Jitterbug, 79
Archer spinners, 40
Arming of hook, 38, 124
Armstrong, A. Joseph, 256
Aronis, Costa, 210
Artificial lures. See Lures, artificial
Art of Angling, The (Brookes), 54, 153, 162, 184
Art of Angling (Barker), 179
Art of Fishing (Brookes), 245
Art of the Creel, The (Chatham & McClain), 234–235
Ascent, 216
Ashaway Line & Twine Manufacturing Company, 127, 130, 138–139, 141
Ashaway Slip Cast, 199, 205, 206
Atlantic Game Fishing (Farrington), 250
Auburn Fish Hook Company, 21

B

B. F. Gladding Co., 130, 135, 141, 142
B. F. Smith Co., 18
Babe-Oreno, 67
Bagley, 96
Bagley Rattling DB3 Magnum, 102
Bag-O-Mad, 93
Bailey and Elliott, 60
Bait, live and natural
    casting with, 38–39
    chumming, 37
    early, 34
    frogs as, 33, 39–40
    ground and paste baits, 34–35
    grubs, 38
    hooks for, 42–43
    making paste, 38
    minnows as, 40–42
    pork rind, 43
    preserving roe, 38
    reasons against using, 33
    roe for trout and salmon, 35
    scouring worms, 37
    unusual, 36
    worms, 34–38
Baitcasting
    books on, 250–252
Bait Casting for the Novice and the Expert, 204
Bait Casting (Robinson), 252
Bait-Casting (Vogt), 33, 250
Bait Casting with a Thermometer (Steel), 257
Bait Mate, 104
BaitRunner, 211
Baldwin Live Minnow Bait, 42
Bamboo rod, 154–159
Banana lures, 65–66
Barbless hook, 24
Barker, Rocky, 256
Barker, Thomas, 179
Bartram, William, 48
Bass-A-Lure, 75
Bass Anglers Sportsman Society, 90, 252
Bass Bait, 56
Bass bugs, 47
Bass Buster crappie jigs, 94
Bass flies, 69–70
Bass-Oreno, 67
Bass Pro Shops, 143, 224
Bass Strip, 43
Bate Patent Serpentine Spinner, 55–56
Bates, Joseph D., 246
Bauer, 216
Baumgartel, Henry, 193
Baxter Brogue, 238
Bayou Boogie, 76, 105
Bean, 143
Beaver Bait Co., 69
Becket hitch, 117
Bedell, Berkley, 78–79
Bedell, Tom, 78
Bellan, 216
Bell guides, 162
Belmar guides, 163
Benson, 208
Bergman, Ray, 248, 250, 252
Berkley, 78, 104–107, 110, 131, 132, 134–135, 148, 172
    Not-A-Knot system, 118
    Trilene, 79
Berners, Dame Juliana, 27–28, 47–48, 137, 145, 181, 244
Beryllium copper rods, 165
Bethune, George Washington, 6–7, 9
Biek's Jack-Knife Gaff Hook, 228
Big O., 90
Big Tin Liz, 72
Bill DeWitt, 83
Bill Harrington Bait Co., 93
Billinghurst, 216
Billinghurst cage reel, 183
Bill Lewis Company Rat-L-Trap, 94
Bill Norman Big N., 91
Bimini twist, 115, 120
Black Bass Fishing (Lincoln), 252
Black Bass Lore (Gallaher), 132
Blade baits
    beginning of, 94
Blood knot, 121
Blood worm, 36

Blue Fox, 92
Blue Fox spinner, 7
Bobber, 30–31
Bobs, 48–50, 56
Bomber, 62, 64, 80, 81
    Mag A, 102
    Water Dog, 102
Book of the Black Bass (Henshall), 138, 153, 246, 247, 249, 256
Book on Angling, A (Francis), 35, 148
Books and periodicals
    changing fishing book market, 257–258
    for collectors, 259–261
    early American books, 245–247
    early references to tackle, 247–250
    English books and English influence, 244–245
    fishing annuals, catalogs and magazines, 252–254
    fly fishing influence, 250
    historical reference books, 262–263
    introduction to, 243
    more facts and less anecdotes, 254–255
    niche books for species, technique or tackle, 256–257
    rise of baitcasting, 250–251
    rise of regional books, 255–256
Boschen, William, 200
Bow-dipsy, 36
Boyer Manufacturing, 30
Bradco, 206
Braided lines
    connections, 119–120
    for fly lines, 140–141
Braided wire knots, 120–121
Bristol, 166, 167, 206
Bronson, 194
Bronson 631, 209
Brookes, Richard, 54, 153, 162, 184
Brooks, Joe, 10, 202, 250
Brown, Bache, 196, 205
Brown, John J., 25, 29–30, 34, 53, 146, 182–183, 189, 226, 245, 247, 254
Bruette, William A., 125
Buel, Julio T., 50–51, 53, 67
Buel spinner, 50, 57
Bumble Bee, 192
Burke Company, 60, 84, 99
Burke Flexo-Products Co., 77, 87
Bush Wacker, 81

C

C. P. Swing, 83, 92
Cabela's, 143, 224
Caddis larva, 36, 38
Caliber, 92
Callmac bugs, 70
Camp, Raymond R., 164
Camp, Samuel G., 152, 250
Campbell, John W., 23
Camuto, Christopher, 256
Cap, 206
Cape Fear Rod Company, 175
Carboloy, 163

Cargem Mignon 33, 199
Carlton, 204
Carr, Teddy, 256
Carroll, Dixie, 254
Carter, William, 189
Castaic Baits, 101
Casting with bait, 38–39
Casting Tackle and Methods (Smith), 152, 250
Casts, 124
Catesby, Mark, 245
Cat gut, 126
Catskill Fly Fishing Center and Museum, 251
Centaure, 206
Centrifugal brake, 191
Chandler, Leon, 140
Chaney, A. Nelson, 249
Charles C. Kellman Company, 70
Charley's Worms, 77
Charlton, 216
Chas. Forsburg & Sons, 235
Chatham, Hugh, 234
Chatter Chub, 106
Childre, Lew, 163, 213
Chippewa Bait, 69
Chrystal Minnow, 58
Chub, 29
Chumming
  early, 37
  standard method of, 37
Circle, Homer, 76, 165
Circle hook, 21
Clark, J. M., 152
Clark Spoon, 77
Classic Woods, 77
Class line, 131
Clearing ring, 220–222
Clerke, Andrew, 152
Clinch knot, 114, 115
Coaxer, 63, 70, 88
Cobra, 132
Coleman Family Fishing, 78
Collectors, 8–9
  books for, 259–261
Colonial Angler's Manual of Flyfishing & Flytying, The (Reinard), 15, 45, 48
Color C-Lector colors, 97
Colored hook, 23
Commercial fishing
  conflict with recreational fishing, 10
  early, 9–11
Compleat, Angler, The (Walton), 6, 9, 14, 38, 46, 48, 50, 151, 179, 182, 244
Comstock, Harry, 58
Conery, 190
Connett, Eugene, 249
Conroy, 190
Contracted reels, 195–196
Cook, Carroll Blaine, 254
Cordon, Francois, 16
Cortland Company, 131, 132, 134–135, 140–143, 216
Cotton, Charles, 6, 38, 244
Cotton Cordell Company, 77, 84, 90, 95
Cotton lines, 125
Coxe, 194
Coxe, J. A., 200
Crandall, Lester, 127

Crane hook, 20
Crankbait Corporation, 102
Crazy Crawler, 83, 84
Creek Chub, 64, 72, 74, 77, 80, 81, 195
  Darter, 76
  Giant Jointed Pikie, 101
  Giant Pikie, 60
  #100 Wiggler, 74
  #200 Wiggler, 74
  Plastic Pikie, 101
  Weed bug, 76
Creel, 233–236
Creme, 77
Creme, Nick, 21, 86–88
Crippled Alewife, 77
Crippled Herring, 77
Croaker, 70
Crosby, 39
Cross Rod & Tackle Co., 150
Crystal Minnow, 52
Cullum & Boren, 30
Cummings, 235
Cuttyhunk, 128

D
D. H. Thompson Co., 240
Dacron, 111, 132
Daiichi, 19
Daiwa, 148, 160, 202, 203, 205, 210, 211, 214
  Millionaires, 192
Dalton, 190
Dame, Stoddard & Kendall, 16
Dardevle, 52, 67, 78, 83, 95
Dare Devil, 52
Darter, 74
Darting Zara, 74
Days and Nights of Salmon Fishing (Scrope), 195
Dazzle Tail, 89
Deally, 190
Decker, 63–64
Decker, Anson B., 63
Dee Thomas flipping rod, 214
DeLong, 87
Depth-O-Therm thermometer, 220
Detroit Glass Minnow Tube Company, 41
Devels Horse, 52
Devon lures, 50
Devons, 62, 83
DeWitt, William, 19, 21
Dexter Minnow, 58
Dexter Spoon, 58
Diamond, 216
Ding Bat, 74
Disgorgers, 236
Dive Bomber, 80
Diving lures, 74
Divine, Fred D., 152
Dixie Wiggler, 69
Doctor, 77
Double-barb hook, 22
Double water knot, 110
Dowagiac, 62
Dr. Juice, 104
Driscoll-Bruch Company, 19, 20
Dry fly, 6
Dry Fly and Fast Water (LaBranche), 250
Dry Fly Fishing in Theory and Practice (Halford), 248
Duckling Feathered Frog, 70
DuPont, 130–132

E
Eagle Claw, 21, 24
Eagle Claw (B. F. Smith), 18
Eagle Claw (Wright & McGill), 19, 20, 42
Eagle Folding Net Company, 231
Early Fishing Plugs of the U.S.A. (Kimball & Kimball), 50
Eaton, 235
Eckhardt Minnow, 40
Edwards, 156
Ehlers, Harry, 89
Electric Fishing Reels Systems, 192
Electric Submarine Bait Co., 104
Elliott, Bob, 256
End loop knot, 116
Enterprise Manufacturing Company, 19, 52, 58, 64, 88
Envy, 134
Eppinger, 20, 52, 78, 81, 95
  Dardevle spoon, 7
Eppinger, Lou, 52, 67
Erie Dearie, 95
Erne St. Claire Tail-Lite, 83
Eureka Wiggler, 93
Evanoff, Vlad, 249
Excalibur, 77
Experienced Angler, The (Venables), 182, 233, 244
Expert Telescoping Pocket Gaff Hook, 228
E-Z spinner fly, 49

F
F. C. Woods & Company, 228
Falcon, 83
Falcon Grip, 19, 20
Farcaster, 194
Fare, Eric C., 49
Farlow, 235
Farnsworth, George, 200
Farrington, Chisie, 164
Farrington, S. Kip Jr., 164, 250
Feathered Wiggler, 70
Featherweight, 161
Fenwick, 78, 132, 172, 177, 214
Ferrules, 149, 161
Fiberglass rods, 172–174
Figure-eight knot, 111
Figure-eight loop knot, 115–117
Figure-eight twist, 121
Fincheroo, 93
Fine Art of Fishing, The (Camp), 152
Fine-wire hook, 20
Finger pulls, 150
Finley-Norwood Machine Shop, 215
Fin-Nor, 163, 201, 202, 211, 215, 216
FireLine, 79
Fish
  stocking, 10–11
  as utilitarian object, 9–10
Fish basket, 233–236
Fishcake lures, 60, 85
Fisherman's knot, 112–113, 115
Fisherman's Luck (Van Dyke), 248

Fish Formula, 104
Fish Hawk, 76
Fishing
  commmerical/recreational conflict, 10
  prejudices against as sport, 11
  prohibition of, on Sunday, 9
  varieties of, 11
Fishin' Glue, 117
Fishing in American Waters (Scott), 56, 186–187, 241, 247–248
Fishing Kits and Equipment (Camp), 250
Fishing knives, 239–240
Fishing Reel Makers of Kentucky (Vernon & Stewart), 188
Fishing suits/jackets/vests, 241
Fishing Tackle, Its Materials and Manufacture (Keene), 246
Fishing Tackle and Kits (Carroll), 254
Fishing Tackle (Frazer), 250
Fishing the Atlantic (Farrington), 250
Fishing the Pacific (Farrington), 250
Fishing the Surf (Camp), 164
Fishing Tourist, The (Hallock), 149, 256
Fishing With Hook and Line (Forester), 247
Fishing With the Fly (Orvis & Chaney), 249
Fish-Ng, 192
Fish pannier, 233–236
Five star, 131
Fix, 206
Fixed hooks, 7
Fix-Reel, 205
Flambeau, 224
Flatfish, 65, 66, 79, 85
Flax, 124–125
Flex Plug lures, 100
Flies
  1875-1900, 61
  1900-1920, 69–70
  in colonial fishing period, 48, 50
  early, 46–47
  1800s-1850s, 53–54
  1940 to 1950, 80
  tools for tying, 240
Flipping, 49, 214
FlipTail, 89
Fli-Tossr line, 141
Floating-diving lures, 74
Floating Feather Minnow Feath-Oreno Minnows, 70
Floating Flies and How to Dress Them (Halford), 249
Floats, 28–31
  bobber stop, 30–31
  early, 28–29
  material for, 29–30
  modern, 30–31
  unusual, 30
Floppy ring guides, 162
Fluorocarbon line, 132–133
Fly books, 225–226
Fly boxes, 225
Fly Champ, 204
Fly Fisher's Text Book (South),

Index   267

Fly fishing
    no-knot systems, 118–119
    saltwater fishing, 53–54, 56–57
Fly-Fishing and Fly-Making (Keene), 246
Fly Fishing in Salt Water (Kreh), 250
Fly leaders, 126
Fly lines, 136–143
    braided construction of, 140–141
    early history of, 137–138
    fast-sinking lines, 142–143
    line-size standard, 142
    nylon, 141
    plastic coatings and changes in design, 142
    PVC and high floating lines, 142–143
    silk, 138–139
    weight-forward and specialty lines, 139
    weights and sizes for, 139–140
Fly reels
    automatic, 203–204
    fly reels defined and described, 195–196
    high tech/big game, 215–216
    for saltwater fishing, 215–216
    simplicity of, 202–204
Fly rod
    evolution of, 7–8
Fly-Rods and Fly-Tackle (Wells), 166
Fly Strip, 43
Forester, Frank, 6, 35, 51, 137, 247, 253
Fork lure, 88
Foul Proof guides, 163
Fox, Charles K., 37, 252
Francis, Francis, 35, 148
Frank Forester's Fishing of the United States and British Provinces (Forester), 247
Frankfort Kentucky Reel, 200
Frazer, Perry D., 250
Fred D. Divine Company, 152, 159
    rod, 158
Free-swinging hooks, 7
Fre-Line, 206, 207
French Mitchell, 148
French Olympique, 83
Freshwater Bass (Bergman), 252
Freshwater Fishing Hall of Fame and Museum, 9
Fresh Water Fishing (Koller), 257
Frictionless Spooler, 192
Frisbee, 235
Frog Casting Frame Gang, 39
Frogs, 69
    artificial pork frogs, 43
    as bait, 33
    frog-hooking harnesses, 33
    harnesses for, 39–40
Fuji, 164
Fullilove, 190

G
Gaddabout Gaddis spoon, 80
Gaffs, 226–229
Gaines Company, 80, 88
Gallaher, Wallace W., 132
Gamakatsu, 19, 22
Game Fisher, 65, 74
Garceau, Leo, 210
Garland Cork-Head Minnow, 96
Gar Wood, 215
Gator Grip Company, 192
Gay, John, 45
Gayle, Clarence, 190
Gayle, George W., 190
Gayle reels, 190
Gel-spun polyethylene line, 111, 134–135
Gem, 216
Genuine Crankbait Brand, 77
Gephart, 166, 167
Gep rod, 150
Ghost and Gobblin lures, 89
Gibbs, Jerry, 102
Glass rods, 170–172
Glenn, 235
Glop, 91
Glow Body Minnow, 104
Glow Worm, 104
Golden Stren, 134
Good-All, 206, 207
Goodspeed, Charles, 184
Gordon, Theodore, 6, 61, 246
Gorges, 13
Gorgstrom, Goth, 213
GPS unit, 219, 233
Graflite, 172
Graphite rods, 172–176
Grasshoppers, 34–35
Great Equalizer, 177
Green, E. A., 154
Green box portable depth finder, 233
Gregory, Myron, 139
Grey, Zane, 22, 129, 249
Grubs
    hooking, 38
Gudebrod Company, 130, 134–135, 143
Guides, 161–165, 177
Gurglehead, 73
Gut leaders, 124, 125

H
H. C. Brush, 55
Hair lines, 123, 124
Halford, Frederic M., 246, 248, 249
Halik Company, 89
Hallock, Charles, 6, 149, 245, 256
Hancock, George, 208
Handitop, 235
Hanson Frog Harness, 40
Harbin, Clyde, 62
Hardloy, 165
Hardy, 235
Hardy Barton, 216
Hardy fly reels, 148
Harrison Hoge, 92
Hart, 106
Haskell
    Minnow, 55, 57
    Musky Minnow, 55
Hastings, James, 59
Hastings Rubber Frog, 58
Havens, G. G., 170
Hawaiian Wiggler, 72–73
Hawg Boss, 77
Hawk Fish, 94
Hawthorne single action reel, 202
Hayes Bass Bug Co., 70
Haynes Bait Company, 69
Heddon, 59–61, 70–72, 74, 76, 94, 95, 150, 166, 191, 204, 206, 213, 216
    Bomber, 77
    Deep Six, 62
    Double Dowagiac Minnow, 61
    Dowagiac Minnow, 58
    Gay Blade, 94
    Glass Eye Vamp, 61
    Jointed Vamp, 83
    King Stanley spoon, 7, 81
    Luny Frogs, 75
    Musky Minnow, 59
    Pyralin Vamp, 83
    River Runt, 62
    Sonar Flash, 94
    Sonic, 94, 105
    Spoony Frog, 81
    Stanley Ace, 74
    Tadpolly, 65, 66
    Tadpolly Spook, 65
    Weedless Widow, 61
    Widget, 62
    Zaragossa, 52
    Zara Spook, 90
Heddon, Charles, 52, 61, 88
Heddon, James, 59, 61, 62, 88
Heddon, William, 61, 88
Helin Tackle Co., 31, 77, 79, 85
    Flatfish, 46, 58, 60
    Rollaflote, 31
Hellbender, 64
Helm-knot, 117
Hendricks raised pillar reel, 185
Hennepin, Louis, 245
Henschel, 216
Henshall, James, 6, 138, 151, 154, 188, 246, 247, 249, 256
Henze, Otto, 201
Herbert, Henry William, 6, 51, 247, 253
Herter, 20, 249
Herter, George Leonard, 246
Herter's reel, 210
Hexagraph rods, 176
Hildebrandt, 7, 58–59, 92, 95
Hildebrandt, Mark, 58
Hill, Loren, 97
Hi-Seas, 131
History of tackle
    speculative nature of, 7
    work and social history influence, 8
Hi-Viz lines, 134
Hofe, Julius, 190
Hofschneider, 78
Holden, George Parker, 159
Holt, John, 256
Hom-Art Bait Co., 73
Homer LeBlanc, 65
Homer Rhode loop, 110, 115
Honeycutt, Blake, 90
Hoochy skirt, 93
Hook, Line, and Sinker (Soucie), 249
Hooks, 13–24. See also specific hooks
    arming of, 38, 124
    for bait, 42–43
    barbless, 24
    bending tools, 17
    changing purpose of, 22
    circle, 21
    colored, 23
    early American hook makers, 19
    from early civilization, 13–14
    early hand-made, 15–16
    early U. S. makers, 16–17
    eye-less, 16
    finishes and designs, 24
    hook attachments for lures, 60
    importing in colonial America, 14–15
    jig hooks, 21
    machine manufacturing of, 17, 19
    modern, 23–24
    single point, 13–14
    specialty, 20
    spring triggering hooks, 18
    transparent, 23
    World War II's affect on, 20
Hoo Nose, 42
Hopkins, 77
Hopkins jigging spoons, 95
Hornet, Inc., 92
Horrocks-Ibbotson Company, 20, 49, 59, 141, 177, 194, 202, 204
Horse hair
    fly fishing line, 137–138
Horton, Everett, 160
Horton Manufacturing Company, 160, 194
Hot'N Tot, 91
Hot Shot, 229
Hotternell Bait Holder, 42
Howald, Arthur, 171
Howald process, 174
Hula Popper, 104
Hula skirt, 73
Humminbird depth finder, 89
Humphreys, 206, 207
Huntington Drone, 77, 78
Hurd Super Caster, 208
Husky Devle, 68

I
Iceland hook, 20
Ice tong hook, 18, 23
Ideal Gaff Hook, 227
Ideal Tackle Co., 30
Identification and Value Guide, Old Fishing Lures and Tackle (Luckey), 61–62
Illingworth reel, 197–198
Imbrie, 152
Immell Bait Co., 69
Improved clinch knot, 115, 121
Inductor, 194
Inductor reel, 214
In-line dropper loop, 110, 112, 115
International Game Fish Association, 134, 251
Intrinsic Phantoms, 55
Invisible knot, 114
Iron Maiden, 40

Islander, 216

J
J. B. Christian, 56
J. M. Mast Mfg. Co., 30
Jackson, Keith, 107
James T. Hastings Company, 90
Jamison, William J., 63, 88
Jamison Company, 22, 58, 59, 63, 68–70, 84
  Shannon Twin Spin, 81
  Underwater Coaxer, 68, 82
Jazz Wiggler, 69
Jelly Worm, 89
Jersey Queen, 64
Jigger, 93
Jig hook, 21
Jigs
  development of, 77
  evolution of, 93–94
Jitterbug, 73
Joe Welsh, 140
John Conroy, 188, 189
John L. Walleye, 77
Johnson, William, 50
Johnson Reel Co., 214
Johnson Worldwide Associates, 78, 148, 205–207
  Caper, 71
  Silver Minnow, 71, 80, 81, 84, 90, 95
  Sprite, 71
Jones, Alan P., 43
Jones, Keith, 102, 105
Joseph M. Ness Co., 42
Julius Vom Hofe casting reel, 185
June Bug spinner, 41, 68
Just Fishing (Bergman), 248
JWA, 217

K
K. B. Explosions, 95
KaBar knife, 239
Kalm, Pehr, 245
Kazoo Reed bugs, 70
Kazoo Wobbler, 76
K-B, 77
K-B spoon, 81
Keene, John Harrington, 240, 246
Kellman, Charles C., 42
Kelso, 204
Kelson, George, 241, 249
Kent, Wayne, 87
Kent Double Spinner Artificial Minnow, 60
Kent Floaters, 65
Kentucky reels, 187–190
Kenyon, John M., 160
Kerr, 208
Kesting, Ted, 132
Ketchum, 39
Ketchum Release, 236
Kevlar, 176
Kimball, Art, 50
Kimball, Scott, 50
Kingfisher Tackle Company, 19, 20
King Wig-Wag, 75
Kirby, Charles, 14
Kitchen Sink lure, 88
K & K Manufacturing Company, 67
Knickerbocker Case Co., 223
Knight, John Alden, 250

Knight Manufacturing, 77, 87
Knight Tube Worm, 100
Knots and connectors. See also specific knots
  braided line connections, 119–120
  braided wire knots, 120–121
  changing and improving, 117
  early knots, 111–112
  early line-to-hook knots, 114
  early line-to-line knots, 112–114
  before eyed hooks, 109
  glue and, 117–118
  importance of, 111
  introduction, 109
  knotting knots in place, 110–111
  leader sleeves for mono and wire, 121
  line-to-line connections, 110–111
  loops, 116–117
  material for line and effect on, 111, 116
  naming, 115
  new knotty wire, 121
  no-knot connections, 118–119
  splicing/splicing needles, 120
  strength of, 118
  testing, 113
  wire knots, 120
Knotted sheet bend, 115
Koller, Larry, 257
Kreeker, 80
Kreh, Lefty, 116, 177, 250
Krider, 156
Kwikfish, 77

L
L. Crandall & Company, 128
L. L. Bean, 40
LaBranche, George M. L., 250
Lamiglas, 177
Lamson, 216
Landing nets, 230–231
Langley, 194, 206
LaRue, Gene, 105
Lawrence, 235
Lazer system lures, 104
Lazy Ike, 65, 66, 77, 97
LCI, 177
Leader, 124
Le Boeuf Creeper, 84
Lee Wulff's Handbook of Freshwater Fishing (Wulff), 114
LeGrande, David, 130
Leonard, 156, 195
Leonard, Hiram L., 156
Les Davis, 77
  Hot Rod, 83
Level-wind mechanisms, 193
Lew Childre Speed Spool, 213
Lewis, Bill, 105–106
Libbey-Owens-Ford Glass Company, 171
Lighted lures, 103–104
Lightning Rod, 79
L'il Tubby, 101
Lincoln, Robert Page, 250, 252
Line counters, 192
Linen, 124–125

Lines, 123–143
  by American Indians, 123
  beginning braiding, 128–129
  braided line connections, 119–120
  class line, 131
  color in, 133–134
  cotton, 125
  Cuttyhunk, 128
  Dacron, 132
  early Colonial lines, 123–126
  early commercial manufacturing of, 127–128
  effect on knots used and, 111
  fluorocarbon, 132–133
  for fly fishing, 136–143
  gel-spun polyethylene, 134–135
  hair lines, 123, 124
  introduction to, 123
  linen, 124–125
  line-size standard, 142
  line-to-line connections, 110–111
  material for, 111
  nylon monofilament, 130–132
  silk, 125–126
  size, 138–140
  test line, 131
  thread lines, 129–130
  walking to make lines, 126–127
  wire, 135–136
Line walks, 126–127
Line winder/dryer, 240–241
Lion Gaff, 227
Little Egypt, 52, 69
Little George, 89
Live Bait Holder Co., 42
Live Minnow Cage, 42
Live-Wire, 75
Lloyd & Co., 103–104
Lobb, Floyd Ferris, 54
Lockhart, E. J., 93
Log Chain Live Bait Hook, 41
Long-shank hook, 20
Loomis, 176, 224
Loop knot, 121
Loops, 116–117
Lowrance Global Map 100, 233
Lucas, Jason, 49, 132, 236, 252
Lucas on Bass Fishing (Lucas), 132, 246, 252
Luckey, Carl, 61–62, 73
Lucky 7 dice lures, 98
Luhr Jensen, 77, 84, 229
  Deep Secret, 102
  Ripple Tail Cicada, 94
LumaLure, 104
Lunker City Fin-S, 100
Lunker City Slug-Go, 100
Lure retriever, 220–222
Lures, artificial
  benefit of, 45–46
  biology and fisheries studies of lure design, 107
  combo hard and soft plastic, 101
  hook attachments, 60
  introduction to, 45–46
  lighted, 103–104
  plastic, 71, 86–89
  pork rind, 69

  rubber, 56, 58
  sonic, 76, 93–94
  vinyl, 89–90
  wood, 59, 61, 96
Lures, artificial, timetable for
  from beginning to 1800s, 46–50
  from 1800s to 1850s, 50–54
  after 1850s to 1875, 54–57
  from 1875 to 1900, 57–61
  1900 to 1920, 61–70
  1940 to 1950, 79–85
  1950 to 1975, 86–94
  1975 to present, 94–107
Luxe, 205
Luxor, 204, 205
Luxor spinning reel, 199
Lyons, Nick, 257
L-Y Yates, 77
  spoon, 81

M
Mackinen Tackle Co., 85
Magazines. See Books and periodicals
Maggots, 36
Magnum Warts, 91
Major, Harlon, 26, 249
Makilure baits, 85
Makinen Tackle Co., 73
Malloch, Peter, 197
Manitou Minnow, 60
Mann, Tom, 87, 89
Mann's Lures, 84, 87, 89, 96
Mann's 20 Plus Deep Hog, 102
Marado, 217
Marathon, 141
Marble's Clincher Gaff, 228
Marinaro, Vince, 37
Martin, 202, 203, 206
Martin Fish Lure Company, 42
Marttiini knives, 239
Martuch, Leon L., 142
Martuch, Leon P., 142
Maruto, 19
Mason, 134–135
Master Biff Plug, 93
Maxima, 131
Maybug Bait, 55
McChristian, Bob Mac, 215
McClain, Dan, 234
McClane, A. J., 83, 180, 210, 246
McClane's New Standard Fishing Encyclopedia and International Angling Guide (McClane), 246
McClellan, Bing, 99
McGill, Andrew, 19
McGregor, Nelson, 193
McKenzie, 143
McManus, Patrick, 254
Medley, 190
Meek, Benjamin F., 189
Meek, Jonathan F., 189
Meek-Horton 2MJ baitcasting reel, 185
Meek & Sons Blue Grass #4 casting reel, 187
Meisselbach, 204, 216
  BakeLite reel, 187
  Catucci Mfg. Co., 201
  Good Luck reel, 184
  side mounted casting reel, 180
  Symplo reel, 217

take-apart reel, 185
Tri-part reels, 186
Mepps, 83
Mepps spinners, 7, 55, 82, 90, 92
Merlin Lures Pathfinder, 93
MetaLure, 77
M-F Manufacturing Co., 72
Mick, Jacob, 64
Milam, Benjamin C., 189
Milam & Son reel, 200
Mildrum, 163
Millsite Rattle Bug, 105
Millsite Tackle Co., 73, 97
Milwaukee reel, 193
Minnow Corset, 40–41
Minnows
 for bait, 35
 chaining up, 41
 clear minnow tubes, 41–42
 held on hook, 40
 lip hooking and corseting, 40–41
 pails for, 237
 traps for, 237
Mister Twister, 22
Mitchell, 205, 206, 217
Modern Bait & Fly Casting (Ripley), 252
Modern Fishing Tackle (Evanoff), 249
Moldcraft, 101
Montague, 166
Montgomery Ward, 235
Monti-spinner, 83
Moonlight Bait Co., 73
Mouse, 69
Mouse Bait, 70
Mousie Devle, 81
Multipliers
 early, 184–187
Murphy, Charles F., 154
Museums, 251
Muskill spinner, 57
Musky Monk
 marathon, 70
Musky Tin Liz, 72
Musky Vamp, 75
Mustad, 17, 19–22, 40, 79

N
Nail knot, 114
National Fishing Lure Collectors Club, 8–9
The National Fresh Water Fishing Hall of Fame and Museum, 134, 251
Natural History of the Fishes of Massachusetts (Smith), 25, 27, 54, 136, 148, 183, 247
Nature's Scent, 104
Ned W. Moran & Co., 56
Needle knot, 114
Nets, 230–231
New Discovery of a Vast Country in America, A (Hennepin), 245
New England Cod Fish Jig, 56
New Frog Tandem, 39
New Tin Liz Snake, 72
Newton, 141
Nibble Nabber, 30
Nichols, Bill, 90
Nifty Minne, 42

No-knot connections, 118–119
 fly fishing and, 118–119
Norman, 96
Norman, Bill, 69
Normark, 92
 Fish 'N Fillet knife, 240
 Rapala knife, 239
Norris, Thaddeus, 6, 22, 25–27, 29, 35, 36, 56, 112, 154, 183, 185, 241, 247, 248
North British Rubber Company, Ltd., 238
Nostealum hook, 20
Nottingham reels, 183, 184
Nylon lines, 130–132, 141

O
O. A. Norland Co., 227
O'Boy Minnow, 75
Obverse barb hook, 22
Ocean City, 194, 199, 201, 206, 214
 reel, 200
 300, 205
O'Conner, James, 190
Off Shore, 229
Offshore Angler, 224
Offshore swivel knot, 115
Old fighter, 69
Oney Johnson, 26
On The Characteristics of Animals or Natural History (Aelian), 47
Oreno, 76
Oriental Wiggler, 83
Oriental Wiggler #3, 69
Orvis, Charles, 195, 246, 249
Orvis Company, 80, 83, 143, 151, 206, 224
Osprey, 52, 67
Osprey box, 81
Ostrum, Ray, 91
Outing Company, 74
Outing Manufacturing Co., 24
Overhand knot, 115
Overhand loop, 115
Ovington, Ray, 250
Owner, 22
Owner America, 19

P
Pachner and Koeher Minnow Saver, 41
Paddle Plug, 73
Palmer, Mark, 193
Palomar, 114
Palomar knot, 120, 121
Pal-O-Mine, 75
Panther Martin, 83
Paragon Minnow, 57
Partridge, 19
Paste
 making, 38
Paste bait, 35
Pate, 216
Paul Bunyan, 78
Paw Paw, 70
 Fire Plug, 62
Peckinpaugh, 70, 80
Pecos, 205
Pecos River Tackle Minnow, 69
Peetz reel, 184
Pelican, 206

Penn International, 201, 202, 211, 216
 Squidder, 201
Penrod, Ken, 256
Pepper, Joe E., 99
Pequea Works, 81
Perfection loop, 115, 116
Perfection Tip, 163, 164
Perrine, 225–226
Perry, George, 74
Peters, 235
Pfeiffer, 42
Pflueger, 19, 55, 56, 58, 64, 75, 85, 88, 103, 191, 195, 213, 216
 All-In-One #3500, 78
 Alpine casting reel, 185
 American spinner, 57
 Chum spoon, 77, 81
 Competitor Wooden Minnow, 64
 Cub handle, 200
 Flying Helgramite, 58
 1495 medalist, 202
 Globe, 64
 Last Word spoon, 81
 McMurray spinner, 57
 Monarch Minnow, 60
 Pipin spoon, 81
 Progress, 216
 Snapie Spinner, 68
 Supreme, 194
 Trory Minnow, 60
 Trory Wooden Minnow, 64
Pflueger, Ernest, 58
Phantom Products Inc., 174
 Minnow, 50
Phillippe, Samuel, 16, 153, 155–156, 249
Phillippe, Solon, 154, 155–156
Phoebe, 83
Piano twist, 120
Pico Perch, 76, 94
Pikie Minnows, 64, 74
Pinnacle, 211, 217
Pinnacle T-2, 199
P & K Company, 19
 Re-Treeve-It reel, 204
Plano Molding Company, 223
Plas-Tak, 224
Plastics
 combo hard and soft lures, 101
 early, 69
 lures, 71
 for saltwater fishing, 100–101
 soft, 99–100
 switch to (1940-1950, 85
Pliers, 233
P-Line, 131
Plug-Oreno, 76
Plunker, 74
Poe, 77, 84
Pole, Edward, 25, 50, 182, 222
Pollywog, 93
Pollywoggler, 43
Popeil Pocket Fisherman, 208
Pop It fly rod lure, 74
Pork Chunk, 43
Porker, 63
Pork rind, 43
 lures and, 69
Porky Getum, 24, 83

Powell, Edwin C., 159
Powell, Walton, 176
Powell Rods, 176
Power Baits, 79, 101, 105
Practical Bait Casting (St. John), 250
Practical Fishing Knots, II (Kreh & Sosin), 116
Pradco Company, 77, 84, 91
Premax, 208
Prescott, 95
Prevost patent Combination Frog Hook, 39
Professional Fly Tying and Tackle Making and Manufacturer's Guide (Herter), 249
Professional Glass and Split-Bamboo Manual and Manufacturer's Guide (Herter), 246
Pultrusion process, 174
Pure Fishing, 78–79, 172

Q
Quantum, 211
 Hypercast, 212
 MT1 Micro, 209
Quilby
 Minnow, 81
 Streamer, 81
 Wab-Tail, 81

R
R. D. Hull, 207
Rapala, Lauri, 91
Rapala Company, 90–92, 107, 148
 Count Down, 62
 Deep diver, 101
Rat-L-Trap, 96, 105–106
Rattles, 105–106
Real Craw, 77
Rebel, 77, 84, 95, 100
 Deep Runner, 62
Records, 134, 206
Red and White
 trolling spoon, 83
 Witch, 81
Red Eye, 78
Redneck lizard, 100
Red Wolf, 78
Reed, Herb, 100
Reef knot, 113–114
Reel cases, 238–239
Reels, 179–217. See also Fly reels
 around World War II, 204–206
 attachments for, 192
 automatic casting features, 212–213
 casting reels after World War II, 213–215
 centrifugal brake for, 191
 closed-face spinning reels, 207–209
 current trends in, 217
 development of spinning, 196–198
 early simple, 182–184
 early multipliers, 184–187
 evolution of, 7–8
 golden age of early casting

reels, 191–194
introduction to, 179–180
Kentucky, 187–190
level-wind mechanisms, 193
magnetic, 214
reels without rods, 180–181
saltwater spinning reels, 209–211
simplicity of, 202–204
trolling reel, 200–201
ultralight, 198–199
winches, 182
windes, 182
wood, 184
Reinard, Ken, 15, 45, 48
Repine, Jim, 256
Research and Model Co., 103–104
Retallic, Ken, 256
Revolution, 65
Richardson, 167
Rio, 143
Riss Findory, 83
Riverside, 77
Roach, 29
Robert Page Lincoln spoon, 80
Robinson, Gilmer G., 252
Rod cases, 238–239
Rods, 145–177
cane, 153
early Colonial rods, 146
early rod construction, 147
early rod design, 148–151
ferrules, 161
ferrules and splices, 149
ferrule system, 168–169
graphite rods, 172–176
guides, 161–165, 177
hollowed out, 159–161
introduction to, 145
modern design, 176–177
for saltwater fishing, 169–170
shortening of, 151–152
solid steel for durability, 167–169
split-bamboo, 154–159
tubular glass, 170–172
tubular steel for strength, 165–167
Roe
early use of, 35
preserving, 38
Roller guides, 163
Roosevelt, Robert Barnwell, 6, 54, 57, 245
Roscoe Vernon Gaddis, 80
Ross Orvis, 216
Ross Thumb Spooler, 192
Royal Wulff, 143
Ru, 206
Rubber Cor sinker, 28
Rubber lures, 56, 58
Rubbermaid, 224
Rush, J. K., 65–66
Rush Tango, 67, 74
Rush Tango lures, 65–66
Ryall, 216
Ryobi, 211

S
S. Allcock Company, 55
S. Doering & Company, 69
Sadu Strobe Lures, 103
Safe Deposit Bait, 57
Sage, 143, 190
Salmon
best bait for, 35
Salmon and the Dry Fly, The (LaBranche), 250
Salmon Fly, The (Kelson), 241, 249
Saltwater fishing
fly fishing, 53–54, 56–57
fly reels for, 215–216
harder soft plastics for, 100–101
1900-1920, 68–69
rods for, 169–170
spinning reel for, 209–211
Salt Water Fishing Tackle (Major), 26, 249
Salt Water Fly Fishing (Brooks), 250
Salt-Water Fly Fishing (Sand), 250
Saltwater hook, 24
Salt-Water Special, 75
Sampo, 26–27
Sand, George X., 250
Schullery, Paul, 53–54, 148
Scientific Anglers, 142, 143, 177, 202, 216
Scooterpooper Sales, Inc., 107
Scotland, James, 16
Scott, Genio, 6, 56, 186–187, 241, 247, 248
Scott, Ray, 90, 252
Scrope, William, 195
Scum Frogs, 90
SeaGuard, 131
Seamaster, 215–216
Sears Roebuck, 223
Sea-Spook, 71, 75
Sea Wonder spinning reel, 199
Seneca, 77
spoon, 83
Serviente, Barry, 258
Sevenstrand, 101
Seward, Tom, 84
Shad roe, 35
Shakespeare Co., 58, 65, 67, 70, 75–76, 80, 131, 134, 166–170, 172, 174, 191, 194, 204, 206, 207, 211, 213, 216
Griteria reel, 185
Revolution, 67
35U, 209
Tru-Art automatic fly reel, 202
Shannon, Jesse P., 63
Shannon Twin Spinner, 22, 63, 68–69, 95
Shimano, 148, 201, 211, 214, 215
Bantam Chronarch, 217
Shimmy Wiggler #5, 69
Shoe Form Company, 19
Short-shanked single hook, 20
Shrimpy-Spook, 71
Shur Bite, 69
Shure Strike, 76
Sidecaster, 197
Sigma, 134
Silk lines, 125–126
for fly fishing, 138–139
Silstar, 211, 217
TF-20, 199
Silver Buddy, 94
Single water knot, 110
Sinkers, 25
early, 27–28
modern style, 28
split shot, 27
Sitgreaves, T. R., 154
Skidder, 69
Skinner, G. M., 55
Skinner fluted spinner, 7, 54, 57
Skipper, 73
Skirts, 73, 93–94
Sliding sinker, 27
Slip float, 30
Slip sheet bend, 115, 117
Slopenose, 62
Smith, Fillmore M., 65
Smith, Jerome V. C., 25, 27, 54, 136, 148, 183, 247
Smith, O. W., 152, 250
Smith Brothers, 231
Smithwick, 77, 96
Smithwick, Jack, 52
Smithwick Devil's Horse, 8
Snag Proof Manufacturing Co., 89, 104
Sneck, 19, 22, 49, 63
Snyder, Charles, 188
Snyder, George, 187
Snyder, John, 188
Sockdolager, 18, 23
Solar lines, 134
Solid Strike, 105
Sonar, 94
Sonic, 76
Sonic lures, 76, 93–94
Sosin, Mark, 116
Soucie, Gary, 249
South, Theophilus, 195
South Bend, 66–67, 70, 76, 78, 80, 81, 130, 166, 191, 193, 204, 211
Bass Obite, 83
Bass-Oreno, 58, 76
Better Bass-Oreno, 58
Cast #1600, 209
Cross Double-built rod, 157
#550 B, 217
Min-Buck Minnow, 74
Nip-I-Diddee, 8
Spincast, 209
Tease-Oreno, 65, 66
Southern Lure Co., 90
Sparano, Vi T., 256
Sparkler fish, 98
Specialty lines, 139
Spider hitch, 120
SpiderWire, 84, 134–135
Spinnerbait, 80–81
invention of, 63
Spinners
development of, 82–83
1900-1920, 68
1940 to 1950, 82–83
1950 to 1975, 92
Spinning (Brown), 205
Spinning for Fresh and Salt Water Fish of North America (McClane), 83, 180
Spinning reels
closed-face, 207–209
development of, 196–198
invention of, 7
for saltwater, 209–211
spinning changes over decades, 211–213
ultralight, 198–199
SpinTail Kicker, 71
Splicing/splicing needles, 120
Split-bamboo rods, 154–159
Spook lure, 71
Spooners, The (Thompson), 52, 54
Spoons
1900-1920, 68
early, 54–55
first, 51, 53
Sportsman's Supply Co., 192
Sportsmen's Encyclopedia (Bruette), 125
Spreaders, 36
Sputterfuss, 73
Square knot, 113–114
Squid hooks, 16
St. John, Larry, 250
Standing Stamping Co., 223
Staro, 205
Statech Spinfly, 141
Steel
Fin, 216
solid steel for durability, 167–169
tubular steel rods, 165
Steel, Frank R., 257
Stewart, Frank, 188
Stewart, William M., 208
Stocking fish, 10–11
benefits/disadvantages of, 11
Stoner, Lew, 159
Storm, 84, 91, 96, 101
thin Fin, 71
Stream-Eze, 98
Stream Liner, 208
Stren, 131, 132, 134
Strike, 105
Strike-It, 76
Striped Bass Wobbler, 76
Stubcaster, 167
Sunfish Tin Liz, 72
Sunset, 141
Sunspot spoon, 81
Super Dowagiac Spook, 71
Superior-Copper, 80
Superior Fishing (Roosevelt), 54
Super Z ferrules, 161
Sure Catch Grasshopper Hook, 40
Sure Catch Minnow Hook, 40
Sure Lure, 65
Surgeon's knot, 112, 115
Surgeon's loop, 115–117
Swastika, 128
Swedish Ambassadeur 5000, 213
Swim Whiz, 65
Swiss EGB Bunker, 83
Swiss Filvit Flirt, 83

Swivel, 25–27
ball-bearing, 26–27
early, 25–26
Swivel sinker, 27

T

Index 271

Tackle bags, 224–225
Tackle boxes, 222–224
Tadpolly lures, 74
Tantilizer, 76
Tarp-Oreno, 76
Taverner, Eric, 198
Techsonic Industries, 89
Teeny, 143
Teflon, 132
Terminal tackle. See also Hooks
   floats and bobbers, 28–31
   introduction to, 25
   sinkers, 27–28
   swivels, 25–27
Test line, 131
Teton, 216
Thinfin, 91
Thomas
   Buoyant Minnow, 83
   Cyclone Spoon, 83
   Fighting Fish, 83
   Hi-Fi Minnow, 83
Thomas, Dee, 176
Thommen, 141
   Dolly Midget, 83
   T-Flirt, 83
Thompson, D. H., 240
Thompson, Harvey W., 52, 54
Thread lines, 129–130
Thread-line spinning, 205
Thunderstick Junior, 84
Tibor, 216
Tiemco, 19
Tiller-hitch, 117
Tin Liz, 72
Tin Liz Minnow, 72
Tin Liz Spintail, 72
Tin Liz Three Fin, 72
Tin Liz Walleye, 72
Tiny Toads, 90
Tockterman, Tony, 29–30
Tonkin cane bamboo, 156, 159
Tony Accardo, 80
Tony Accetta, 77
Tony Accetta Pet, 7, 77
Topwater lures, 94
Transparent hook, 23
Travel Diary of an Angler (Van Dyke), 250
Travels into North America (Kalm), 245
Travels of William Bartram, The (Bartram), 245
Treatise on Fishing With an Angle (Berners), 27–28, 47–48, 137, 145, 244
Trebles, 20
Trenton Mfg. Co., 73
Trilene knot, 115
Trilene XL, 132
Trilene XT, 132
Triple Fish, 131
Troller, 83
Trolling spoons, 77
Troll-Oreno, 67
Tronick Treink Co., 223
Trout, 39
   best bait for, 35
Troutangos, 66
Trout (Bergman), 250
Trout Fishing From All Angles (Taverner), 198

Trout flies, 69
Troutiger Tangos, 66
True Temper, 10, 167
Trumpet guides, 162
Tru-Turn, 22–24
Tubby Tackle, 101
Tube lures, 100
Tubifex worm, 36
Tubular guides, 162
Tubular steel rods, 165
Tucked sheet bend, 115
Tule fishing, 94
Turle knot, 114, 115
Twin Bass Bait, 56
Tycoon Tackle, 215

U
Ugly Stik, 174
Umco, 222
Uncle Josh Bait Company, 43, 52
Undertake, 93
Uni-knot, 115
United Fishing Association, 11
Universal Angler, The (Venables), 244
U.S. Line, 141
Uslan, 156
Ustonson, Onesimus, 182
Utica, 204

V
Van Dyke, Henry, 250
Van Staal, 211
Van Vleck hook, 5, 14, 22
Varmac, 163
Velek, Frank, 92
Venables, Robert, 182, 244
Venom, 106
Vernley, 202
Vernon, Steven, 188, 200
Versitex, 134–135
Vinyl lures, 89–90
Virgin Mermaid lure, 52, 98
VMC, 17, 131, 134–135
Voedisch Brothers, 140
Vogt, William C., 33, 250
Vom Hofe, 195
Vom Hofe, Edward, 190
Vom Hofe, Julius, 200
Vortex, 84, 103

W
W. D. Chapman, 56, 57
W. H. McManies, 235
W. J. Jamison Company, 24, 40
Waddle Bug, 73
Wading pants/stockings, 238
Wagtail Minnow Mfg. Co., 93
Walk-the-dog lure, 74
Waltco Products, 167
Walton, Izaak, 6, 9, 14, 38, 46, 48, 50, 146, 151, 179, 182, 233, 244
Walton Feather Tail, 74
Warren Fish Gaff, 226
Water Gremlin, 28, 41
Water-knot, 112–113
Water Witch, 93
Waukazoo Surface Spinner, 76
Wawasee, 216
Weber, 101
Weber, Ron, 91, 239

Weber Company, 19
Wee Dee, 74
Weedless Collared Bait, 59
Weedless hook, 18
Wee Warts, 91
Weezel, 81
   Sparrow, 70
   spoon, 81
   Wessner Feather Weezel, 68
Weight-forward lines, 139
Welles, Henry S., 65
Wells, H. P., 166
Western Filament, 134–135
WetCel lines, 142
Wheeler, Cornelius, 193
Whip finish, 115
Whopper Stopper, 76, 94, 96, 105, 222
Whopper Stopper, Hellbender, 90, 102
Whopper Stopper Hellcat, 96
Whopper Stopper spinnerbait, 97
Wicked Wiggler, 81
Wiggle Fish, 74
Wiggle Wart, 91
Wiggle Worm, 87
Wilder-Dilg series, 70
William Mills and Sons, 156
Williams, 78
Williams, Lacey Y., 24
Wilson, 78
Winans & Whistler, 207
Winans & Whistler rod, 196
Winches, 182
Winchester, 76, 167
Windes, 182
Winged Dardevle, 81
Winona, 216
Winston rods, 159
Wire
   braided wire knots, 120–121
   leader sleeves for mono and wire, 121
   lines, 135–136
   new knotty wire, 121
Wire knots, 120
Wisconsin Pharmacal, 104
Wm. Mills & Son's, 55
Wob-L-Rite, 77, 83
Wolverine Ocean city, 204
Woodies, 106
Wood lures, 59, 61, 96
Wood reels, 184
Woodstream, 224
Worden, 66, 77, 84, 92
   Combination Minnow, 8
   Minnow, 74
Worden, B. F., 66
Worms, artificial
   evolution of, 21–22
   soft plastic, 86–89, 99–100
Worms, natural
   baiting and hooking, 38
   buying, 34
   as early bait, 34
   gathering methods, 34
   types of, 35–36
Wright, Stan, 19
Wright & McGill Co., 19, 22, 42, 72–73, 133, 207
Wulff, Lee, 114, 241
Wulff Manufacturing Company,

227

Y
Yakima Bait Co., 77, 181
Yankee Aero Bass Bait, 99
Yawman & Erbe Company, 203
   Automatic Combination reel, 180
Yellow Kid, 64
Young, Fred, 90
Young, J. W., 203

Z
Zap-A-Gap, 117
Zara Spook, 100
Zebco, 176, 207, 209, 211
   Cardinal 3, 210
Zern, Ed, 254
Zero Hour Bomb Company, 207